Enterprise Systems Education in the 21st Century

Andrew Targowski, Western Michigan University, USA

J. Michael Tarn, Western Michigan University, USA

 Information Science Publishing

Hershey • London • Melbourne • Singapore

Acquisitions Editor:	Michelle Potter
Development Editor:	Kristin Roth
Senior Managing Editor:	Jennifer Neidig
Managing Editor:	Sara Reed
Copy Editor:	Larissa Vinci
Typesetter:	Marko Primorac
Cover Design:	Lisa Tosheff
Printed at:	Integrated Book Technology

Published in the United States of America by
Information Science Publishing (an imprint of Idea Group Inc.)
701 E. Chocolate Avenue
Hershey PA 17033
Tel: 717-533-8845
Fax: 717-533-8661
E-mail: cust@idea-group.com
Web site: http://www.idea-group.com

and in the United Kingdom by
Information Science Publishing (an imprint of Idea Group Inc.)
3 Henrietta Street
Covent Garden
London WC2E 8LU
Tel: 44 20 7240 0856
Fax: 44 20 7379 3313
Web site: http://www.eurospan.co.uk

Library of Congress Cataloging-in-Publication Data

Enterprise systems education in the 21st century / Andrew S. Targowski and J. Michael Tarn, editors.
    p. cm.
  Summary: "This book presents methods of reengineering business curricula in order to use ES solutions. It also helps ES vendors understand the higher education environment so they can support college and university programs"--Provided by publisher.
  Includes bibliographical references and index.
  ISBN 1-59904-349-1 (hardcover : alk. paper) -- ISBN 1-59904-350-5 (softcover : alk. paper) -- ISBN 1-59904-351-3 (ebook : alk. paper)
  1. Business education. 2. Business--Computer programs. 3. Curriculum planning. I. Targowski, Andrzej. II. Tarn, J. Michael, 1960-
  HF1106.E58 2007
  658.4'0380711--dc22
                         2006015167

British Cataloguing in Publication Data
A Cataloguing in Publication record for this book is available from the British Library.

All work contributed to this book is new, previously-unpublished material. The view expressed in this book are those of the authors, but not necessarily of the publisher.

Enterprise Systems Education in the 21ˢᵗ Century

Table of Contents

Preface

At the beginning of the 21st century, the civilizations of the World entered into the next modern wave of globalization, driven by world evolving transportation systems and information technology (IT), which triggered a concept of the "death of distance" (Cairncross, 1997). The latter also "flattens" the world (Friedman, 2005), in which businesses are looking for the producers and servers providing the lowest cost possible from undeveloped or developing countries. The United States, the most advanced country in manufacturing and IT as well as some Western European countries have adopted a strategy to outsource some operational/designing jobs to countries with low wages. In effect, these outsourcing countries have lost complex systems and a need for large numbers of engineers and IT professionals. This trend has also impacted colleges which are facing declining number of students in the said areas.

Because of this downward trend, some American universities are trying to adapt their information systems programs to the needs of the current industrial shift. It is indeed a healthy reaction to this industrial shift since those programs that could not adapt to a new challenge may face extinction. This book describes the best practices of some universities reengineering their educational programs around the concept of business process integration (BPI) within a framework of enterprise-wide information systems, with the support of enterprise resource planning (ERP) software's academic version from such leading vendors as SAP, Microsoft, and Oracle. The concept of the book is shown in Figure P-1.

The concept elucidates that the industrial trends and needs shape the academic curricula. It is because IS/CIS/MIS/IT programs are professional studies that must respond to the industrial challenges.

Table P-1 illustrates the companies' effort to optimize IT development and operations. Almost all types of the listed improvements lead to the establishment of robust enterprise-

Figure P-1. The concept of the book

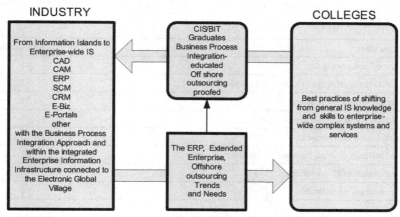

wide processes and systems. Good news is that 18% of outsourcing companies are bringing back in-house IT services. Some companies have brought back their services even more extensively (e.g., hotels — 38%, natural resources — 30%, communications — 29%) (InformationWeek, 2005).

The passage of the Sarbanes-Oxley Act 2002 mandates increases in information processing requirements for public companies, which has in turn led to greatly increased needs for more reliable enterprise-wide IS and also increased job opportunities for computer business applications graduates. Furthermore, the 500 most IT innovative companies still invest large amount of funds in IT, on average 3% of annual revenues. However, in 2005 they invested less ($293 million) than in 2001 ($484 million), which means that the enterprise information infrastructure has been built and now its optimization is taking place (InformationWeek, 2005, p. 38). As for today's situation, Carr (2003) may need to re-evaluate the standpoint of "IT Doesn't Matter." IT does matter, but is not a novelty anymore. It is maturing and becoming a strong electronic-information infrastructure for the 21st century company, competing in the global economy.

The book is the first title in enterprise systems education. It intends to provide higher education with a direct resource, guidelines, and examples for developing an ES curriculum, teaching specific business process of ES, teaching specific IT topics in ES, and learning industrial support of ES education. The book consists of 20 chapters which are further organized into four sections.

Section I contains five chapters sharing experiences at the level of curricular development, which explores the strategic issues in the support and implementation of ERP education. A positive shift from the traditional CIS/MIS to the contemporary BIT (business information technology) majors and minors is suggested. The BIT approach reflects the Octopus Strategy, where besides a vertically oriented professional major/minor IS/CIS/MIS/BIT, IT technology penetrates almost every kind of business function and other functions as well. For example, this approach and strategy lead to the development of such courses as Accounting IT, Marketing IT, Health IT, Art IT, Music IT, Communication IT, and so forth. An important step in teaching IT at business schools is to incorporate ERP software in teaching,

Table P-1. Optimization efforts in 2005 — what steps has your company taken to optimize the efficiency of its business processes in the past 12 months (Source: InformationWeek research survey)

Optimization steps	% of Responders
Increase use of automation	85
Improved data integration between systems or departments	82
Reengineered existing applications	79
Established enterprise technology standards	76
Business-process optimization	73
Established business-process frameworks and defined processes	62
Centralized control of IT operations	62
Brought in strategic consultants	60
Outsourced IT operations domestically	33
Outsourced IT operations offshore	29
Brought outsourced functions back in-house	18

Note: Multiple responses allowed

which exemplifies the first attempt to allow students directly to learn the integration of all business-oriented information in an enterprise via a hands-on experience.

Chapter I analyzes the critical success factors for implementing ERP systems as a vehicle for business curriculum integration at a large state university. This chapter documents the history of a College of Business Administration that implemented ERP systems in their coursework with the original goal of integrating the curriculum across disciplines. An analysis of the reason why the college was unable to achieve its goal is provided. This analysis results in lessons learned that can be useful in building technological relationships with third party organizations.

In **Chapter II**, the ERP education program at the Department of Information Business of the Vienna University of Economics and BA is described. Especially emphasized is the embedding into the study programs both at the department and university levels. Due to a major change in the degree programs offered by the university, including the introduction of a completely new Information Systems bachelor and master program, changes to the ERP education program became necessary. The author reports several quantitative data on the lectures both before and after the changes, including satisfaction measures. Some lessons are condensed for other institutions that are planning to introduce ERP into their curricula.

Chapter III indicates that many of the entry-level positions that graduates traditionally entered have diminished due to the economic downturn and to companies outsourcing positions to off shore companies. This chapter presents the path that one Australian University school took in introducing multiple programs in an endeavour to compliment traditional course delivery and to better connect a University School with ICT industry requirements. The programs included the use of SAP hosting centers for access to ERP systems, conducting a visiting expert teaching delivery model for SAP content and multiple SAP certification programs. The results of these programs show that flexibility in delivery mode and effective merging of curriculum and certification content is crucial to achieving successful programs.

Chapter IV introduces a concept of the re-engineered CIS (computer information systems) curriculum accomplished at the beginning of the 21st century through a few initiatives taken by the Department of Business Information Systems at Western Michigan University's Haworth Business College, over the time period of 2000-2005. These initiatives led to the shift from teaching the knowledge and skills of universal/generic computer information systems to more integrated knowledge and skills about how to develop complex systems such as ERP (enterprise resource planning) and e-enterprise. This curriculum shift is a response to the shift of industrial information infrastructure from information islands to the gradually integrated online (Web-driven) infrastructure of systems and services. The revised CIS program at Western Michigan University is supported by the use of ERP-like SAP R/3 and MS Great Plains software.

Chapter V presents a revised graduate CIS concentration in the MBA program at Western Michigan University's Haworth College of Business. The new MBA-CIS concentration has been designed with a strong focus on ERP systems management, and it is proposed in response to industrial needs and to meet MBA students' interests. The existing MBA-CIS concentration was developed in mid-1990s on the premise that future IT professionals must have mastery in technical IT skills in managing computing information resources. The recent trend in IT outsourcing triggers a new question — "What kind of IT training and education should be delivered to Americans to keep them employable in the United States?" A new premise resulted from the present environment changes that require our graduate students to have balanced knowledge in both IT skills and business processes (i.e., knowing how to apply IT to the development of business applications that support integrated business processes and enterprise operations).

Section II has six chapters which share practice in teaching the application of IT in particular business processes (e.g., supply chain management [SCM], human resources [HR], sales and distribution [SD], operations management [OM], and enterprise capstone courses of the IS/CIS/MIS/BIT majors/minors).

Chapter VI describes an enterprise resource planning (ERP) system as a system that integrates all the different functionalities within an enterprise which is used to manage the basic commercial functions in a business. This chapter describes the use of business processes and ERP systems as a mechanism to provide the integration in the capstone course. The various modules taught in the class are described and issues with the modules are raised and discussed.

Chapter VII introduces a concept of the capstone course of the CIS/BIT program at the Western Michigan University. The course is composed of lectures and five projects, which are related to each other. The lectures provide knowledge that supports every project (skills). The end-product of this course is prototyped software of an enterprise performance management system, which is demonstrated by each team as an integrated software package. The course is divided in three following parts: Part I: Enterprise system definition (classic knowledge and skills), Part II: Business process integration (trend-oriented approach), Part III: Enterprise system development (ERP prototype-demo software).

Chapter VIII emphasizes that information technology has become a critical component for human resource (HR) professionals. Human resource information systems (HRIS) have helped many HR departments automate routine processes, eliminate unnecessary work, and play a strategic role in driving employee performance. Many IT firms are now forming alliances with universities to popularize their products. This chapter first investigates the utility and the choice of various HRIS options available to an organization. Next, it evaluates the utility of universities forming alliances with enterprise resource planning (ERP) firms to enrich their business curricula. Finally, the experiences of a college of business at a large university in Midwestern United States with the implementation of IT in the human resource management (HRM) curriculum are examined.

Chapter IX describes how enterprise systems technology is used to enhance the teaching of operations management through development and operation of a virtual manufacturing enterprise. An ongoing, real-time simulation is conducted in which operations management issues in the fictitious factory must be addressed on a daily basis. The virtual manufacturing enterprise is integrated into an operations management course to facilitate understanding of the dynamic and interrelated nature of operations planning and control in a complex manufacturing environment. Enterprise software supports the primary learning objective of understanding how operations management decisions affect customer service, capacity, inventory, and costs.

Chapter X states that in order to maintain a competitive position in today's marketplace, companies must demand a greater level of enterprise efficiency. In today's rapidly changing market, experts argue that it is no longer about becoming a powerhouse but simply about remaining competitive. That is why automating and linking the supply chain has become so imperative. Supply chain management systems link all of the company's customers, suppliers, factories, warehouses, distributors, carriers, and trading partners. These systems integrate all the key business processes across the supply chain of a company. This chapter explains the objectives of supply chain management and how SAP's supply chain management system helps companies fulfill these objectives.

Chapter XI states that in order to become globally competitive in today's dynamic business environment, organizations have to come closer to customers and deliver value added services and products in the shortest possible time. The primary business process through which this is achieved is the sales and distribution process. However, the sales and distribution process is just one part of an enterprise resource planning (ERP) system. This chapter focuses on the sales and distribution (SD) process of SAP's ERP system. This chapter will assist in learning about the basic functions that make up this process and how it affects the other modules in the ERP system. This chapter looks at the purchasing process and the materials requirements planning (MRP) process and how all the three processes are linked together to form one complete business process.

Section III includes six chapters dealing with specific issues of the enterprise-wide approach, such as the enterprise information infrastructure (service course for all business sophomores), how to customize the SAP R/3 software using the ABAP/4 language, how to configure this software for the whole company or how to develop an enterprise portal.

Chapter XII deals with sharing information in between business schools, which are attempting to integrate their curricula with enterprise software, particularly enterprise resource planning (ERP) software. Although the introduction of ERP into the undergraduate academic curriculum offers students a potentially deeper understanding of business processes in a global, information-centric environment. Connecting a new global economy with enterprise systems requires a course, which is much broader than ERP and should place enterprise systems in a much larger information-communication technology (ICT) context. This chapter presents a teaching model that provides that context, emphasizing the critical role of systems components and relationships, the central function of information in problem solving, and business perspectives of information from infrastructure to applications.

Chapter XIII states that the main role of enterprise systems is to support business operations efficiently and effectively and to create competitive advantage. Nevertheless to reap the benefits of using enterprise systems, it is essential to align the information technology goals with business goals and to establish the appropriate enterprise architecture (EA) and supporting enterprise information architecture (EIA). For students to understand the linkage between the EA and EIA and to learn the subject, a hybrid academic and industrial approach to teaching EA and EIA is proposed. This proposed hybrid approach covers theory, framework, principle and best practice of the EA and EIA in the beginning, and then moves to a practical and comprehensive approach in delivering the subject matter — EA and EIA. A real world EA and EIA project is used to illustrate the efficacy of these architectures.

Chapter XIV indicates that as more and more companies are implementing ERP to support daily business transactions, the needs for ERP trained employees are increasing as well. Industry demand has prompted many universities to consider incorporating ERP into their curriculum. Information systems programs in many universities have started offering courses that include ERP education. However, most universities have faced multi-faceted challenges related to lab setup, training, software support, and curriculum design. In this chapter, a guideline for development and teaching an ERP based course with MS Great Plains™ is provided. Teaching approach is discussed and an ERP based business curriculum is proposed. Effectiveness of the curriculum design in the classroom is analyzed based on a single semester trial of the course in two classrooms.

Chapter XV explains the trend that the business world has recognized the importance of managing business processes rather than functions. As a result business education has begun to embrace this transformation, although the organizational barriers between departments in most business schools have limited the success of teaching business from a process-oriented perspective. On the other hand, ERP technology provides an opportunity to illustrate the management of integrated business processes. One approach to using ERP software to teach business processes is through a dedicated configuration class. In this class structure, students configure an ERP system to manage the basic business processes of a small company. Because of the integrated nature of ERP systems, students must configure the system in a number of functional areas — accounting, operations, sales, etc.— many of which are not in a student's major. The necessity of configuring an ERP system in a number of functional areas illustrates the importance of having a background in all basic business functions to successfully manage a business enterprise. This chapter provides a review of an ERP configuration course that is currently being taught at Western Michigan University using SAP R/3 business software. The context of the course, its mechanics, key learning points and areas for future development are presented.

Chapter XVI analyzes programming language ABAP/4 as the fundamental programming tool used for the development of SAP R/3 ERP system. While other OO languages such as Java, J2EE are receiving their attention in new ERP module development, ABAP/4 will continue to play an important role in SAP R/3 customizations that are often required to meet the special application needs of most SAP adopters. In this chapter, ABAP/4 language — its programming environment, types of customization for SAP R/3, teaching pedagogy, and the development of ABAP application are discussed. In specific, a simple example of ABAP/4 program that employs the sample database (flight) is included to illustrate an online application that employs both internal and external tables for data processing using SAP SQL statements. Moreover, a three-thread teaching approach is presented to highlight how ABAP/4 learning could be enhanced by experiencing (SAP), coding (ABAP programs), and simulating (an ABAP business module). Limitations, suggestions, and future trend of ABAP/4 application development are also addressed with a concluding remark.

Chapter XVII offers an idea how enterprise portals present a great opportunity to bridge online applications with the backend business systems. Although enterprise portals are now widely adopted in the business environment, the literature has been scarce in studies on how an enterprise portal course is better delivered in the information systems curriculum. The goal of this chapter is to discuss the potential issues and challenges arising from the delivery of such a course, and to propose a comprehensive teaching framework. The framework consists of three teaching modules (i.e., portal basics, portal management and portal development) to better cover enterprise portals with topics ranging from technical details to business decisions.

Section IV contains three chapters depicting the continuous efforts done by the three major ERP software vendors whose approach to supporting universities in using their demo-solutions in academic courses are provided. This section should be particularly interested for those universities that plan to reorient their curriculum towards the approach presented in this book.

Chapter XVIII focuses on a very popular enterprise system, SAP, and summarizes the outcomes of a global survey on the status quo of SAP-related education. Based on the feedback of 305 lecturers and more than 700 students, it reports on the main factors of Enterprise Systems education including critical success factors, alternative hosting models, and students' perceptions. The results show among others an overall increasing interest in advanced SAP solutions and international collaboration, and a high satisfaction with the concept of using application hosting centers. Integrating enterprise systems solutions in the curriculum of not only universities but all types of institutes of higher learning has been a major challenge for nearly ten years. Enterprise systems education is surprisingly well documented in a number of papers on information systems education. However, most publications in this area report on the individual experiences of an institution or an academic.

Chapter XIX describes how the Microsoft Dynamics™ Academic Alliance (MDAA) helps address the challenge of teaching enterprise systems by donating business solution software (e.g., MS Great Plains) to higher educational institutions for classroom use. This chapter discusses the background of the MDAA and the types of systems available for its members. The chapter content is designed to be helpful for both business educators and administrators as they plan and implement technology into their curricula. MDAA provides another popular platform for higher education. Microsoft typically becomes a strong competitor when it enters a given software market At this time Microsoft offers enterprise software for small and medium size companies, which is a plus in comparison to other vendors which used to aim at the large firms.

Chapter XX indicates that Oracle is becoming a major player in the industry, particularly after its acquisition of PeopeSoft. Oracle enterprise system, E-Business Suite, is not only suitable for large and medium enterprises but also small companies. Oracle E-Business Suite is an appealing alternative for institutions to consider in regard to integrating enterprise systems into their curricula. The literature of the integration of enterprise system into academic curriculum and challenges of such integration are briefly reviewed. Oracle Academic Initiative, Oracle E-Business Suite and Oracle enterprise system related education — Oracle University's practice are introduced. One university's experience in integrating E-Business Suite into a capstone information management course is discussed. The vision enterprise case that Oracle University uses to train its customers is suggested as a viable alternative option for academic institutions.

The book contains chapters describing how to teach the enterprise BPI with ERP demos, it does not contain descriptions of those universities' cases which decided to specialize in a single vendor software (e.g., University of California in Chico, which specializes in SAP). Although the UC in Chico is very successful in job placements of its graduates, its approach is comparably unique and not widely adopted yet.

In conclusion, the book reflects the contingency approach, which is at the right timing (2006+), but it does not guarantee that it will last forever. Shifting focus of IT education from general skills to business process-driven IT skills seems to be a successful strategy for the 2000s. However, it is too soon to judge how it impacts on students' potential for better jobs and their security. Further research should be undertaken to trace the industrial practices and attitude towards "local" more expensive and better educated labor force versus "offshore-outsourced" less expensive one. The IS/CIS/MIS/BIT faculty should study how the BPI/ERP-oriented curriculum has actually made a change in the careers of students who took the reengineered program, whether students were able to find better paying jobs, and whether their level of satisfaction was higher.

REFERENCES

Carr, N. (2003, May). IT doesn't matter. *Harvard Business Review*, 41-49.

Cairncross, F. (1997). *The death of distance*. Boston: Harvard Business School Press.

Friedman, T. (2005). *The world is flat*. New York: Farrar, Straus, and Giroux.

InformationWeek. (2005, September 19). *17th Annual Survey of 500 most IT innovative companies*.

Acknowledgments

We are indebted to many individuals who contributed to the development of this first scholarly book in Enterprise Systems Education in the world.

First, we would like to thank all reviewers for their constructive comments on and invaluable suggestions to each chapter, which essentially ensure the academic value and quality of this book. Our professional gratitude is directed toward all of our authors from academia to industry for their excellent contributions to this book.

Our special thanks go to the publishing team at Idea Group Publishing, in particular to our development editor, Ms. Kristin Roth, who advised and helped us not only to keep the project on schedule, but also to resolve several tough issues, and Dr. Mehdi Khosrow-Pour who motivated us to take on this pioneering project.

Finally, we would like to give our hearty thanks to Andrew's wife, Irmina, and Michael's wife, Lee, and his lovely children, Charity, Christina, and Michael, for their love and patience to support us for completing this project.

Andrew Targowski and Michael Tarn
Kalamazoo, Michigan, USA

Section I

Developing an ES Curriculum

Chapter I

Critical Success Factors for Implementing ERP Systems as a Vehicle for Business Curriculum Integration at a Large State University

Kenneth E. Murphy, Willamette University, USA

ABSTRACT

This chapter documents and analyzes an initiative in which the College of Business Administration implemented an ERP system in their coursework with the goal of integrating curriculum across disciplines. While the narrative will not attempt to provide the precise reason that the College did not achieve its goal, it will point to a number of challenges that arise in such initiatives. Analysis of these events is provided in order to assist other educational organizations in determining critical success factors for entering in technology alliances relationships with third party providers.

INTRODUCTION

In 1998, the College of Business Administration (CBA) within a large public University engaged in the endeavor of integrating its business curriculum via the implementation an enterprise resource planning (ERP) system. Over the next five years, significant investments of time, money, and faculty and staff resources were put toward the initiative, but in the end, the college failed to achieve its initial objective. Was the objective too aggressive or was the execution of the plan flawed? This chapter provides a description of the ERP initiative from its conception, analyzes the outcomes, and presents those factors that if they had been better anticipated may have helped alter the results.

The CBA is a unit within a large state university in the southern United States. The university has a total enrollment of over 30,000 students and is located in a large metropolitan area. The CBA is the largest of the university's professional schools, enrolling approximately 4500 undergraduate and graduate students each year. The CBA is organized into five academic units, the departments Finance, Decision Sciences and Information Systems, Management and International Business, Marketing and Business Ethics, and a School of Accounting. The CBA offers a broad variety of undergraduate business majors managed within each of the departments as well as a significant number of Masters Degree programs including MBA and specialized Masters of Science degrees. The College is accredited by the Association for the Advancement of Collegiate Schools of Business (AACSB) International (CBA, 2005).

Business curricula, in both graduate and undergraduate programs, is generally composed of a set of courses that are known as the "core" that represent a fundamental set of content in which all students must be proficient. The core is a significant percentage of the entire business degree program and generally includes courses in management, marketing, accounting, finance, operations, management science and statistics, international business, business law, and ethics. Large business colleges, like the CBA that tend to be functionally organized, manage core courses by allowing each of the departments to determine the relevant material for the specific courses that they are assigned to administer. Departments traditionally manage these courses in isolation without considering the content in core courses of other departments. In recent years, many collegiate schools of business have considered integration of core coursework across departments in order to increase the quality and relevance of the business education experience. This integration takes on a variety of forms in practice including the use of common case studies across courses, team teaching, and/or the creation of new multi-disciplinary courses. The incorporation of ERP systems in the curriculum has also been viewed as another possible mechanism for achieving this cross-functional integration.

ERP systems became popular in the mid to late 1990s with the goal of replacing legacy functional systems in accounting, human resources, order and inventory management and customer service with a unified application. ERP systems are divided into modules along the lines of the old standalone systems except that these modules access the same database. Each functional department still has their own application, except now the data is linked so that, for example, finance personnel can view the order management system to see if an order has been shipped. Among other stated goals, ERP systems can integrate financial and customer information across business units, standardize and speed up manufacturing processes, reduce inventory, and standardize HR information (Koch, 2005).

This chapter begins by telling the story of a college leadership that bravely struck out in a new direction with the goal of integrating management education across the disciplines by using ERP technology. It describes as objectively as possible the experience of deploying the ERP system across the curriculum. It then provides a critical analysis of this initiative both from an operational as well as the strategic perspective in order to understand why the initiatives original goals were not met. The result is a set of insights and recommendations for academic administrators and innovators who wish to proceed down a similar path.

USING CRITICAL SUCCESS FACTORS TO EVALUATE SUCCESS OF TECHNOLOGY INITIATIVES

Many universities have implemented ERP systems with the goal of updating their curriculum (Antonucci & Zur Meuhlen, 2001; Becerra-Fernandez, Murphy, & Simon, 2000; Corbitt & Mensching, 2000; Fedorowicz, Gelinas, Usoff, & Hachey, 2004; Strong, Johnson, & Mistry, 2004; Watson & Schneider, 1999). The most typical functional areas of implementation include the accounting, operations, and information systems departments. For example in accounting, McCombs and Sharifi (2002) describe the implementation of Oracle Financials in an accounting course, and Wygal and Hartman (2003) describe how ERP concepts have been implemented in a series of accounting courses through an initiative known as Advancing Curriculum Change in Technology.

ERP curriculum examples from the operations and systems areas are even more widespread. Watson and Schneider (1999) provide an early description of enterprise systems curriculum within operations and information systems. Their approach is to break the necessary ERP knowledge into a series of reusable components that can be integrated into a curriculum where needed. Hawking and McCarthy (2000) describe incorporating ERP into an IS curriculum via industry projects. These authors provide a further description of an e-learning ERP curriculum for the Asia-Pacific region (Hawking & McCarthy, 2001). Davis and Comeau (2004) outline a capstone course focusing on enterprise integration in the e-business concentration in the University of New Brunswick. The course is comprised of both hands-on ERP exercises and management oriented materials. Ritchie-Dunham, Morrice, Scott, and Anderson (2000) describe a strategic supply chain simulation in which an organization with non-integrated systems is compared to one that is integrated with enterprise systems. The simulated organization includes the main functions of an enterprise and is meant to quantitatively demonstrate the benefits of ERP systems. Bradford, Vijayaraman, and Chandra (2003) and MacKinnon (2004) provide surveys comparing the ERP offerings of schools in general and in the SAP University Alliance respectively.

Integrating the curriculum has been one of the most challenging goals to achieve in a meaningful way with respect to management education. Although there appears to be general agreement that it is beneficial to "demonstrate the interrelatedness of the various business functions and how they work together within the firm" (Pharr, 2000), one can find many examples of the problems encountered within these efforts (Closs & Stank, 1999; Ginger, Wang, & Tritton, 1999; Stover, Morris, Pharr, Byers, & Reyes, 1997). These problems include challenges with course design and presentation as well as the attitudes of faculty and the resources and infrastructure provided for the initiative. One recent study found that level of support by administrators for this process does seem related to integration success (Pharr, 2003).

The cross-functional and business process orientation of an ERP system lends itself well to their use as a vehicle for curriculum integration. In Becerra-Fernandez et al. (2000) the authors outline the integration of three MBA courses into a single combined team taught course based on an ERP. Joseph and George (2002) argue that ERP has the potential to bring about more effective pedagogy through the ability to approach problems from several different viewpoints. They continue stating that ERP "provides a 'nervous system' that can help the different units to see the value of working cohesively" (Joseph & George, 2002). Cannon et al. (2004) describe a curriculum integration initiative in which a company is described in a case study and simultaneously implemented in an ERP system. The authors describe a number of phases in the evolution of this case study and the implementation of the ERP system and eventually realized that the case study should be the focus of future integration efforts.

This chapter utilizes a version of the critical success factors (CSF) technique to analyze the ERP initiative at the CBA. Beginning with Rockart (1979), IS researchers have empirically identified factors that are most important for ensuring success in both IS planning and implementation. In the context of assessing a CEO's information needs, Rockart (1979) defines critical success factors as "the limited number of areas in which results, if they are satisfactory, will ensure successful competitive performance for the organization." Rockart proposed a method that includes iterative interviews with corporate executives in order to obtain an organization's critical success factors from executives for obtaining their current information needs. This technique was further developed and applied in a variety of settings including MIS planning and systems requirements analysis (Boynton & Zmud, 1984), project management (Slevin & Pinto, 1987), and business process reengineering (Bashein, Markus, & Riley, 1994).

In the ERP literature, many authors have endeavored to create generalized CSFs for ERP implementation. Bingi, Sharma, and Godla (1999) were among the first to recognize the critical implementation concerns of top management commitment, reengineering, integration with other systems, obtaining skilled consultants and employees for the project and employee training. Holland and Light (1999) divide their listing of CSFs into strategic and tactical levels employing as well as augmenting the work of Slevin and Pinto (1987). Somers and Nelson (2001) conducted an extensive review of more than 100 ERP implementations and arrived at a list of 22 CSFs. They created an executive survey and sampled 700 organizations receiving 86 responses for the degree of importance of the CSFs on a five point scale. They also asked respondents to indicate which stage of Cooper and Zmud's (1990) implementation framework (initiation, adoption, adaptation, acceptance, routinization, and infusion) that each CSF was most important. The results indicated that nine of the 22 CSF with mean importance greater than four and all but one with mean importance greater than three. They also found the six implementation stages had significantly different lists of most important CSFs (Somers & Nelson, 2001).

Nah, Lau, and Kuang (2001) performed a structured literature search and found 10 articles all but one published between 1998 and 2000 that had empirically sought CSFs in ERP or MRP II implementations. Based on this activity, the authors identified 11 CSFs for ERP implementation success and identified the phases of Markus, Axline, Petrie, and Tanis (2000) ERP life cycle model in which these factors were most important. To further validate this work Nah, Zuckweiler, and Lau (2003) surveyed 54 CIOs of Fortune 1000 companies in which they were asked to evaluate the importance of each of the CSFs on a 1 (not criti-

Table 1. Critical success factors in ERP implementation (Nah et al., 2003)

Factor	Average Score (5 point Scale)
Top Management Support	4.76
Project Champion	4.67
ERP Teamwork and Composition	4.65
Project Management	4.59
Change Management Culture and Program	4.50
Communication	4.39
Business Plan and Vision	4.31
BPR	4.22
Software Testing and Trouble Shooting	4.20
Monitoring and Evaluation of Performance	4.19
Appropriate Business and Legacy IT Systems	3.48

cal or important) to 5 (extremely critical and important) scale. The CSF research of these authors is summarized in Table 1.

In this chapter, the critical success factor approach will be based on the narrative history and documents of work on the ERP initiative at the CBA. Using this information as input for analysis, a comparison will be made; between what happened at the CBA and the critical success factors from Nah et al., (2003) and a second paper by Fedorowicz et al., (2004) which outlines 12 points for the successful implementation of ERP systems across the curriculum (See Table 2). The result then will indicate which of these factors are most

Table 2. Twelve tips for ERP integration (Fedorowicz et al., 2004)

The Twelve Tips
1. Go with what you know
2. Practice knowledge diffusion
3. Get it straight from the horse's mouth
4. Don't re-invent the wheel or make others do the same
5. New training approach, new training challenges
6. Outsource non-core competencies
7. Develop and maintain helpful relationships
8. Ask for help
9. Have realistic expectations
10. Let students learn from their mistakes
11. Provide good customer support
12. But what does it really look like?

important for success in implementations of ERP systems, this specific university setting or if there are additional factors that should be added to the list.

THE ERP INITIATIVE AT THE COLLEGE OF BUSINESS

The Dean of the CBA was the leader in initiating the idea to implement an ERP system as a tool for supporting teaching in the CBA. In her conversations with business leaders across the country, she had found that many of their organizations were facing complex and expensive implementations in ERP systems. The business leaders were aware of how resource intensive these ERP implementations were in practice and that their organizations had relatively little expertise in this arena. Based in part on the need for ERP skills the Dean determined that incorporating ERP technology in the curriculum could create a unique niche for the college, enhance and update faculty skills as well as introduce cutting-edge technology. A colleague of the Dean who had significant experience as an ERP Human Resources consultant was a second major influence. She put the Dean in contact with the American division of a German company, SAP,[1] to discuss membership in their budding corporate-academic alliance in late 1997.

SAP A.G., founded by five former IBM employees and located in Waldorf, Germany, has been in the software business since 1972. Throughout its existence, SAP has been and continues to be the leading vendor of ERP systems across the globe. Their most successful product has been the client-server application known as R/3 (Real-Time Version 3). Today, the company dominates the business applications market especially for the largest businesses and governmental organizations and counts Microsoft, IBM, HP, and Intel as well as many others among their clients. As the third largest software vendor in the world, there are over 96,000 installations of R/3 with 12 million users in 120 countries. SAP is currently pushing toward modularizing their product as well as become a provider of enterprise architecture infrastructure under the Netweaver initiative (SAP, 2005).

SAP has had an alliance program with universities since 1996. Early members of what was called the SAP University Alliance in the United States included Drexel University in Philadelphia (Drexel, 2005), Central Michigan University (Central Michigan, 2005), California State University at Chico (CSU Chico, 2005), and Louisiana State University (LSU, 2005). The number of universities in the alliance with SAP grew quickly through the late 1990s and early 2000s reaching at least several hundred institutions worldwide today. Today, SAP's major competitors in the ERP marketplace including Microsoft and Oracle have alliances that contain many member universities as well.

To obtain membership in the SAP University Alliance the university must present a proposal outlining the institution's plans to utilize the R/3 system in the curriculum. The CBA submitted its initial proposal to SAP America in June of 1998. The central goal outlined therein was to achieve an "enterprise-wide educational strategy" which was defined as the "readjustment of educational delivery, moving away from a focus on the standard functional areas toward an integrated, business process approach" (CBA, 1998). To accomplish this, the participating faculty members in the CBA proposed to proceed in a series of incremental stages that they felt would facilitate radical change in delivery of the business curriculum. Three major stages were identified for the evolution:

1.   Establishing enterprise-wide presence at the CBA
2.   Expanding delivery of enterprise-wide courses to the functional areas of Logistics, Information Systems, Accounting, Operations, and Marketing
3.   Creation of a new integrated core course in the MBA program and a new innovative major in the undergraduate program that will emphasize business processes. The undergraduate major was tentatively to be named "Enterprise-Wide Computing."

The first step of this strategy involved the development of an introductory course on the enterprise information systems. The initial course was to be taught at the graduate level in the fall semester of 1998. The second stage of this strategy was to integrate enterprise information systems principles and examples into courses in the functional disciplines including Logistics, Management Information Systems, Accounting, Operations, and Marketing. Courses that would use the R/3 system were forecasted to be ready for roll out over the next year and a half (from spring semester 1999 through spring semester 2000). Students were to gain experience in using SAP R/3 in the functional disciplines through exercises and projects that utilized the system.

In the third stage a new integrated course offering was to be created, building on the experience gained in stages one and two. This new course, for the graduate business program, was to replace several functional core courses (operations, accounting, and marketing) with a single "combined" course that was to be integrated across functions and would focus on business processes. Elements from operations, marketing, logistics, finance, accounting,

Table 3. Timeline for enterprise-wide curriculum integration

Fall 1998	Spring 1999	Fall 1999	Spring 2000	Fall 2000
Enterprise Information Systems (1)	Principles of Logistics (2)	Logistics Technology (2)	Global Logistics (2)	Integrated Graduate Core (3)
	Introduction to Business Information Systems (2)			Enterprise-Wide Computing Major (3)
	Organizational Information Systems (2)			
	Designing and Managing the Information Based Organization (2)			
	Current Issues in Auditing (2)			
	Global Operations Management (2)			

Note: Original proposed stage of development is indicated in parentheses.

and information systems were to be integrated into a single set of course materials that would be delivered by a team of faculty. The SAP R/3 system will be utilized throughout this "integrated core" to demonstrate the flow of information and level of integration that is necessary in modern business processes.

An additional component of stage three was to create an innovative new major entitled Enterprise-Wide Computing an alternative to the traditional undergraduate Management Information Systems major with the goal of developing students who handle both the technical as well as managerial issues that arise in ERP implementation and operations. Some of the courses included in the major were the traditional MIS course while others focused only on ERP (e.g., SAP R/3 administration). Intensive course development for the stage three initiatives was to take place during the 2000-01 academic year. A proposed timeline with the courses that would incorporate SAP as a component is shown in Table 3.

Table 4. Faculty titles and courses from June 1998 (SAP university alliance proposal)

Faculty/Staff Member Number	Title	Proposed Courses (Stage)
1	Dean and Professor of Management Information Systems	• Designing and Managing the Information Based Organization (2)
2	Director and Professor School of Accounting	• Current Issues in Auditing (2)
3	Professor of Logistics (Marketing)	• Principles of Logistics (2) • Logistics Technology (2) • Global Logistics (2)
4	Professor of Decision Sciences	• Principles of Logistics (2) • Global Operations Management (2)
5	Associate Professor of Information Systems	• Logistics Technology (2) • Organizational Information Systems (2)
6	Associate Professor of Accounting	• Enterprise Information Systems (1)
7	Assistant Professor of Information Systems	• Organizational Information Systems (2)
8	Assistant Professor of Information Systems	• Global Logistics (2) • Global Operations Management (2)
9	Instructor of Information Systems	• Introduction to Business Information Systems (2)
10	Director of Technology for CBA	• Introduction to Business Information Systems (2)

Ten faculty and staff were involved in writing the original proposal, which included six faculty members from Decision Sciences and Information Systems, two from the School of Accounting, a logistics professor from the Marketing department who was also an associate Dean as well as the Director of Technology at the CBA. The Dean was the initiative's leader, but the responsibility for initial operations fell to the Professor of Logistics. See Table 4 for a list of the faculty titles and proposed courses from the initial proposal to the SAP University Alliance.

There was no fee to join the Alliance with SAP, however, any university in the alliance was required to pay an annual fee to license the use of the R/3 application. At the time of joining the alliance, there were three levels of membership and CBA leadership chose the 2nd level at an annual cost of $7500. This membership level included a one-time benefit of 105 free person-days of training on the R/3 system at SAP education centers. Most of the faculty members who were a part of the proposal intended to attend one or more of these training courses often starting with an introductory course and then heading to intermediate or advanced level courses. Faculty members were generally sent to one or more training courses if they indicated interest in supporting the initiative. Subsequent to proposal submission several new faculty members joined the initiative as well (see Table 5).

In addition to the annual license fee, the College was also required to provide the hardware to support the application as well as any costs for travel and lodging training courses which would be necessary as training took place at SAP education centers. Table 6 displays a list of the training courses attended or scheduled by the set of involved faculty members as of summer 1998.

Table 5. Additional faculty joining the initiative in 1998-2000

Faculty/Staff Member Number	Title	Rationale
11	Associate Professor of Information Systems	Taught database course/In charge of Masters of Science in Management Information Systems (MS in MIS) program
12	Department Chair and Professor of Marketing	Considered teaching a Customer Relationship Management course
13	Associate Professor of Information Systems	Teaching ERP Courses in the Masters of Science in Management Information Systems (MS in MIS) program
14	Assistant Professor of Information Systems	Teaching ERP Courses in the Bachelors of Business Administration Masters of Management Information Systems (MS in MIS) concentration
15	Instructor of Information Systems (PhD Student)	Former ERP HR Consultant and Ph.D. Student

Table 6. CBA ERP initiative initial training plan at SAP America

SAP Training Course Name	Location	Training Days	Faculty Attending
Financial and Management Accounting	Houston	5	2, 6
Implementation Planning for R/3	Dallas/Philadelphia	2	9, 11
Technical Core Competencies	Houston	5	9, 11
Customer Order Management	Philadelphia/Boston	5	5, 8, 12
Logistics Information Systems	Chicago	2	5
Logistics Information Systems (2)	Chicago	2	5
R/3 Architecture	Houston	2	11
R/3 Basis Technology	Atlanta	2	9, 11
R/3 Business Processes	Dallas/Irvine	3	2, 5, 6, 11, 12

A student with a background in engineering who had completed a Masters degree at the CBA was hired to be the system administrator for the server that would house the SAP system. Among the responsibilities of the system administrator were to install, bring up, and support the SAP R/3 system for the CBA. The SAP R/3 system was to be brought up using the International Demonstration and Evaluation System (IDES) training database. IDES represented a pseudo-company that the SAP company itself used as a training and demonstration system for the functionality of the R/3 product. The system administrator was sent to several technical training courses at SAP as well.

The implementation of ERP in the curriculum seemed timely. Faculty team members were excited about working with a new and in-demand technology, and they hoped that this innovation would enhance the reputation of the college. Students, who were aware of the Y2K problem, had heard that ERP was a major initiative at many companies. They were also quite interested in getting their hands on the technology as a way of getting at plum professional services positions that seemed to be plentiful in the late 1990s. The administration including the Dean hoped that the initiative would bring new prominence to the CBA.

EXECUTING THE PLAN PART 1: THE IMPLEMENTATION OF ENTERPRISE SYSTEMS CURRICULUM (1998-2000 ACADEMIC YEARS)

SAP America accepted the proposal and admitted the CBA to the University Alliance by the end of summer 1998. From the beginning, the initiative was beset by a number of issues that resulted in delays. The first issue was that took it longer than expected for the University and SAP legal teams to agree to the formal letter of understanding. The time to read, edit, and process the legal agreement between was far longer than expected. The

University had not been a member of such an alliance in the past and the time to process it through the University's legal department was not planned for. The final letter of understanding was not completed until several months into the fall semester of 1998.

A second major challenge involved the installation of the SAP R/3 system and the IDES training database. System installation was lengthy and required a large number of patches to complete the process. Mistakes in choice of patches or memory allocation made early in the installation would not been realized until hours or perhaps days later. At the beginning the system administrator did not have a good understanding of complexity of the sophisticated ERP system, R/3. As an example, in standard configuration the system's calendar dictates that month-end closing must be accomplished before any subsequent processing can occur. System closing had to be done by a user with proper authorization. Inexperience with ERP systems both from the perspective of instructors and the technical staff member was in part responsible for these delays. For these reasons the system was not operational until early in 1999.

While many of the faculty members who originally supported the initiative attended training courses at SAP, almost none of these faculty members incorporated the system into their courses. One of the major reasons was that training on the system at SAP did not lend itself naturally to a way that the R/3 system could be easily used in the classroom. Training at SAP was built around demonstrating software functionality of the system for the corporate customers of the company. A week long training course might focus solely on the order management process and provide deep detail on the nuances of the system to support these activities. This did not lend itself well to a specific course module or topic in part because course were generally designed around functions and departments and not processes.

In the beginning, CBA faculty members in the initiative had been excited about working as a team and the possibilities that the R/3 application might provide for their courses. However, after attending the training sessions there were no subsequent incentives to either motivate these nor help instructors to follow through on incorporating the system into their course materials. Beyond the system administrator no additional personnel resources who understood both the particular needs of the instructor in the classroom and the detail with respect to the complex R/3 system.

During this early period, two new faculty members were hired at assistant professor level into the Decision Sciences and Information Systems department. One had worked with the SAP system as a PhD student, and the other was very interested in ERP systems from both a teaching and research perspective. These faculty members, (listed as numbers 13 and 14 in Table 5,) were both willing and motivated to include the SAP R/3 system in their courses. A PhD student, (listed a number 15 in Table 5) who had been an SAP consultant in the HR area was also one of the early adopters of using the technology in the classroom.

The instructors that did implement the SAP R/3 system in their courses during the 1998-2000 academic years only presented introductory coursework or overviews of ERP systems within the information systems area. Faculty members incorporating the system had a hard time finding textbooks or other course materials to use in the classroom. Relevant course content often had to be created by the faculty member teaching the class or pulled together from widely disparate sources. In some of the courses the ERP system was simply demonstrated to, rather than used by the students. Table 7 shows the coursework that used or demonstrated the system in the 1998-2000 academic years.

Technical problems continued to affect the R/3 system's integrity at the CBA and support from SAP America was not easy to obtain. It was not clear exactly why support was lack-

Table 7. Course offerings 1998-2001 utilizing or demonstrating SAP R/3 technology

Semester	Course Title	Instructor	Program	Enrollment
Fall 1998	Enterprise Information Systems	6	MBA	45
Spring 1998	Enterprise Information Systems	13	MBA	45
Fall 1999	Enterprise Information Systems	13	MBA	22
	Organization Information Systems	1	Executive MBA	25
	Organization Information Systems	7	MBA	58
	Enterprise Information Systems	14	BBA MIS	34
Spring 2000	Organization Information Systems	7	MBA	50
	Information Systems Development	13	MS in MIS	41
	Information Systems Configuration	15	MS in MIS	41
	Design and Implementation of Information Systems	14	BBA MIS	45
Summer 2000	Enterprise Systems Development	10	MS in MIS	41
	Development and Integration of ERP Applications	14	BBA MIS	45

ing from SAP America, but there are several possible reasons. University alliance members represented customers of little value to SAP as they did not pay the standard licensing fees. The lack of understanding of technical issues related to the IDES training database which was the purview of the training organization and not the personnel in the University Alliance group within SAP America. Couple these observations with the fact that during this period the number of customers and implementations of SAP R/3 in the private sector were booming and technical expertise with the technology was in general hard to find. The high-profile, front page, "failures" of SAP implementations in the corporate world were well documented and there is no doubt that the company wanted to avoid repeats of that situation.

Toward the end of 1999, faculty members in the Department of Decision Sciences and Information Systems documented their view of how the technology would be incorporated into the curriculum at the CBA (Becerra-Fernandez et al., 2000). Two programs incorporating the R/3 system were proposed, an enterprise resource management track as a part of the undergraduate management information systems program and the integration of the system into the existing Masters of Science in Management Information Systems program. Both programs infused the ERP idea into the existing curriculum by including essentially the following three classes:

1.   **Business Process Modeling:** a course that would define and demonstrate the use of modern business processes in organizations

2.   **Configuration of ERP Systems:** a course in which the actual technical implementation or configuration of ERP systems would be demonstrated
3.   **ERP System Administration:** a course that would demonstrate the administration concepts including technical installation of R/3, security implementation, role administration and general system operations

The article's authors describe the vision for an integrated curriculum based on combining operations, marketing, and accounting courses. It is stated that this course would be completed by August of 2000. The article goes on to present some of the challenges faced by the college in implementing the system including training issues, lack of technological know-how, the lack of incentives, significant resource requirements and the organizational barriers between departments. The article seems to deviate in vision from the original proposal presented to the SAP Corporation. In this article, it seems that use of system would be focused mainly on the information systems curriculum.

EXECUTING THE PLAN PART 2: CHANGE AND GROWTH IN THE ERP INITIATIVE (ACADEMIC YEARS 2000-2003)

During the summer of 2000, two major changes took place with respect to the organization supporting the ERP initiative at the CBA. First the operational leadership was changed from an the Professor of Logistics to an Assistant Professor of Information Systems after the former left the University, and second a new system administrator was hired after the old administrator resigned her position at the University. The decision to put the assistant professor of information systems in charge was largely based on that professor's desire to take on the responsibilities involved with the initiative. The Dean, who was still highly supportive of the initiative, had little choice but to appoint this professor as no other leader emerged.

The new system administrator was a former student with a technical background both in information systems and in finance, but similar to the case of the first system administrator he had no experience with ERP systems or systems administration. The university also had to obtain an H1B visa for the student before hiring him as the systems administrator. One major difference between the two administrators was the depth of the interest in ERP systems. The new administrator was highly motivated to succeed in his new role supporting ERP at the CBA.

Over the three academic years from 2000-2003 the new director instituted a number of new initiatives to reinvigorate the use of the system. During this time, a number of new faculty members and instructors became involved with teaching in the ERP oriented curriculum (See Table 8). A curriculum award was applied for at SAP America and the CBA was selected to receive the award in 2001. This provided the College with additional (and needed) training days at SAP. This time the initiative's leadership was much more selective both with the training courses attended and with who attended those courses. Faculty members were required to have already incorporated this system into their courses before being permitted to attend training.

Table 8. Additional faculty who joined the ERP initiative 2000-2003

Faculty Number	Title	Rationale
16	Assistant Professor of Accounting	Willing to teach ERP courses in the School of Accounting
17	Instructor of Accounting	Willing to teach ERP courses in the School of Accounting
18	Instructor of Accounting (PhD Student)	Willing to teach ERP courses in the School of Accounting
19	Instructor of Information Systems	Interested in ERP systems
20	Instructor of Accounting	Interested in ERP systems
21	SAP R/3 System Administrator	Required ERP training for systems administrator duties and willing to teach in the Department of Decision Sciences and Information Systems
22	Assistant Professor of Information Systems	Willing to teach ERP courses in the Department of Decision Sciences and Information Systems

One way that new faculty members were inspired to become involved was by being offered a financial stipend to begin teaching courses, which used SAP R/3. By this time a significant amount of organizational expertise existed in part represented by a number of working exercises for the SAP system, which had been developed and catalogued. Any instructor could use any of these exercises on the system in their courses. This greatly speeded integration of system concepts into a broader variety of courses (see Table 9).

Even though a larger number of instructors became involved the coursework remained largely disciplined based. The focus was specifically in two departments: Accounting and Decision Science and Information Systems. In the School of Accounting ERP systems were now being viewed as "hot" technology and it was hoped that all students would gain some experience in using these systems. Several, but not all, of the faculty teaching the accounting information systems courses incorporated R/3 exercises in their coursework. In the Management Information Systems major, it was felt that students would gain necessary depth using the system if they used the system in several courses. Eventually a three-course sequence was established using R/3, which included:

1. Enterprise Information Systems
2. Implementing Enterprise Systems
3. Enterprise Reporting

Table 9. Course offerings 2000-2003 academic years utilizing ERP technology

Semester	Course Title	Instructor(s)	Program
Fall 2000	Organization Information Systems	1	Exec MBA
	Organization Information Systems	13	MS MIS
	Process Design and Configuration	15	MS MIS
	Enterprise Information Systems	14	BBA MIS
Spring 2001	Organization Information Systems	13	MS MIS
	Process Design and Configuration	15	MS MIS
	Enterprise Information Systems	14	BBA MIS
	Systems Analysis and Design	14	BBA MIS
Summer 2001	Enterprise Information Systems	14	BBA MIS
Fall 2001	Organization Information Systems	7	MS MIS
	Adv. Acc. Information Systems	17	MS Acc
	Acc. IS Analysis and Design	18	MS Acc
	Enterprise Information Systems	8	MBA
	Accounting Information Systems	16, 18	BBA Acc
	Configuring Enterprise Systems	8	BBA MIS
	Enterprise Information Systems	8	BBA MIS
Spring 2002	EDP Auditing	17	MS Acc
	Adv. Acc. Information Systems	17	MS Acc
	Accounting Information Systems	16, 18	BBA Acc
	Configuring Enterprise Systems	8	BBA MIS
	Enterprise Information Systems	8	BBA MIS
	Process Design	15	MS MIS
Summer 2002	Adv. Acc. Information Systems	17	MS Acc
	Configuring Enterprise Systems	8	BBA MIS
	Enterprise Information Systems	8	BBA MIS
	Systems Analysis and Design	19	BBA MIS
Fall 2002	Accounting Information Systems	20	BBA Acc
	Adv. Acc. Information Systems	17	MS Acc
	Acc. IS Analysis and Design	18	MS Acc
	Configuring EIS	18	MS Acc
	Enterprise Information Systems	21, 22	BBA MIS
	Systems Analysis and Design	19	BBA MIS
	Enterprise Information Systems	15	MS MIS
Spring 2003	Accounting Information Systems	16, 18	BBA Acc
	Data Warehousing and Anal	8	MS Acc
	Adv. Acc. Information Systems	17	MS Acc
	Configuring Enterprise Systems	18	MS Acc
	Configuring Enterprise Systems	18	BBA MIS
	Enterprise Information Systems	8, 22	BBA MIS
	Enterprise Reporting (ABAP)	8	BBA MIS
	Enterprise Information Systems	15	MS MIS

The first two courses were similar to those previously outlined and in Becerra-Fernandez (2000), an introduction focusing on business processes and on the use of ERP systems, and a course in which the students actually configured all the basic modules of the R/3 system. This course was largely based on a training course offered by the SAP University Alliance and an outside consultant. The Enterprise Reporting course focused on the ABAP/4[2] programming language in order to create custom reports and interfaces the system. This skill was thought to be in high demand by corporate customers of the SAP technology. Again this course was based on training provided though the SAP University Alliance and California State University at Chico.

The ability to offer these courses was directly a result of the increasing sophistication of the services offered by the SAP University Alliance during this period. The alliance began offering specific training sessions aimed directly at specific topics for faculty using the R/3 system. The CBA hosted one such training seminar. These training sessions provided instruction on content and processes for teaching the curriculum to students. The material as taught could become a standalone course or part of such a course. A variety of sessions were offered providing training on SAP's basic R/3 technology and peripheral applications like customer relationship management.

The technical infrastructure supporting the ERP initiative at the CBA grew significantly in this period as well. The new system administrator in his intent to learn, innovate, and grow the initiative repeatedly asked for more resources. Among other items, he requested that test servers be available for evaluating various aspects of systems management as well as servers for the ever broader variety of classes that were offered. Depending on the goal of the course it can be risky for system integrity to have several classes operating on the same server. During this period the SAP data warehouse (SAP Business Warehouse) was also acquired from SAP America. SAP Business Warehouse was utilized in the newly reconstituted Masters of Accounting program to illustrate the use of advance decision support systems. The number servers supporting the initiative grew from one to five by the summer of 2002.

In 1998, one faculty member had visited the Personal Computer Division within IBM in Raleigh, North Carolina to observe a large-scale ERP implementation. This was the first of what would be several visits for a small group of CBA faculty to IBM to observe ERP implementation and factors leading to its success. A relationship with IBM was established, and in 1999, several students were sent to IBM for internships. The internship at IBM provided the students the opportunity to take part in a real ERP implementation. From 1999 until 2001 over 20 of the best MIS and Computer Science students were sent to work with IBM. No ERP or SAP experience was required as the CBA and IBM desired the best students for this internship opportunity.

The period from 2000 forward was marked by serious changes in the technology world. Even before the events of September 2001, there was evidence of an economic and technological slowdown. This had both a positive and a negative effect on the CBA. Initially enrollments for the programs offered at the CBA increased as many unemployed workers headed back to school. Later however, particularly in the computer oriented majors, like management information systems, enrollments fell significantly. The most likely case was the perception that jobs in information systems were simply not available in the volume previously seen.

The downturn in the economy eventually affected revenues at the State, which in turn changed the funding environment for the University as a whole. All units including the CBA were required to tighten their belts. The general trends were parallel by the shifting of internal priorities for the CBA. A movement from an entrepreneurial stage in which programs proliferated to a quality improvement initiative reduced the size of the new revenue generating programs. This reduced the Dean's flexibility to allocate money to the ERP initiative.

In the fall of 2003, for the first time, the Dean proposed reducing or even eliminating investment in the ERP initiative. The initiative had not realized success in the form of significant additional funds or in great reputation improvements for the CBA. Students were not flocking to take courses using the technology nor were employers breaking down the doors to hire students who took ERP courses. The overhead to keep the initiative going was significant. Cutbacks were planned and made in the level of investment in the salary for the systems administrator and in new technology purchases. There was also talk of moving the ERP system out of the CBA to a department in the School of Engineering. In the summer of 2003, the director of the ERP initiative at the CBA left the institution.

ANALYSIS AND REFLECTION OF ENTERPRISE SYSTEMS INITIATIVES IN UNIVERSITIES

This section provides analysis to obtain insight as to why the original objectives of curriculum integration were not achieved using the ERP system. Not surprisingly it was a combination of challenges faced by the CBA that led to the eventually demise of the initiative. The issues faced can roughly be divided into environmental, strategic, and operational categories and each of these areas had a role.

During the 2000-2001 and subsequent academic years, there was a perception many factors changed both in the internal and external environments at the CBA. Externally, the bursting of the IT "bubble" and subsequent change in economic climate had the effect of significantly reducing the investment in ERP systems and the number of employment opportunities in IT. In general, the business world took a much more defensive position with respect to IT investments, and all ERP vendors also suffered. Not surprisingly the professional service firms stopped hiring as well as the business for ERP services declined.

As previously mentioned, the CBA first benefited from the economic slowdown in that program sizes grew and new programs with specific specializations were implemented. In part this growth in diversity and offerings was also a reflection of the entrepreneurial stage that the CBA was in. Later, however, the CBA's strategy shifted and program quality became more important than size. This led to small class sizes and, in turn, less disposable income which led to a reevaluation of spending priorities.

The ERP initiative at the CBA suffered from a number of operational challenges with respect to its administration and organization. There were many issues were respect to return on the ERP initiative investment. Investments in the initiative were significant with respect to the systems administrator's salary, technology investments, licensing fees and miscellaneous other costs including travel to training and conferences. There was no obvious way to recover these costs directly from the students, and there was no additional in-flow of money as a result of having the technology available. It was not clear if this situation would be rationalized at any time in the future.

Table 10. Summary of turnover in CBA ERP initiative faculty/staff 1998-2003

Faculty Member	Rank	Number of Training Sessions Attended at SAP	Courses Taught	Notes
1	Dean and Professor of Management Information Systems	0	3	
2	Director and Professor School of Accounting	2	0	Left Institution
3	Professor of Logistics (Marketing)	0	0	Left Institution
4	Professor of Decision Sciences	0	0	
5	Associate Professor of Information Systems	6	0	Left Institution
6	Associate Professor of Accounting	2	1	Left Institution
7	Assistant Professor of Information Systems	0	3	
8	Assistant Professor of Information Systems	1	10	Became Initiative Director and (later) Left Institution
9	Instructor of Information Systems	3	1	
10	Director of Technology for CBA	0	0	
11	Associate Professor of Information Systems	5	0	
12	Department Chair and Professor of Marketing	2	0	

Table 10. continued

Faculty Member	Rank	Number of Training Sessions Attended at SAP	Courses Taught	Notes
13	Associate Professor of Information Systems	2	5	Left Institution
14	Assistant Professor of Information Systems	2	9	Left Institution
15	Instructor of Information Systems (Ph.D. Student)	0	5	
16	Assistant Professor of Accounting	0	6	
17	Instructor of Accounting	1	8	
18	Instructor of Accounting (Ph.D. Student)	1	9	
19	Instructor of Information Systems	0	2	
20	Instructor of Accounting	0	1	
21	SAP R/3 System Administrator	3	1	
22	Assistant Professor of Information Systems	2	2	

A major issue that continually occurred throughout was faculty and staff turnover. (See Table 10) To address the question of why the original faculty members lost interest in the initiative is challenging, however, some of the reasons include:

1. Research productivity is rewarded at large, research-oriented universities and not teaching innovation.
2. The ERP system was complex to learn and faculty members didn't perceive that effort spent in this manner was worth it; Moreover the system's complexity was not well-understood in the first place.

3.   Integration of the ERP system concepts into the classroom was difficult because of the lack of textbooks or other course materials on the subject.
4.   Even if relevant course materials could be brought together a major "headache" was the lack of a good data set. The IDES training database simply did not provide the level of functionality required in order to be broadly useful for students in disciplines outside the accounting and information systems disciplines.

Student interest in the initiative also waned for a number of reasons:

1.   The general lack of positions in information systems arena which is part of the more general trend of declining enrollments in MIS majors and CS majors across the country today.
2.   The lack of obvious positions in industry using ERP oriented skills that they had obtained in the classroom.
3.   The lack of many faculty members stating the importance of the initiative to students, that is, the lack of institutional message on the importance of ERP systems. The CBA as a whole never adopted a process model for how organizations operate. Such a model could have enabled the use of the SAP system as a demonstration mechanism.

These observations lead to recommendations for institutions who, like the CBA, wish to become members in complex technology alliances. The first, on a strategic level, regards the shift in the CBA's objectives. Originally the CBA set out with the goal of moving from silo-ed courses to integrated core. After 2000 the evidence shows that the college evolved back toward departmental oriented courses using advanced technology. These goals are both worthy, but have very different implications for how they are to be carried out. In the former case faculty from all departments must be involved whereas this is not the case in the latter setting.

It is not clear why the CBA gave up on its original vision of integrating the curriculum across departments. However, schools that have gone through the exercise of integration have experienced the challenges associated with it. The lack of cross-functional course content, agreement on delivery and institutional support are all factors that have been cited as barriers (Pharr, 2000). Moreover coupled with a complex technology that was not well understood by faculty members especially outside of accounting and information systems made this an almost insurmountable challenge. Add to this the lack of real incentives to integrate the curriculum from leadership at the college, and it is unlikely to occur.

In the research surveying use of ERP systems at colleges of business, one sees that many schools focus this use primarily in the information systems and accounting arenas (Bradford et al., 2003; MacKinnon, 2004). Although ERP systems are cross-functional in nature and do support a complete set of business processes, they are better suited for the teaching of information systems and accounting than to marketing and finance. This is due to the type of content generally taught in these courses, which tend toward strategic versus operational decision making. In any case the goals set for the initiative must be clearly stated and used as a guide to implementing the initiative. They should also be reasonable in the sense that many factors can affect the success of such an initiative.

A second key factor required for any institution embarking on technology oriented initiatives is to gain a real understanding of the technology itself in advance to joining the initiative. This can be done by a single trusted member of the university, but this person must have some understanding of the following:

1.   Goals of the organization with respect to the use of the technology in the classroom.
2.   The data that the system provides to use in the classroom setting.
3.   The complexity in learning how to use the system.
4.   The realities of the teaching environment in terms of goals of instruction in order to successfully assess the technology.

The last point is particularly important. Beyond an understanding of what the technology can and cannot do for the college instructor, one must understand the various levels of the technology use. Will the student be a user of the built-in business processes (keystroke activities), a business-technological interface implementer (programmer) or configuration expert (implementation expert)? Will the technology be utilized as a management decision-making aid (data warehouse) or for some other purpose? These are some key questions that should be carefully thought through before choosing the system.

These decisions tie quite closely to the requirement for an effective data set for teaching using the technology. Without a reasonable data set that is both simple enough for instructors and students to understand within the limits of a single course or set of courses and complex enough to be both interesting and provide for some reality in using the technology, a major reason for using a specific technology is lost. Moreover, for economies of scale, it makes sense to use the same data and interface in multiple courses if it is possible. In order to do this the data must be cross-functional in nature.

Instructors and faculty members are central to any such initiative. The complexity of ERP technologies dictates that any faculty members selected or who choose to be involved must understand that this involvement is for the long term, preferably for at least three to five years. Plans for the use of such technology should incorporate this view. Faculty members should be released from other responsibilities where possible and work on such an initiative should be acknowledged both within the normal review structure and though additional rewards and incentives. It is risky for untenured faculty members, PhD students, and instructors to be involved in such efforts, especially at research universities, as this often leads to unfortunate outcomes for those personnel.

Key to using advanced technologies is effective technical support. In addition to having personnel who are experienced in the system's operation, when supporting an educational initiative it is also useful to have personnel who understand the capabilities of the technology and the needs of instructors in the classroom. This capability is useful for colleges seeking to implement complex technologies. The second system administrator understood these needs at the CBA much better than the first.

Student interest in these initiatives must be sustained by the institution and its instructors as well. Students should be repeatedly advised as to exactly what their opportunities might be if they obtain this technology expertise. The institution has a role in making sure that these employment opportunities are available and making clear what the potential career paths are. This may require teaming with career placement organizations, holding events for potential employers and bringing in speakers to classes to discuss ERP careers.

The last component of the educational lifecycle for students is their choice of career. ERP systems were initially popular amongst students because of the perceived number of professional services opportunities of the late 1990s. Any college focusing on deep ERP skills must have alliance with organizations that value these skills and hire accordingly. Though the CBA had a strong alliance with IBM and even placed students in an ERP project at the company, the company did not hire students for their ERP skills. Initiative managers did not spend the time to develop a significant set of relationships with the right employers. This may in part have also been related to the perceived lack of users of SAP R/3 in the region in which the University was located.

In Table 11, the success of the initiative is summarized against the eleven critical success factors for ERP implementation of Nah et al. (2003).

Table 11. Analysis of critical success factors in ERP implementation for the CBA (Based on Nah et al., 2003)

Factor	Summary
Top Management Support	Excellent support with respect to funding for 1998-2003.
Project Champion	Lack of external and powerful champion.
ERP Teamwork and Composition	Very significant turnover in participating faculty members (See Table 10).
Project Management	Lack of formal management and recognition of the implementation of the initiative in the 1998-2000 period.
Change Management Culture and Program	Lack of a plan for culture change (however, three new courses were developed in the Decision Sciences and Information Systems Department and the system was incorporated in numerous courses).
Communication	Reasonably good internal communications, but lacked contact with a sufficient number of external stakeholders.
Business Plan and Vision	Reasonable short term planning, but changed vision midstream
BPR	N/A
Software Testing and Trouble Shooting	Very poor skills with technology in 1998-2000, however this improved over time.
Monitoring and Evaluation of Performance	Reasonable monitoring, number of students exposed to the technology grew every year reaching almost 600 in 2002-03
Appropriate Business and Legacy IT Systems	N/A

CONCLUSION

The success of the ERP initiative at the CBA can be evaluated in a number of ways. In terms of its size with respect to the number of students experiencing ERP systems in courses, the number of faculty members who taught and used the system one might say that the initiative was very successful. In the period of the last two years, 2001-2003, approximately 1000 students took classes from over ten faculty members on at least four different R/3 servers. Students utilized the business processes built in the system, configured, and customized the system. Accounting students also used the SAP Business Warehouse data warehousing technology in their graduate program. During the initiative a successful alliance was struck with IBM's PC Division and several research papers as well as over 20 student internships that often subsequently became jobs resulted.

Evaluated strategically one might reach different conclusions. The college was not able to integrate the curriculum using ERP technology. The reasons for this are many, and not the responsibility of any particular faction within the CBA. Integrating management curriculum has proved to be very challenging in practice and adding advanced technology increases the complexity of the task. Perhaps it is enough to introduce students to the technology and leave it to their future employers to bring them up to speed. Still a very significant resource investment in the ERP initiative did not return either on the initial goal of an integrated curriculum nor tangible economic manner.

The list below presents a set of recommendations for anyone embarking on such a technology alliance initiative as the CBA did with SAP. Many of these recommendations are perhaps self-evident, but never more so than when looking in a rearview mirror. In parentheses the link is shown between these recommendations and the twelve tips of Fedorowicz et al. (2004) from Table 2.

1. Develop a long-term (3-5 year) vision for the technology alliance
2. Determine one or more faculty members or other personnel with the proper stature to be the project champion
3. Determine relevant metrics for measuring the initiative's success
4. Set reasonable goals for the initiative over each year (Tip 9)
5. Provide effective support and incentives for faculty members supporting the program (Tip 5)
6. Build relationships with (hopefully large) organizations who are users of the technology (Tip 3, 7)
7. Understand the goals of the technology vendor and actively manage the relationship for mutual gain (Tip 7)
8. Reinforce knowledge sharing and interaction between faculty across departments (Tip 2, 4)

The goal of incorporating world-class technology in an academic setting is highly compelling from a number of perspectives. Most management faculty members are altruistic enough to want to deliver the highest quality and relevant educational experience for their students. By definition faculty members enjoy learning challenges themselves and developing their own state of the art skills. Educational institutions compete from the perspective of reputation and advanced technology initiatives lend themselves well to this type of publicity. Though compelling, careful thought and planning should accompany any alliance choice involving advanced technology as the resource investments not just financial will be significant. Ensuring that measures of success are established up front will help to clarify their viability.

REFERENCES

Antonucci, Y. L., Corbitt, G., Stewart, G., & Harris, A. L. (2004). Enterprise systems education: Where are we? Where are we going? *Journal of Information Systems Education, 15*(3), 227-234.

Antonucci, Y. L., & Zur Muehlen, M. (2001). Deployment of business to business scenarios in ERP education: Evaluation and experiences from an international collaboration. In *Proceedings of the 7th Americas Conference on Information Systems* (pp. 998-1004).

Bashein, B. J., Markus, M. L., & Riley, P. (1994, Spring). Preconditions for BPR success and how to prevent failures. *Information Systems Management*, 7-13.

Becerra-Fernandez, I., Murphy, K. E., & Simon, S. J. (2000). Integrating ERP in the business school curriculum. *Communications of the ACM, 43*(3), 39-41.

Bingi, P., Sharma, M., & Godla, J. (1999). Critical issues affecting an ERP implementation. *Information Systems Management, 16*(3) 7-14.

Boynton, A. C., & Zmud, R. W. (1984). An assessment of critical success factors. *Sloan Management Review*, 17-27.

Bradford, M., Vijayaraman, B. S., & Chandra, A. (2003). The status of ERP integration in business school curricula: Results of a survey of business schools. *Communications of the Association for Information Systems, 12*, 437-456.

CBA. (1998, June). *Enterprise-wide education strategy proposal*. Unpublished proposal to SAP America.

CBA. (2005). Retrieved August 20, 2005, from http://cba.fiu.edu/web/profile.htm

Central Michigan. (2005). Retrieved August 20, 2005, from http://sapua.cba.cmich.edu/default.asp

Closs, D. J., & Stank, T. P. (1999). A cross-functional curriculum for supply chain education at Michigan State University. *Journal of Business Logistics, 20*(1), 59-72.

Cooper, R. B., & Zmud, R. W. (1990). Information technology research: A technological diffusion approach. *Management Science, 36*(2), 123-139.

Corbitt, G., & Mensching, J. (2000). Integrating SAP R/3 into a college of business curriculum: Lessons learned. *Information Technology and Management, 1*, 247-258.

CSU Chico. (2005). Retrieved August 20, 2005, from http://sap.cob.csuchico.edu

Davis, C. H., & Comeau, J. (2004). Enterprise integration in business education: Design and outcomes of a capstone ERP-based undergraduate e-business management course. *Journal of Information Systems Education, 15*(3), 287-300.

Drexel. (2005). Retrieved August 20, 2005, from http://www.drexel.edu/IRT/SAP

Fedorowicz, J., Gelinas, U. J., Usoff, C., & Hachey, G. (2004). Twelve tips for successfully integrating enterprise systems across the curriculum. *Journal of Information Systems Education, 15*(3), 235-244.

Ginger, C., Wang, D., & Tritton, L. (1999). Integrating disciplines in an undergraduate curriculum. *Journal of Forestry, 97*(1), 17.

Hawking, P., & McCarthy, B. (2000). Industry collaboration: A practical approach for ERP education. In *Proceedings of the 4th Australasian Computing Education Conference* (pp. 129-133).

Hawking, P., & McCarthy, B. (2001). The ERP eLearning model for the delivery of ERP (SAP R/3) curriculum into the Asian region. In *Proceedings of the Informing Science Conference* (pp. 257-261).

Holland, C., & Light, B. (1999). A critical success factors model for ERP implementation. *IEEE Software, 16*(3), 30-35.

Johnson, T., Lorents, A. C., Morgan, J., & Ozmun, J. (2004). A customized ERP/SAP model for curriculum integration. *Journal of Information Systems Education, 15*(3), 245-254.

Joseph, G., & George, A. (2002). ERP, learning communities, and curriculum integration. *Journal of Information Systems Education, 13.*

Koch, C. (2005). The ABCs of ERP. *CIO Magazine.* Retrieved June 8, 2005, from http://www.cio.com/research/erp/edit/erpbasics.html

LSU. (2005). Retrieved August 20, 2005, from http://www.bus.lsu.edu/centers/sapucc/

MacKinnon, R. J. (2004). A comparison of the ERP offerings of AACSB accredited Universities belonging to the SAPUA. In *Proceedings of the 7th Annual Conference of the Southern Association of Information Systems* (pp. 206-212).

Markus, M. L., Axline, S., Petrie, D., & Tanis, C. (2000). Learning from adopters' experiences with ERP: Problems encountered and success achieved. *Journal of Information Technology, 15*, 245-265.

McCombs, G. B., & Sharifi, M. (2002, Winter). Design and implementation of an ERP oracle financials course. *Journal of Computer Information Systems*, 71-73, 2002-2003.

Nah, F. F., Lau, J. F., & Kuang, J. (2001). Critical factors for successful implementation of enterprise systems. *Business Process Management Journal, 7*, 285-296.

Nah, F. F., Zuckweiler, K., & Lau, J. L. (2003). ERP implementation: Chief information officers' perceptions of critical success factors. *International Journal of Human-Computer Interaction, 16*(1), 5-22.

Pharr, S. W. (2000, September/October). Foundational considerations for the establishing an integrated business common core curriculum. *Journal of Education for Business, 76*, 20-23.

Pharr, S. W. (2003). Integration of the core business curriculum: Levels of involvement and support provided. *Marketing Education Review, 13*(1), 21-31.

Ritchie-Dunham, J., Morrice, D. J., Scott, J., & Anderson, E. G. (2000). A strategic supply chain simulation model. In J. A. Joines, R. R. Barton, K. Kang, & P. A. Fishwick (Eds.), *Proceedings of the 2000 Winter Simulation Conference* (pp. 1260-1264).

Rockart, J. (1979, March-April). Chief executives define their own data needs. *Harvard Business Review*, 81-93.

SAP. (2005). Retrieved August 20, 2005, from http://www.sap.com/company/history.epx

Slevin, D. P., & Pinto, J. K. (1987, Fall). Balancing strategy and tactics in project implementation. *Sloan Management Review*, 33-44.

Somers, T. M., & Nelson K. G. (2001). *The impact of critical success factors across the stages of enterprise resource planning implementations.* Paper presented at the Hawaii International Conference on System Sciences.

Stover, D., Morris, J. S., Pharr, S. W., Byers, C. R., & Reyes, M. G. (1997). Breaking down the silo: Attaining an integrated business common core. *American Business Review*, *15*(2), 1-11.

Strong, D. M., Johnson, S. A., & Mistry, J. J. (2004). Integrating enterprise decision-making modules into undergraduate management and industrial engineering curricula. *Journal of Information Systems Education*, *15*(3), 301-313.

Watson, E. E., & Schneider, H. (1999). Using ERP systems in education. *Communications of the Association of Information Systems*, *1*(9), 1-46.

Wygal, D. E., & Hartman, B. P. (2003). Partnering for change: Infusing enterprise resource planning in the accounting curriculum. *Management Accounting Quarterly*, *4*(4), 63-67.

ENDNOTES

[1]   SAP stands for System Analysis and Program Development (http://www.sap.com/company/history.epx)

[2]   ABAP/4 is SAP's proprietary programming language. The R/3 system uses ABAP/4 for customization.

Chapter II

Implementing ERP Education in a Changing Environment and Different Degree Programs

Stefen Koch, Vienna University of Economics and BA, Austria

ABSTRACT

In this chapter, the ERP education program at the Department of Information Business of the Vienna University of Economics and BA is described. Especially emphasized is the embedding into the study programs both at the department and university-level. Due to a major change in the degree programs offered by the university, including the introduction of a completely new information systems bachelor and master program, changes to the ERP education program became necessary and are described. We also report several quantitative data on the lectures both before and after the changes, including satisfaction measures. From this, we try to condense some lessons for other institutions who are planning to introduce ERP into their curricula.

INTRODUCTION

Any education program can not be separated from the environment surrounding it, both on the department- and the university-level, but always needs to fit into larger programs. In this chapter, we will detail how enterprise resource planning (ERP) education with SAP R/3 has been fitted into a department, and into a changing environment of study programs offered by the university.

ERP education is today seen as a cornerstone of information systems (IS) education in general, and is part of many model curricula (e.g., Gorgone & Gray, 1999; Hawking, Ramp & Shackelton, 2001) have demonstrated that ERP can be fitted into several parts of the IS'97 model curriculum. It is influenced by several concepts like business process modeling that have become important to even larger communities like the consultant business overall. In addition, it is a changing field, as most vendors develop their products and include new functionalities like e-business, supply chain management, customer relationship management, or data mining applications, sometimes at a staggering rate (Joseph & George, 2002).

Educating students in ERP has always been a challenging task. Current ERP systems are very complex and because of the large amount of functionality offered, not easy to grasp. In addition, most areas demand specialist business know-how to understand, which is often missing especially in IS students. For students of more business-oriented degree programs, ERP offers a good starting point to enter the world of IS, and it is of high importance for them. Still today, many business administration areas mostly teach theory, without considering the tools in place in real-life companies. For many areas of business administration, foremost accounting, these tools are ERP solutions. It therefore seems of high importance for business administration students to learn about these systems and get to know their capabilities and limitations. In addition, as naturally spanning functional boundaries, ERP solutions can be used to overcome these divisions in education (Becerra-Fernandez, Murphy, Simon, 2000; Joseph & George, 2002).

VIENNA UNIVERSITY OF ECONOMICS AND BA AND ITS STUDIES

Overview

The Vienna University of Economics and BA was founded in 1898 as the Imperial Export Academy and got its current name in 1975. In 2004 the university gained autonomy implementing the University Act 2002. Currently, six degree programs, a doctoral study, and several post-graduate programs are offered to the 21,766 students (as of winter semester 2003/04). The staff numbers about 400 faculty, and 320 administrative personnel. In the last years, about 2,500 students newly enrolled each year. The Vienna University of Economics and BA has a distinctly international focus, documented by the fact that about every second student has experience abroad, 172 partner universities worldwide and nearly 21% of international students. The University is also a member of the Community of European Management Schools (CEMS) network, offering a master degree. There are several programs with focus on Central and Eastern Europe in place, including a special Executive MBA, a Master Class Eastern Europe and the JOSZEF Program geared specifically to East-West management training for students from Austria, Central- and Eastern Europe (Vienna University of Economics and BA, 2004).

Studies Before Winter 2002

From the mid of the 1980s onwards, the Vienna University of Economics and BA has offered eight-semester master programs in the fields of business administration, economics, business education, and commerce.

Within these studies, the education in IT related areas encompassed a two-hour introductory course on IT, followed by another two-hour laboratory course covering an area chosen by the lecturer. Both were positioned early in the programs and constituted the only mandatory IT education.

During their graduate study from the 5th semester onwards, students had to choose, depending on their master program, one or two specialist business administration options, each being a program of 12 weekly hours of classes. About 30 different programs were offered, including marketing, banking, insurance, human resource and others. Of special interest are the IT-related specialist options, offered by the three departments of the Institute of Information Processing and Information Business, termed Information Business (offered by the Department of Information Business), Production Management (offered by the Department of Industrial Information Processing, later renamed to Production Management), and Management Information Systems (offered by the identically named department). Within the first two of these, education in ERP was offered. The program implemented at the Department of Information Business will be detailed in this chapter, while the Department of Production Management focuses on logistics processes and business warehouse (Prosser & Ossimitz, 2001; Prosser, Taudes, & Weiss, 2001).

Current Studies

In the term starting Winter of 2002, the Vienna University of Economics and BA changed the curricula for all studies and in addition made several new studies available. One of the most profound changes was a common two-semester introductory phase in which students are required to complete a total of 34 weekly hours of classes. Of these 34 hours, only six are specific to the chosen degree program to facilitate easy switching between degree programs at the beginning, the rest is composed of business administration (including an introduction to business information systems), economics, law, mathematics, statistics, and foreign language.

The university continued, in a changed curriculum, the eight-semester master programs of Business Administration, Economics, Business Education, and Commerce (renamed to International Business Administration). In addition, a master program Business and Economics was introduced, with specialist areas business and law, management dcience and social economics. Besides the common introductory phase, main changes were the establishment of optional competence areas of 22 weekly hours of classes combining two different areas, and increasing the hours of specialist business administration options by four hours to 16 weekly hours of classes. This number had unofficially been reached by most programs even before by prescribing additional lectures to be taken.

The most important change pertaining to the ERP education was the creation of a completely new, six-semester bachelor's program in Information Systems, with an accompanying three semester master program.

The structure of the IS bachelor program (see also Figure 1) follows the other degree programs and participates in the common two-semester introductory phase of 34 weekly hours of classes. The six hours specific to the IS program are filled by a course on principles

Figure 1. Structure of information systems bachelor program (simplified)

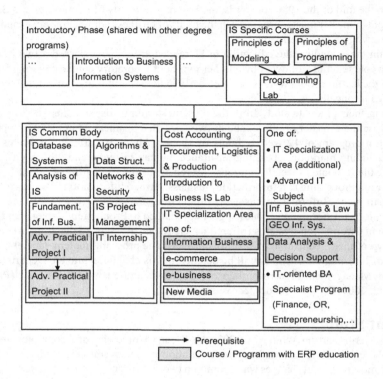

of modeling, containing lectures on the entity-relationship model, business process modeling techniques and the unified modeling language (Rumbaugh, Jacobson, & Booch, 1998), together with a short introduction to software development. The next course is Principles of Programming, which basically teaches Java programming, enforcing the object-oriented paradigm. If both courses are successfully completed, a two-hour laboratory class on programming concludes the segment, in which students have to perform several small and one larger programming exercises in Java, including analysis and design with UML.

After the introductory phase, the curriculum includes two additional business administration classes, the lab class Introduction to Business Information Systems, which features mostly office applications, internet basics and a small database application, and the common body of IS knowledge. This common body includes courses like Database Systems or IS Project Management and Teamwork, an IT internship with a company (de Brock, 2001) and Advanced Practical Project I and II. In addition, students have to choose one IT specialization areas (information business, e-commerce, e-business, or new media), plus either an additional IT specialization area or an advanced IT subject combining an IT specialization with another subject like IT-law, or an IT-oriented business administration specialist program. Each of these options consists of 16 weekly hours of classes.

ERP education is offered most prominently as an Advanced Practical Project I and II within the common body of knowledge by the Department of Information Business. By the same department in the IT specialization area Information Business, and by the Department of Production Management in the IT specialization area e-business and the advanced IT subjects data analysis and decision support respectively GEO information systems.

ERP EDUCATION AT THE DEPARTMENT OF INFORMATION BUSINESS

Situation Until Winter 2002

Introduction and Organization

Like any other specialist business administration option, information business was a program of 12 weekly hours of classes. These classes were divided between practice-oriented classes and lectures (see Figure 2 for an overview). Practice-oriented classes contained evaluations of students' performance, while mastery of contents of the lectures was evaluated with one exam at the end of the whole program. Officially, two classes at two hours per week each are more practice-oriented, an implementation project, and a seminar with scientific term paper. The successful completion of the implementation project is necessary to start with the seminar. If both are successfully finished, the student can take the program's final exam. The different lectures should be heard before or while taking the practice-oriented classes. As the implementation project deals with a small team of students completing an IS implementation project, another class has been introduced to give the students not familiar with the necessary technical knowledge in their chosen implementation variant the chance to learn these. The skills taught in the respective four weekly hours workshop, or successful completion of the workshop itself were necessary to start the implementation project. During the term the workshop was taken, students were advised to hear the two core lectures, Information

Figure 2. Structure of information business specialist program

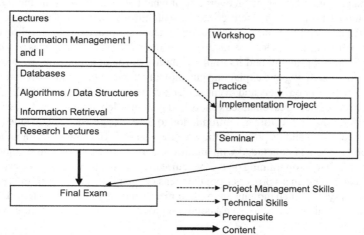

Copyright © 2007, Idea Group Inc. Copying or distributing in print or electronic forms without written permission of Idea Group Inc. is prohibited.

Management I and II, which mostly dealt with IS project management (e.g., process models and project planning) and therefore provided the necessary background knowledge to plan and execute the implementation project. The main reason for having students largely autonomously perform a complete, if small, IS implementation project was to raise their awareness of possible problems when they assume management responsibility. Combining skills from different courses, these implementation projects therefore served as capstone projects (Denton & Spangler, 2001; Gupta & Wachter, 1998).

The lectures completing the Information Business program included one out of a set of databases, algorithms/data structures and information retrieval, and two out of a varying set of research-oriented classes including open source software, user interface design, expert systems, decision support systems, and similar.

Most of the time, several different combinations of workshop and implementation project were offered for the students to choose from, corresponding to different possibilities of implementing an information system in an organization. The possible choices included: Object-oriented programming with C/C++ (later on Java), internet technologies (scripting languages with database connection like Perl or PHP), database implementation with SQL and Oracle, and implementation of a standard software package.

During the first years the set of workshop and implementation project with standard software package was taught using BaaN, and starting with Winter 1999 was switched to using SAP R/3 due to difficulties in the cooperation with BaaN and the market situation. The following descriptions pertain to the situation after the change to SAP R/3. Until the end of 2003, the SAP installation at the Department of Production Management was used, afterwards an own server (at costs of about 2,000 EUR) was purchased, and is now operating SAP R/3 4.7 Enterprise in cooperation with the academic application service provider Education Competence Center (ECC) of the Technical University Vienna. Software, and training for the lecturers using introductory courses, is sponsored by SAP AG.

Contents and Teaching Methods

The organization of the first course, the four-weekly-hours workshop, contained two different elements, with the first one being of a theoretical, the second, longer one, of a practical nature.

The first part aimed at giving an overview of what ERP is, and what the methodological background is. Therefore the lectures included an introduction with definitions, market overview, ERP pros and cons and a generic implementation process model, followed by a lecture on data modeling and a lecture on process modeling. Data modeling was taught using the Entity-Relationship model and its implementation in relational databases, knowledge later on used for visualizing and explaining customizing transactions, and process modeling was taught using both Petri-nets and event-driven process chains (Scheer, 2000).

While these first lectures remained vendor and system independent, afterwards SAP R/3 was emphasized. In a first lecture, an introduction to SAP was given. This included a short history of the company and its products, the organization of SAP R/3 itself with underlying software architecture and concluded with an introduction to the graphical user interface.

Afterwards, hands-on training on the system started, with the first part concerned with performing relevant business process from the areas of finanican and controlling (modules F1 and CO) on a system, then moving on to customizing and changing the system. The main reason for doing it this way was to have a common ground for viewing a working system in

Figure 3. Excerpt from lecture using entity-relationship concepts to illustrate SAP R/3 customizing transactions (Adapted from German original)

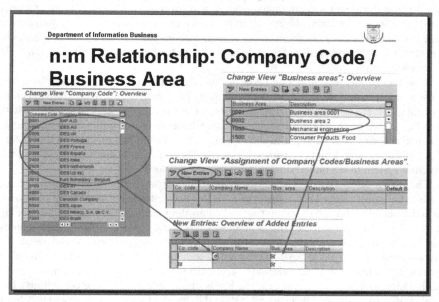

production, afterwards allowing each student to change it. Out of scarcity in storage space, all students worked on the same client, using their assigned two-digit login number as part of any key for objects they created, e.g. creating an account 1131## with ## standing for the login number. During the years of working in this way, no problems of one student deleting or changing another's objects ever occurred. In the first part, both modules were explained, also using entity-relationship models to document relations between organizational structures, and the most important master data like accounts including receivable and payable, cost centers, cost elements, activity types or internal orders were described and sets created by the students. Then several business processes were enacted (using also the created master data sets), first in demonstration by the lecturer, then by the students. These included among others general ledger documents, invoices, payments, reposting of costs, activity allocation, settlement of internal orders and diverse reports. In the second part, an introduction to customizing in SAP R/3 was given, especially emphasizing work with the implementation guides (IMGs). Drawing from the skills taught in the entity-relationship lecture before, customizing transactions and especially their precedence were illustrated using the underlying data model and the implementation of the concept of keys in relational databases (see Figure 3).

Then students performed several customizing transactions, leading to each students creating and customizing from scratch a working company code with associated controlling area. As the students in the following implementation project needed to work largely alone with the system, special emphasis was laid on demonstrating work on business processes in the system and how to find and enact the corresponding customizing transactions if errors were encountered. For example, after defining a new company code, entering a new general ledger account document was attempted, resulting in several error messages (e.g., number range 01 is missing for 2004). Using the implementation guide, the necessary transaction (define document number ranges in financial accounting) was looked up and the data entered (also using the transaction define document type to illustrate why number range 01 was necessary in this case).

Assessment was based on a one-hour test on the theoretical background (which was also used as selective criteria if there were too many prospective students, as only 25 computers are available in the classroom), with one set of business process descriptions with data to be enacted on the system for each module similar to the examples from the course. A personal assessment session at the end in which each student had to work on the system in front of the lecturer who posed some problems, leading from business processes in the production system to the underlying customizing transactions.

The main problems encountered by the students stem from two major cause: deficiencies in business administration knowledge and SAP R/3 user interface issues. Lack of knowledge and especially practice in accounting and controlling leads to many students not being able to understand what some business processes represent, e.g. are unsure what accounts to use in credit or debit to represent a real-life transaction. This problem is confounded by the terminology employed in SAP R/3, which at some points differs from the terms used in the respective business administration courses. Giving more background on the business administration side would be very helpful, but is impossible due to time constraints. The second main cause of problems is the SAP R/3 GUI, mostly two issues: Many transactions contain numerous fields, which are not mandatory, but a large proportion of students tries to fill them, which either is problematic due to missing data, or causes other problems in later steps of the processes. In addition, the search interface for selecting data to enter into a field offers several possible ways to search, which often are not distinguished by the students. For example, when selecting an account, the user can search within the chart of accounts or the company code, the difference between which, although explained, is often lost when actually working. These problems could be largely circumvented by heavily customizing the system, e.g. by hiding several fields, but this both represents major effort to be invested and also would possibly reduce transferability to real-life systems.

Regarding the SAP courses (and also prior BaaN), next to no students had the necessary technical knowledge to directly enter the implementation project, but had to take the described workshop beforehand.

In the implementation project, students had to work in pairs, each pair choosing an existing or imaginary company to implement SAP R/3 for. First, an enterprise model had to be created, including a description, organization chart, data model and business process description for accounting processes and at least three processes pertaining to other areas. After this document was cleared by the lecturer, implementation and documentation work started. For the described company, the modules FI and CO, plus one of the modeled business processes pertaining to an additional module had to be implemented. This forced the students to become familiar with one additional module of their own choice. The implementation had to be carefully documented, together with the project organization, plan and effort data. Assessment was based on scope and quality of the implementation, and the quality and clarity of the documentation. This is somewhat similar to the approach detailed by Stewart and Roseman (2001) in that students have to cover a complete project.

Changes Caused by New Studies

Introduction and Organization

The Department of Information Business took responsibility for a large part of the core classes for students of the newly introduced IS program. This includes the Advanced Practical Project I and II, into which the former four weekly hours workshop and the implementation project were fitted. Therefore, internet technologies (scripting languages with database connections like Perl or PHP), database implementation with SQL and Oracle, and ERP are currently offered. The object-oriented programming package had been relocated to the introductory phase and made mandatory for all IS students. Also offered is an IT specialization area Information Business to IS students. During this, students have to take an additional Advanced Practical Project I and II, where again the ERP option is available, if not chosen within the common body of knowledge.

While the specialist Business Administration area Information Business is still offered to students of Business Administration and International Business Administration (now encompassing 16 weekly hours of classes, reflecting the former reality in now officially including the four hours formerly assigned to the workshop). Out of necessity, due to personnel shortage most classes had to be shared between all of these degree programs including the IS bachelor program. Therefore all classes are now based on skills in object-oriented programming and in modeling techniques as taught in the IS study beginner courses. Therefore, to enable sharing of classes between IS students having these core classes, and BA students, these core classes had to be decreed as mandatory for BA students within the specialist Business Administration area, thus preventing further choice between different implementation variants including ERP, in fact forcing students to take the object-oriented programming option. Therefore, the ERP program is no longer available to BA students.

Contents and Teaching Methods

The former four weekly hours workshop on SAP R/3 became the two-hour Advanced Practical Project I, necessitating severe changes. The most severe change was the elimination of the lectures on data and process modeling. As all students now come from the IS degree program, each one has had to pass the Principles of Modeling class in the introductory phase, which features the necessary skills. Therefore, these building blocks were no longer necessary, but "outsourced," together with the respective test. In addition, the students are more intimately familiar with principles of database systems. On the other hand, the IS students now partaking in the class have less business administration background than their predecessors, necessitating more explanations in accounting, especially controlling, to follow the class. Overall, while some elements have been eliminated from the class, the new time frame allotted enforces faster proceedings, which has already been criticized by some students. In fact, work will have to be done to further decrease the contents of this course. The implementation project became the Advanced Practical Project II, without major changes.

Empirical Data

There are three major sources of empirical data: The number of students starting and passing each course (see Table 1), results from the university's feedback program using students' anonymous questionnaires available from some courses (see Table 2), and data from the students' self-selection into different modules besides accounting during the implementation

Table 1. Number of students starting and passing ERP courses

Type of Class	Term	Students at start	Students having passed
Workshop	Winter 1999	68	25
	Winter 2000	40	23
	Winter 2001	54	20
	Winter 2002	69	33
Advanced Practical Project I	Winter 2003	16	12
	Summer 2004	16	11
	Winter 2004	21	18
	Summer 2005	26	26
	Subtotal	310	168
Implementation Project	Summer 2000	28	16
	Summer 2001	20	15
	Summer 2002	15	13
	Summer 2003	28	26
Advanced Practical Project II	Winter 2003	15	12
	Summer 2004	9	8
	Winter 2004	22	22
	Summer 2005	23	23
	Subtotal	16-0	135
Total		470	303

project (see Table 3). The last point might provide valuable insight into which modules to enforce, or which modules to include into the coverage in courses to come.

While the workshop and implementation project had been held in a two-term alternating cycle, since the introduction of new studies the Advanced Practical Projects I and II now both take place in the same term, blocked one after the other. This allows both for faster graduation of the students, and also limits the problems of long breaks, during which much content is forgotten.

What we have seen is a high rate of dropout in the workshops, but not the implementation projects. This is caused by two distinct effects: first, students having passed the workshop already made a severe commitment to the program and therefore will try their best to pass the implementation project. Second, many students entered the workshops, which had no limitations of any kind, out of curiosity for the area of ERP, and especially SAP R/3, but

Table 2. Results from students' feedback on ERP courses

Type of Class	Term	# of Questionnaires	Lecture consistent with pre-defined targets	Quality of Notes, Handouts	General Satisfaction
Workshop	Winter 1999	25	5.82 / 8	6.47 / 8	6.35 / 8
	Winter 2002	31	7.25 / 8	7.13 / 8	7.45 / 8
Advanced Practical Project I	Summer 2004	16	6.49 / 8	5.85 / 8	6.46 / 8
	Mean		6.52 / 8	6.48 / 8	6.75 / 8
Implementation Project	Summer 2001	9	6.39 / 8	5.06 / 8	5.39 / 8
Advanced Practical Project II	Summer 2004	7	7.33 / 8	5.81 / 8	7.15 / 8
	Mean		6.86 / 8	5.44 / 8	6.27 / 8
Mean			6.67 / 8	6.06 / 8	6.56 / 8

not wishing to partake in the information business education program it was part of. Many of these dropped out after a while, and some did not take the final examination, as a grade would have been useless for their further progress in their degree program. In addition, if there were too many interested students, the one hour test on the theoretical part was used to filter down to 50 people, as only this many seats with computer access are available in the classroom for the following hands-on part of the course.

The relatively steep drop-off in students since introduction of the advanced practical projects stems mostly from the fact that the IS program has started in Winter 2002, and the respective classes are not introductory but have several prerequisites. Therefore, not many students are already eligible to take these classes. In addition, the IS degree program has distinctly fewer students than the BA program the workshop and implementation project had been part of.

Several things can be seen from the students' feedback (see Table 2). Generally, the quality of the workshop-type of class is improving over time, although the change resulting from new environmental conditions led to a decrease in students' perception. This might be caused by changes in the lecture itself, which did not work out, but also by changed expectations and skills of the students joining. Regardless, the course needs to be continuously adapted and improved to reach the good results from before.

Although there is only one set of feedback less for the implementation project type of class, the results are worse than for the first course in the series. Mostly, this will stem from the more challenging contents, in which the students have to work for the most part alone, including skills from other courses as well. While this is not welcomed by them, it is needed to prepare them for their jobs later, as we know from experience that complete training and

Table 3. SAP R/3 modules self-selected by students during implementation projects

Term	Number of Projects	MM	SD	HR	N/A
Summer 2000	9	3	2	2	2
Summer 2001	8	3	2	3	
Summer 2002	7	2	2	3	
Summer 2003	13	9	1	3	
Winter 2003	6	4	1	1	
Summer 2004	4	2	1	1	
Winter 2004	11	4	1	6	
Summer 2005	11	5	3	3	
Total	69 100%	32 ~46%	13 ~19%	22 ~32%	2 ~3%

preparation is, at least in the ERP sector, not available for newcomers in companies. The trend that the Practical Project II shows better performance is encouraging, but might be due to the better general IS education of this group of students.

Regarding the modules chosen by the students in the implementation projects (see Table 3), it seems interesting that materials management is the dominant choice. One possible explanation would be the way courses at the university level are taught on these topics. Logistics and related areas are emphasizing quantitative models, which can be more easily transferred to or found in ERP solutions, while education in marketing and human resource is more qualitatively oriented. Therefore students might be led to think of ERP solutions as more suitable for the first form of processes.

Unfortunately, no data is available on whether the students use the skills from the ERP education program in their jobs. The general data available from a questionnaire sent to graduates of the department indicates that about 22% become consultants, and 19% overall later work in the area of account and controlling. Regarding their first job, 30% claimed to have benefited from the technical skills acquired at the department. This can be coupled with data from the Austrian job market: An analysis, based on job offers from print and online media, showed that SAP-related jobs, foremost consultants, account for 42% of the offers in the category IT-jobs mixed. Most sought after are skills in the modules finance and controlling (AMS, 2002). The current situation is similar, with SAP-related jobs still being increasingly in supply, both within the IT and the consulting area (AMS Barometer of Jobs and Qualifications, http://www.ams.or.at/neu/2339.htm, accessed November 18, 2005). It can be concluded from these figures, and from the penetration of SAP R/3 into organizations in Austria (which leads to SAP-skills sought even in most business job offers in areas like human resources or accounting), that a large proportion of the students will be actively using their skills and that a significant part will have acquired jobs centered on ERP, especially in consulting.

LESSONS LEARNED

There are several lessons from holding the described ERP education program over several years, and with different groups of students. These lessons should be applicable to most similar programs. First, skills in databases, especially entity-relationship modeling, should be acquired before the ERP education proceeds. This can be done either in the same course beforehand, or another course scheduled earlier. In addition, skills in business process modeling are advised. Also strongly encouraged is to start the ERP education after the relevant business administration courses (e.g., concerning accounting or controlling), but ideally shortly afterwards. We found that students had largely forgotten several key concepts, as several semesters had passed in our case. Another possibility would be to integrate ERP education in these business administration courses (e.g., teach SAP R/3 CO module together with general controlling), but this is often hampered by the lecturers themselves, who are not familiar with the system. In general, ERP courses offer a good possibility for a capstone project (Denton & Spangler, 2001; Gupta & Wachter, 1998) to combine information systems, business administration, and project management skills. Other elements of the ERP courses found to be helpful were to discuss a production system before customizing, to customize both structures from scratch and perform changes to existing ones, to especially enforce the interplay between problems in operation and customizing and to allow the self-selection of students to modules during the implementation project, as this tends to increase motivation.

CONCLUSION

We have demonstrated how ERP education can be incorporated in different programs, even in different degree programs. In addition, we have shown how the ERP education was adapted to changing environmental conditions. We have also given some empirical data on the education program during the whole time interval and tried to condense some lessons learned from these experiences.

ERP education currently remains an important part of both IS and BA education. What we see as a future trend is a movement towards integration into different functional areas of BA, forming a prerequisite towards bridging divisions in education between functional areas and leading to learning communities (Becerra-Fernandez et al., 2000; Joseph & George, 2002). While this is a process that takes a long time, it seems worthwhile to relegate the "business" side of ERP education to the accounting or finance departments. Then the IS departments would be able to more accurately focus on the issues behind these topics with ERP. We are proud to report, that starting this term, the Department of Strategic Management and Management Control and Consulting offered a course on controlling information systems using SAP R/3 for students of business administration partaking in their specialized education program, demonstrating a start of this trend.

REFERENCES

AMS—Arbeitsmarktservice Österreich. (2002). *Der Stellenmarkt in Österreich 2001 - End-bericht (Job Market in Austria 2001, Final Report)*, AMS, Wien.

Becerra-Fernandez, I., Murphy, K. E., & Simon, S. J. (2000). Integrating ERP in the business school curriculum. *Communications of the ACM, 43*(4), 39-41.

de Brock, E. O. (2001). Integrating real practical experience in ICT education. *Journal of Information Systems Education, 12*(3), 133-140.

Denton, J. W., & Spangler, W. E. (2001). Effectiveness of an integrated pre-capstone project in learning information systems concepts. *Journal of Information Systems Education, 12*(3), 149-156.

Gorgone, J. T., & Gray, P. (1999). Graduate IS curriculum for the millennium: Background, processes, and recommendation. *Journal of Information Systems Education, 10*(3&4), 6-14.

Gupta, J. N. D., & Wachter, R. M. (1998). A capstone course in the information systems curriculum. *International Journal of Information Management, 18*(6), 427-441.

Hawking, P., Ramp, A., & Shackelton, P. (2001). IS'97 model curriculum and enterprise resource planning systems. *Business Process Management Journal, 7*(3), 225-233.

Joseph, G., & George, A. (2002). ERP, learning communities and curriculum integration. *Journal of Information Systems Education, 13*(1), 51-58.

Prosser, A., & Ossimitz, M. L. (2001). *Data warehouse management using SAP BW*. Stuttgart: UTB für Wissenschaft.

Prosser, A., Taudes, A., & Weiss, K. (1991). *Integration management with SAP R/3*. Wien: WUV Universitätsverlag.

Rumbaugh, J., Jacobson, I., & Booch, G. (1998). *The unified modeling language reference manual*. Boston, MA: Addison-Wesley.

Scheer, A. W. (2000). *ARIS–Business process modeling* (3rd ed.). Berlin: Springer.

Stewart, G., & Roseman, M. (2001). Industry-oriented design of ERP-related curriculum — an Australian initiative. *Business Process Management Journal, 7*(3), 234-242.

Vienna University of Economics and BA. (2004). *Facts and figures 2004*. Retrieved May 4, 2004, from http://www.wu-wien.ac.at/rektorat/KeyData.htm

Chapter III

ERP Education:
Hosting, Visiting, and Certifying

Andrew Stein, Victoria University, Australia

Paul Hawking, Victoria University, Australia

Brendan McCarthy, Victoria University, Australia

ABSTRACT

In recent times, there have been discussions by computing professionals about how to best respond to developments in the information technology and communications industry. At the same time, there has been a downturn in employment opportunities in this industry (ICT Skills Snapshot, 2004). Recent research also indicates that many of the entry-level positions that graduates traditionally entered have diminished due to the economic downturn and to companies outsourcing positions to off shore companies. This chapter presents the path that the Victoria University (Australia) school of Information Systems took in introducing multiple programs in an endeavour to compliment traditional course delivery and to better connect a University School with ICT industry requirements. The programs included the use of SAP hosting centres for access to ERP systems, conducting an ERP visiting expert teaching delivery model for SAP content and multiple SAP certification programs. The results of these programs as described in this paper show that flexibility in delivery mode and effective merging of ERP curriculum and ERP certification content is crucial to achieving successful programs.

INTRODUCTION

Many universities have committed considerable time and resources in modifying their curriculum to incorporate enterprise resource planning systems (ERP) (Hawking, Shackleton, & Ramp, 2001; Lederer-Antonucci, 1999; Watson & Schneider, 1999). For many universities it has been a struggle even though ERP vendors have developed a number of initiatives to facilitate curriculum development. As companies' ERP system usage has become more strategic in nature, ERP curriculum must evolve to reflect this usage. Information systems curriculum in universities has undergone rapid and continuous change in response to the evolution of industry requirements. Over a period of 40 years, the information systems (IS) discipline has become an essential component in the employment of information technology personnel in business and government organisations. In recent times there have been discussions by IS Professionals how to best respond to developments in the information technology and communications industry (Hawking & McCarthy, 2000). The industry now requires a broad range of skills that support the development, implementation, and maintenance of e-business solutions. A recent Australian report identified skill shortages in security/risk management, enterprise resource planning (ERP) systems, data warehousing and customer relationship management (CRM) (ICT Skills Snapshot, 2003). At the same time, there has been a downturn in employment opportunities in this industry (ICT Skills Snapshot, 2003. This chapter discusses the evolution of ERP education and the issues it now faces. It provides an example of how one university is addressing the "second wave" of ERP education and the challenges that educators face in preparing students for rapidly developing software environments.

ERP SKILLS AND
CURRICULUM APPROACHES

The shortage of ERP related skills in not a recent phenomenon. A survey by Hewitt Associates (1999) found that people with ERP skills were in short supply, and consequently in high demand experiencing rapid changes in their market value. In Australia, an IT Skills Shortage study (ICT Skills Snapshot, 2003) commissioned by the Government, found skill shortages in enterprise wide systems, and more specifically SAP R/3 and PeopleSoft implementation and administration. The Department of Immigration and Multicultural Affairs in their Migration Occupations in Demand List (MODL, 2000) identified information technology specialists with SAP R/3 skills as people who would be encouraged to migrate to Australia.

In accordance with this demand, many universities identified the value of incorporating ERP systems into their curriculum. ERP systems can be used to reinforce many of the concepts covered in the business discipline (Becerra-Fernandez, Murphy, & Simon, 2000; Hawking et al., 2001). The ERP vendors argue that their products incorporate "world's best practice" for many of the business processes they support, making them an ideal teaching tool (Hawking, 1999; Watson & Schneider, 1999), while at the same time increasing the employment prospects of graduates. Universities also realised the importance of providing students with "hands on" experience with particular ERP systems and formed strategic alliances with ERP system vendors to gain access to these systems. The ERP vendor benefited from these alliances by increasing the supply of skilled graduates that can support their product thereby enhancing its marketability and lowering the cost of implementation.

Universities who decided to introduce ERP related curriculum were faced with a number of barriers. For many universities getting access to an ERP system to provide "hands on" learning environment was not a major issue, however, the lack of ERP related skills of academic staff and accordingly the development of appropriate curriculum material was and still is a major hurdle. SAP, the leading ERP vendor has established the SAP University Alliance, the largest ERP university alliance with more than 400 universities worldwide accessing their ERP system (SAP R/3). They have introduced a number of initiatives to facilitate the incorporation of their system into university curriculum. Initially when universities joined the alliance they were provided with free training for academic staff and access to training materials. The amount of training made available and the restrictions how the training materials could be used varied from country to country and to a certain extent from university to university within the same country.

The transporting of SAP training materials into a university environment, as many universities attempted to do, was not a simple process. The training materials were often version dependent and utilized preconfigured data that was not readily available in the universities' systems. The SAP training exercises were often just snapshots to reinforce particular features of the system, and therefore were not comprehensive exercises illustrating end-to-end processes that are often relevant in ERP education. For example, staff soon came across the problems associated with opening and closing posting periods that often prevented certain transactions from being completed in the system. Another major problem was the need to protect and not share data and code in the educational setting. In commercial organisation code sharing often forms the basis for teams and work tasks, however this is not desirable in an educational setting. This problem required "tweaking" of roles and permissions in the SAP environment. These concepts are not covered in training courses even though it impacts on many processes.

The ERP curriculum employed by universities could be classified into one of four different curriculum approaches or a fifth, being a hybrid of the four:

1.   Training into ERP
2.   ERP via business processes
3.   Information systems approach
4.   ERP concepts
5.   The hybrid

The first, which is least preferred by academic institutions, focuses on the instruction or training in a *particular* ERP system. There has been increasing pressure from both students and industry for universities to offer subjects based on this type of curriculum direction. In the case of SAP, the Alliance specifies that specific training of SAP R/3 is the domain of SAP. The second curriculum approach retains the focus on business processes but uses the ERP system to assist in the presentation of information and skills development. Most ERP system vendors argue that their particular system incorporates *best business practice* and, as a consequence, students use the system to enhance their understanding of the processes and their interrelationships, especially in areas like supply chain management. The third approach is the use of ERP systems to teach and reinforce information system concepts. ERP systems provide students with the opportunity to study a real world example of a business information system, often incorporating *state of the art* technology. The final curriculum direction is to teach about ERP systems and concepts. This is different from the first curriculum approach outlined above in that it deals with *general* ERP issues and the implications for an organisation for implementing this type of information system.

CERTIFICATION: AN AVENUE FOR INDUSTRY COLLABORATION?

IT industry certification programs are seen as a respected and widely-established vehicle for attaining specific, practically based expertise — areas that many tertiary courses seem to lack or with which they have chosen not to be involved (Basu, 2002; McCain, 2001). Some tertiary institutions (mainly TAFE) have taken certification programs on board enthusiastically, to the extent that they are supplementing their own programs in quite a significant way (ITT, 2000). Others have ignored such programs labelling them as being too training or proprietary oriented to be considered as educative (the "high-brow" response) (Flynn, 2001). In very recent times selection data (university selection popularity polls) have caught up with the significant downturn of employment experienced in the IT industry during 2001-2003. These trends place a greater burden on the University sector to react positively towards "adding value" to their offerings. For University IT/IS courses to be more industry relevant, practically focused and to add value in tune with industry and government funding pressure, IT/IS certification needs to be looked at a lot more seriously than it has been to date (McCain, 2001).

CERTIFICATION PROGRAM IMPLEMENTATION

The implementation of certification programs has been ad hoc and reactionary and little has been done to investigate the implementation of IT certification programs within tertiary IT/IS programs (McCain, 2001; Rothke, 2000). There are several distinct certification classifications:

- **Industry body certification:** ACS, PPP programs,
- **Proprietary certification programs:** MCSE, CNE, CISCO,
- **Industry generalised certification programs:** A+, i-Net+, Network+,
- **Specific purpose certification:** SAP professional
- **Academic certification:** degree, certificate & short course programs

Assuming the case can be made to enhance existing programs with certification programs the "why" is answered, the "how" can therefore be crucial to success. A wider classification of certification programs is presented in Table 1.

The discussion section will focus on describing the hosting, visiting, and certifying programs that VUT adopted to deliver ERP content. The endpoint of this work is to analyse the programs and provide a focus for the improvement in implementation of these programs

Table 1. Certification models with example programs

Certification Model	Example Program
Value-Added, End-On	ACS PPP program: Employment Driven, End-On
Distance Learning	Charles Sturt University, Microsoft, CISCO, Sun
Full Fee (Tertiary)	
Full Fee (Private)	
Hybrid (Tertiary/Private),	James Cook University, ITTI Master of IT
Curriculum Inclusive	VU TAFE: Cisco Accreditation-Curriculum Inclusive in Separate Subject
Mapping to Industry Certification	PowerLan Microsoft Certification: Hybrid, Curriculum Inclusive, Mapping
Specific Subject	SAP Professional Program
Industry Employment (Co-Operative Education)	Citrix Certification: Specific purpose, Employment Driven, End-On

within the School of Information Systems, Victoria University. The formal research questions for this chapter are:

- What types of delivery programs would augment ERP learning at VU?
- Which model(s) is best suited to the needs of the School of IS?

DISCUSSION
ERP Education at VUT

Victoria University has been a member of the SAP University Alliance since 1998. It adopted a faculty approach to the introduction of ERP curriculum. It was seen as a tool that could reinforce many of the business and information systems concepts taught across the faculty. The university now has approximately twenty-five subjects at both the undergraduate and postgraduate levels that incorporate SAP and related products. These subjects form part of master degree program that is taught in Australia, Singapore, and China. Even though the university has a well-established curriculum, it was also faced with the dilemma of how it could take advantage of the educational potential of SAP's "second wave" components. Second wave components include CRM, SCM, and SRM suites. These modules are all designed to get added value out of the core SAP R/3 implementation. Each of these second wave components is a full installation in itself and requires considerable expertise to set up and develop educational programs. Staff needed to go on steep learning curves in firstly learning how to use say a CRM suite and then further work in fine-tuning for students access. It was felt that existing staff were stretched to the limit and time and effort to develop this new curriculum would be insurmountable.

Hosting Programs

The acquired knowledge of academics involved in ERP education is difficult to encapsulate and therefore the curriculum is often dependent on relatively few staff. Usually there is a core of academics that have spent many hours working on the system; when these core academics leave or change direction, then the curriculum usually flounders. This has been evident in Australia where from the original thirteen universities involved in the SAP alliance only seven remain. Some universities were able to develop and retain their ERP skills while others struggled. SAP (Americas) established the SAP Curriculum Awards and Curriculum Congress in an attempt to facilitate the problems many universities were facing. The Congress was designed to bring together academics involved in ERP education where they could share their experiences and to be made aware of new product developments. The Awards identified and financially rewarded exemplary programs, however there was limited sharing of the exemplary curriculum. Some universities considered the curricula their competitive edge and intellectual property or conversely it was not documented to a level that made it accessible to others. Recently SAP has established their education and research portal, "Innovation Watch,"[1] to facilitate collaboration between universities. The site includes a range of "plug and play" curriculum materials however not all university alliance members has access to it or are even aware of it. The quality of the curriculum varies enormously and some is far from "plug and play." Due to escalating demands associated with administering new versions SAP R/3 and to facilitate the entrance of new universities into the alliance SAP established a number of application hosting centres around the world in universities with established ERP curriculum offerings. The hosting model varied from country to country with some only providing access to systems rather than curriculum. However SAP considered that the increasing support universities required could be provided by the hosting centres and therefore lessen the burden on SAP. At VUT the SAP hosting centre out of another Australian University provided access to the SAP BW product. The subject Data Warehousing has been delivered multiple times both in Australia and Singapore using this hosting centre. Currently there are about 10 SAP UCC (University Competence Centres) in the world. Some examples include Queensland University of Technology (Australia), National Central University (Taiwan) & CSU Chico (USA). Hosting brings most advantage when the high cost of initial and ongoing installation of SAP is taken into account. One disadvantage of the hosting model is the need to use a "vanilla" instance rather than a tailored solution.

Visiting Programs

As a pilot program in 2002, the university identified academics from around the world that had the skills, curriculum, and access to systems to teach the specialist solutions. An academic was invited to teach their curriculum at Victoria University through a concentrated mode (one week). This also relied on Victoria University students accessing the visiting lecturer's ERP system and any "add on" solutions in their university via the Internet. The pilot had a number of obvious benefits, firstly, the visiting academic provided access to the curriculum skills and system, and secondly, resident staff received professional development as they assisted in the class, thirdly, students gained access to education they would not readily receive, and finally it provided the foundation for future collaboration between the participating universities. Due to the success of the pilot in the ERP program several subjects were offered via this method in 2003/4/5.

- **2003 ERP Applications:** (Shell Course), SAP Configuration
- **2004 ERP Applications:** (Shell Course), SAP Solution Manger
- **2005 ERP Applications:** (Shell Course), SAP Data Warehousing
- **2005 ERP Applications:** (Shell Course), SAP Configuration

The collaboration has resulted in Victoria University staff being invited to other universities to teach curriculum that was unavailable in these universities. The visiting program yields greatest advantage in the import and transfer of knowledge between the participant organisations. If no effort is made to facilitate that transfer then the advantage of this model is diminished.

ERP Certification at VU (Course Mapping)

Two certification models were developed and used in the ERP masters. The first saw SAP certification being mapped into subjects in the masters. The second involved specific SAP certification being delivered in conjunction with an ERP masters subject. As the VU approach uses several elements of certification it could be classified as a hybrid. The first approach of certification of ERP education came about through the linking of subject content with SAP accredited programs. Students upon completion of subjects receive SAP industry accreditation certificates that they can use to further their career prospects. Whilst no quantitative evidence has been collected as to the effectiveness of certification to the students employment prospect's much anecdotal evidence suggests that the certificates not only help students get "in the door" but also give them credence in interview situations. This SAP certification model is displayed in Figure 1.

The second approach of certification of ERP education came about through the complete delivery of a certification module through the delivery of subject content combined with a certification test. Students upon completion of subjects, SAP Portal, complete the test receive SAP industry accreditation certificates that they can use to further their career prospects. An example of this model in application is shown in the delivery of SAP Portal certification via a course termed ERP Developments in Winter term 2005. This course was

Figure 1. ERP end-on certification implementation model

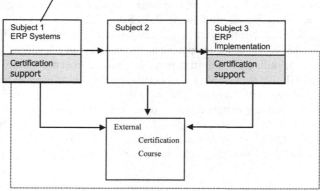

Figure 2. ERP course mapping certification implementation model

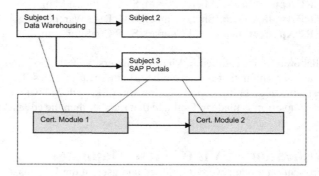

delivered in condensed mode and was fully subscribed. It covered both the theory and SAP Portal Certification content. This SAP certification model is displayed in Figure 2.

CONCLUSION

"Mobile, flexible, highly-trained, industry-focused, experienced…" cries that are heard from the information technology industry in relation to the expertise that is expected from tertiary graduates these days. Until the recent cyclical downturn of the computer industry demand had been extremely high for graduates from tertiary institutions that could fit the chameleon-like nature of the computer industry's graduate skills deficit gap (DES, 2001; DHFE, 2000; Knight, 2001; NOIE, 2003). Much of this deficit was due to the rapidly changing nature and focus of the industry itself. It still is. The information technology industry is constantly evolving, with localised demand for graduates with skills in the latest technology upgrade (software and hardware). This demand exhibits much of the "here today, gone tomorrow" mentality that pervades industries that focus on new and developing but much hyped innovations. The modern marketing machine has trained many of us to "keep up with the technological Jones." Industry decision makers too, have been seduced by the hard sell. This trend is clearly manifested in the need to have employees and consequently IT graduates trained in the latest innovative hardware and software. Industry has been very quick to sound the alarm bells when there is a shortfall in the skills base (ICT Skills Snapshot, 2004).

Certification literature points to the benefits and pitfalls of certification. These are described in Table 2. The benefits that underpin the use of certification at Victoria University all relate to the transfer of skills from industry environs to educational programs. Undertaking SAP certification, ITIL, i-Net+ and Microsoft certification at VU attempt to better prepare students as they exit university programs and make the transition to the workforce.

Additionally IT industry certification programs are seen as a respected and widely-established vehicle for attaining specific, practically based expertise — areas that many tertiary courses seem to lack or with which they have chosen not to be involved. In very recent times, selection data (university selection popularity polls) have caught up with the

Table 2. Benefits and pitfalls of certification programs

Strengths	Weaknesses
Adding value to degree programs	Exist to support training industry
Work related experience	Proprietary nature
Practical rather than just theoretical focus	Lack of educational rigor
"Up-to-Date" nature of certification programs	Often lacks "real-world" experience
Specific targeted content very relevant to employers	Industry partnership inadequate or unstable
Industry liaison opportunities	Too focused
Adjunct to education programs offering verifiable	Training oriented rather than education oriented
testing of skills and knowledge	"Value-for-money" ignorance of certification
Potential employment advantages for graduates	Too market and popularity driven
Precursor to licensing requirements	

significant downturn of employment experienced in the IT industry during 2001-2003. These trends place a greater burden on the University sector to react positively towards "adding value" to their offerings.

Universities who have worked very hard to develop ERP curriculum are now faced with the dilemma of evolving their curriculum to reflect the evolution of ERP systems and industry requirements. The evolution of ERP systems from an operational to a more strategic focus requires a different skill set to support this transition. The visiting professor delivery method could be further extended whereby a directory of specialist academics could be established by SAP and distributed to alliance members. These academics could be provided with additional support from SAP to assist them to further develop their curriculum with the goal of making it portable to other universities. The hosting centres could become solution specific rather than trying to implement all new wave solutions. Each centre would focus on one solution and client universities would access different hosting centers dependent on their curriculum requirements. This would enable the hosting centers to specialize and develop specialist curriculum. Universities and ERP vendors need to develop strategies how to best address this skill deficit. There will need to be far greater collaboration than exists at present. The Victoria University School of Information Systems has therefore seen it as a necessary strategy to implement certification into course material. At the time of writing it is unsure whether other SAP Alliance Universities in the USA are offering SAP certification, but there is little doubt that this model for SAP delivery could work in US aligned Universities. Certification is not without its critics but the results so far show that students are very interested being provided multiple endpoints to there study. This paper has focused on identifying the various forms of ERP curriculum delivery must complement traditional course delivery. SAP hosting centres, ERP visiting and SAP certification all provide relevance to tertiary education and enrich the student experience.

REFERENCES

Becerra-Fernandez, I., Murphy, K. E., & Simon, S. J. (2000). Enterprise resource planning: Integrating ERP in the business school curriculum. *Communications of the ACM, 43*(4), 39-41.

Bennett, C. (2000, November). *Welcoming address.* Presented at the Sapphire Conference, Application Hosting Centre, Singapore.

Basu, K. S. (2002). Training strategies in the emerging hi-tech banking environment. *Indian Journal of Training and Development, XXXI* (4), 13-22.

CAP, Gemini, and Ernst & Young. (2002). *Adaptive ERP.* Retrieved January 25, 2003, from www.cgey.com/solutions/erpeea/media/AdaptiveERPPOV.pdf

CSC. (2001). *Critical issues of information systems management.* Retrieved November 25, 2002, from http://www.csc.com/aboutus/uploads/CI_report.pdf

Davenport, T., Harris, J., & Cantrell, S. (2002). *The return of enterprise solutions.* Wellesley, MA: Accenture, Accenture Institute for High Performance Metrics.

Deloitte Consulting Report. (1999). *ERP's second wave.* Atlanta, GA: Deloitte Consulting.

Deloitte, Touche, and Tohmatsu. (1999). Future demand for IT&T skills in Australia 1999-2004. IT&T Skills Workforce. *A report developed for the Australian government.* Retrieved May 25, 1999, from http://www.noie.com.au

Department for Education and Skills Report (DES). (2001). An assessment of skill needs in information and communication technology/Dept for education and skills. In *Skills dialogue: Listening to employers,* (Vol. II, pp. 68). Nottingham, UK: Department for Education and Skills.

Department of Higher and Further Education Task Force Report (DHFE). (2000). A study of the Northern Ireland labour market for IT skills: A report prepared by the Priority Skills Unit. In *A Northern Ireland Skills Task Force report, Department of Higher, and Further Education* (p. 68). Belfast, Ireland: Northern Ireland Economic Research Centre.

Flynn, W. J. (2001). More than a matter of degree: Credentialing, certification and community college. *The Catalyst, 30*(3), 3-12.

Hawking, P. (1999, May 31-June 2). The teaching of enterprise resource planning systems (Sap R/3) in Australian universities. In *Proceedings of the 9th Pan Pacific Conference*, Fiji.

Hawking, P., & McCarthy, B. (2000). Industry collaboration: A practical approach for ERP education. In *Proceedings of the Australasian Conference on Computing Education*, Melbourne, Australia (pp. 129-133).

Hawking, P., Shackleton, P., & Ramp, A. (2001). IS' 97 model curriculum and enterprise resource planning systems. *Business Process Management Journal, 7*(3), 225-233.

Hewitt Associates. (1999). *Hot technology study: Scarcity of it professionals means big pay raises.* Retrieved May 25, 2003, from http://www.hewitt.com/compsurveys

ICT Skills Snapshot. (2004). *The state of ICT skills in Victoria.* Department of Infrastructure. Retrieved July 25, 2004, from http://www.itskillshub.com.au/render/exec/render_content.asp?subgroup=courses&file=it+jobs+market+brighter%2Ehtml&title=IT+jobs+market+brighter

ITT. (2000). Industry report. Information-technology training: Teaching computer skills to American workers. *Training, 37*(10), 62-71.

Knight K. S. (2001). Raising the bar on certification. *The Catalyst, 30*(3), 13-17.

Lederer-Antonucci, Y. (1999). Enabling the business school curriculum with ERP software experiences of the SAP University Alliance. In *Proceedings of the IBSCA'99*, Atlanta, GA.

McCain M. (2001). Business approach to credentialing. *Community College Journal, American Association of Community Colleges, 71*(5), 40-41.

Mehaut, P. (1999). Training, skills, learning: How can new models be developed? *Vocational Training European Journal, 3*(18), 3-7

MODL. (2000). *Migration to Australia—skilled migration, migration occupations in demand list*. Retrieved July 25, 2001, from http://www.immi.gov.au/allforms/modl.htm

Nolan and Norton Institute. (2000). *SAP Benchmarking Report 2000, KPMG White Paper,* Melbourne, Australia.

National Office Industry Education (NOIE). (2003). *Project overview — ICT skill needs*. Retrieved July 25, 2004, from http://www.itskillshub.com.au/render/exec/render_content.asp?subgroup=courses&file=it+jobs+market+brighter%2Ehtml&title=IT+jobs+market+brighter

Rosemann, M., Scott, J., & Watson, E. (2000). Collaborative ERP education: Experiences from a first pilot. In H. M. Chung (Ed.), *Proceedings of the 6th Americas Conference on Information Systems (AMCIS '00)*, Long Beach, CA (pp. 2055-2060).

Rothke, B. C. (2000). The professional certification predicament. *Computer Security Journal, 16*(4), 29-35

Watson, E., & Schneider, H. (1999). Using ERP systems in education. *Communication of the Association for Information Systems, 1*(9), 4.

ENDNOTE

[1]   Services.sap.com/iw

Chapter IV

The Business Process-Driven Undergraduate IS Curriculum:
A Transition from Classical CIS to Emerging BIT

Andrew Targowski, Western Michigan University, USA

Bernard Han, Western Michigan University, USA

ABSTRACT

This chapter introduces a concept of the re-engineered CIS (computer information systems) curriculum accomplished at the beginning of the 21st century through a few initiatives taken by the Department of Business Information Systems at Western Michigan University's Haworth Business College, over the time period of 2000-2005. These initiatives led to the shift from teaching universal/generic computer information systems' knowledge and skills to more integrational knowledge and skills about how to develop complex systems such as ERP (enterprise resource planning) and e-enterprise. This curriculum shift is a response to the industries' information infrastructure's shift from information islands to the gradually integrated online (Web-driven) infrastructure of systems and services. The revised CIS program at WMU is supported by the use of ERP-like SAP R/3 and MS Great Plains software. The authors hope that the presented curriculum re-engineering concept facilitates the understanding of how the business process-driven CIS/BIT program can be implemented in academic practice.

INTRODUCTION

The purpose of this chapter is to present the re-engineered CIS (computer information systems) curriculum accomplished at the beginning of the 21ˢᵗ century through a few initiatives taken by the Department of Business Information System at Western Michigan University's Haworth Business College,[1] over the time period of 2000-2005. These initiatives led to the shift from teaching universal/generic computer information systems' knowledge and skills to more integrational knowledge and skills about how to develop complex systems such as ERP (enterprise resource planning) and e-enterprise. This curriculum shift is a response to the industries' information infrastructure' shift; from information islands, to the gradually integrated online (Web-driven) infrastructure of systems and services. The revised CIS program at WMU is supported by the use of ERP-like SAP R/3 and MS Great Plains software. The whole transformation process was gradual. In 2000, all CIS courses were restructured to focus on IT knowledge and skills that were essential for the development of an enterprise-wide information system. Soon after the revision, a new curriculum — E-Business Design was developed to meet the e-business needs. In the same time, another interdisciplinary major—Telecommunication & Information Management (TIM) was also developed to meet the emerging industry demand for graduates who can manage the convergence of digital and telephony networks. The sluggish economy recovery, coupled with the continuous offshore outsourcing, motivated our CIS faculty to visit the CIO/CTO of six major corporations in the Southwest Michigan to identify the company needs and, in particular, the expectation of knowledge and skills for future CIS graduates before they enter the real world. Our findings were finally transformed into a new initiative — reengineering the CIS curriculum with a paradigm shift from a technology-based program to a new one focused on using IT for business process integration (BPI). All these transformations have happened at a very fast pace, especially, in the manufacturing-rich state of Michigan which has lost its core competency and cut its higher education budget every year over 2001-2005. Because of this, additional burdens were laid upon the CIS faculty,[1] who made fast changes in the CIS curriculum but were criticized by other departments and the administration for moving too fast.

THE EVOLUTION OF IT EDUCATION

The modern electronic stored-program computers were first developed in Germany (Konrad Zuse's Z3 was operational in 1941) and at U.S. universities in the 1940s, mainly in response to military needs during World War II. Among those computers was the "large systems of linear algebraic equations" solver at Iowa State College (1937-1942), the Mark I or IBM Automatic Sequence Controlled Calculator at Harvard (1939-1944), the ENIAC (Electronic Numerical Integrator and Computer) at the University of Pennsylvania (1945-1950), the ORDVAC (Ordnance Variable Automatic Computer), the ILLIAC (Illinois Automatic Computer) at the University of Illinois (1948-1952), the MSUDC (Michigan

State University Discrete Computer) at Michigan State University, the Whirlwind I at the Massachusetts Institute of Technology (1947-1950), and the SWAC (Standards Western Automatic Computer) at the University of California at Los Angeles. The construction of computers by the industry began at Bell in 1938 and the Bell Model V was delivered in 1946. Remington Rand delivered the first commercial computer, UNIVAC I, in March 1951. Very soon IBM built 701 in 1953 and 650 in 1955 for business applications, which competed with UNIVAC 80 and 90. These lamp-driven computers belonged to the First Generation. When the transistor was developed in 1948, the Second Generation of computers (after 1959) included UNIVAC M460, IBM 7030 and in the area of data processing computers: NCR 304, NCR 315, RCA 501, IBM 7070, IBM 1400. The application of large-scale integrated circuitry led to the Third Generation of computers introduced between 1964 and 1975, among them the most popular were IBM 360 and 370 (Hamblen, 1983).

A lengthy gap took place between the conception of computers at universities and their applications in education programs. The first academic computer center was opened in the mid 1950s and the computer revolution took place at universities from 1960 to 1965. Some cases of teaching hardware and binary arithmetic began in the 1950s, taught mostly by the staff from computer centers. Soon, departments of mathematics and engineering began to collaborate to establish the discipline of computer science. The first such effort was provided in 1959-1962 at the University of Michigan, University of Houston, and Stanford University, the latter and the Perdue University organized the Department of Computer Science in 1962. The ACM (Association of Computer Machinery) published the famous Curriculum 68 document (later followed by Curriculum 78), which had tremendous impact on the further development of computer science education. Ever since, the computer science program became very popular and successful. In 1989, the ACM took another effort to generalize and expand computer science into more a universal program — computing (Denning et al., 1989). This new title was a definition of a whole discipline rather than simply a change of department titles from computer science to computing.

Computer science has always been perceived as a formal, mathematical discipline, which called for precise definitions and solutions. In contrast "application computing" in business and institutions opted for descriptive definitions and has rejected the language of mathematics as a tool of normalization inside its own discipline. Today, IT in business, having been in practice for more than 50 years (since UNIVAC I, but de facto for 100+ years since the introduction of punch cards), is nearly taking over the computer world from the computer science domain; at least from the point of view of the economic and employment of IT specialists.

In the 1960s first academic courses in business data processing were taught; mostly limited to data programming in assembly, auto code and later in COBOL language. Data processing indicated computing applied to administrative and commercial applications, generally taught at two-year colleges. The programs were housed in a department of computer science, computer technology, or data processing; or given as an option in mathematics, engineering, or business administration. Nowadays, these kind of programs are housed in a department located at a business college.

The Curricula 68 and 78 emphasized the mathematical and scientific content of computer science education, and the IEEE Computer Society (1977) report was on computer engineering paid little attention to the business-oriented computer study. In 1972, ACM's Curriculum Committee on Computer Education for Management designed curricula in the field of "information systems" of organizations. Although this overview concerns U.S.

and Canada, the same evolution took place in Europe (under the name *informatique*) beginning in 195, in Southern America in the early 1970s, and in Southeast Asia around the mid-1970s.

In the 1960s a series of data processing computer families such as IBM 1400 and 360, later 370 (in the 1970s) with random access storage were introduced in tens of thousands units, which wave triggered a process of designing management information systems (MIS). With disk storage and online display it seemed to many that it would be easy to provide customized information for any management need. Consequently, many, but not all, academic data processing programs changed their titles to the MIS or CIS programs, the latter emphasizing more on technical skills. These programs' core courses were specialized in COBOL programming, system analysis and design, and later, an added course on database design. Thousands

Figure 1. The evolution of IT education

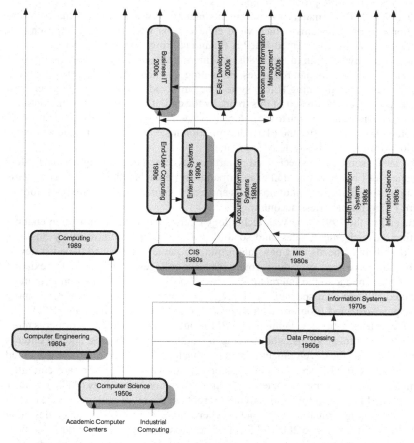

Note: Disciplines in a shadow indicate the major trends.

of graduates from these programs found quick employment in business and administration, significantly advancing the scope of computerization at those places. Even today, there are many IS programs that teach how to develop the so-called legacy systems.

The success of the MIS and IS programs has something to do with a concept of the application portfolio. Application portfolio argued that there are so many possible computer applications that a head of the MIS department can be lost, so instead of managing "chaos," they should focus on five to seven "sure" applications (e.g., payroll, inventory control, production planning, etc.). This methodology stopped the design of advanced systems for years, and instead programmers worked on installing legacy systems within "islands of automation."

Even IBM listened to this appeal and stopped selling its advanced software COPICS (Communication-oriented Production Information Control Systems) for enterprise-wide computing. However, three IBM employees in Germany founded a company named SAP, which converted the concepts used in COPICS into SAP R/2 and R/3. These products were very successful, and managed to capture 30% of the worldwide market. Furthermore, IBM is engaged in reselling these products to end-users.

In the 1970s, MRP I (material requirements planning) was a very popular solution for production planning systems, which were enhanced by CRP (capacity requirements planning). Both new systems created MRP II (manufacturing resources planning), which became another trendy solution in the 1980s. Adding more business applications for such functions as management, human resources, marketing, finance, and so forth to MRP II, a new enterprise resources planning (ERP) system began invading minds of IT leaders and their business processes. As a result of this trend, by the end of the 1990s, some universities began to revise curricula and switch to the enterprise systems programs. At the graduate level of MBA, some universities offer the ERP concentration instead of CIS or IT concentration as a reflection of the enterprise systems approach.

In The 1980s some more specialized programs have been developing, such as Information Science for library automation of information systems, health information systems (HIS) for supporting management of hospitals and health centers, and accounting information systems (AIS) for paperless accounting.

By the end of the 1990s, the Web technology opened a new communication channel for marketing, advertisement, sales, and so forth, "*electronizing*" almost every business function. Consequently, needs for a new major/minor became obvious and the e-biz development programs have been spreading around business colleges in addition to the existing programs. Very soon, due to the Internet popularity, almost every department in a business college wanted to have own specialized IT program, which lead to the merging of more general computer-oriented program such as business information technology (BIT). The difference between the e-biz development and BIT programs is such that the former is more oriented towards IT professionals, who develop and administer Web sites, and the latter is more oriented towards the development of specific, business functions or process-oriented applications that are used by business professionals. Similar to BIT, there are emerging programs in other academic areas. For example, art information technology (AIT), music IT (MIT), sport IT (SIT), and so forth. This trend has roots in the cross-college service course on end-user computing, which mostly teaches Microsoft Office and home page design at the introductory 100 level. The 200/300 level of the cross-college service course is more oriented towards the enterprise information infrastructure, introduction to enterprise systems, the system approach, and the transformation from an industrial to informated enterprise, followed by consideration on information and civilization and information and culture. This course at many colleges is still taught as the "MIS" course.

THE IMPACT OF MANUFACTURING AND IT OUTSOURCING UPON IT EDUCATION

In the 2000s, an estimated 12% of American companies offshore manufacturing jobs to foreign countries. In 2000-2005, about 3 million direct manufacturing jobs have been lost in the United States with four to five million support jobs disappearing with them (AC-CRA, 2004). Many U.S. based airlines are linked via computers and telephone lines with reservation clerks in Ireland where labor costs are low and education is high. Many American computer firms have technical help-desk support in India. There is less current demand for engineers, IT students, and MBAs in the United States. The middle class is shrinking even as health care and energy costs are rising rapidly. Greed appears to run rampant in corporate executive suites as dislocated workers struggle with unemployment and severe financial pressures. Trade deficits in the U.S. are growing to about $700 billion by the end of 2005 (http://www.census.gov/indicator/www/ustrade.html).

Escalating off shoring threatens to eliminate IT skills-knowledge foundation for more complex jobs creating an IT knowledge gap. We are experiencing a transformation shift in work and opportunity. Some have suggested that the shift is similar to the movement from an agricultural to an industrial society, but we did not eliminate agricultural with the industrial movement. Rather, the productivity of agriculture was increased. The industrial wave allowed us to make payments with goods. Now we pay with debt. Also we in the U.S. subcontract foreigners for not only manufacturing product for us, but also conducting R & D, which means doing "thinking for us."

The solution to outsourcing is long-term thinking and innovation. The timing of innovation is notoriously unpredictable. New jobs will require more knowledge, but how many jobs will there be? When will we see them? They will require dealing with complexity, but we need less complex work to prepare us for more complex work. We cannot teach classical music if we have disbanded the symphony orchestra. Outsourcing and off shoring must be viewed from the perspective of long-term investment as well as short-term profits.

On the other hand, outsourcing and off shoring are really nothing more than traditional market competition expanded in a global economy, and enabled by an increasingly robust information infrastructure. Market economies are relentless in their drive for efficiency and productivity. Historic barriers of transportation logistics, off-site management, and knowledge transfer have been greatly reduced by information and transportation technologies. There are obvious short-term financial benefits available to companies by moving well defined systems and processes to lower cost areas of the world. Short-term effects on developed societies are less attractive than they are to companies, with less available jobs and fewer opportunities. Long-term consequences for everyone are open to debate, and potentially foreboding.

So far, for example in the state of Michigan, the computer science and CIS/MIS programs have lost at least 40% of the students, who do not want to graduate from programs with a very limited employment opportunity. Companies offshore about 40-50,000 IT jobs per year, which is equal to the output of graduates from those programs in U.S. Companies still want to hire IT specialists but with more advanced skills. It is still possible, since there is some pool of such specialists in U.S. But, very soon without entry-level jobs, this country will not produce more advanced IT specialists (Rienzo & Targowski 2006). The globalization of IT jobs triggers dramatic changes in the IT profession.

CHANGES IN THE IT PROFESSION

One thing has always been true is that the fast advancement of computing makes *information technology* (IT) constantly change over the past five decades. The rapidly changing nature of the IT field makes itself a moving target for all industries, not to mention the educators of IT. As a matter of fact, IT has been viewed as a ubiquitous commodity since its basic functions (e.g., data storage, data processing, networking, etc.) become available to all organizations at virtually the same costs. Therefore, today's issue is not whether IT can or cannot provide its functions, rather it is if the costs and risks involved in IT investment could be fully justified by its return on investment (ROI) for the corporate strategic use of IT (Carr, 2003).

There have been tremendous changes in the computer business applications profession over the past few years:

1. Programming tasks are being outsourced to offshore service providers by many corporations, which limit the number of entry positions for college graduates. Not all business applications will be in-housed developed. Due to the modularity of IT applications and the routine nature of business processes, any none-core business operations, if they need be automated, will be defined as *commodities* outsourced to the third party for operational support or code development.
2. Potential employers seek college graduates who are skillful in handling the business processes integration projects with the support of networked computers in secured and easy to recover environments. CIS graduates should know more about business, business, and business. IT should be considered a tools to integrate business processes to make organizations and corporations more efficient, effective, secure, and reliable to meet the best interests of all their constituents. IT education should focus more on the general knowledge and skills in using, maintaining, and developing enterprise-wide information systems such as ERP and EAI (enterprise application integration).
3. The passage of the Sarbanes-Oxley Act 2002 mandates increased information processing requirements for public companies, which has in turn led to greatly increased opportunities for computer business applications graduates. These changes steer the curriculum changes of the computer science and CIS/MIS/IS program. There is little doubt that IT functions will continue to be expanded and integrated with business processes to support today's extended corporation operations. All applications will either be in-house supported through an ERP or commoditized and outsourced to a low-cost provider (Benemati & Mahaney 2004).

FUTURE IT JOBS

The commoditization of IT applications may shift IT professionals focus from micro technical application development to macro system planning to project management of corporate computing resources that support enterprise-wide business processing with the goal of cost reductions, productivity improvement, and enhancement of value-added business activities. The IT professionals should be prepared to:

- Identify corporate core competences
- Know how to prioritize and define IT tasks
- Determine if the IT task is a commodity that ought to be either in-house developed or offshore outsourced to cut down the costs or minimize the risks for the corporation as a whole

Note that many of the IT jobs being sent offshore, are the entry-level positions such as application programmer, help desk receptionist, hardware/software technical support, call center staff, and so forth. The nature of primary IT jobs that will remain in the United States are of greater complexity (Weisman, 2003). Therefore, the possible IT jobs in the future, while not limited to, are the following:

- IT project manager
- Business analyst
- Application integrator
- Information security officer
- ERP system consultant
- Information resource manager
- E-business designer
- Corporate portal content manager
- Business intelligence specialist
- Other

By and large, corporations will still need IT managers with strategic vision and business process knowledge. According to Gartner report, skills such as application design, system integration, enterprise information architecture, IT resource management, client relationship/business process management, and technology integration with extended corporate partners will remain in house (Traylor, 2003).

THE FUNCTION VS. PROCESS IN BUSINESS AND THEIR REPERCUSSIONS FOR EDUCATION

Business Environment Change

Corporate globalization is a clear trend, and more and more companies will continue to go overseas to locate business partners in support of low-cost production to maximize corporate profits. This globalization movement makes corporate planning more complex due to the involvement of increased business partners and business processes that could be co-developed (shared) or outsourced to partners. A direct ramification of such globalization has deeply affected corporate investment in IT and its management. Possible changes include corporate workflow redesign, shift of less-critical processes overseas, and the integration of existing business processes through new IT products. Subsequently, the conventional "make-or-buy" decision becomes an issue encountered by all corporate IT executives and management.

Due to the environment change, the CIS curriculum also needs a paradigm shift to ensure that our graduates truly have IT knowledge and skills that are sufficient to help business owners solve their problems by maximizing the bang out of each buck spent in IT investment. Simply put, a graduate who knows only technology itself (e.g., coding, prototyping, Web site development, etc.) is not good enough. CIS graduates must have a solid grasp on all business functions (e.g., accounting, marketing, finance, etc.), business processes (e.g., purchasing, sales distribution, etc.), and, more importantly, how to asses and manage IT projects that deal with various business functions and processes in support of corporate-wide information processing. Very likely, EAI (enterprise application integration) will need to be used to support necessary business process integration (BPI), which leads corporations to be more cost-effective and performance-efficient.

From Business Function to Business Process

A business function concept was triggered by the development of *bureaucracy*, whose concept was created by a German philosopher Max Weber at the end of the 19th century. The rapid growth of the Industrial Wave needed more specialized office workers. In that time bureaucracy meant progressive solution, because functional specialization provided higher productivity. However, the rising volume of paper-driven transactions slowed down their flow across an enterprise, due to the so-called "silos" effect. In the 1990s the attention in developing IS was switched from a function to process-driven information solutions, as it is shown in Figure 2.

Figure 2. Business functions vs. process

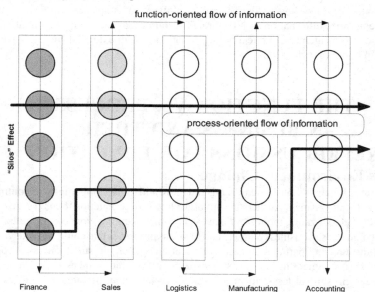

Figure 2 illustrates a shift from a vertical-horizontal flow of information to a horizontal one, which increases the velocity of information throughout the enterprise and collaborating stakeholders. Examples of process-driven information solutions are as follows:

- **Promote to deliver:**
  o   Marketing
  o   Quote and order processing
  o   Transportation
  o   Documentation
  o   After sales service
  o   Warranty and guarantees
- **Procure to pay:**
  o   Vendor sourcing RFQ
  o   Purchase requisition
  o   Purchase ordering
  o   Purchase contracts
  o   Inbound logistics
  o   Supplier invoicing
  o   Supplier payment
  o   Supplier performance

Figure 3. The general architecture of R/3 software system (the Targowski model)

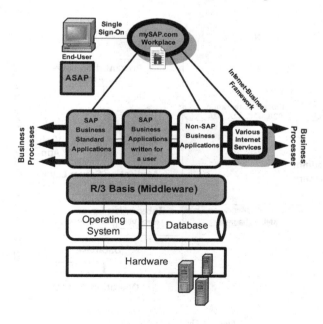

A good software example of process-driven information solutions is SAP R/3 ERP-like software, which has informated 800 standard business processes and provides open sockets for plug-in customized business processes. Figure 3 presents a graphic model to highlight the architecture of SAP R/3. The SAP architectures reflects the business process approach to the creation of the enterprise-wide software, which despite of computerizing 800 standard processes is open to customized ones and to interaction with Web-driven services. Therefore, this software is so good example for students to teach them in the comprehensive approach to the business process management (BPM) in the enterprise-wide solution.

An appropriate handling of business processes leads towards the business process integration (BPI) across an enterprise, which is shown in Figure 4. This Figure shows different layers of integration, which leads to a very complex software. In a case of SAP there are about 500,000,000 lines of code and 80,000 tables. Of course, the CIS student should be exposed to such complexity in order to be prepared to handle difficult industrial project when they move to the real world.

Based upon the presented business applications integration, under the form of ERP, CIM, and business process concepts applied throughout the industries at the beginning of the 21st century, the CIS faculty of the Department of Business Information Systems at Western Michigan University's Haworth College of Business, undertook an initiative to transform their undergraduate curriculum from the classical CIS program (technology-based) to the BIT program (business process based). More details about the curriculum transformation are presented in the next section of this chapter.

The concept of an extended enterprise supports the proposed curriculum transformation, and is depicted by a graphical model in Figure 5. This model shows the growing number

Figure 4. The BPI architecture

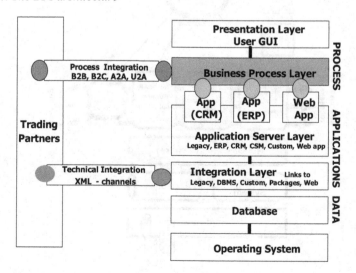

Figure 4 The BPI Architecture

Figure 5. The architecture of the extended enterprise systems (the Targowski model)

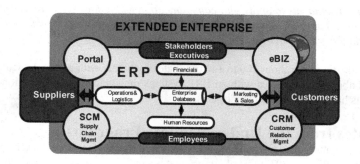

of complex systems, which collaborate with the ERP system within a framework of the extended enterprise to the vendors (SCM) and customers (CRM) with the support of e-business and e-portals. Of course, that such complex platform cannot be off shore outsourced, hence the students' chance for better jobs is in taking on these kind of systems. Needless to say it is a huge challenge for the professors, who do not have enough experience with these systems and have to learn on the fly, with a very little support for training from the short budget-managed colleges.

FROM THE CLASSICAL CIS
TO THE BIT PROGRAM

Formed in 1981/82 the Computer Information Systems Program at the Business Information Systems Department is one of six main programs (four departments and the BIS department has two independent units; CIS program and BCM-Business Communication Management program) in the Haworth College of Business (HCoB). CIS offers three undergraduate majors; CIS, TIM (Telecommunication & Information Management, an interdisciplinary major with the School of Communication at College of Arts and Sciences), and e-BizD (e-business design) and one graduate ERP (enterprise resources planning) concentration in the MBA program. There are currently 8 tenure-track faculty members and three full-time instructors. The CIS faculty teaches classes for the three undergraduate majors, the graduate concentration as well as three service courses for all students from the college and the University. The three service courses are: CIS102–End-User Computing, BUS270 — Information and Communication Enterprise Infrastructure, and BUS618 — IT Management.

The vision of the CIS program is:

To prepare students to work in informated and electronic businesses in the modern global economy driven by knowledge workers using information infrastructure.

The mission of the CIS program is:

To educate students to apply info-communication technology (ICT) in order to develop and operate informated, knowledge-based, and network-driven enterprise in the global environment.

Currently, there are about 100 to 140 graduates each year with a baccalaureate degree in CIS, and about 10 graduates with an ERP systems management concentration. Due to this, students have two distinct career paths.

Graduates from the Undergraduate Program

The employment data (provided by our career and student employment service office) show that, from 1998 to 2003, most of our graduates can find a job within three months, and were recruited by a variety of industries that include accounting, banking, information consulting, health care, insurance, manufacturing, and public utilities. Since our old curriculum was focused on the technology-based training for system development, a good percentage of our graduates found entry-level jobs that involve system analysis and design, application development, network administration, database design and development, Web site design, and Web administration. Due to increasing offshore outsourcing, less entry-level jobs were available over the past three years. Not until recently were our graduates able to find positions that include network manager, system maintenance technician, and business analyst. As compared to four years ago, the annual salary is in the neighborhood of high 30K and low 40K, a five thousand drop from five years ago.

While more and more internships are offered since Fall 2004, there is no significant growth of full-time positions. With our revised curriculum focused on business processes and ERP applications, future graduates are expected to be hired as business consultants and analysts more than as application programmers and database designers.

Graduates of MBA-ERP Concentration

Since the year 2001, most of our MBA graduates with an ERP (CIS) concentration are employees who have a full-time job in nearby corporations. Their career interests are quite different from those of early international students, who tried to learn technical skills to find a job within the IT department. The current MBA-ERP graduates are more interested in applying IT knowledge/skills to improve their current jobs on hands, or seeking some managerial position within the same division that needs both IT and business knowledge. Currently, most of our MBA students are employed by Pfizer, Kellogg, Perrigo, Denso, and Stryker. Receiving an MBA with an ERP concentration may not guarantee career relocation. However, it does provide them opportunity to be more productive and able to secure their career especially during the uncertainties when corporations often exercise layoffs to cut down the operation costs.

THE 2000 CIS CURRICULUM MODEL

The CIS curriculum model in 2000 is depicted in Figure 6, which shows clear categorization of course levels and their progression from information systems programming, via design, development to management, assuring the curriculum completeness.

Figure 6. CIS major cirriculum model — 2000 at the Western Michigan University

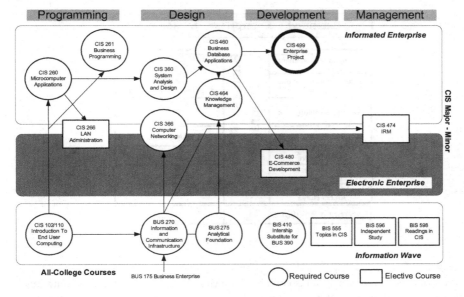

Since year 2000, many small changes have been introduced to the above model. Major changes were introduced in year 2004, by then the CIS program has lost about 40% of students (from 500 to 300). We think that the decline[2] was caused by the IT and manufacturing outsourcing. The scope of changes will be presented hereinafter.

AN INITIATIVE FOR CURRICULUM REVISION IN 2004

A revised curriculum was proposed based on the actual findings of corporate IT needs and market demands. After consultation with the CIS Advisory Council in November 2004, the CIS faculty decided to pursue a complete transformation of the classical CIS program into a business process-drive program that supports BPI using the following framework:

- Solid grasp on business applications and processes,
- Efficient management of IT projects,
- Innovative use of IT for value-added activities,
- Hands-on Exercise using existing ERP tools (e.g., SAP, Microsoft Great Plains).

A Paradigm Shift

To face the environment change and to meet future corporate needs, the CIS curriculum requires a paradigm shift (i.e., it must move from our current technology-based design to a new one that blends IT through the understanding of businesses and their integration), (i.e., a BPI-driven IT curriculum). Figure 7 highlights the model of BPI-driven CIS curriculum,

Figure 7. A model of BPI-driven CIS curriculum

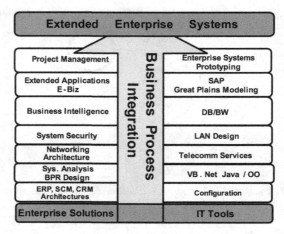

where extended enterprise systems contain modules such as SCM, ERP, CRM, and other. This model shows how enterprise system solutions are supported by IT tools, which learn students through the right set of courses. This kind of approach assures at this moment that the CIS graduates may apply for higher levels of jobs, beyond the legacy practice of beginning as just a programmer. Therefore, the syndrome of off shore outsourcing (of programming) can be minimized.

As it shown previously, all CIS subjects are integrated while covered by different courses, through the "business process integration" approach. That is, the knowledge and concepts of business process will be woven into and practiced in every CIS course, from the beginning college IT core course (i.e., BUS270 — Information and Communication Infrastructure) to the final CIS capstone course (i.e., CIS499 — Enterprise Project). More details follow.

Table 1. Revised BPI-driven CIS curriculum

CIS Course	Traditional Topics	Business Process Topics	ERP Topics
CIS 2600 — Business Programming	• Programming concepts, • Loops/If Then Else Logics, • Structured programming techniques.	• Business application modules, • VBA tools for process development.	• ERP Data Entry Forms, Customizations • WSP ABAP/ Great Plains VBA.

Table 1. continued

CIS 2800 — OO/Web Programming	• OO Programming Concepts, • Programming logics and flowchart, • Tools - Perl, Visual Basic, Java, JSP, PHP.	• Business process module concept, • J2EE concept.	• Programming examples illustrating ERP systems, • WSP Java for e-Portal.
CIS 3260 — Business Networking	• LAN setting and installation, • OSI Model, • Networking Essentials.	• Enterprise network design and administration (Intranets).	• B2B and B2C networks (Extranets), • Secured Netweaver framework.
CIS 3600 — Systems Analysis and Design	• System analysis methodologies, • Business requirements analysis, • Systems Modeling and SDLC concept.	• Work flow analysis, • Business process modeling, • Project management hands-on.	• Modules in ERP systems, • Business Process Integration concepts.
CIS 3620 — Project Management	• Project management methodology, • PERT/CPM and resource leveling, • Milestones/Tasks/Deadline management.	• Business Process modeling, • Business Case studies focused on process management.	• Business process configuration, • SAP solution manager, • Great Plains Reporting tools.
CIS 3660 — Enterprise Network Security	• Information assurance and integrity, • Network Security Fundamentals.	• Business network defense and countermeasures, • Intranet as BPI tools.	• ERP network security management, • Netweaver framework.
CIS 3900 — Business Web Architecture	• XHTML, XML, CSS, JavaScript, • Graphics, Design and Layout, • Web Architecture.	• Project Management, Project Flow, • Group Dynamics.	• Web Services (e.g., SAP iViews), • System Integration.

Curriculum Implementation Framework

In brief, "business process" related topics will be identified for each CIS course, and they will be delivered together with traditional subjects. To enhance the students' learning and teaching effectiveness, all subjects identified for each course will be integrated by hands-on exercises using some current ERP software. Two popular ERP tools that could be considered for use in this BPI-driven curriculum are SAP and Microsoft Business Solutions such as Great Plains. A course-topic matrix as shown in Table 1 is used to define the revised course content for this proposed BPI-driven CIS curriculum.

Expected Educational Results

With the revised BPI-driven CIS curriculum, our graduates are expected to develop the following knowledge and skills before they enter the real world:

- **Solid grasp on business functions and processes:** Since IT knowledge/skills are delivered throughout with business processes/functions knowledge, students are expected to have a solid grasp on business knowledge.
- **Efficient management of IT projects:** Today, information technologies are more application integrators than stand-alone tools in solving business problems. Using the BPI approach, IT is employed with business knowledge to ensure its proper use for corporate core competence build-up.
- **Innovative use of IT for value-added activities:** Through the emphasis of BPI, more creative use of IT in extending value-chains between business partners are highly expected.
- **Hands-on exercise tools:** A number of existing software that supports Enterprise Information Systems includes SAP, PeopleSoft, and Great Plains. Fortunately, our college has access to two ERP.
- **Software packages:** SAP and Microsoft Great Plains. While we are not limited to these two products, they can be immediately used for our revised BPI-driven curriculum.

At the same time, the CIS courses are converted into BIT courses with necessary changes in title and content. Details are shown in Table 2.

Table 2. The transition from the CIS to BIT program and its expected learning outcomes

CIS Program Objectives	BIT Program Objectives	Learning Outcomes
To teach the state-of-the-art information technologies	To teach the state-of-the-art information technologies in business processes and enterprise	1. Apply recently-developed IT technologies in support of business processes. 2. Ability in using information technology in automating business processes in an enterprise.

Table 2. continued

To prepare graduate for the dynamic market needs	To prepare graduate for the dynamic market needs close to business processes of an enterprise	1. Understand general business processive needs that are to be integrated by information technologies. 2. Ability in exploring new computerized solution to meet the market changing needs.
To develop IT-oriented curriculum that meet stakeholders' needs	To develop IT-oriented curriculum that meet stakeholders' needs In the times of outsourcing	1. Demonstrate integrated business knowledge with proper use of information technologies for problem solving of business processes integration. 2. Ability in communicating with non-IT users and using IT for productivity/effectiveness improvements.
CIS Core Courses	**BIT Core Courses**	**Learning Outcomes of BIT Courses**
CIS 260/261 Business Programming A and B	**BIT 2600** Business Programming	1. Understand logical reasoning and program structures applied in BPI 2. Writing computer program using current business programming languages (Visual Basic).
CIS 280 Internet Programming	**BIT 2800** Internet Programming	2. Understand the role of Internet applications in e-business across business processes of an enterprises.
CIS 326 LAN Administration	**BIT 3260** Business Networking	1. Understand network essentials and the functionality of LANs, MANs., WANs., and GANs in support of exchanging info-communication in A2A, B2B, B2C settings. 2. Ability in planning, design, and administering computer/business networks and managing their security issues.

Table 2. continued

CIS 360 Systems Analysis and Design	BIT 3600 Business Process Modeling	1. Understand how information systems are developed in support of business processes and enterprise needs. 2. Apply major design methodologies and graphic modeling tools for information systems supporting BPI.
BIS362 Advanced Programming	BIT 3620 IT Project Management	1. Understand how to manage a complex IT projects in the globalizing environment, including off shore and in-shore outsourcing.
CIS 366 Computer Networking	BIT 3660 Business Networking Security	1. Understand large scale network planning and their functions in support of business info-communication. 2. Ability in designing computer network architecture and various network deployment strategies.
CIS 390 Business Web Architecture	BIT 3900 Business Web Architecture	1. Understand how to develop and implement effective Websites to support e-business. 2. Apply human computer interaction theories to support information systems management.
CIS 460 Business Database Applications	BIT 4600 Data Modeling and Warehousing	1. Ability in designing, developing, and implementing databases and warehouses over a client/server platform, including data mining. 2. Apply knowledge in developing front-end interface for remote database/warehouse processing.
CIS 464 Business Data Mining	BIT 4640 Business Intelligence and Data Mining	1. Understand the role of knowledge management and data mining techniques applied in business intelligence. 2. Apply knowledge management and data mining in support of business operations and management.

Table 2. continued

CIS 490 E-Commerce Development	BIT 4900 E-Commerce Development	1. Ability in developing an e-commerce applications 2. Apply various web skills in e-commerce administration.
CIS 499 Enterprise Project	BIT 4990 Enterprise Project	1. Understand enterprise application architecture 2. Ability in developing enterprise systems
CIS 555 SAP programming using ABAP/4	BIT 5550 SAP programming using ABAP/4	1. Understand fundamental ABAP/4 programming syntaxes and coding technique in BPI projects. 2. Ability in developing SAP-like interface, report, and fundamental dialog applications

THE FUTURE OF IT EDUCATION IN THE U.S.

The future of IT education in U.S. is uncertain. If the process of offshore outsourcing continues and the industrial/institutional employers only recruit experienced IT professionals, then before long they will consume all qualified candidates and the colleges will eliminate or shrink the computer-oriented programs because of the lack of student enrollment. In the same time, the states budget deficit will further increase due to the reduction of manufacturing and its services, which used to bring in sufficient taxes. For example, the 2005 State of Michigan Budget is at the level of the 1995 Budget, but after correction for inflation this budget is at the level of 1972. The State of Michigan in years 2001-2005 appropriated $300 million less for higher education, which will cause the shut-down of two universities with 15,000 students each (Rienzo & Targowski 2005).

Furthermore, if the U.S. loses manufacturing, then it will also lose system complexity. Consequently, the U.S. will not require advanced information systems and talents for their development and operations.

How long can a situation last when the enterprise's nervous system (a metaphor for information systems) and blood system (a metaphor for information infrastructure) are in the hands of IT specialists who live thousands of miles away? It is a big puzzle. Today, many companies are already bring back their help centers to the U.S. since it is very difficult to advise users when help is thousands of miles away from the processes that are to be fixed.

There is an old saying that the American Society is a self-poisoning society and at the same time a self-repairing one. It means that the offshore outsourcing wave may weaken in the future and the situation may return to the business it used to be. Certainly, this is a long-term prediction, but in the mean time the damage has already done to the IT education in the U.S. A similar damage has also done to the companies, even though they are "happy" about being able to offshore outsourcing their manufacturing and IT projects. However, their gains are short-term.

CONCLUSION

So far the development process of IT education in U.S. goes by the strategy of "development by division," which reflects many nature and civilization domains' practices, particularly in biology and finance (e.g., diversified portfolio of stocks). When will the full enterprise processes consolidation take place? It is too soon to predict, however the ERP, CIM, and e-enterprise approaches indicate the first steps in this direction.

Off shore outsourcing of IT and manufacturing projects have been intensified at the beginning of the 21st century. They have created damages to the IT education initiatives, which cultivate defensive strategies to protect the already built "territories."

Shifting focus of IT education from general skills to business process-driven IT skills seems to be a successful strategy for the 2000s, however it is too soon to judge how it impacts the students' potential for better jobs and job security. Further research should be undertaken to trace the industrial practices and attitude towards a "local" more expensive and better educated labor force versus a "outsourced" less expensive one. In future research the WMU CIS faculty is going to study how the ERP-related curriculum has actually made a change in the careers of students who take the re-engineered program. For example, we will examine whether students have been able to find better paying jobs and if their levels of satisfaction have increased.

REFERENCES

ACCRA. (2004). *How is offshoring impacting the American economy*. Retrieved January 22, 2005, from http://www.accra.org/newsletter/offshoring.htm

Anonymous. (2003). Juggling outsourcing stats. *Communication of the ACM, 46*(9), 11.

Benemati, S., & Mahaney, R. (2004, August 5-8). The future job market for information system graduates. In *Proceedings of the 10th Americas Conference on Information Systems*, New York.

Bernstein, A. (2004, December 6). Shaking up trade theory. *BusinessWeek,* 116-120.

Carr, N. (2003, May). IT doesn't matter. *Harvard Business Review,* 41-49.

Denning, P. J., Comer, D. E., Gries, D., Mulder, M. C., Tucker, A., Turner, A. J., et al. (1989, January). Computing as a discipline. *Communications of the ACM, 32*(1), 9-23.

Hamblen, J. W. (1983). Computers in colleges and universities. In A. Ralston & E. D. Reilly, Jr. (Eds.), *Encyclopedia of computer science and engineering*. New York: Van Norstand Reinhold Co.

Murphy, C., & Chabrow, E. (2003, November 17). The programmer's future. *Information Week*.

Rienzo, T., & Targowski, A. (2006). Outsourcing premises and consequences. In V. P. Singh (Ed.), *Outsourcing and offshoring in the 21st century: A socio-economic perspective*. Hershey, PA: Idea Group Publishing.

Rosen, S. (1983). Contemporary and future history of computers. In A. Ralston & E. D. Reilly, Jr. (Eds.), *Encyclopedia of computer science and engineering*. New York: Van Norstand Reinhold Co.

Targowski, A. (2003). *Electronic enterprise, strategy, and architecture*. Hershey, PA: Idea Group Publishing.

Traylor, P. (2003). Outsourcing. *CFO, 19*(15), 24.

Weisman, R. (2003, December 3). IT careers that will bounce back. *E-Commerce Times*.

Wilkes, M. V. (1983). Early history of computers. In A. Ralston & E. D. Reilly, Jr. Eds.), *Encyclopedia of computer science and engineering*. New York: Van Norstand Reinhold Co.

ENDNOTES

[1]   The WMU-HCoB-CIS faculty involved in the presented curriculum revising initiatives were composed of the following ones: professors: Bernard Han (Department Chair), Andrew Targowski (Department and College Curriculum Committees Chair), Kuriakose Athappilly; associate professors: Alan Rea (the e-BizD program coordinator), Mike Tarn (the TIM program coordinator); assistant professors: Pairin Katerattanakul (the CIS/BIT program coordinator), Kuanchin Chen, and Muhammad Razi; instructors: Jim Danenberg, Thomas Rienzo, Tom Zembrowski, Anne-Mary Oulai.

[2]   This kind of decline is noticed at all Michigan computer programs, according to the Conference of these programs chairs. Needles to say that the State of Michigan is the manufacturing state where the auto industry is dominating industry.

Chapter V

The ERP-Oriented Graduate IT Program

Andrew Targowski, Western Michigan University, USA

Bernard Han, Western Michigan University, USA

ABSTRACT

The purpose of this chapter is to present a revised graduate CIS concentration in the MBA program at Western Michigan University's Haworth College of Business. The new MBA-CIS concentration has been designed with a strong focus on ERP systems management, and it is proposed in response to industrial needs and to meet MBA students' interests. The existing MBA-CIS concentration was developed in mid-1990s on the premise that future IT professionals must have mastery in technical IT skills in managing computing information resources. The recent trend in IT outsourcing triggers a new question — "What kind of IT training and education should be delivered to Americans to keep them employable in the United States?" A new premise resulted from the present environment changes that require our graduate students to have balanced knowledge in both IT skills and business processes (i.e., knowing how to apply IT to the development of business applications that support integrated business processes and enterprise operations). The authors hope that this chapter will contribute to the new issues facing the Academia in the 21st century in respect to IT education.

THE NEED FOR RE-ENGINEERING OF THE MBA-CIS CONCENTRATION

The existing MBA-CIS concentration was developed in mid-1990s on the premise that future IT professionals must have mastery in technical IT skills in managing computing information resources. This curriculum orientation was quite popular for international students who are often young with strong technical skills but lack extensive business experience. Therefore, courses were often designed to target students with interests more in technology itself than in those business processes that employ technologies. Similarly, faculty members who were assigned to teach graduate-level CIS courses have focused more on the technology per se than its functional role in business processes.

In brief, the major factors that have impacted our MBA-CIS Concentration are:

1. After the 9-11 terrorist attack in 2001, the course enrollment has declined more than 50% because of a big drop in international students due to difficulties in getting student visas.

2. For the sake of cost reductions, IT outsourcing has been increasingly adopted by big corporations since 2003. By and large, more technical routine jobs such as application programming and module development have been outsourced offshore. The IT triggers a new question — "What kind of IT training and education will keep Americans employable in the United States?"

3. The current corporate IT investments highlight the importance of the deployment and/or modifications of existing enterprise-wide ERP (enterprise resource planning), CIM (computer integrated manufacturing), and many others. A few prominent of such enterprise systems include SAP, Oracle (acquired both Peoplesoft and J.D. Edwards), and Microsoft Great Plains.

The aforementioned factors lay a new premise for our MBA-CIS education that should provide our graduate students with a balanced knowledge and skills in:

how to develop enterprise-wide business applications with a strong focus more on the integrated business processes than on specialized facet of IT skills.

Simply put, an IT employee for any corporations today must stay closer to the business process (that uses IT) than to the technical knowledge or use of IT (e.g., computer programming, Web design, etc.). A business IT professional should be capable in operating an IT-driven extended enterprise, where ERP systems are at the center of the enterprise as shown in Figure 1. Process management is not another form of automation, a new killer-application or a fashionable new management theory. Process management discovers what you do and then manages the lifecycle of improvement and optimization, in a way that translates directly to operation. Whether you wish to adopt industry best practices for efficiency or pursue competitive differentiation, you will need process management. Based on a solid mathematical foundation, the BPM breakthrough is for business people. Designed top down in accordance with a company's strategy, business processes can now be unhindered by the constraints of existing IT systems (Smith & Fingar, 2002). The business process management approach can be customized in such a manner that, despite Car's (2004) claim that

Figure 1. The evolution of IT business applications and curricula responses in education

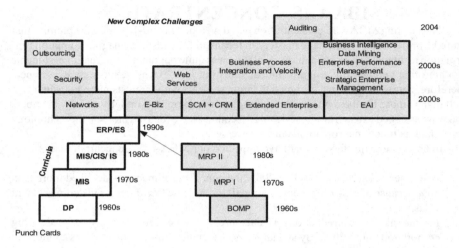

"IT becomes ubiquitous-commodity inputs," properly implemented it is and will be still the essential infrastructure for business operations as long as information is and will be the basic substance of human cognition and control.

AN MBA-CIS WITH AN ERP SYSTEM MANAGEMENT ORIENTATION

To fulfill the new premise addressed above, the CIS faculty[1] at the Department of Business Information Systems at Haworth College of Business, WMU has unanimously agreed that our new MBA-CIS Concentration should be oriented towards the ERP systems management. More specifically, our new CIS curriculum is aimed at all MBA students who are already involved or will be working for businesses that employ or will employ advanced ERP systems.

The historic origin of ERP is in inventory management and control packages. In 1970s, it came with the emergence of material requirements planning (MRP) and distribution resource planning (DRP), which focused on automating all aspects of production master scheduling and centralized inventory planning, respectively. During the 1980s, the misnamed MRP II (manufacturing tesource planning) systems emerged to extend MRP's traditional focus on production processes into other business function, including order processing, manufacturing, and distribution. In the early 1990s, MRP II was further extended to cover areas of engineering, finance, human resources, project management, and others. In other words, it was expanded with a complete "breadth" of activities within a business enterprise. The further trend shifts business leads from "making to stock" to "make to order" with competitive aggressive deliveries, leads-times, flexibility and further integration with corporate suppliers and customers, in responses to greater product mass-customization.

Figure 2. The MBA-ERP concentration within the enterprise-systems-driven majors at the Western Michigan University — 2005

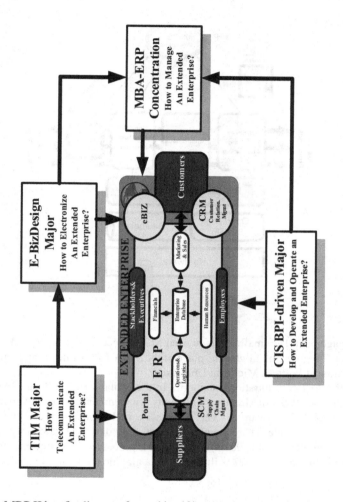

Hence, MRP II has finally transformed itself into an ERP system. But the latter differs not only in system contents but also in more advanced IT. An ERP often provides a graphical user interface, rational database management systems, some 4th generation programming languages, CASE tools in application development, and a client/server architecture that supports open-system portability. Also, while MRP II has traditionally focused on the planning and scheduling on internal resources, an ERP strives to plan and schedule supplier resources as well, based on the dynamic customer demands and schedules. The evolution of ERP is depicted in Figure 1. As accepted by most corporations today, ERP is considered as a strategic business solution that integrates all the business functions, including manufacturing, financial, and distribution. To ensure a proper revision, our CIS faculty has revised all CIS graduate courses in the MBA program with a strong orientation towards the ERP

Figure 3. The general architecture of the ERP SAP R/3 software system (the Targowski model)

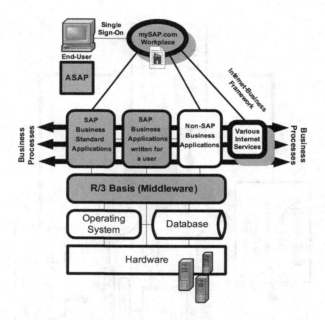

systems management. Hereinafter, this revised MBA concentration is termed "MBA-ERP Concentration." Figure 2 highlights the place of the MBA-ERP Concentration among other IT-driven majors at Western Michigan University.

The MBA-ERP concentration is supported by the available ERP software SAP R/3 for all MBA students since Western Michigan University is a member of SAP University Alliance. As we know SAP-R/3 software is a very large-scale ERP system that contains with more than 500,000 lines of code. There are more than 20 fully developed functional modules in SAP R/3 and it employs about 800 different business processes. Nevertheless, its education IDES version is limited. SAP R/3 is illustrated in a graphic model in Figure 3.

THE MBA PROGRAM AT WESTERN MICHIGAN UNIVERSITY

The MBA-ERP concentration should be viewed within the context of a bigger picture, which is detailed in the following curriculum format.

MBA Program Admission Criteria

1.   A GMAT score of 530 or higher with a GPA of 2.75 or higher for the last two years in an accredited undergraduate university program.
2.   MBA Co-operative program requires a minimum 3.00 GPA.

3. A minimum verbal score of 24 on GMAT.
4. A minimum quantitative score of 32 on GMAT.
5. A minimum GMAT writing score of 3.5.
6. Professional work experience of 2 years or acceptable alternative for regular MBA admission.
7. TOEFL score is not less than 550.
    - Program Requirements
8. Prerequisites/Basic Core (12 hours).
    - ACTY 601 Accountancy
    - ECON 601 Basic Economic Analysis
    - FIN 602 Corporate Finance
    - LAW 604 Legal Regulatory and Political Aspects of Business
9. Business Context (9 hours)
    - BUS 615 Global Business and Intercultural Communication
    - BUS 616 Business Policy and the Social and Ethical Environment
    - BUS 618 Information Technology Management
10. Functional Core (15 hours)
    - ACTY 611 Managerial Accounting
    - FCL 612 Financial Management
    - MKTG 613 Customer-driven Marketing Management
    - MKTG 614 Business Process Management
    - MGMT 617 Managing Human Resources and Behavior
11. Concentration Elective (9 hours) (including among others the MBA-ERP).
12. Integrative Business Solution (3 hours).

A SET OF MBA-ERP GRADUATE COURSES

The following aims have been defined for the MBA-ERP Concentration at WMU in 2004:

Vision Statement

Prepare students to work in informated and electronic businesses in a new, globalizing economy driven by knowledge workers using info-communication infrastructure.

Mission Statement

Educate students in applying info-communication technology (ICT) to develop and operate informated, knowledge and network-driven enterprises in the global environment.

Goal Statement

Prepare business specialists to develop, operate, and manage ERP business processes and their systems in the enterprise-wide info-communication infrastructure of the Global environment.

A set of the MBA-ERP courses should reflect the ERP system's logic in the context of the extended enterprise environment. The ERP system is the application software complex

Figure 4. The major applications of the ERP system

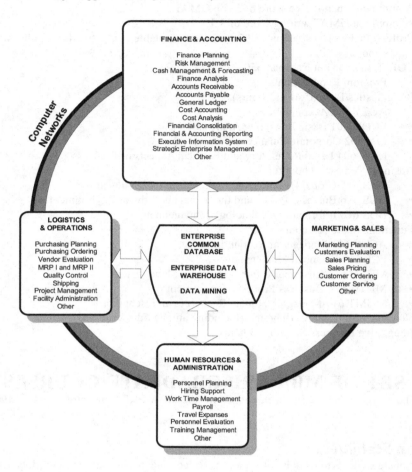

applied in managing almost all business data and applications in the framework of a common database, data warehouse, and data mining as it is shown in Figure 4.

In teaching the ERP concentration in the MBA program the emphasis is put on the issue of how to *manage* an extended enterprise with its core ERP applications. Furthermore, this concentration has only three elective classes, which should be selected from a wide set of ERP-oriented classes, according to each student's preferences.

Also it is necessary to point out that a student should not be "trained" by limiting to a given ERP package, rather he or she should be taught in a broad perspective that covers ERP management issues such that he/she may become a future business executive or a specialist in ERP. Of course in the process of conducting these courses a student has to complete projects involving a demo solutions using SAP R/3 and/or Microsoft Great Plains, one of the most successful ERP for small-to-medium-sized business.

Given the above general requirements, a set of the ERP-oriented CIS classes have been included in the MBA-ERP Concentration at WMU in 2004:

- CIS 620 ERP System Configuration
- CIS 630 ERP Data Management
- CIS 662 ERP Project Management
- CIS 664 ERP Data Mining
- CIS 666 ERP Network & Security Management
- CIS 670 ERP Portal Management
- CIS 710 Independent Research
- CIS 710 Professional Experience

Note: All MBA students are required to take the BUS 618 IT Management course, therefore it is not included in the set of the MBA-ERP concentration. Its syllabus is provided next, followed by the syllabus of CIS 620 ERP System Configuration to illustrate the set of listed courses.

Course Description

BUS 618 enables the student to understand the use of information technology as part of business strategy. Issues surrounding information technology such as information and communication systems and services, and enterprise-wide systems — traditional, networked, and virtual — in organizations, will be explored. The growing convergence of technologies — computer video, and telecommunications — within sophisticated information networks, will also be examined. Students should gain knowledge about strategic issues involving information technology management, as well as the development of specific computer skills.

Required Materials

- Andrew Targowski: Electronic Enterprise, Strategy and Architecture, IRM Press, 2003
- BUS 618 SAP Course Pack

Course Objectives

After completing this course students should be able to:

1. Recognize, analyze, and suggest various types of information-communication systems/services that are encountered in everyday life and in the business world
2. Integrate business and IT strategies and services, and analyze their strategic impact on the business world
3. Identify issues and implications of IT management

Career Goal

Graduates of this course will be prepared to work as follows:

1.   Business professional as an IT end-user and IT committee member
2.   Business executive-IT oriented, (ex. general manager, business function manager)
3.   Information technology executive (ex. CIO, application development manager, operations manager, network administrator, etc.)

Course Structure

The purpose of this course is to prepare managers with adequate knowledge and skills in the area of information-communication systems/services. The students, therefore, will be actively involved in:

1.   **Class, lectures, and discussions:** To gain a conceptual understanding of information-communication systems/services   and related technologies.
2.   **Project reports:** To gain a theoretical knowledge and understanding of information-communication systems/services.
3.   **Project presentation:** To gain a hands-on experience of IT project presentation to the enterprise's executives. The presentations are computer-supported in Power Point.

Course Theme

How general managers are using IT services to change organizations. The underlying thread woven throughout this course encompasses these three areas:

1.   **Knowledge (lectures and exams):** 50% of grades
2.   **Skills (projects and presentations):** 25% of grades
3.   **Attitude (readiness and project quality):** 25% of grades

Projects

Project 1:	SAP Navigation
Project 2:	SAP Transactions Processing (Sales Order Processing)
Project 3:	Data Mining — if Demo is available in Summer II 2004
Project 4a:	The Integration of Business and System Strategies
Project 4b:	Power Point Presentations of Project 4 and 5
Project 5a:	Plan An IT-Driven Enterprise
Project 5b:	Spreadsheet for Budgeting and Project Managementt in Project 5

Team Project/Cases

A. Project Report

This should be about 10-15 pages long (typed, 1.5-spaced). The table of content is provided in the syllabus. Cases should be selected from the student's practice.

Common elements of a project report:

Title Page
Table of Contents
Executive Summary
Introduction
Report Main Body
Conclusion
Self-evaluation by each student

a.   What did you learn in this project?
b.   How are you going to apply this project's skills in your profession?
c.   How are you going to apply this project's skills in your life?
d.   Other

References
Appendix

Table 1. Skills/Projects of a BUS 618 graduate

Target Groups / IT Skills Coverage	Target Groups of BUS 618		
	IT End-Users To learn how to apply the most popular IT Techniques	*IT Executives* To learn the business side of IT	*Business Executives* To learn the IT side of business
IT Technical Skills (Hands-on) (30%)	Enterprise software P1 - SAP Navigation P2 – SAP Transactions Processing Office productive software P4b – PowerPoint/Visio P5b – SS-Excel, MS Project	P3 Data Mining due to Software availability	
IT Conceptual Skills (Management) (70%)	Case analysis from your work or Fortune 500 for P4 and P5 - transformed into a managerial picture of an IT-driven enterprise	P4 – Business & System Strategies Integration P5 - IT-oriented Enterprise Planning	

B. Project Presentation:

The presentation should be your professional best, which can last 20-30 minutes. Visual aids will affect your presentation grade. Generate interest in the case. Number of questions asked by other students in the class and the interaction and discussion will determine part of the success of presentation. Students are expected to read the assigned case of the week ahead of class, and actively participate in the discussion.

Points Distribution

PROJECTS	MAX PTS
Project 1	50
Project 2	50
Project 3	Demo
Project 4	175
Project 4a	25
Project 5a	175
Project 5b	25
Mid-Term Exam	250
Final Exam	250

Team Firing and Resigning Policy

Although students are expected to participate in their assigned teams, the course does provide a last resort mechanism to quit a team or fire non-performing members. Anyone leaving a team is responsible for finding another team to join in the same class section. If students leaving assigned teams are unable to join other teams, they must complete all designated project activities by themselves, and will be eligible for no more than 80 percent of the maximum points possible for each group project.

Firing

Non-performing group members can be dismissed using the following process:

1. Team creates and signs a group dismissal policy.
2. Group provides specific requirements for non-performing members and documents them in writing.
3. Group notifies instructor of non-performance and provides documentation in step 2.
4. Group produces a memo notifying non-performer that he/she is off the team and copies instructor.

Resigning

Students believing they are unfairly performing a disproportionate share of project work may resign from a team using the following process:

1. Compose a memo to the team describing specific reasons for dissatisfaction and specific changes desired. Memo must state that resignation will follow if changes are not implemented. Instructor must be copied.

2.   Compose resignation memo and resign from team. Copy instructor.

Remember, anyone leaving his or her assigned team must find another team in the same section, or complete all future assignments individually, and be eligible for no more than 80 percent of group project points.

Academic Honesty:

You are responsible for making yourself aware of and understanding the policies and procedures in the (Undergraduate Catalog (pp. 268-269)/Graduate Catalog (pp. 26-27)) that pertain to academic integrity. These policies include cheating, fabrication, falsification and forgery, multiple submission, plagiarism, complicity and computer misuse. If there is reason to believe you have been involved in academic dishonesty, you will be referred to the Office of Student Conduct. You will be given the opportunity to review the charge(s). If you believe you are not responsible, you will have the opportunity for a hearing. You should consult with your instructor if you are uncertain about an issue of academic honesty prior to the submission of an assignment or test.

Attendance Policy:

Given the nature of this course and the value added by attending the class, attendance is mandatory. Students are expected to contribute in the class and have the responsibility, not only for their own learning, but also to contribute to the learning of their fellow students. Students with four or more class absences shall lose 50% of total points counted towards the course grade. In the event a student must miss more than three classes because of extenuating circumstances such as a lengthy illness, or other reasonable cause, the instructor of the course can make allowances at their discretion.

Late Assignment Policy:

All assignments are due by the end of the class period on the date in the syllabus. Late assignments will be docked 5% of the maximum grade obtainable for that assignment if late up to one week, 10% if over one week late. The course instructor can take into account extenuating circumstances such as illness at their discretion.

Late Exams Policy:

Students are expected to take exams when scheduled. In the event a student misses an exam, they must arrange with the instructor for a make-up. This option is at the discretion of the instructor.

Make-Up Exams:

Make-up exams will be given if the student has a valid University-approved excuse. Once again, most scheduling problems should be discussed with the instructor prior to the exam.

Final Grading Scale

A	=	95.0-100.0
BA	=	89.0-94.99
B	=	83.0-88.99
CB	=	76.0-82.99
C	=	70.0-75.99
D	=	60.0-64.99
DC	=	65.0-69.99
E	=	Below 60.0

Project 1: SAP Navigation

Objective: To learn how SAP organizes the enterprise-wide software

1.	Executive summary	5
2.	Describe the concept of main menu.	5
3.	Describe the concept of navigation	10
4.	Describe the concept of generating certain types of data	10
5.	Evaluate the potential application of SAP in your company.	10
6.	Write self-evaluation	5
7.	References	5
8.	Points total	50

Project 2: SAP Purchasing Order Processing

Objective: To learn how SAP handles a business process through the example of a purchasing order

1. Executive summary   5
2. Answer the following questions about the purchasing order.   20
   a. What is the purchase requisition number?
   b. What is the storage location number?
   c. What is the vendor of your purchased goods?
3. Screenshots of the following completed transaction   10
   a. Create Purchasing Requisition.
   b. Create Purchasing Order: Overview of Requisition Items.
   c. Goods Receipt.
   d. G/L Account Balance Display.
   e. Invoice Receipt.
   f. Post Outgoing Payments.
4. Write self-evaluation   10
5. References   5
   Points total   50

Team Project 4
Project 4a
The Integration of a Business Strategy with an IT Strategy
Project 4b–Power Point Presentation   25

Objective: To learn how to support business aims by IT aims to achieve a competitive advantage

Table 5. Class schedule (activities in capital letters are lectures)

SESSION	ACTIVITIES	DUE TIME	SOURCE
1	a) Class Concept b) MANAGEMENT OF EII c) C. Project 4 Strategies Integration, Introduction	Session 7	Chapter 8
2	a) DEVELOPMENT OF EII b) Project 1 — SAP Navigation c) C. Project 4 — Team Work	Session 4	Chapter 7 SAP Lab
3	Martin Luther King Jr. Holiday		
4	a) ENTERPRISE INFORMATION INFRASTRUCTURE b) B. Project 4 — Team Work		Chapter 3
5	a) APPLICATION LAYER b) Project 2 — SAP Purchasing Order Processing c) C. Project 4 — Team Work	Session 6	Chapter 4
6	a) Project 4 — Team Work b) Exam Review		Power Point
7	a) Presentation of project 4 b) Mid-term Exam		
8	a) Enterprise Configurations b) Project 5 — Plan an IT-driven Enterprise-Introduction	Session 12	Chapter 2
9	a) ENTERPRISE ELECTRONIZATION AND INTEGRATION b) Project 5 — Team Work		Chapter 5
10	a) THE INTERNET ECOSYSTEM b) Project 5–Team Work		Chapter 6
11	a) Project 5 — Team Work		
12	a) Final Presentation of Project 5		
13	a) Class Summary b) Exam Review		
14	Final Exam		

1.	Executive Summary	35
2.	Select a company from your practice	
3.	Define the case's business aims (Model 8-6)	50
	a. Industrial strategy.	
	b. Business creed.	
	c. Business mission.	
	d. Business culture.	
	e. Business goal.	
	f. Business objectives.	
	g. Business tasks.	
	h. Business activities.	
	i. Business strategy.	
	j. Business policy.	
	k. Business practice.	
4.	Define the case's IT aims (Model 89)	50
	a. IT creed.	
	b. IT mission.	
	c. IT paradigm-goal.	
	d. IT strategy.	
	• IT target results.	
	• Application strategic domains.	
	• IT differential advantage.	
	• Strategic thrust.	
5.	Rationalize the defined IT aims	30
6.	Self-evaluation (each teammate).	10
7.	References	
	Total	200

Team Project 5

Project 5a — Plan an IT-driven enterprise
Project 5b— MS Spreadsheet and Project Mgmt Applications
Objective: To learn how to computerize an enterprise

1.	Executive summary.	10
2.	For a Project 1 select an IT-driven enterprise configuration	30
	a. Evaluate the case's enterprise IT aims in terms of IT advancement.	
	b. Provide stages of IT-driven enterprise configurations that are right for the case (apply a Gantt chart–timeline MS Project).	
	c. Design a graphic model of an IT-driven enterprise configuration with all specific solutions for the case.	
3.	Select a strategic application system domain and defined its architecture	20
4.	Define *developmental* issues associated with the implementation of the selected IT-driven enterprise configuration	40
	Apply advanced spreadsheet for budgeting-5a.	25
5.	Define management issues associated with the *operations* of the selected IT-driven enterprise configuration.	40
	Apply advanced spreadsheet for budgeting-5a	25
6.	Self-evaluation (each teammate)	10
7.	References	
	Points Total	200

A syllabus of CIS 620 ERP System Configuration is described next.

Western Michigan University
Haworth College of Business

BIS Dept, CIS Program

CIS 620
ERP SYSTEM CONFIGURATION
Master Syllabus
Spring/Fall 20XX
Classroom:
Professor Name:
Professor Office:
Contact Information:
Mailbox: 3310 Schneider Hall
Office Hours
Course Site
http://homepages.wmich.edu/~netID

MBA GOAL

To provide excellent targeted education, primarily for business professionals and international students.

1. COURSE DESCRIPTION

Through hands-on experiences, students learn how to configure an integrated enterprise requirements planning (ERP) system to manage a firm's business processes and gain a better understanding of the nature of these processes. Management issues associated with implementing these packages are also explored. Cross-listed with MGMT 620, ERP System Configuration.

2. PREREQUISITES

- ACTY 611: Managerial Accounting, MGMT/MKTG 614: Business Process Management, BUS 618: IT Management.

3. COURSE MATERIALS AND TEXTBOOKS

- Brady, Monk, and Wagner, Concepts in Enterprise Resource Planning. Course Technologies, 2001. (ISBN: 0619015934).

4. COURSE OBJECTIVES

1. Understand the nature of complex business processes in today's multi-facility, multi-national firms.
2. Understand how to configure general-purpose enterprise requirements planning (ERP) systems to match a firm's business processes.

3.   Understand the integration of financial and managerial accounting with materials management processes.
4.   Understand the organizational management issues in ERP system implementation.

5.   COURSE OUTCOMES

After taking this course, the student should have:

1.   The ability to describe business activities in terms of interrelated processes.
2.   Fluency with an actual ERP software package.
3.   An appreciation of the integration of accounting with business processes.

6.   COURSE REQUIREMENTS

The following scale defines the grade the student will receive based on the total points earned in the semester:

A   =   95.0-100.0
BA   =   89.0-94.99
B   =   83.0-88.99
CB   =   76.0-82.99
C   =   70.0-75.99
DC   =   65.0-69.99
D   =   60.0-64.99
E   =   Below 60.0

Points will be awarded as follows:

*   **Midterm exam:** 30 points
*   **Final exam:** 40 points
*   **In-class configuration:** 10 points
*   **Configuration project:** 20 points

Midterm Exam

The midterm exam will consist of multiple choice and true-false questions on concepts covered in class and in the exercises. These exams will be administered using WebCT during the class period.

Final Exam

A comprehensive final exam, similar construction to the midterm exam, will be administered using WebCT on the last day of class.

7.   GENERAL SCHEDULE

The topics covered and lecture schedule are listed in Table 6.

8. GENERAL INFORMATION

Academic Integrity

You are responsible for making yourself aware of and understanding the policies and procedures in the (Undergraduate Catalog (pp. 268-269)/Graduate Catalog (pp. 26-27)) that pertain to academic integrity. These policies include cheating, fabrication, falsification and forgery, multiple submission, plagiarism, complicity and computer misuse. If there is reason to believe you have been involved in academic dishonesty, you will be referred to the Office of Student Conduct. You will be given the opportunity to review the charge(s). If you believe you are not responsible, you will have the opportunity for a hearing. You should consult with your instructor if you are uncertain about an issue of academic honesty prior to the submission of an assignment or test. Also please note the University's policy on computer misuse: "Computer misuse is disruptive or illegal use of computer resources." Any evidence of academic dishonesty may be pursued by the instructor. This code can be found at http://www.wmich.edu/oit/planning/policies.html.

9. BRIEF PROJECT DESCRIPTION

The first half of the course will consist of a hands-on, but directed, configuration exercise based on the company in *Concepts in Enterprise Resource Planning*. The next quarter of the course will cover the managerial aspects of implementing an ERP system. During the last quarter of the course, the student will demonstrate what they have learned by configuring a new company in the ERP system.

Table 6. Topics covered

Lecture	Topics
1-2	SAP R/3 System Navigation Company Code and Accounts
3-4	Materials Management Organizational Structures G/L Account Creation
5-6	Vendor Records Material Master Data
7-8	Setup for Posting Documents Materials Management Config. for Goods Receipt
9	Setup for Automatic Account Determination
10	Setup for Controlling
11	Setup for Production Planning Configuration for MRP
12-13	Setup for Sales Sales Order Process

EMPLOYMENT OPPORTUNITIES

An MBA with the completion of our new CIS concentration will be able to find jobs with the following positions:

1. Business executives skillful in IT
2. Business power end-users of ERP
2. ERP project leaders and managers
3. ERP database administrators
4. ERP network and security administrators
5. ERP portal developers
6. ERP info-infrastructure developers
7. ERP data mining analysts
8. IT executives

CONCLUSION

1. The CIS concentration in the MBA program is loosing students for the CIS programs. Most of prior students major in CIS were recruited from foreign countries, and they are usually interested in learning technical computer skills at the graduate level.
2. The CIS concentration should transform from the technical orientation towards the managerial orientation to suit the local business students who may have a limited technical background.
3. The proposed MBA-ERP concentration is the answer to the dilemma created by the current IT trend–technical jobs outsourcing. The new concentration is focused more on business processes and integration by employing ERP applications.
4. Will it be the "last" solution for the MBA programs? Of course, it will not be. We will witness several transformations in this area along with the transformation of enterprises, affected by technology and globalization.

REFERENCES

Adam, F., & Sammon, D. (2004). *The enterprise resource planning decade: Lessons learned and issues for the future*. Hershey, PA: Idea Group Publishing.

Car, N. G. (2004). *Does IT matter? Information technology and the corrosion of competitive advantage*. Boston: Harvard Business School Publishing Corporation.

Smith, H., & Fingar, P. (2002). *Business process management — the third wave*. Tampa, FL: Mephan-Kiffer Press.

Summer, M. (2005). *Enterprise resource planning*. Upper Saddle River, NJ: Pearson, Prentice Hall.

Targowski, A. (2003). *Electronic enterprise, strategy, and architecture*. Hershey, PA: Idea Group Publishing.

ENDNOTE

[1]   The WMU-HCoB-CIS graduate faculty involved in the presented curriculum revising initiatives were composed of the following ones: professors: Bernard Han (Department Chair), Andrew Targowski (Department and College Curriculum Committees Chair), Kuriakose Athappilly; associate professors: Alan Rea (the e-BizD Program Coordinator), Mike Tarn (the TIM Program Coordinator); assistant professors: Pairin Katerattanakul (the CIS/BIT Program Coordinator), Kuanchin Chen, and Muhammad Razi.

Section II

Examples —
How to Teach Specific
Business Processes of ES

Chapter VI

Teaching ERP Concepts in a Capstone Course

T. M. Rajkumar, Miami University, USA

Mahesh Sarma, Miami University, USA

ABSTRACT

An enterprise resource planning (ERP) system is a system that integrates all the different functionalities within an enterprise and which is used to manage the basic commercial functions in a business. Capstone courses are used to integrate materials from different disciplines. This paper describes the use of business processes and ERP systems as a mechanism to provide the integration in the capstone course. The various modules taught in the class are described and issues with the modules are raised and discussed.

INTRODUCTION

Traditionally, universities have offered functionally oriented, discipline specific courses and have been criticized for stove piping and producing graduates who lack the multi-disciplinary focus, knowledge and relationships among the different functional areas that are required to succeed in the business world (Cannon, Klein, Koste, & Magal, 2004). Responding to this, universities have tried a number of integration approaches, such as simulation courses, business process orientation, integrative cases and so forth. One mechanism universities have used to implement the business process integration approach is to use ERP based courses. ERP courses provide a mechanism to change the delivery of education from a functional orientation of accounting, finance, marketing etc to that of a business process oriented approach, the ultimate goal of which is the integration of the curriculum across functions (Beccera-Fernandez, Murphy, & Simon, 2000).

A common model that is practiced in many business schools is for the business core courses to provide an introduction to the discipline and lay the foundation for the integration that is achieved in the capstone experience. The aim of this chapter is to describe an integrative capstone course using ERP specifically the use of SAP at Miami University. We start by providing some context to the capstone courses offered at Miami's School of Business. We then describe the different modules taught in the course.

Capstone Course Context within Miami

Miami University emphasizes liberal education in its undergraduate programs. The four principles of liberal education, namely:

- Thinking critically
- Understanding contexts
- Engaging with other learners
- Reflecting and acting must all be embedded in the capstone course

Miami University capstone courses are designed to culminate a liberal education curriculum, as distinct, from culminating a major. The capstone encourages students to integrate aspects of their major with concepts from other related disciplines.

In addition to the liberal education requirement, all business school capstones must be horizontally integrative and provide for the development of multiple skill sets. The business core courses form the foundation of most business school capstones. In many business capstone courses, the student is encouraged to think in terms of not only their major but apply their skill, knowledge, and methods learned in the other business disciplines.

In general, capstone courses do not have a prerequisite beyond the business core. The MIS core as is currently taught at Miami does not have any use of ERP software by the students. The students are exposed to ERP and other enterprise system software, and depending on the instructor, sometimes have seen an ERP demo in the class. This essentially means that the students when they come in to the ERP capstone course have not been exposed to any significant ERP experience, and the course as designed and taught takes this limitation into account.

BACKGROUND AND OVERVIEW

The ERP capstone course is conducted over the period of a semester with a class size of typically 25 students. This class size helps the instructor focus on the problems of each individual student. A class size larger than this tends to become unmanageable due to various problems that students face while working on ERP software. The different modules that are covered in the course are as listed next. Each module is explained in detail in the topics that follow:

1. Business process and business process re-engineering
2. Event process chain diagrams
3. Business process hands-on activities
4. Decision making features of an ERP system
5. Business warehouse

6.   Management issues in ERP
7.   ERP implementation and support

Since there is a range of topics that are covered in the course, the instructor has the flexibility to focus on the topics that seem the most important from the instructor's and student's points of view. However, all these topics are covered, either briefly or in detail, in the course. An important point to be noted is that the theory for the modules is explained first while the module itself is presented later as far as possible but in some of the modules, the theory, and the modules are explained together. The theory part of the module focuses on the theoretical aspects of the topics covered in class while the module itself looks at it from a student's point of view. Another important point is that Module 3 (i.e., business process hand on activities starts off in the second or third week of the semester and goes on until the end of the semester). This module focuses on the students using an actual ERP system. So, this module is used and explained in conjunction with the rest of the modules so that the theoretical and practical aspects of the course go hand-in-hand.

COURSE MODULES
Business Process and Business Process Re-engineering
Module Theory

The first module that we focus on in this class is that of a business process and the notion of business process re-engineering. We also cover data flow diagrams and entity-relationship diagrams because traditionally, in an IT course, the business process is analyzed using a data flow diagram and an entity relationship diagram. It is this perspective that is first introduced in this module. We start with the different definitions of a business process; for example; Hammer and Champy (1993) define "Business process as a collection of activities that take one or more inputs and produce outputs that is of value to a customer." The notion of a business process as one of coordination of work whereby a set of skills and routines exploited to create a capability that cannot easily be matched by others is also introduced. Simultaneously, the notion that ERP systems are software that automate and integrate business processes and using a shared data and practice is emphasized (Sumner, 2005). Also, ERP systems introduce best practices and therefore, the notion that a successful implementation requires business process re-engineering is then introduced.

Business process reengineering (BPR) is " The activity by which an enterprise reexamines its goals and- how it achieves them, followed by a disciplined approach of business process redesign; A method that supports this activity" (GWU, 2005). Process redesign from an organizational perspective is the strategic capability to:

- Configure business process faster, for example by losing wait time, outsourcing to a partner who can execute swifter, or allow for mass customization;
- Execute business process faster for example by capturing information digitally, and propagating it digitally, using the digital information to get insight into the process and its status and gaining quicker customer feedback; or,
- Learn faster through processes for example by growing reusable knowledge around the process through all who touch it (El Sawy, 2000).

A discussion of process redesign and a case is introduced here. Also, the theoretical aspects of data flow diagrams and entity-relationship diagrams are introduced here. Data flow diagrams focus on the logical flow of data within a system. DFDs show how the data is processed by the system in terms of inputs and outputs. DFDs are one of the simplest and most powerful techniques available to the systems analyst for process modeling (Kamath, Dalal, Chaugule, Sivaraman, & Kolarik, 2003). ER diagram is a modeling tool that helps to organize data into entities and helps to create relationships between those entities. Done correctly, this helps to create a good database structure using which data can be stored and retrieved in the most efficient manner.

In the case of an integrated enterprise system, it becomes all the more important to understand the business process in order to carry out business processing. The different business processes are broken down into separate views and these views are then again linked back together to form a whole business process (Ferdian & Weinburg, 2001).

Module

While this module is explained in class, students also start Module 3 (i.e., starting off with exercises performed on an actual ERP system). The first exercise performed by the students is the order-cash exercise. Though students have difficulty understanding the importance of these exercises, these exercises are started early in the semester so that they can understand the business processes in an organization. In order to substantiate the students understanding of the business process, some time is spent in taking them through a data flow diagram (DFD) and an E-R diagram for this process. A DFD for the order-cash process is shown in Figure 1. The student can easily follow and understand this diagram and recognize the inputs that are needed and how the inputs are transformed into corresponding outputs by the process within the system.

Understanding E-R diagrams helps the student understand what entities are stored by the system, the relationships, and the basic structure behind the entities. A very basic E-R diagram for the order-cash process is shown in Figure 2.

Students from MIS have seen both these techniques, and accounting students in general also are knowledgeable about E-R diagrams. Students from other majors understand the diagram as they are laid out, but do not know enough of the mechanics to draw the diagrams themselves. Hence, assignments are given out as a group work. Every group is made up of students from different majors and there is at least one MIS major or minor in each group that knows the techniques and can help the group complete assignments. In general, if we go through procure-pay process in class, then the students develop the DFD and E-R diagram for the order-cash process or vice-versa.

Event Process Chain Diagrams

Module Theory

While traditional information systems use structured or object oriented analysis, most ERP vendors have their own analysis diagrams. It becomes essential to understand the diagramming method that ERP software uses because business processes are modeled within the software using these techniques. SAP uses the event process chain (EPC) diagram to provide reference diagrams. The reference EPC diagrams links (a) the business functions (what should be done), (b) the organizational elements such as who should do and where it should be done, and (c) the data or information together by a common process flow. Thus,

Figure 1. DFD for order — cash

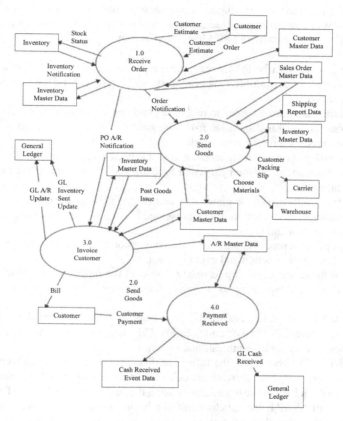

Figure 2. E-R diagram for order — cash

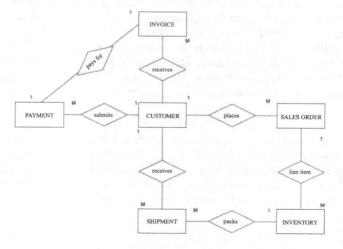

the EPC diagram shows the flow of the business process from a control point of view. The most important addition that EPC diagrams provide over a data flow diagram is the notion of control logic "When something should be done and in what order" (Kamath et al., 2003).

Some of the elements in an EPC chain are (Ferdian et al., 2001):

- **Event:** Events describe the circumstances a process works or the state in which the process results. For example, "materials on stock" is an event and these are represented by a hexagon.
- **Function:** Functions are used to model the tasks or activities within a company and they describe the transformation from one state in a process to the other. A function is represented by a rounded rectangle.
- **Organizational unit:** An organizational unit is used to represent which person in the company is responsible for a particular function and is represented by an ellipse with a vertical line.
- **Object:** An information or material object can be used as an input to a function or as an output from a function. It is represented by a rectangle and examples would be materials, orders and so forth.
- **Process path:** A process path shows the connection between different processes and is represented by function and event symbol.
- **Control flow:** A control flow is used to connect the functions and process paths in order to create a sequence and is represented by a dashed arrow.

A simple EPC diagram showing the steps leading to the creation of a sales order is represented in Figure 3 (Curran & Ladd, 2000). This diagram shows the basic sales order process without the data and organizational structure.

Until SAP R/3 Version 4.6, the reference diagrams (EPC diagrams) were available within the base product. The reference models also are useful to show the techniques used to implement SAP's ERP in the organization using the accelerated SAP (ASAP) methodology. A key part of ASAP is the development of a business blueprint, a visual model of the business future state that allows the project team to focus on just the business processes in R/3 needed by the organization. The reference models provide what SAP calls "best practices in business processes." Hence, these models can be analyzed to identify the required business processes and determine the gaps between the organizations business process and the reference models. ASAP also provides a question and answer database to help with the analysis, identify the gaps, and document the organizations requirements. Once the gaps are known, alternative solutions can then be identified. The business blueprint is then realized by making the required system settings for various parameters. These customizing activities are performed using the implementation management guide (IMG).

Module

Microsoft's Visio has the elements to draw simple EPC diagrams. It is easy to use this tool in the class, as students are able to pick Visio up on their own to draw diagrams. However, special purpose software such as the architecture for integrated information system (ARIS) (Scheer, 2004) exists and is widely used in industry. ARIS provides the functional, organizational, data, control and resource views and stores the diagrams in a repository.

Figure 3. EPC diagram for an order (Curran et al., 2000)

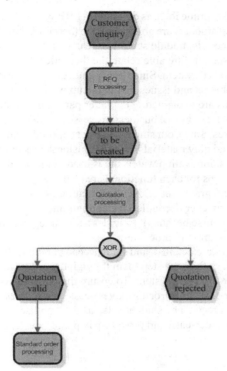

Each of these views can be modeled separately and then combined with each other. This integration of views within ARIS allows the user to jump between different levels of detail and complexity. While there are educational discounts for ARIS, it is a separate program that has to be obtained and used by the institution. While the authors have not used it in their classes, it is useful to demonstrate this software and its capabilities for requirements analysis.

As stated earlier, until SAP R/3 Version 4.6, the reference diagrams (EPC diagrams) were available within the base product and we could show them in the classroom. Once the students saw the reference diagrams, they understood the importance of analyzing the business process in terms of EPC. It was also useful to the students to see the complexity of the business processes modeled within the software. However, since version 4.7, this capability to view the reference models and the EPC diagrams does not exist, as it has now been separated and spun off into its own product.

Our approach has been to show the IMG feature of the software in class but not take the students through any configuration of the software within this capstone class. Figure 4, shows a simplistic view of the ASAP process.

Business Process Hands on Activities

Module

As stated earlier, this module focuses on using an ERP system and this module is started in week 2 or week 3 so that students are able to link the theoretical aspects of the course with an actual EP system. Since this module starts very early in the semester and goes on until the end of the semester, students are able relate the theoretical topics they learn in class to the practical nature of an ERP system. Since many students use an ERP system for the first time, there are many problems and issues that come up while using the system, and some of the issues and problems are explained in the latter part of this module.

To demonstrate understanding of business processes, students use SAP software to run standard business processes. Since, our students are not exposed to any ERP tool prior to this class, a mix of the plug and play materials, and the Business Process Integration–I (BPI-1) course available from SAP innovation watch site is used in this module. The plug and play materials provide a set of labs for each functional area (such as production, accounting etc). In contrast, BPI-1 is an integrated set of exercises that takes the student through configuring a pen company. We however decoupled the configuration and we took just the first 20 exercises from the BPI-1 course because it provides a nice integrated demonstration of both the order-cash and the procure-pay processes.

While the instructions are detailed, and students can complete the exercises, our observation is that, it is necessary for us to step them through the processes and explain in detail what is going on in the process and system. To ensure they understood what was going on, they had to redo the order-cash, and procure-pay process, in a *separated fashion* as opposed to the earlier integrated process. The students also as a group had to turn in a DFD and an E-R diagram for both the order-cash and procure-pay processes. Other possible extensions

Figure 4. Simple ASAP configuration

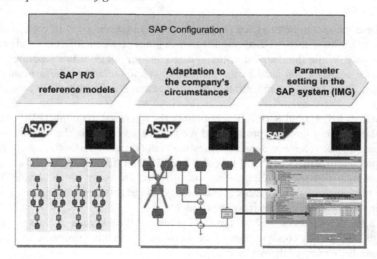

are to require the student to accomplish the sales return process using SAP's online help which provides the steps needed to accomplish that task.

The plug and play material from SAP innovation watch site was used for production planning, human resources and accounting exercises. Our experience, is that despite being seniors, students some time do not know or remember the basics of different areas, so terms such as materials requirements planning, master planning schedule etc have to be reintroduced and concepts discussed in the class. While we did not require the students to draw the process diagrams here, an emphasis on these helped the students to understand the concepts better.

Issues with SAP Labs

- **Issue 1:** The plug and play material uses the standard SAP preconfigured company IDES. IDES is populated with data representative of multiple industries and created by SAP to demonstrate SAP functionalities to prospective clients. The different exercises in plug and play sometimes use different companies within IDES and hence, the students do not completely understand the companies. The material appears to be out of context for the students (Federowicz, Gelinas, & Usoff, 2004) and the students do not completely value the exercises they perform. When this happens, students question the relative worth of learning SAP and lack enthusiasm for the course.

- **Issue 2:** In addition, since IDES is both complex and data intensive, classroom use tends to lack in depth and limits us to using exercises adapted from other universities (Cannon et al., 2004). In contrast, the Pen Company represented within BPI-1 is a simple company and allows the faculty and students to experiment more and use their own data. Federowicz et al. (2004) reports that students understand better when they use their own data even within IDES. The authors have both taken the BPI-I training course offered by SAP for faculty and found it very useful. The BPI-1 course is used by other universities in their integration classes.

- **Issue 3:** While SAP offers a number of training courses geared towards faculty, getting many faculty members to go to these classes continues to be a problem. If a faculty member who is trained in SAP leaves the university or changes direction, the courses start to flounder (Hawking, McCarthy, & Stein, 2004). An option that we have tried is to offer the initial BPI exercises ourselves in a half day training session training to faculty members within our school. This has kindled the interest of some of the faculty members who are going to the SAP training sessions. Such intra-campus workshops lead to both knowledge diffusion and lesser frustration for new faculty (Federowicz et al., 2004).

Decision Making Features of an ERP (SAP) System

Module Theory

The data is the most important part of any information system but this data has to be available to people who make decisions at the right time and in the right format. An ERP system has huge amounts of data and usually managers view the required data in the form of reports. Reports in SAP are in general programs that are written using the advanced business-application programming (ABAP) language to retrieve and read data from the SAP R/3

Figure 5. BPI — integrated order-cash and procure-pay process (Rushmore Group, 2005)

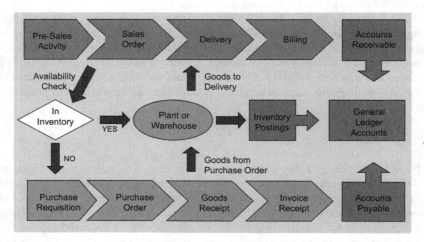

database. In the R/3 system, reports can be created or they can be just viewed. If managers in a company want to view reports, they can use the executive information system (EIS) to retrieve data needed by them. The EIS system provides the information needed to make decisions by combining the data from internal and external sources. SAP R/3 also provides the general report selection tree which combines all the reports in one location for easy retrieval of necessary data.

If users want to create reports, they can use ABAP queries or ABAP program. Users do not need any programming experience in order to create these queries. ABAP queries retrieve the necessary data from any table in the SAP R/3 database. If users want to retrieve data about the human resources module, they can use SAP R/3 Ad-hoc queries. The reports can be configured so that the user can view it, either over the Internet or Intranet.

There are a few important things to be noted to understand reporting in the SAP R/3 system (Larocca, 2000):

- Reports are programs in the SAP system. The data for the reports within SAP come from different views in the SAP system and are stored in fields stored in different tables. These tables are connected by relationships. The data for the reports are retrieved from these tables and the output is the formatted report.
- Selection screens are necessary to produce the desired output. These screens help the user to specify what data is to be generated in the output.
- There is a difference between reports and lists. As seen above the reports are functions that produce the output while lists are the final result. Since reports can be run anytime to produce the necessary output, it is in real-time while lists only display the output at a particular point of time.

Module

The students performed three different types of reporting exercises (1) executing pre-canned reports, (2) ad-hoc queries and ABAP programs and (3) business warehouse exercises. In the first exercises, students used the report tree to extract simple data such as the birthday list for this month. The goal is to allow the users to get familiar with using selection lists, enter different selection criteria, and execute the report. In the next exercise, students were asked to sort, drill down and find the top 10 customers, analyze what they purchased and be able to execute charts. This exercise was adapted from a reporting exercise (given in the SAP Innovation 2003 Congress) and available on the SAP innovation watch site. The purpose of this is primarily to show students that pre-canned reports do have some decision-making capabilities.

When users want quick access to reports that do not exist in pre-canned reports, they can execute SAP ABAP Queries or ABAP programs. Both these exercises are demonstration exercises, where the students are stepped through the entire process in the labs in class. For the ABAP query, the students use the ABAP workbench to create a query of customers. The students can pick the criteria and the fields for the query. In an ABAP query, the students do not write any program, but pick the fields and criteria from a table. In contrast, with ABAP programs, students write code.

For the ABAP programs, a simple "Hello World" program was used to step them through the process of creating a program. Next, a simple report using a SQL query was written to extract flight timings from the flights database. Column headings were then added and the report was customized. A selection screen was then added to the report to take in input from the user. These extensions show the user how to use the very powerful SQL queries to extract data and present it using SAP guidelines.

While we have not given any assignment here, it is possible to provide group assignments, because there is at least one MIS student in each group. The other issue here is that to perform the exercises, students need access to the ABAP part of SAP. This is typically on a client that is different from the IDES or BPI client, as the host institution is reluctant to allow users to write programs on systems that are shared by multiple universities. Hence, the data is not integrated with any of the clients they have seen in earlier exercises.

Business Warehouse

Module Theory

Wah (2000) asks the question "Do ERP systems really foster better decision making?" ERP systems are considered transaction processing systems, but can contain some decision support elements, for example, a whole range of reports and ability to create your own reports exist within SAP. In a study on potential adaptors of ERP systems, Holsapple and Sena (2003) find that adaptors perceive ERP systems as providing decision support capability.

There are some decision support characteristics since these systems integrate knowledge and provide reporting tools for users to examine and analyze functional data, though providing such tools is not the primary purpose of ERP systems. Business intelligence offerings from SAP and other vendors provide DSS capabilities that are not fully developed in their core products. A reason these are separate products is because businesses use many different transaction processing applications, and information from all of them are needed to perform global analysis of data (Yurong & Houcon, 2000).

The business information warehouse is SAP's data warehousing solution. BW is a separate system from the R/3 transaction processing system. BW data structures are optimized for reporting data efficiently and quickly. In contrast, SAP R/3's data structures are optimized for recording data efficiently and quickly. BW reduces data processing load on SAP R/3. In general, the data is stored in an aggregated format and incorporates internal and external sources of data into one single data repository. The SAP BW model is based on the building blocks of InfoObjects which are used to describe information and business processes. Some of the key elements in SAP's BW model are (thespot4sap):

- **DataSources:** Data sources are flat data structures containing data that belong together and are responsible for staging and extracting data.
- **InfoSources:** InfoSources are the group of InfoObjects that belong together from a business point of view.
- **Operational data store (ODS) objects:** An ODS object is a dataset which is formed as a result of merging data from one or more info sources.
- **InfoCubes:** InfoCubes are multidimensional data storage containers for reporting and analysis of data. They consist of keys figures and characteristics of which latter is organized as dimensions facilitating users to analyze data from various business perspectives such as geographical area or types of sales channel.
- **InfoProviders:** InfoProviders refer to all the data objects that are present in the SAP BW systems.
- **MultiProviders:** A MultiProvider is a virtual information provider that is a combination of any two physical or virtual info providers. Their main purpose is to make this data accessible for reports and analysis.

Figure 6. SAP demo cube: Star Schema

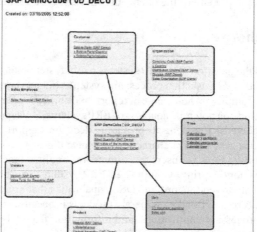

The SAP BW design is based on the star schema design. This design has a central database table surrounded by dimension tables. These dimension tables contain references to pointer tables that point to master data tables. These master data tables contain master data objects stored as InfoObjects. Figure 6 illustrates a simple star schema of the sales demo cube in SAP.

Module

Users can use the business explorer (BEx Analyzer) and Excel add-in that provides online analytical processing functions on the multidimensional info cubes in BW. Both pre-programmed reports and ad-hoc queries can be run using BEx analyzer. The students use the star schema and demo cube shown in Figure 6 to write an ad-hoc BW Query. In order to do this they have to specify the dimensions, key figures in business explorer (BEx Analyzer). When the query is executed the results are brought into Excel as a pivot table. Standard pivot table analysis such as changing the dimensions and characteristics can be performed in BW. The students are again led through the process. To refresh them about pivot table analysis, a standard pivot table exercise in Excel is also given. This exercise gives students the perspective of what it is to run a query in a data warehouse, and exposes the students to decision support capabilities.

SAP has data mining features built into the SAP BW product. However, none of the data mining features are discussed in the capstone class, basically due to lack of time. The extraction, transformation, and loading of data into a cube are also not done.

Management Issues in ERP

Module Theory

A variety of management and technical issues related to ERP and their successful implementation and operation are covered in this module. The topics include change management, project management, critical success factors for ERP, IT, and ERP audit, Web services etc are dealt with in class.

Change Management

Leavitt's model of organizational change (Figure 7) is introduced and the interdependence between the four factors — technology, structure, people, and task is emphasized. Leavitt's model of organizational change illustrates the importance of aligning task, structure, people, and technology in order to effectively bring about change. It also provides a basic framework for managers to start thinking about how to fit these components together in order to best manage their knowledge. A change in one leads to a change in the others. ERP implementations involve a change in technology that affect the tasks the employees perform and require people to take on new roles or responsibilities. Hence, ERP implementations tend to bring changes in an organization. Effective management of the change is a key success factor for ERP implementations. It is essential that the people involved are able to accept the changes and make it happen. Rather than viewing change management purely as a set of soft factors, if change management is viewed as a business process like any other the organization carries out, then change management can be managed more effectively (Abolhassan, 2003). The ideas that change management can be planned, managed and the strategies for change such as the rational-empirical, normative-reeducation, power-coercive and environmental-adaptive approaches (Marchewka, 2003) are discussed.

Figure 7. Leavitt's factors in business change (El Sawy, 2000)

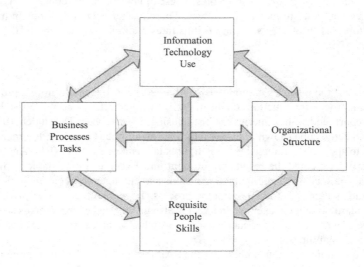

IT and ERP Audit

IT audit is "the process of identifying risks that threaten business and system processes, observing the controls in place to mitigate those risks, and recommending additional controls to further protect the processes." Ever since the Sarbanes Oxley (2002) act has passed, IT audit has grown in significance, and organizations are spending large amounts of money to be in compliance with the act. Sarbanes Oxley is not the only motivator, the purpose of IT audits is to safeguard assets, maintain data integrity, effectively achieve organizational objectives, and consume resources efficiently.

Process audits are top-down reviews of business processes (purchasing, accounting, etc.) without regard to physical location or organizational structure. They provide management with an overall evaluation of the adequacy and effectiveness of controls over the process as a whole. Use of the top down approach enables auditors to understand top management's perception of the purpose of the process, the critical success factors associated with the process, how the process is expected to function, and the information used to manage and control the process.

ERP audits are different and difficult because:

- It covers many different business functions which makes associated security, risks and control more important.
- Technical complexity such as residing on multiple computers, systems allow flexible configuration and customization.
- Event-driven and real time processing means traditional batch controls are no longer available.
- Modules automatically create entries in the database for each other, a design flaw in one module causes unexpected problems elsewhere and auditors need to understand the interactions and flow of information.

- Many IT department functions (including security) are performed within the application making segregation of responsibilities difficult (Van Mien & Noakes-Fry, 2004).

Authorization checks are critical in determining whether duties are appropriately segregated. However, the authorization process is extremely complex and there are some 50000-60000 transactions in SAP. This makes authorization checks difficult, and extensive expertise is required to effectively audit and control ERP systems and implementations.

Vendors are responding to these needs with software tools. SAP for example, provides an audit workbench called audit information system (AIS) with capabilities for real time and continuous monitoring. The AIS serves as a centralized repository for queries, views, and reports of interest to auditors. However, this tool still requires SAP knowledge to interpret results and the dependency on the vendor creates problems for some companies.

Web Services

Web services are XML data standards along with communication standards (Kalakota & Robinson 2003). A lab exercise is done in class using Microsoft's .NET technologies that provides a simple calculator service, and then a client to connect to Amazons Web service. This is done to show that it is fairly easy to develop Web services and use them for business purposes. More importantly, the class discussion is focused on how different Web services can be integrated to provide service oriented architectures. Service oriented architectures enable cross-enterprise processes such as the order-to-cash process and are the foundation of digitization initiatives (Kalakota & Robinson, 2003). Enterprise vendors such as SAP are also building these types of service oriented architectures into their products.

Module

The managerial section topics in this module are in general researched by the students and presented in class as a lecture to the other students. This is to ensure that students learn from their peers. Topics vary and at times include topics such as business process outsourcing, case studies of ERP implementations such as the CISCO: Implementing ERP case study from Harvard Business School Publishing, product life cycle management, encryption and privacy laws, project management, innovation management, identity management and so forth. Most times we make sure that at least the above three topics of change management, IT auditing and Web services are discussed and covered in class. As students present the topics, sometimes the depth of what they provide varies. We supplement and provide additional perspectives in class. Our feedback indicates that students like the managerial section very much as they have some leeway in topics and put effort into researching and presenting the topics. Studies have found that when there is a managerial perspective and issues discussed along with the technical foundation, the course is better appreciated by the students (Davis & Comeau, 2004).

ERP Implementation and Support
Module Theory

Once students are exposed to the different modules earlier in the class, they are introduced to areas of ERP implementation and support. The topics in this module include the evaluation and selection of an ERP system, the critical success factors to be considered in the implementation and the factors in evaluating the performance of an ERP system.

Evaluation and Selection of an ERP system

Since each company has its own set of business processes, the steps for evaluating and selecting and ERP system for each company may be different. However, there are some common steps that every company can take to evaluate and select an ERP system some of which are listed below (Relevant Business Systems):

- Take a cross-functional view to implementation — people from different levels and different departments or the company should be involved in the selection of an ERP system. This will help in the sharing of information as well as usher in a positive and team-oriented approach to implementation.
- The company's resources like personnel, technology and workflows should be assessed so that the areas that are most critical to the growth of the company can be focused on.
- The organization's core competencies and strategic goals have to be identified so that an EP system that best fits the company's long range strategy is selected.
- A model along with the metrics for success has to be developed in order to achieve the goals of the organization.

Critical Success Factors in implementation

One of the main purposes of ERP technology is to support the business processes that achieve a company's long range objectives. There are many critical factors to be considered to successfully implement an ERP system, some of which are (Donovan, 2004):

- Evaluate the business processes and business strategies of the company. Since this is an area that can slow system deployment, companies may tend to ignore this factor. By identifying and correcting flawed business processes, the company may be able to offset problems that come up during implementation.
- Decide business strategies that will help the company achieve a competitive advantage over its rivals.
- Acquire flexible ERP systems that are able to accommodate changing business conditions.
- Try to move away from functional silos and concentrate on cross-functional business processes.

Evaluating System Performance

According to Rakesh Radhakrishnan in "Performance Evaluation and Measurement of E-Business /ERP systems," there are nine basic steps used to evaluate and measure the performance of an E-Business/ERP system:

1. Definition of performance requirements such as minimal acceptable response time for all end-to-end tasks and acceptable network latency of an interface.
2. Creation of a test bed with all components in place.
3. Configuration of entire infrastructure based on vendor recommendations.
4. Execution of unit tests for each application in the package to ensure all required functions work.

5. Execution of integration test to ensure compatibility and connectivity between all components.
6. Launch monitoring tools for underlying systems including operating systems, databases and middleware.
7. Creation of baseline reference of the response times for all key tasks when the system is not under stress.
8. Creation of baseline reference of response times for all key tasks under varying load Conditions.
9. If requirements are not met, make necessary changes in the hardware, software and networks and repeat the tests.

CONCLUSION

With the rapid advances in information technology, companies are changing the way they do business. Companies are realizing the importance of having a good ERP system so that there is a smooth flow of information within the company. From an academic point of view, business process and ERP systems provide a natural mechanism to integrate material from multiple disciplines. This chapter looked at the use of SAP's ERP system in a business capstone course. We looked at the importance of business process re-engineering, process analysis and design techniques and the labs that we used in this class. We also looked at the different reporting features of SAP's R/3 system and the importance of the business warehouse. Implementation and use of ERP in organizations are fraught with problems. Hence, a management module is used to discuss managerial issues in the class along with the technical perspective provided in the labs. Our observation is that students welcome the use of ERP systems and process orientation as the integrative mechanism for the capstone course.

REFERENCES

Abolhassan, F. (2003). The change management process implemented at IDS Scheer. In A. W. Scheer, F. Abolhassan, W. Jost, & M. Kirchmer (Eds.), *Business process change management: ARIS in practice* (pp. 15-22). Berlin, Germany: Springer Verlaag.

Beccera-Fernandez, I, Murphy, K. E., & Simon, S. J (2000). Integrating ERP in the business school curriculum. Communications of the ACM, *43*(4), 39-41.

Cannon, D. M., Klein, H. A., Koste, L. L., & Magal, S. R. (2004, November-December). Curriculum integration using enterprise resource planning: An integrative case approach. *Journal of Education for Business, 80*(2), 93-101.

Curran, T., & Ladd, A. (2000). S*AP R/3 business blueprint: Understanding enterprise supply chain management* (2nd ed.). New Jersey: Prentice Hall.

Davis, C. H., & Comeau, J. (2004). Enterprise integration in business education: Design and outcomes of a capstone ERP-based undergraduate e-business management course. *Journal of Information System Education, 15*(3), 287-300.

Donovan, M. (2004). *ERP: Successful implementation the first time.* Retrieved April 19, 2005, from http://www.refresher.com/!erp1.html

El Sawy, O. (2000). *Redesigning enterprise processes for e-business*. New York: McGraw Hill/Irwin.

ERP selection process survival guide, The. *Relevant Business Systems*, 4-5.

Federowicz, J., Gelinas, U. C., & Usoff, C. (2004). Twelve tips for successfully integrating the enterprise across the curriculum. *Journal of Information System Education, 15*(3), 235-244.

Ferdian, J. W. L., & Weinburg, A. (2001). *A comparison of event-driven process chains and UML activity diagram for denoting business processes.* Harburg, Germany: Technische Universität Hamburg-Harburg.

GWU. (2005). *Data warehouse: Glossary.* Retrieved April 16, 2005, from http://uis.georgetown.edu/departments/eets/dw/GLOSSARY0816.htm

Hammer, M., & Champy, J. (1993). *Re-engineering the corporation: A manifesto for business revolution.* London: Nicholas Brealey Publishing Ltd.

Hawking, P., McCarthy, B., & Stein, A. (2004). Second wave ERP education. *Journal of Information System Education, 15*(3), 327-332.

Holsapple, C. W., & Sena, M. (2003). The decision-support characteristics of ERP systems. *International Journal of Human-Computer Interaction, 16*(1), 101-123.

Kalakota, R., & Robinson, M. (2003). *Services blueprint: Roadmap for execution.* Redwood City, CA: Addison Wesley.

Kamath, M., Dalal, N. P., Chaugule, A., Sivaraman, E., & Kolarik, W. J. (2003). A review of enterprise modeling techniques. In V. Prabhu, S. Kumara, & M. Kamath (Eds.), *Scalable enterprise systems: An introduction to recent advances* (pp. 1-32). Boston: Kluwer Academic Publishers.

Larocca, D. (2000). *SAP R/3 reporting tools.* New York: McGraw Hill.

Marchewka, J. T. (2003). *Information technology project management.* New York: John Wiley.

Radhakrishnan, R. (2004). *Performance evaluation & measurement of e-business/ERP systems.* McLean, VA: Sun Microsystems, Inc.

Relevant Business Systems (2005). *The ERP selection process survival guide.* San Ramon, CA: Relevant Business Systems.

Rushmore Group (2005, January 4). *R/3 Client-server integrated solution.* Paper presented at the Business Process Integration-1, Baton Rouge, LA.

Scheer, A. (2004). ARIS toolset: A software product is born. *Information Systems, 19*(9), 607-624.

Sumner, M. (2005). *Enterprise resource planning.* Upper Saddle River, NJ: Prentice Hall.

thespot4sap. (2005). *SAP BW.* Retrieved April 19, 2005, from http://www.thespot4sap.com/articles/SAP_BW_Introduction.asp

Van Mien, A. D., Noakes-Fry, K. (2004, February). *How to tackle five major threats in your ERP system* (Gartner Report No. TU-20-7534).

Wah, L. (2000). Give ERP a chance. Management Review, *89*(3), 20-24.

Yurong, Y., & Houcun, H. (2000, March-April). Data warehousing and the Internets impact on ERP. *IT Pro*, 35-40.

ChapterVII

Teaching an Enterprise Project as a Capstone Course of the CIS/BIT Program

Andrew Targowski, Western Michigan University, USA

ABSTRACT

This chapter introduces a concept of the capstone course of the CIS/BIT program at the Western Michigan University. The course is composed of lectures and five projects, which are related to each other. The lectures provide knowledge that supports every project. The end-product of this course is prototyped software of an enterprise performance management system, which is demonstrated by each team as an integrated software package. The course is divided in three following parts: Part I: Enterprise System Definition (Classic Knowledge and Skills), Part II: Business Process Integration (Trend-oriented approach), Part III: Enterprise System Development (ERP Prototype-Demo Software). The author hopes that the presented capstone's course concept facilitates the understanding of the business process-driven CIS/BIT program.

INTRODUCTION

The purpose of this chapter is to share the author's experience in teaching this course at Western Michigan University – Haworth College of Business in the CIS/BIT program over the last 20 years (1985-2005). While the course has been evolving in its shape, its main philosophy remains only slightly changed.

At the beginning of the class, the students are typically lost, because they do not have the skills to accomplish a given task, which appears at first too large in scope to conquer. Furthermore, the students usually would like to know how to pass the course with the least amount of effort on their part, a goal that is complicated by the initial reaction of being overwhelmed by the tasks required of them. It is tremendously challenging for the instructor to convince the students that according to the system life cycle development (SLCD), the beginnings of understanding the project tasks include a lot of "unknowns." However, as the students learn the problem solving process, along with the gained knowledge & skills and passing time, they finish the task successfully. The first six weeks are the most difficult for the students and instructor in gaining mutual confidence.

In reality, nowadays, as far as the students' career is concerned, they usually are most interested in taking jobs as Web masters or network administrators. Only a few students are interested in pursuing careers as application programmers or developers. The former requires programming, which being off-shore outsourced and the latter requires much more thinking in terms of whole organization processes, which looks too difficult to them. Therefore, this course is rather a "must" for them and not necessarily always taken 100% voluntarily. As the term progresses, many realize that in order to be a good Web master and network administrator one must know enterprise organization quite well. Needless to say that in the near future, the most jobs will be offered in application development from the business process integration point of view. Why? Because the job market for Web masters and network administrators is saturated. On the other hand, the outsourcing policy requires strong administration of these kinds of projects in a given place of business processes operations.

THE PURPOSE OF THE CAPSTONE COURSE IN THE CIS/BPI-ORIENTED CURRICULUM

The purpose of the capstone course BIT 4990 Enterprise Project is to apply the whole knowledge and skills that the students have already learned in programming, system analysis & design, and database courses. In this course, this knowledge and skills will be applied in prototyping a moderate complexity project, which will touch the issues of the enterprise-wide systems.

The *Course Objectives* for Students are as follows:

1.   To learn the state of the art knowledge of:
     a.   Information engineering
     b.   Application software engineering
     c.   Project management
2.   To provide the student with the knowledge and skills of a:
     a.   Application programmer
     b.   System designer

    c.   Software engineer
    d.   Project leader

The *Course Theme* is about:

- Classic knowledge and skills of subsystems integration into an enterprise-wide software, applying
- The business process integration approach
- ERP prototype-demo software

The course is composed of lectures and five projects, which are related to each other. In fact, the lectures provide knowledge that supports every project. The end-product of this course is prototyped software of an enterprise performance management system, which is demonstrated by each team as an integrated software package.

The course is divided in three following parts:

- **Part I:** Enterprise System Definition (Classic Knowledge and Skills)
- **Part II:** Business Process Integration (Trend-oriented approach)
- **Part III:** Enterprise System Development (ERP Prototype-Demo Software)

In Part I, which is about the "enterprise" development *classic knowledge and skills* in the framework of *Information Engineering*, the activities (lectures and projects) are provided on the following topics:

- A concept of six Information Tools Delivery Centers (Planning, *Development*, Maintenance, Data, Network, and Information Help Desk) are presented as the background for the description of the Development Center, and its methodologies and strategies of design.
- How to define enterprise system complex architecture (the enterprise system approach) from *bottom-up* analysis leading from individual processes to subsystems and systems, a lecture and related Project 1 are offered.
- How to define enterprise system complex architecture from *top-down* analysis, a lecture, and Project 2 on one business process definition is required.

In Part II, which is about the "business process integration" the course prepares the student to a new emerging trend of knowing more about a business process than about its programming. In this part, the following issues of *Information Engineering* are addressed:

- How to understand the MIS architecture, which is the main system of a business, and Because this is a project management class, the student will define a CPM network for the class' activities, using the MS Project software as an experience of the Project Management methodology.

In Part II, the issues of *Application Software Engineering* are addressed, since this is a course in the CIS/BIT technology and the student cannot speak about "technology," but he/she has to know how to deliver it to the level of business practice. Hence, the following activities are planned for the students:

- In order to be more practice-oriented in prototyping the EPMS, a student makes Project 4 on SAP navigation and sales order processing, which provides some exposure to a real solution. Based on this solution, a student is obliged to design/program own solution according or even better than "*feel and look*" of a SAP solution.
- The lecture on the architecture of enterprise performance management system, because this system will be a subject of a software prototype in Project 5. Since the EPMS is based on a set of key indicators, hence the lecture covers also a concept of a balance scorecard. Both the EPMS and balance scorecard are the key systems of contemporary IT/management practice in the Fortune 1000 companies. In other words, the students learn the state of the art of the business system applications development.
- This course is not a course on SAP or other enterprise large package, but is a course on how to design and program a complex business system, therefore a student has show his or her own ability in creating more innovative solutions than common practice. Hence he or she is asked to design a more advanced solution than SAP. Of course, the students are surprised whether or not they can do it. In order to prove that they

Figure 1. The relations of the BIT 4990 Enterprise Project content

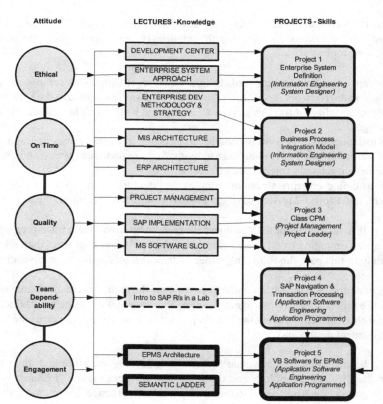

can do it, a lecture on the semantic ladder is offered, which explains such concepts as data, information, concept, knowledge, and wisdom processings. As we know SAP-like software is mainly limited to data vs. information processing, while the project 5 goes beyond this scope and requires that a student will design and program in all units of cognition (previously above), what actually leads towards the application of artificial intelligence.

- At the end of the course, the students program project 2 (a student's concept of an EPMS of a business process) into a prototype software package, by integrating different subsystems (developed by each team) into a common solution (common menu), developed by the team 2. This common package is presented by all the students in a class by the end of a semester. In most of the cases the students are proud of the presented solution and no longer complain about the fuzziness of the approach, which has such a character at the beginning of the semester.

The relationship among projects and lectures is described in Figure 1.

THE ORGANIZATION OF THE CAPSTONE COURSE

This course should simulate conditions close to the future work environment, in which will work students after completing this course and graduating from the university. Therefore three kinds of teams are applied:

- **Team 1:** Project Management, its charge is to manage the whole project and their workers, another word — the students. This team is responsible for:
  o   Selection of a company for which the EPMS will be designed (it can be a local or national or global company)
  o   Supervising of the selection of teammates
  o   Opening each session and providing its agenda
  o   Communicating the project's tasks and issues
  o   Solving problems of teams
  o   Interfacing between a professor and the students
  o   Other
- **Team 2:** Project Integration & Consulting is responsible for all technical aspects of the project, for example:
  o   Establishing a level of VB expertise among developmental teams' members and advising how to minimize the gap in this area
  o   Developing a common menu for all subsystems and assembling all subsystems into one system
  o   Supervising the final presentation of the Project 5
  o   Other
- **Teams 3:** Ten Developmental Teams are in charge of developing a business process chosen from a set of such processes of SAP R/3, among their duties are:
  o   Making all projects
  o   Presenting in a classroom the Project 5

Figure 2. The organization of the CIS/BIT 4990 Enterprise Project course

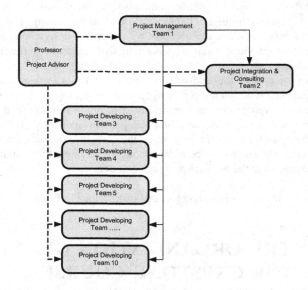

This course is the students' course, they supervise, design, program, and present their own solutions, while a professor is only an advisor to them. However, it would be too premature to think that Teams 1 and 2 can act without a professor's strong supervision. Therefore, 30 minutes before each session, these both teams meet with the professor, who advises them what to do during the coming session. Since these teams have additional tasks, they do not make the Project Team 2 is in charge of assembling all subsystems into a system under a common menu.

To make the class more involved in the current issues of the enterprise systems development, each team presents a press review on this subject, about 10 minutes at the beginning of almost each session. Since this is the last course, each student is obliged to organize a folder with class lectures, projects, syllabus, resume, and other materials, which can be shown to the future employers.

The course organization is shown in Figure 2.

THE MASTER SYLLABUS OF
THE CAPSTONE COURSE

An example of the master syllabus of the CIS/BIT capstone course is provided next:

Western Michigan University
Haworth College of Business
Department of Business Information Systems

BIT 4990 Enterprise Project
Fall /Winter/Spring/Summer 2005

- **Undergraduate Program Goal:** HCOB's goal is to provide comprehensive, afford-able, high quality undergraduate business education that meets the needs of students and employers.
- **BBA Objective:** (1) Understand essential business knowledge, (2) Make effective decisions, (3) Understand and use computer-based systems and infrastructures.

Faculty Name		Office Address		Office Hours		Office Phone	
E-mail Address		Time		Class Room		Other	

- **Course Theme:** (a) Classic knowledge and skills of subsystems integration into an enterprise-wide software, applying the (b) business process integration approach and (c) ERP prototype-demo software.
- **Course Description:** This is a capstone course of the CIS curriculum. Applications of computer, programming, and system knowledge and skills gained from the previous classes are applied in developing an enterprise-wide software project. Some industrial enterprise-wide packages are reviewed such as SAP, MS Great Plains, and other. A team approach is applied to develop and integrate different computerized business processes into an integrated software system. Project management techniques and computer simulated solutions are formally presented to emphasize team dynamics and management skills.

Prerequisite: BIT 4600 Business Data Base Applications

Textbook
A. **Targowski:** Electronic Enterprise, Strategy, and Architecture, Harrisburg PA: Idea Group Publishing, 2003.
B. SAP Course Pack

Course Objectives for Students
1. To learn the state of the art knowledge of:
    a. Information Engineering
    b. Application Software Engineering
    c. Project Management
2. To provide the student with the knowledge and skills of a:
    d. Application Programmer
    e. System Designer
    f. Software Engineer
    g. Project leader
3. To recognize the **value** of **enterprise-wide IS** in today's competitive business environment and how **to manage it** (attitude).

- **Enterprise project definition:** Enterprise project includes the interactions among subsystems supporting different business processes through a common menu.
- **Content Integration:** The BIT 4990 class is about the integration of a modern enterprise's information subsystems (reflecting **integrated business processes**) into one **ERP-prototype-demo software** system. A case study project reflecting feel and

Table 1. Course topics and schedule (titles in capital letters are lectures)

Session	Topic	Chapter
1	Class Concept	
2	Project Teams Organization	
3	**Part I: Enterprise System Definition (Classic Knowledge and Skills)** THE DEVELOPMENT CENTER	Chapter 7
4	THE SYSTEM APPROACH TOWARDS THE ENTERPRISE A. ENTERPRISE TERMS AND CONCEPTS B. PRINCIPLE OF ENTERPRISE SYSTEM DEVELOPMENT C. Project 1--Enterprise System Definition, due: session 7	Chapters 3, 4, 7
5	THE ENTERPRISE-WIDE IM APPROACH A. ENTERPRISE-WIDE IMS COMPLEX B. DATA-DRIVEN VS. SYSTEM-DRIVEN DESIGN C. APPLICATION PORTFOLIO VS. FEDERATED SYSTEM METHODOLOGY	Chapter 7
6	Team Work on Project 1	
7	**Part II: Business Process Integration** a. Intro to Project 2–Business Process Integration Model	Chapter 4
8	MIS ARCHITECTURE	Chapter 4
9	ERP ARCHITECTURE	Chapter 4
10	Exam review	
11	Exam 1	
12	Team Work on Project 2	
13	Student Project 2 Presentations	
14	Student Project 2 Presentations	
15	PROJECT MANAGEMENT	
16	Project 3: Class CPM	
17	Fall/Spring Recess	
18	Fall/Spring Recess	
19	**Part III: Enterprise System Development (ERP Prototype-Demo Software)** Introduction to Project 4: SAP Navigation and Transaction Processing	SAP Lab
20	EPM SYSTEM ARCHITECTURE	
21	Introduction to Project 5: VB Software for an MIS Subsystem--EPM (Enterprise Performance Management based on a balance scorecard)	Chapter 4
22	THE SEMANTIC LADDER	Chapter 4
23	Team Work on Project 5	

Table 1. continued

24	Installation of EPM's Main Menu in VB	
25	A. SAP IMPLEMENTATION B. Team Work on Project 5	
26	A. MICROSOFT SOFTWARE SLCD B. Team Work on Project 5	
27	Team Work on Project 5	
28	Student Project 5 Presentation	
29	Final Exam Review and Class Summary	
30	Final Exam	

look of a commercial software such as SAP or MS Great Plains is undertaken by a team and presented to the class. Some **basic knowledge and skills** of enterprise-wide software design will be offered too.

Project Organization

A class will analyze, design, and program a Management Information Systems Federation's (MISF) enterprise performance management system (EPMS) for a case company. There will be the following number of teams:

Team 1 Project Management
a.   Coordination of teams work (grades and attendance recording)
b.   SAP R/3 for IDES standards
c.   All project assignments but no. 4
d.   Teams' ERP reviews coordination
e.   Software validation
f.   Organization of presentations
g.   Final project presentation leadership

Team 1 System Integration
a.   Technical consulting on projects all teams
b.   Teams' EPMs integration into a common menu-driven SAP-like solution
c.   All project assignments but no. 4
d.   Software validation
e.   Final project presentation leadership

Team 3-10 Systems Developers
a.   All projects
b.   Final presentation
c.   ERP reviews

Instructor: The Project Advisor
Following SAP R/3 module-applications can be developed:

1. Enterprise controlling
2. Controlling
3. Treasury
4. Financial accounting
5. Sales and distribution
6. Material management
7. Production
8. Quality management
9. Customer service
10. Human resources

Assignments

- Project 1: Enterprise system definition
- Project 2: Business processes integration model
- Project 3: Course CPM
- Project 4: SAP navigation and transaction processing
- Project 5: VB Software for the MIS subsystem — EPM (enterprise performance management)

Table 2. Team #   Project 1 design an enterprise information system

	Objective: To learn skills how to conceptualize a complex Enterprise Information System	Points
1	Executive summary	5
2	Introduction (The approach to complete the project)	5
3	Design the "*Srombrero*" model for a selected company	10
4	Define a set of business processes (System-1a)	10
5	Define limited relationships within the defined set (System-2)	20
6	Define subsystems of the defined set (System-3)	10
7	Define the Cybernetic Model of the defined set of subsystems	20
8	Conclusion	5
9	Self-evaluation: a. What did you learned in this project? b. How will you apply this project's skills in your IT profession? c. How will you apply this project's skills in your personal life? d. Other	10
10	References	5
11	Points Total	100
12	Points achieved	

Table 3. Team #   Project 2 design a model of an EPMS for a given business process

	Objective: **To learn skills how to design Information Components, which will be a subject of application programming in Project 5**	Points
1	Executive summary	5
2	Introduction (The approach to complete the project)	5
3	Define a Bill of System Processor (BOSP): a. Information Subsystems b. Information Functions c. Information Activities d. Software Programs e. Software Module (for a selected software program)	20
4	Design a set of 4 Key Performance Indicators (KPI)for the selected business process, one KPI for each perspective of a balance scorecard: • Financial Perspective • Customer Perspective • Operation Perspective • Innovation Perspective	40
5	Design a content and format of Scheduled Reports	25
6	Design a content and format of Alert Reports	10
7	Design key data elements of a database, necessary to process these reports	15
8	Design data necessary to update the database	10
9	Define additional IT requirements for the EPMS that will be passed to an application programmer (Project 5)	
10	Conclusion	5
11	Self-evaluation: a. What did you learned in this project? b. How will you apply this project's skills in your IT profession? c. How will you apply this project's skills in your personal life? d. Other	10
12	References	5
13	Points Total	150
14	Points achieved	

Table 4. Team #   Project 3 Design an Activities Network of the CIS/BIT 4990 Course with CPM

	Objective: **To learn skills how to control and manage an IT Project**	Points
1	Executive summary	5
2	Introduction (The approach to complete the project)	5

Table 4. continued

3	Define minimum 25 activities of this course	10
4	Design a Gantt Chart for those activities	20
5	Design a 3–tier network of 25 + activities for this course	20
6	Define a critical path	10
7	Define steps how to achieve the due date of the project	10
8	Conclusion	5
9	Self-evaluation: a. What did you learned in this project? b. How will you apply this project's skills in your IT profession? c. How will you apply this project's skills in your personal life? d. Other	10
10	References	5
11	Points Total	100
12	Points achieved	

Table 5. Team #   Project 4 SAP purchasing order processing

	Objective: **To learn skills how to process a transaction in a complex Enterprise Software Package (SAP or MS Great Plains)**	**Points**
1	Executive summary	5
2	Introduction (The approach to complete the project)	5
3	Define minimum 25 activities of this course	10
4	Design a Gantt Chart for those activities	20
5	Design a 3–tier network of 25 + activities for this course	20
6	Define a critical path	10
7	Define steps how to achieve the due date of the project	10
8	Conclusion	5
9	Self-evaluation: a. What did you learned in this project? b. How will you apply this project's skills in your IT profession? c. How will you apply this project's skills in your personal life? d. Other	10
10	References	5
11	Points Total	100
12	Points achieved	

Table 6. Team #   Project 5 Design Software for the MIS-EPMS

	Objective: **To learn skills how to develop a user-friendly application**	**Points**
1	Executive summary	5
2	Introduction (The approach to complete the project)	5
3	Define your prototype's methodology and strategy	10
4	Develop VB software providing screenshots for: a. Data processing (measurements of planned and actual PKI) b. Information processing (change of each KPI) c. Concept processing (state of affairs: normal, conflict, success, failure, based on pre-planned ranges of KPI for each state) d. Knowledge processing (three solutions for each concept state) e. Wisdom processing (choice of a solution from the knowledge stage)	100
5	Evaluation of GUI: a. User-friendly b. Average c. Failure	55
6	Conclusion	10
7	Self-evaluation: a. What did you learned in this project? b. How will you apply this project's skills in your IT profession? c. How will you apply this project's skills in your personal live? d. Other	10
8	References	5
9	Points Total	200
10	Points achieved	

Total Grading Scale

Final Grading Scale
A	=	95.0-100.0
BA	=	89.0-94.99
B	=	83.0-88.99
CB	=	76.0-82.99
C	=	70.0-75.99
DC	=	65.0-69.99
D	=	60.0-64.99
E	=	Below 60.0

Grading Policy

Projects: 650 points
- Project 1:   100 points
- Project 2:   150 points
- Project 3:   100 points
- Project 4:   100 points
- Project 5:   200 points

Exams: 300
- 2 exams each
  150 points: 300

Other: 50
- Folder: 30
- Press Review: 20

Total Points: 1000

Key Outcomes

To successfully complete the CIS 499 class, the BBA student should demonstrate the ability to:

1. Apply enterprise-wide IS concepts in business theory and practice
2. Plan and develop enterprise-wide solutions required in the future workplace

Lecture

More specifically, after completing the course lectures, students will be able to:

3. Explain the various approaches in developing enterprise-wide IS
4. Demonstrate how to manage enterprise-wide IS project
5. Explain how to achieve competitive advantage by developing enterprise-wide IS.
6. Describe the ethical, legal, and social implications of applying enterprise-wide IS

Projects

After completing the projects, students will be able to:

7. Demonstrate enterprise-wide IS proficiency in selection and application of appropriate project management techniques
8. Demonstrate essential enterprise-wide IS knowledge that is applied in business decision-making

Academic Honesty

Western Michigan University's Policy on Academic Honesty, stated in the Undergraduate Catalog 1997-1999, page 58, will be enforced fully in this course. Violations of this Policy include cheating, fabrication, falsification, forgery, multiple submission, plagiarism, complicity, and computer misuse, as described in the Catalog. Students found in violation of this Policy will be disciplined, which may include suspension or expulsion from the University. If you have any questions concerning what may constitute academic dishonesty, please consult the catalog or discuss questions with the faculty member in charge of the course.

Attendance Policy

Given the nature of this course and the value added by attending the class, attendance is mandatory. Students are expected to contribute in the class and have the responsibility, not only for their own learning, but also to contribute to the learning of their fellow students. Students with four or more class absences shall lose 1/2 grade from their overall course grade. In the event a student must miss more than 3 classes because of extenuating circumstances such as a lengthy illness, or other reasonable cause, the instructor of the course can make allowances at their discretion.

Late Assignment Policy

All assignments are due by the end of the class period on the date in the syllabus. Late assignments will be docked 5% of the maximum grade obtainable for that assignment if late up to one week, 10% if over one week late. The course instructor can take into account extenuating circumstances such as illness at their discretion.

Late Exams Policy

Students are expected to take exams when scheduled. In the event a student misses an exam, they must arrange with the instructor for a make-up. This option is at the discretion of the instructor.

CONCLUSION

The Enterprise Project course is a demanding course as well for the students as for the professor, since it integrates business and IT knowledge and skills in the times when the students' attitude is declining.

Regardless, whether a student wants to be an application developer or not, this course teaches him/her main stream knowledge and skills of the IT profession. If a student does not show engagement in the course's activities, he or she should consider whether the IT profession is right for him or her.

This course requires strong conceptualization of solutions, which is not a strong ability of young, undergraduate students with a very limited business practice, however, the students should be not discouraged by this, vice versa they should learn and learn how to develop this kind of skills, which is more and more required by the employers, who outsource the most simple IT tasks and look for business conceptualists and IT integrators. A professor should encourage the students to be more optimistic about their potential and ability.

REFERENCES

Targowski, A. (1990). *The architecture and planning of enterprise-wide IMS*. Harrisburg, PA: Idea Group Publishing.

Targowski, A. (2003). *Electronic enterprise, strategy, and architecture*. Hershey, PA: Idea Group Publishing.

Targowski, A., & Han, B. (2006). The business process-driven undergraduate transition from the CIS to BIT program. In A. Targowski & M. Tarn (Eds.), *Enterprise systems education in the 21st century*. Hershey, PA: Idea Group Publishing.

Chapter VIII

Teaching Human Resource Management Using SAP

Satish P. Deshpande, Western Michigan University, USA

Andrew Targowski, Western Michigan University, USA

ABSTRACT

Information technology has become a critical component for human resource (HR) professionals. Human resource information systems (HRIS) have helped many HR departments automate routine processes, eliminate unnecessary work, and play a strategic role in driving employee performance. Many IT firms are now forming alliances with universities to popularize their products. This chapter first investigates the utility and the choice of various HRIS options available to an organization. Next, it evaluates the utility of universities forming alliances with enterprise resource planning (ERP) firms to enrich their business curricula. Finally, the experiences of a college of business at a large university in Midwestern United States with the implementation of IT in the human resource management (HRM) curriculum are examined.

INTRODUCTION

Human resource (HR) departments in organizations have evolved a lot over time. It is an open secret that in the past, the human resource function within an organization did not have the same status as other functions. These departments started off as "personnel departments" whose job was to take care of payroll, employee records and ensure that the company had enough able-bodied people to run the production line. Over time, their responsibilities broadened and included activities such as recruiting, training, promoting, terminating, record keeping, employee relations, and meeting various legal requirements (Mathis & Jackson, 2003). In the last decade, globalization, organizational restructuring, and increased competition, forced companies to reexamine the role of HR function within the organization. Many companies are realizing that only HR gives them the strategic edge needed to manage a workforce effectively and efficiently (Greengard, 2000; Noe, Hollenbeck, Gerhart, & Wright, 2003). Nowadays, HR professionals are responsible for optimizing employee skills, maximizing their potential as valuable resources, and are important players in long-range strategic planning (Losey, 1999).

A major reason for this change is that management research in recent years has consistently found that the management of human resources is the most important factor in developing sustainable competitive advantage over time (Gratton, Hope-Hailey, Stiles, & Truss, 1999; Losey, 1999, Pfeffer, 1994). In addition, research suggests that factors traditionally associated with strategic success of a firm like product and process technology, access to financial resources and economies of scale are no longer sufficient to sustain a firm's competitive edge in the marketplace. These traditional factors provide very little advantage today and are expected to be even more insignificant in the future (Noe et al., 2003).

One way to cut down on administrative overheads and be a strategic partner in managing the firm is for the HR department to use information technology (Greengard, 2000). IT has helped many HR departments automate routine processes and eliminate unnecessary and non-value added work. This allows HR departments to be more efficient, use less paperwork, and ensure better information is available for making HR decisions (Mathis & Jackson, 2003). In addition, it allows HR Managers to free up time from filling out paperwork and ensuring administrative compliance to not only HR planning but also be a strategic partner to other functions with in the organization. The role of HR as a strategic partner includes establishing activities that contribute to superior organizational performance, advising on mergers, acquisitions, & downsizing, redesigning work processes, and demonstrating on a continuous basis that HR contributes to the financial viability of the organization (Mathis & Jackson, 2003).

A study conducted by the Gartner Group suggests that companies that use technology effectively to manage the human resource function will have a tremendous advantage over those that do not (Targowski & Deshpande, 2001). According to Targowski and Deshpande (2001), benefits of the use of HRIS include:

a.   Using an internal Web site or intranet to empower managers and employees to perform administrative tasks on their own than depend on the human resource department.

b.   Incremental leaps in efficiency and response time of various traditionally labor-intensive human resource activities. Not only is work duplication eliminated, but also various processes are streamlined and made more efficient. HR staff can spend less time on day-to-day administrative issues, and more time on strategic decision making and planning.

c.   Better knowledge management which leads to a firm's competitive advantage in the marketplace and better stakeholders' satisfaction.

d.   Using the HRIS, various business performance calculations like return on training, turnover costs, and human-value added can be used to impress the top management that the human resource function is an equal strategic partner and critical to meet various organizational objectives.

Table 1 provides a detailed list of various uses of an HRIS as identified by Mathis and Jackson (2003, p. 59). In spite of this, according to a survey conducted by Deloitte & Touche and Lawson Software, less than 20% of the human resource managers indicated that their organization has the technology to provide expeditious human resource information for business planning (Targowski & Deshpande, 2001).

Table 1. Uses of HRIS

HR Functions	HRIS Outputs
1. Employee and Labor Relations	Union negotiation costing Auditing records Attitude survey results Exit interview analysis Employee work history
2. Staffing	Recruiting sources Applicant tracking Job offer refusal analysis
3. HR Planning and Analysis	Organization charts Staffing projections Skills inventories Turnover analysis Absenteeism analysis Restructuring costing Internal job matching
4. Compensation and Benefits	Pay structures Wage/Salary costing Flexible benefit administration Vacation usage Benefits usage analysis
5. Training and Development	Employee training profiles Training needs assessments Succession planning Career interests and experience
6. Equal Employment	Affirmative Action plan Applicant tracking Workforce utilization Availability analysis
7. Health and Safety	Safety training Accident records OSHA 200 report Material data records

CHOICES OF AN HRIS

There are over 100 vendors for HR related software systems and it is nearly impossible to examine all of them (Gunsauley, 2002). While some HRIS packages are extensive, others are barebone. Many support add-on programs by third parties that can extend the functionality of the HR package. The process to select an HRIS is critical because a company typically has to live with the decision for at least eight years (Fox, 1998). But, it is a time consuming and cumbersome process. The selection process can take anywhere between three to nine months and may involve hiring a consultant to recommend the appropriate system (Targowski & Deshpande, 2001). Gartner Group's Magic Quadrant for Administrative Application Strategies is a good tool to get basic information on the various major players in different market segments (www4.gartner.com).

One option for firms is to consider stand-alone HR software. There are a number of firms in this market segment including NuView Systems (www.nuviewinc.com), Meta4 (www.meta4.com), Best Software (www.bestsoftware.com), and Track-it Solutions (www. itsolutions.intuit.com). MyHRIS by NuView Systems is a comprehensive, Web-native HR management solution that covers all facets of HR Management.

Another option for firms is to use ERP (enterprise resource planning) systems developed by firms like SAP (www.sap.com), PeopleSoft (www.peoplesoft.com), Oracle (www. oracle.com), and Bann (www.baan.com) (Targowski, 2003). ERP software combines computer systems of all departments into a single, integrated software program that runs using a single database. This ensures that different departments in an organization can easily share information and communicate with each other. For example, SAP R/3 Human Resources can be used independently or with other SAP R/3 applications including ones for finance, project management, logistics, production and operations management, and accounting. Integration ensures that any change in data in one system flows to the other systems. Thus, if an employee adds a dependent under her/his health care plan, this is recorded in SAP R/3 Human Resources. SAP R/3 Payroll will automatically update the employee's payroll deduction and SAP R/3 Financial will automatically provide a new check to the insurance provider. Thus while the data is only entered at one place, the entire system is automatically updated. While ERP systems can be expensive, they provide "real-time" data for managers to make informed decisions.

University Alliance Programs

In order to ensure that the next generation of business leaders have this core competency, a number of universities are forming alliances with ERP software companies to enrich their curriculum. One ERP software provider that is very active in this area is SAP. SAP is a market-leader in ERP software in the world. It has 12 million users and over 60,000 installations worldwide (www.sap.com/company/investor/aboutsap/). SAP employs over 28,000 people in more than 50 countries. For the last six years, it has been making its market-leading, client/server-based enterprise software, the R/3 System, available to the higher education community through its University Alliance Program. The annual membership in the program costs a university $8000. As a part of the program, SAP provides setup and training of faculty. SAP also provides a training database that can be used by faculty for various projects and exercises.

This program benefits SAP directly in a number of ways. First, it supports the development of graduate and undergraduate students who can apply SAP technology in practical applications. Second, it establishes a long-term teaching and research relationship with major universities. Third, it develops a network of teachers and researchers who contribute to new applications of various SAP solutions. Finally, it creates a pool of technically qualified business students who may have a preference for SAP applications. For universities, this is an inexpensive way to get the latest information technology in an environment of budget cuts. Students get to understand how different segments of a business interact with each other and learn a new marketable skill. It is an excellent recruiting tool and gives graduating students a competitive edge in the marketplace.

Human resources is a major component of the SAP R/3 System. In fact, over 60% of all tables in the R/3 System are HR related. HR training is provided to practitioners and educators in three broad areas: payroll, planning and administration, and time management. All three areas involve a basic course in human resources that gives a broad overview of the important functions of the SAP R/3 System. Training in payroll involves additional courses that cover topics like configuration of master data, time recording of benefits, travel management, compensation planning, and tax reporting. Training in planning and administration covers topics such as configuration of master data, personnel development, training and event management, compensation, and reporting. Time management involves courses like recording time sheets, time evaluation, shift planning, and organizational management. Each of these courses may involve two to five days of training by SAP trainers.

Thus, joining the SAP University Alliance allows university faculty to get the same training as SAP users at no cost. It also allows professors to interact with SAP professionals as well as with managers of companies that use SAP. In addition, they can attend professional meetings sponsored by SAP or SAP users (e.g., the Innovation Congress and state-level SAP Users Conferences). SAP also has special meetings and conferences open only for faculty using SAP. Universities can also send curriculum or research proposals for cash, hardware, and software as a part of SAP's annual awards program. Currently around 92 universities in the United States and 25 universities/colleges in Canada are members of the SAP University Alliance Program. In addition, around 20 universities in Latin America also participate in this program.

Using Information Technology (IT) in HR Curriculum

We will now examine the experiences of a business school at large university in Midwestern United States with the implementation of IT in the HRM curriculum. Even though IT was implemented at the Masters of Business Administration (MBA) level, for simplicity, we will only examine implementation in the undergraduate program. This business school is AACSB accredited and offers a major in Human Resource Management (HRM) as a part of the Bachelors of Business Administration (BBA) degree program.

This business school developed an integrated curriculum in the Fall of 1998 with a particular emphasis on the ongoing changes in business practice from a functional (e.g., human resources, accounting, finance, marketing, etc.) to an integrated process view. Significant changes were made in the graduate (MBA) and undergraduate curricula. Major changes in the undergraduate curriculum included an introductory course in business administration, a course on information and technology usage, a course on process and productivity improvement, and the electronic portfolio. These are required courses for all students regardless of their majors.

A major aim of these changes was to ensure that the faculty effectively transfer the current knowledge and skills required for business to their students. A precondition to this is that the faculty must have the opportunity to update their understanding of business and have access to the current tools needed to transfer this knowledge to students. To improve effectiveness of business decisions, businesses over the years have moved forward using various computer software programs. Thus, it is critical that today's business students understand how ERP software integrates, standardizes, and synchronizes business processes. Accordingly, in April of 2002, a group of business faculty, after undergoing training, introduced SAP's R/3 software into the curriculum with the ultimate objective of teaching discipline specific skills and enhancing their understanding about integrated business processes. So an HRM student would not only learn HRIS, but would also understand how the HRIS (as a part of the ERP) interacts with other information systems within the company.

By fall of 2003, eight courses had introduced some SAP applications in their curriculum. Courses that involved a heavy use of SAP software (e.g., programming and configuration of SAP) had a course fee of $22 while other courses had a course fee of $11. Three of these are courses required for all undergraduate business students. In these courses, business students are exposed to a set of ERP topics regardless of their major or area of specialization. These topics include navigation, various enterprise applications, and examining how technology can be used to facilitate the integration of functional activities to maximize the performance of entire organization.

In the HRM program, SAP was introduced in the Employee Relations class. This was a required class for all HR students and the instructor of this class was the first HR faculty member to undergo SAP training. Subsequently two more HR faculty who specialized in diversity management and staffing underwent SAP training. In the Employee Relations class HRIS topics were covered for three weeks. HRM students first did an SAP exercise on setting up an organizational structures and reporting relationships. They then did a case study on HRIS implementation. Finally, they discussed issues related to Web based employee self-service. We will examine the HRIS issues covered in this class in detail.

The SAP exercise in this class on a fictitious company covers the following topics:

a.   Create an organizational unit (e.g., Fatfoods, Inc.)
b.   Create functional areas of business unit (e.g., HR, manufacturing, finance, marketing, public relations)
c.   Create sub-units within functional areas of business (e.g., under HR they would create the following sub-units: compensation and benefits, recruitment and selection, industrial relations, etc.)
d.   Creates positions and jobs in sub-units (e.g., under compensation and benefits unit, they would create the following positions: compensation and benefits manager, compensation analyst, benefits analyst, etc.)
e.   Create job descriptions for different jobs/positions
f.   Assign a departmental head (e.g., compensation and benefits manager will be assigned as the head of the compensation and benefits unit)
g.   Assign people to different positions (e.g., make John Smith the compensation and benefits manager)
h.   View organizational structure of organizational units, jobs, and positions

In addition to working on the SAP HR exercise, students in this class also do a case study. The case-study is on how HR partnered with IT in an international paper company to overhaul HR processes by implementing SAP HR and a Web portal for employee self-service. This company is a forest products company that employs 100,000 employees worldwide. Till 2001, the company was mired in inconsistent undocumented HR processes and several legacy systems. The HR Department could not even generate an accurate company-wide headcount report (Roberts, 2002a). An earlier attempt to transform HR in the mid-1990's failed because the company introduced technology without paying attention to people and processes within the organization. The case emphasizes that HR leadership, experienced and knowledgeable IT consultant, HR-IT partnership, executive sponsorship, and buy-in by rank and file HR staff are critical for an HRIS project to succeed in an organization.

Finally, the course discusses the utility of setting up a Web portal for employee self-service. HR departments can shift the responsibility for updating employee records on the employees themselves. Employee self-service is designed from the start to be self-explanatory and easy to use. Users are guided via a protocol similar to that commonly found in an automated teller machine. Employee can typically access these self-service systems through touch-screen kiosks at the workplace or a computer at the workplace or home by accessing a Web page. Some of the commonly found self-service applications discussed in class are changing personal data, changing banking data, benefits selection during open enrollment, time entry and time off, and training enrollment.

There are two ways to implement HRIS into the curriculum. One way is to expose HRM students to HRIS is to have a separate course on HRIS. The other way is to incorporate HRIS in traditional HR courses like Staffing, Compensation, Managing Diversity, and Employee Relations. Table 2 shows how HRIS skills that can be taught to the HRM students in different HRM related classes. It was initially expected that the latter model will be used in the HR program and SAP would be gradually introduced in different HR courses. But recently, the Management Department decided to review all its majors (including HR) to ensure that they meet the needs of its stakeholders. The HR faculty, as a part of the review process, decided not to pick which approach to use to teach HRIS until feedback was received from a focus group of potential and current employers on the existing program. There was also a discussion on using other systems like Microsoft's Great Plains in addition to SAP. Till a final decision has been made, SAP will be continued in the Employee Relations course alone.

Teaching and Operational Issues to be Considered

The following are some teaching and operational issues that must be considered by educators while using an HRIS in the classroom:

a.   Educators must understand that an HRIS is like a high-speed clerk and not an end. It is the job of a manager to come up with processes that ensure that this enabling technology is used effectively.

b.   A number of unforeseen problems will arise the first few times the course is taught. It is advisable that an IT person be available as an HR instructor may not be able to troubleshoot all the bugs and technical problems that may arise which may be system or SAP related.

Table 2. SAP HR applications for HRM students

HR Courses Typically Required of All Human Resource Majors	
Course	HRIS topics that may be reinforced using SAP HR
1. Employee Relations	Organization management including setting up organizational structures and reporting relationships. Case study on HRIS implementation, and employee self service.
2. Staffing	Job analysis, recruitment, and selection process.
3. Diversity Management	Preparation of equal employment opportunity and various government required statistics.
4. Compensation and Benefits	Managing pay structures, payroll, incentives, and benefits.
5. Training and Development	Training, development, and travel management.

c.   Students access SAP R/3 on the Web. The instructor must prepare a backup lecture in a traditional HR topic just in case the system goes down and/or SAP R/3 is not accessible.

d.   Instructors have a limited number of lecture periods to cover various topics. Introduction of HRIS topic may require dilution or elimination of some traditional HR topics.

e.   Like other software, SAP comes up with updates and newer versions of R/3 at a regular interval. Instructors need to familiarize themselves with the functional changes that take place between SAP R/3 releases.

CONCLUSION

Management of HR has become a critical competency in a business. Many organizations are placing more demands on HR departments. As today's business environment places premium on effective management of the workforce and employee development, information technology can have a tremendous impact on the human resource function. It allows HR employees to store, retrieve, and process large amounts of information quickly and efficiently. HR staff can spend less time on day-to-day administrative issues, and more time on strategic decision making and planning. In addition, Web-based applications allow employees to access and modify their personal data anytime and anywhere. Many IT firms are forming alliances with colleges of business to ensure that new graduates have the skill-set in technology that are currently used by potential employers. This is a win-win for both IT firms (spread their technology to future managers) and universities (teach their students valuable skill-sets at very low costs). This technology can easily be incorporated in existing curriculum as shown in the HRM program discussed in the chapter.

REFERENCES

Fox, F. J. (1998, August). Do it yourself HRMS evaluations. *HR Magazine, 43*(9), 28-33.

Gratton, L., Hope-Hailey, V., Stiles, P., & Truss, C. (1999). Linking individual performance to business strategy: The people process model. *Human Resource Management, 38*(1), 17-31.

Greengard, S. (2000). Technology finally advances HR. *Workforce, 79*(1), 38-41.

Gunsauley, C. (2002, April 1). A wealth of choice. *Employee Benefit News, 16*(4), 19-20.

Losey, M. R. (1999). Mastering the competencies of HR management. *Human Resource Management, 38*(2), 99-102.

Mathis, R. L., & Jackson, J. H. (2003). *Human resource management* (10th ed.). Manson, OH: Thompson South-Western.

Noe, R. A., Hollenbeck, J. R., Gerhart, B., & Wright, P. M. (2003*). Human resource management: Gaining a competitive advantage* (4th ed.). Boston: McGraw Hill.

Pfeffer, J. (1994). *Competitive advantage through people.* Boston: HBR Press.

Roberts, B. (2002a). Processes first, technology second. *HR Magazine 47*(6), 41-45.

Roberts, B. (2002b). Count on business value. *HR Magazine 47*(8), 65-71.

Targowski, A. (2001). *Enterprise information infrastructure* (2nd ed.). Boston: Pearson Custom Publishing.

Targowski, A. (2003). *Electronic enterprise: Strategy and architecture* (2nd ed.). Hershey, PA: Idea Group Publishing.

Targowski, A., & Deshpande, S. P. (2001). The utility and selection of an HRIS. *Advances in Competitiveness Research, 9*(1), 42-56.

www4.gartner.com

www.sap.com/company/investor/aboutsap

Chapter IX

Teaching Operations Management with Enterprise Software

R. Lawrence LaForge, Clemson University, USA

ABSTRACT

Enterprise systems technology is used to enhance the teaching of operations management through development and operation of a virtual manufacturing enterprise. An ongoing, real-time simulation is conducted in which operations management issues in the fictitious factory must be addressed on a daily basis. The virtual manufacturing enterprise is integrated into an operations management course to facilitate understanding of the dynamic and interrelated nature of operations planning and control in a complex manufacturing environment. Enterprise software supports the primary learning objective of understanding how operations management decisions affect customer service, capacity, inventory, and costs.

INTRODUCTION

This chapter presents an approach to teaching operations management (OM) with enterprise systems technology. The approach described here is based on the premise that the topics taught in operations management courses are dynamic and interrelated. Therefore, the teaching and learning of operations management should address not only the content of each specific topic, but also the dynamic interrelationships among the topics.

The integration of OM topics is extremely difficult to accomplish in a traditional classroom setting. There are several excellent OM textbooks available in the market, and they generally provide information needed to study the content of OM topics such as aggregate sales and operations planning, master production scheduling, material planning and control, capacity planning and control, and production activity control. However, textbooks are a static medium that cannot capture the dynamic interrelationships between and among the topics. The topics in an OM textbook must necessarily be presented in sequential fashion organized by chapter or unit, and conventional testing typically focuses on the content (issues, concepts, tools, techniques) related to each topic. True insights into the connections among the topics are extremely difficult or impossible to glean from even the best textbooks.

As an example of the interrelationship of operations management issues, consider the topics of aggregate planning and production activity control. Aggregate sales and operations planning deals with the company's overall strategy for meeting anticipated demand of broadly-defined product families over a planning horizon of 12-18 months. Production activity control, on the other hand, deals with day-to-day (or hour-to-hour) scheduling and sequencing issues for internal shop orders to make component parts or assemblies needed for specific products. The two topics are at extreme ends of the continuum and are invariably covered in completely different sections of the typical OM text, but they are in fact highly interrelated. While we might be tempted to seek sophisticated algorithms and models to help with complex scheduling issues that occur on a daily basis, it may be that our day-to-day scheduling issues are the result of poor overall planning at the product family level.

The previous argument suggests that conventional classroom lectures, textbook readings, and end-of-chapter exercises are *necessary* but *not sufficient* to gain insights needed to understand operations management. This chapter describes an ongoing project in which the desired synergy is addressed by the introduction and use of enterprise-wide system (ES) technology in the operations management classroom.

The objectives of this chapter are to raise the level of awareness regarding the need for active learning approaches to operations management, to describe in detail an approach to teaching OM with enterprise technology, and to discuss lessons learned that may be of benefit to other scholars and teachers interested in this approach.

BACKGROUND

The practice and teaching of operations management has been impacted significantly by advancements in information technology (Manetti, 2001; Rondeau & Litteral, 2001). The development of material requirements planning (MRP) systems in the 1970's revolutionized thinking about how to manage materials in a manufacturing environment. This provided an alternative to economic lot size models that assumed that demand for all inventory items was independent, and it promoted more of a systems perspective to materials management. This was followed by manufacturing resource planning (MRPII) systems that provided additional functionality related to capacity planning, limited financial analysis, and "what-if" planning. More recent enterprise resource planning (ERP) systems aim to link together the various functional areas of operations, accounting, finance, customer relationship management, and human resources. ERP systems can be enhanced with advanced planning system (APS) modules for obtaining near-optimal scheduling, manufacturing execution system (MES) modules for shop floor control, and/or supply chain management (SCM) modules designed to integrate planning and execution with suppliers and customers.

A key aspect of this evolution is integration. Organizations have made significant investments in hardware, software, and training to install, maintain, and use enterprise-wide systems designed to better integrate their activities (Hitt, Wu, & Zhou, 2002; Mabert, Soni, & Venkataramanan, 2000). It is logical to assume that collegiate schools of business would also value, and seek to achieve, higher levels of integration in the topics taught in the curriculum (Cannon, Klein, Koste, & Magal, 2004; LaForge & Busing, 2000).

In operations management, the objective of topic integration could be pursued in two ways. One way is to seek greater insights into the interrelationships of topics taught in a given OM course. Another way is to focus on the impact of operations management decisions on other functional areas in the organization such as accounting, finance, marketing, and human resources or on inter-organizational issues with suppliers and customers. That is, the goal could be integration within a given course and/or integration across courses. This chapter provides details on the first approach, which has been implemented under the assumption that one must achieve a high level of understanding of operations management issues before assessing their impact on other areas. However, the chapter also includes a discussion of efforts to achieve "across course" integration, which builds on the application of enterprise software in the operations management course described next.

THE OPERATIONS MANAGEMENT COURSE

The section describes an operations management course that has been enhanced by the use of enterprise software. The course is an advanced, undergraduate course in operations planning and control taken by primarily by management majors at Clemson University. The course topics are aggregate sales and operations planning, master production scheduling, material planning and control, capacity planning and control, and production activity control. The textbook used in the course is a primary study reference for the *Certified in Production and Inventory Management* (CPIM) examinations offered by APICS — The Society for Operations Management. Traditional classroom activities such as textbook readings, lectures, end-of-chapter exercises, and testing of content are involved.

A primary learning objective of the course is to understand and appreciate the dynamic interrelationships among the course topics. As discussed earlier, the traditional classroom activities are necessary to establish content knowledge of each major topic, but do not address the integration of the OM activities in a meaningful way. The issue of integration of OM topics in the course is addressed in the same way that a manufacturing company would address the issue of integration of key OM activities in its facilities — through the introduction of information systems technology. The technology is used to create and operate a virtual manufacturing enterprise in which the OM issues under study are carried out simultaneously on a daily basis. The virtual manufacturing enterprise is the focal point for active learning opportunities that address the integration issues and learning objectives. Table 1 shows details from the course syllabus regarding the body of knowledge and learning objectives.

Table 1. Syllabus information for the OM course

Management 402
Operations Planning and Control
Clemson University

NATURE OF THE COURSE:

This course examines important concepts and procedures involved in managing the operations of a business enterprise. All class meetings take place in the Manufacturing Management Laboratory. This laboratory provides access to a realistic simulation of a business operation utilizing a state-of-the-art enterprise resource planning (ERP) system that is widely used in industry.

Students will study important concepts, issues, and procedures of an operations planning and control system, and then put this knowledge to work in a virtual manufacturing enterprise that is supported by the ERP system. Class meetings will be a combination of lecture and student participation. The basic concepts and procedures will be presented through instructor lecture, reading assignments, and class/homework exercises. The concepts will be reinforced through "hands on" experience with the ERP system and the virtual enterprise. Particular attention will be paid to the interaction of planning/control activities, and how decisions made at one level of the planning process affect output and performance at lower levels.

A model manufacturing company — Orange Office Products — is used to illustrate many of the topics in the course. Orange Office Products is a fictitious manufacturer of office furniture equipment that was developed specifically for use in this course. The database for Orange Office Products has been installed on the ERP system, providing live information about products, inventory levels, plant capacity, manufacturing orders, purchase orders, and much more.

Orange Office Products is an ongoing, real-time simulation of a manufacturing operation. The database changes daily to reflect the activities of the company. Students in Management 402 will observe and participate in many of these important operations management activities.

MAJOR TOPICS IN THE COURSE:

1.   Overview of Planning and Control Systems
2.   Material Planning and Control
3.   Production Activity Control
4.   Aggregate Sales & Operations Planning
5.   Master Production Scheduling
6.   Capacity Planning

OBJECTIVES OF THE COURSE:

Students who complete this course should be able to:

1.   Explain the basic components of an operations planning and control system;
2.   Understand the interrelationships among planning and control activities in a business operation, and their impact on customer service, inventory, capacity, and costs.
3.   Develop, apply, and interpret the results of basic procedures for inventory planning, capacity management, shop floor control, aggregate production planning, and master scheduling;
4.   Understand and appreciate the importance of operations management and the role of information technology in modern planning and control systems.

Figure 1. Components of the virtual manufacturing enterprise

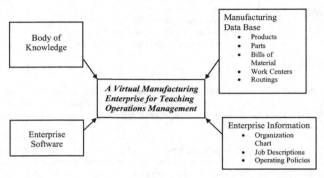

In the following section, the virtual manufacturing enterprise is described in terms of four components necessary to create and maintain it. This will be followed by a detailed description of how the virtual enterprise is used to address the learning objective.

The Virtual Manufacturing Enterprise

The virtual manufacturing enterprise can be described by the four components shown in Figure 1. These elements consist of the body of knowledge, manufacturing database, enterprise software, and enterprise information. The following sections explain the four components of the virtual manufacturing enterprise and address key issues in developing each component.

Body of Knowledge

The most important component of this approach to teaching operations management is a clear statement of the body of knowledge to be taught. All other components of the virtual manufacturing enterprise, and all other activities, should be undertaken with the objective of addressing or supporting the body of knowledge in some way. This is important because without a clear statement of the body of knowledge, one may fall into the trap of teaching what a software package does rather than teaching what the curriculum says. As shown in Table 1, the body of knowledge for the OM course described here consists of concepts, issues, and tools for performing the previously-mentioned topics of aggregate sales and operations planning, master production scheduling, material planning and control, capacity planning and control, and production activity control.

Manufacturing Database

The database provides needed details of products, parts, bills of material, routings, work centers, customers, and suppliers. These details are essential for developing a realistic enterprise model capable of capturing the issues in the body of knowledge. While realism is needed, this does not mean that the database must consist of hundreds of products and thousands of parts. Realism in the database can and should be achieved through complex interrelationships among the elements, not through sheer size. Experience here suggests that size of the database is not as important as well conceived connections among the elements.

An original database for a fictitious manufacturing enterprise was created for the operations management course in this project. The decision to create an original database, rather than use sample data provided by the software vendor, was made to allow complete control over the size of the data set and the interacting components that result in operations management issues addressed in the course.

The fictitious manufacturer produces metal-based office furniture products. This environment was chosen because the products are common items that are easy to conceptualize for students with little or no practical experience in operations management. The database contains technical descriptions of five standard office furniture products that are manufactured in a make-to-stock environment: (a) three-shelf adjustable book case, (b) three-drawer file cabinet, (c) two-drawer work desk, (d) standard desk chair, and (e) one-shelf credenza. In addition to manufacturing details, a chart of accounts and other financial information were created to facilitate use of the virtual enterprise in accounting and other business courses, as discussed later in the chapter.

The inventory portion of the manufacturing database consists of 45 total items, including the five finished products. Twenty-two of the items are manufactured in house, while 23 are purchased from suppliers. The manufactured items typically consist of metal parts (handles, frames, brackets, shelf units, etc.), while the purchased items include raw sheet metal, hardware, paint, packaging materials, wooden parts, and accessories.

Bills of material were created to link the items needed to make each product. These documents are multi-level in nature, reflecting a process that flows from purchased materials to manufactured parts to assemblies to final products. Several items are common to different products, including handles, shelf units, and a major drawer assembly.

The manufactured items in each bill of material are made in a production facility consisting of nine distinct work centers. A routing file was created for each manufactured item that identifies the work center sequence required and the standard setup time and standard run time per unit for processing the item. Multiple operations are required to make each manufactured item. Defined shift lengths dictate the available capacity of each work center.

The database supports the body of knowledge by being small enough to allow manual calculation and tracking of some issues, but large enough to capture complex interrelationships impacted by operations management decisions. The major challenge in creating the manufacturing database was establishing parameter values (routing steps, standards for setup times and run times, work center capacities, planned lead times, etc.) that result in shop loads that introduce meaningful operations management issues to students. Capacity planning modules in the enterprise software assist in this issue by providing projected workloads for a given configuration of parameter values, facilitating adjustment of planning parameters as necessary. Development of the database is an ongoing activity, allowing the introduction of new parts, revised routings, adjusted planned lead times, and various other issues.

Enterprise Resource Planning Software

Introduction of enterprise resource planning software into an academic course obviously requires an answer to the following question: What software should be used? In this context, software should be viewed as the enabling technology that allows issues in the body of knowledge to "come to life" in a dynamic and realistic way. The functionality needed in the software is defined by the body of knowledge. Ideally, software selection should focus on systems that implement generally-accepted methods to address and integrate issues under study. That is, the software should be consistent with the methods described in the text and established in the curriculum. What the software does is give life to the issues and help create a dynamic and meaningful context for studying them.

Realistically, other issues come into play in the software selection decision. Costs associated with hardware, implementation, training, and maintenance must be considered. With the budget constraints and limited technical support that exist at many universities, these issues must be carefully weighed to ensure that the system can be sustained. However, the compatibility of the software with the body of knowledge must be the overriding consideration. It would be indefensible to introduce a software system into the curriculum simply because it was available or easy to maintain without regard to the value it adds to pre-established learning objectives for the subject matter in the course or curriculum. The teaching approach should not be software specific.

Fortunately, there are many software options available that are consistent with generally-accepted practices in operations management. In addition, many software vendors have special pricing arrangements, or make free donations of software and support, for educational institutions using their products in the curriculum. Over the twenty years in which the project described here has been under development, four different software systems, each from a different vendor, have been utilized.

Current enterprise software system support for this project comes from the Microsoft Dynamics Academic Alliance. This alliance not only provides software, but also support, training, and opportunities to interact with faculty at other institutions. Specifically, the activities in the virtual manufacturing enterprise are supported by the Manufacturing Series of Microsoft Dynamics GP 9.0. The system runs on a Dell PowerEdge Server 2600, with the client applications available through the Clemson University network to smart classrooms and laboratories throughout the campus.

Enterprise Information

This component of the virtual manufacturing enterprise refers to a description of the enterprise in sufficient detail to establish the context in which the simulated company operates. This background information is important for students to get the feel of a realistic enterprise. In addition to background information on the company, this material also includes defined roles in the virtual manufacturing enterprise that relate to the body of knowledge, as well as policies and operating procedures. Details of this information will be presented later in the chapter.

OPERATING THE VIRTUAL MANUFACTURING ENTERPRISE

The virtual enterprise is operated in a continuous, real-time mode without regard to the starting and ending dates of academic terms. The calendar in the enterprise system is maintained so that the factory is closed on academic holidays and other "down time" in the academic calendar. However, the database is never reset back to initial conditions. In this manner, the virtual manufacturing enterprise is, in every sense, a going concern.

Daily decision making and transaction processing are required in the virtual manufacturing enterprise just they are in a real company. The virtual factory operates in real-time mode in that daily decisions must be made on matters related to accepting customer orders, shipping products, updating operating plans, managing materials, allocating capacity, and implementing scheduled work activity. A number of random events can be incorporated into the virtual factory that must be considered in the daily decision making, such as actual customer demand, vendor performance, and unexpected down time in work centers. Daily transaction processing is required to report all decisions, activities, and events affecting the virtual enterprise and keep the database up to date. Each day materials and products are moving through the virtual factory from receipts of raw materials, and processing of manufacturing and customer orders. At any time that an inquiry is made into the information system, the user sees current dates related to all activities. In short, the system is live and operated on a day-to-day basis.

The previous operational decisions were made to achieve the realism needed for meaningful active learning tasks that capture the dynamic interrelationships among the operations management topics taught in the course. Without such realism, only static inquiries into the system would be possible. While important to achieving the learning objectives of the course, this realism comes with a price. There is an "overhead" associated with operating the virtual enterprise in the form of instructor or graduate assistant time needed to perform the daily decision making and transaction processing necessary to keep the database current. To minimize the overhead of the daily routine, all activities are periodically evaluated to ensure that they add value with regard to accomplishing the learning objectives.

New features or issues that could be incorporated into the operation of the virtual factory are considered by weighing the potential value added to student learning against the additional overhead required to implement and maintain the new feature. For example, should routines be added to introduce uncertainty into all activities of the factory (e.g., processing times, lead times, customer demand, machine availability), or will uncertainty in final customer demand introduce enough uncertainty to create a meaningful scenario? In this project, uncertainty in final customer demand suffices, but that may not necessarily be the case in other situations with more experienced students in graduate programs, or in courses with different learning objectives.

USING THE VIRTUAL ENTERPRISE TO ACHIEVE THE LEARNING OBJECTIVES

The virtual enterprise is integrated into the operations management course in two ways that are described in detail in the following sections. First, activities are described for integrating the virtual factory into routine class activities. Next, a major project is described in which selected students assume managerial roles in the virtual enterprise and participate in daily decision making and transaction processing.

Class Activities Using the Virtual Manufacturing Enterprise

Students in the operations management course are seated at a work station and have access to the live ERP system during all class sessions. This enables the instructor to enhance traditional classroom instruction with the live system, providing a meaningful context for the course topics. The virtual manufacturing enterprise enhances, but does not replace, traditional classroom activities such as lectures, discussion, and problem solving. After basic concepts and methods for a particular topic, such as material planning, have been addressed, students access data in the live system to explore key issues within the context of the virtual enterprise.

There are generally three objectives in using the virtual factory and enterprise software in the manner described above to enhance traditional classroom instruction: (1) identifying key concepts or issues, (2) verifying outputs of planning functions, and (3) understanding dynamic interrelationships.

Identifying Key Concepts or Issues

This provides a meaningful context for key concepts in the text that might appear to students to be abstract, and it facilitates more meaningful discussion of the issues. Rather than memorize a concept or definition, students have an opportunity to see practical implications of the issue. For example, material planning activities in the MRP module of the system rely on user-supplied parameters referred to as planned lead times. Memorizing the definition of "planned lead time" is one thing, but coming to grips with the fact that MRP-based planning cannot begin until we enter these numbers, understanding what one must do to establish reasonable values for this planning parameter, and realizing the implications of using "bad" numbers are much more valuable lessons for operations management students.

Verifying Outputs of Planning Functions

This enables students to test their knowledge of planning methods with live data in the ERP system. With a carefully constructed database that is realistic in connecting the various elements but small in size, students can manually verify some outputs of the system. For example, the MRP record for a purchased item in the database may show a planned order release on the current date for certain quantity of the item. This means that we should launch a purchase order today to the supplier of the item for the specified quantity. Without the planned purchase order, we will not have sufficient quantity of the item to meet projected requirements for the item in the future. While most ERP training would focus on the transaction processing necessary to create and release the purchase order, the focus here is on the planning logic that resulted in the order recommendation in the first place. Why is the system telling us to do this?

Operations management students who have studied the basic logic of material requirements planning should be able to answer the above question by accessing relevant data from the live system (current master production schedule, bills of material, planned lead times, available inventory, and open orders), and applying the same MRP logic used to work end-of-chapter problems in the text. Successful completion of this exercise goes beyond simply accessing information in a computer system — it requires knowledge of how that information has been generated and, therefore, provides insights into the usefulness and potential limitations associated with the information. Further, because the virtual factory operates on a real time calendar and is updated daily, students can test their skills repeatedly since the numbers are constantly changing with new conditions in the factory.

Understanding Dynamic Interrelationships

This is a key learning objective and is facilitated by the live system in which the various operations planning and control activities are taking place simultaneously. Some key

Table 2. Using the virtual manufacturing enterprise for class activities

Identifying Key Concepts and Issues

Using the live system to access data and discuss issues related to:

- Importance of planned lead times
- Impact of ordering policies
- Importance of inventory record accuracy
- Meaning and use of "floor stock"
- Impact of standard queue times in scheduling
- Differences between backward and forward scheduling

Verifying Outputs of Planning Functions

Applying standard methods in the textbook to verify data in the live system related to:

- Projected available inventory
- Available to promise
- Order recommendations in material requirements planning (MRP)
- Rescheduling messages for open orders
- Operation due dates for scheduled manufacturing orders
- Projected work center loads

Understanding Dynamic Interrelationships

Using the live system to assess cause-and-effect relationships, such as:

- Changes in the material plan needed to accommodate a special customer order
- Capacity needed for a change in the master production schedule
- Effect of reducing planned lead times on shop capacity
- Impact of shop downtime on meeting the master production schedule
- Effect of reducing setup times on shop capacity
- Impact of different scheduling approaches in the shop
- Material planning actions needed to overcome scrap on the production floor

links between planning activities can be examined in classroom sessions in which changes are introduced into the system. For example, a change in the master production schedule of a finished product could be made during a class session to accommodate an unusually large customer order. This in turn will trigger a series of changes in material plans, capacity needs, and work center schedules that are explainable, tractable, and predictable. Working through these changes gives students insights into the dynamics of operations management that are not possible in a traditional setting. These are extremely important insights that help students understand trade-offs involved in balancing customer service objectives with inventory and capacity issues.

Table 2 provides additional examples of the use of the virtual manufacturing enterprise and ERP system to enhance class activities.

Class Project in the Virtual Manufacturing Enterprise

In the first half of the semester, all daily decision making and transaction processing necessary to run the virtual factory are done by the instructor and graduate assistant assigned to the project. During this period, students in the operations management course are engaged with the enterprise system through the class activities described above, but are limited to inquiry capabilities and have no decision making or transaction processing authority in the system.

At approximately mid semester, selected students take an active role in the daily management of the virtual enterprise as part of a course project. In the target OM course, selection is based on student performance, motivation, and career interest. Participating students perform all project activities during special laboratory hours held outside of the normal class meeting time, and must agree that a formal assessment of their performance in the project will become their final examination grade in the course. In this manner, the participants substitute an active learning project that addresses all course concepts for the traditional cumulative final examination.

The student roles relate to the body of knowledge in the course. The three major roles related to the target course are master production scheduler, inventory planner, and work center manager. Multiple students can occupy each of these roles at the same time. In addi-

Table 3. Key OM roles in the virtual manufacturing enterprise

---

Plant Manager (graduate assistant)

Responsible for all activities of the Virtual Manufacturing Enterprise.

Materials Manager

Coordinates activities to provide material needed to meet the master production schedule. Monitors material needs and order status, anticipates problem situations, and coordinates activities to solve problems in a timely fashion. Serves in a supervisory position and does not perform daily transactions related to materials management.

Production Manager

Coordinates shop floor activities required to meet the master production schedule. Monitors work in process, order priorities and capacity at each work center. Anticipates problem situations and coordinates activities to solve problems in a timely fashion. Serves in a supervisory position and does not perform daily transactions related to shop activity.

Master Production Schedulers

Develop and maintain the master production schedule for assigned end items. Receive and enter customer orders, adjust master schedule quantities as needed to meet demand and finished goods inventory targets, receive completed finished goods into inventory, process sales shipments to customers, and track customer service levels. Responsible for all decision making and transaction processing related to the master production schedule.

Inventory Planners

Initiate and monitor actions to obtain needed assemblies, components, and materials to meet the master production schedule. Responsible for all decision making and transaction processing to order, schedule/reschedule dues dates, and receive assigned inventory items.

Work Center Managers

Responsible for managing assigned work centers to meet manufacturing plans. Manage work center capacity, establish and execute daily job schedules, and coordinate operations with related work centers. Responsible for decision making, transaction processing, and reporting requirements in the assigned work area.

---

tion, roles are defined for the plant manager, materials manager, and production manager. The plant manager role is performed by an assigned graduate assistant with significant work experience in operations management, while the materials manager and production manager are undergraduate students enrolled in a special independent study course who completed the target operations management course in a previous semester (and therefore previously served as master production scheduler, inventory planner, or work center manager). Brief job descriptions of each of these key roles are provided in Table 3.

The student roles require content knowledge of operations management topics acquired through traditional classroom activities. It is for that reason that assigned student roles go into effect near the midpoint of the semester, at which time the student team replaces the instructor and graduate assistant in the daily decision making and transaction processing necessary to keep the system live and current.

Enterprise policies are published that provide general guidelines for student activity in the virtual manufacturing enterprise and specific rules for assigned roles. General policies apply to all student participants and deal with communication and reporting responsibilities. Rules for specific roles place requirements and responsibilities on students as they deal with unexpected situations in performing their assigned duties. For example, work center managers may schedule overtime in their assigned work center in a given day, but only if they submit a request at least one day in advance with appropriate justification and receive approval from the plant manager. Master production schedulers may make any changes in the master schedule they feel necessary, but changes in the very near term must be justified in writing since these changes affect material and capacity plans that have already been implemented. The master production schedulers must be able to explain the impact of changes they propose. These and other policies force students to use the information system to plan ahead, anticipate problems, and communicate with each other.

During the second half of the semester, all decision making and transaction processing are conducted by the student team. Factory conditions resulting from these decisions provide the data used in the classroom activities during the second half of the semester as described in the previous section.

Weekly factory performance metrics are computed and posted in a public place so that factory performance can be viewed by all students and observers, whether or not they are direct participants in the project. These metrics include total sales shipments, customer service level (percent of customer orders shipped on time and complete), overtime hours worked in the facility, work in process inventory, finished goods inventory, and total inventory. Factory performance for several previous semesters is available so that students can see their performance relative to previous classes and to periods in which the instructor and graduate assistant were managing the factory. The formal performance assessment of each student at the conclusion of the project includes both individual performance and factory performance.

Project results continually show that successful management of the virtual factory requires more than simple content knowledge of operations management tools and techniques presented in textbooks. The dynamics of the virtual enterprise require students to deal with uncertainties and ambiguities, to make decisions in real time, and to coordinate their activities and understand how their roles and operations management decisions are interrelated. Successful completion of the project requires not only technical competence in operations management and expertise in using enterprise software, but also teamwork, communication, and leadership.

Overall Effectiveness of the Approach

There are a number of indicators that the use of enterprise software to teach OM as described above is effective. Three indicators discussed below include the success of former students, continuing support from the business community, and external recognition from academic and professional societies.

Student participants in the project have been well received in the job market, and many report that their hands-on experience with enterprise systems was a major factor in attracting interest from potential employers. Many former students hold positions of major responsibility in manufacturing firms, and have supported the program through donations and testimonials.

In the twenty years that the project has been under development, over $1.5 million in hardware, software, and support services has been donated by industrial partners and supporters. The project began in the mid 1980s with assistance from IBM, who provided MAPICS II software running on an IBM System 36 minicomputer. The project evolved with later versions of MAPICS designed for the AS400 series of IBM computers. Various software packages such as JOBSCOPE and FACTOR have been donated and utilized in the manufacturing simulation as the project evolved. Recent support from Microsoft Business Solutions has facilitated more of a total enterprise approach that integrates the virtual factory with accounting courses at Clemson, as described in the "Future Trends" section below. This continuing and evolving industrial support is an indicator of the relevance of the approach, and has enabled the project to stay on the cutting edge of information technology.

The project has also received significant external recognition through formal awards from academic and professional societies and business organizations, including the Decision Sciences Institute, the Academy of Business, and Microsoft Business Solutions, as well as special recognition from the Carnegie Foundation for the Advancement of Teaching and the Council for the Advancement and Support of Education (CASE). In addition, instructors in the project have won numerous teaching awards from campus student groups.

FUTURE TRENDS

Integration of topics in the business curriculum is likely to be more important in the future as firms continue to rely on enterprise systems to link activities and processes internally and with external suppliers and customers. Enterprise systems are a potentially important resource for collegiate schools of business because they facilitate meaningful integration in the curriculum. As the operations management project described in this chapter continues to evolve, efforts have been undertaken to utilize the virtual manufacturing enterprise in other business courses as well.

The first step in this process involves various accounting courses at Clemson University. Daily operational decision making and transaction processing in the virtual manufacturing enterprise generate accounting data that are examined and processed in a number of different accounting courses. Introductory accounting courses use the ongoing live model to illustrate business events that are discussed in accounting texts, while intermediate accounting students work on financial problems that occur in the virtual enterprise and develop accounting adjustments as needed. This provides opportunities for accounting instructors to address issues involving asset purchases, accounts receivable write-offs, mortgage loan amortizations, and other problems, all in a dynamic environment created by the virtual manufacturing enterprise.

A logical extension of these activities is the development of courses that combine teams of management, accounting, and other business students working together to manage the virtual enterprise. This type of across-course integration could be the wave of the future in business schools, and it will likely blur the boundaries between traditional courses in functional areas of business such as operations, accounting, finance, marketing, and human resources. Such activities require careful planning to ensure that the body of knowledge in each functional area is clearly identified, the learning objectives are clear, and student participants have sufficient content knowledge to engage in their assigned role in the virtual enterprise and benefit from the experience. The enterprise system technology to accomplish this is readily available — the challenge is for business schools to develop meaningful ways to employ it.

CONCLUSION

An approach to teaching operations management has been presented in which enterprise software brings to life key issues in managing the production operations of a business. A key feature of the approach is the realism created by using enterprise software to operate the virtual factory in an ongoing, real-time mode in which various operations management issues related to customer service, inventory, scheduling, and capacity occur simultaneously. The approach provides a way to enhance understanding of operations management topics, as well as a vehicle for students to better understand the integration of operations management with other functional areas of business such as accounting, finance, and marketing. An important by-product of the approach is the hands-on experience students receive with enterprise software that is widely used in the business world.

REFERENCES

Cannon, D. M., Klein, H. A., Koste, L. L., & Magal, S. R. (2004). Curriculum integration using enterprise resource planning: An integrative case approach. *Journal of Education for Business, 80*(2), 93-101.

Hitt, L. M., Wu, D. J., & Zhou, X. (2002). Investment in enterprise resource planning: Business impact and productivity measures. *Journal of Management Information Systems, 19*(1), 71-98.

LaForge, R. L., & Busing, M. E. (1998). The use of industrial software to create experiential learning activities in operations management courses. *Production and Operations Management, 7*(3), 325-334.

Mabert, V. A., Soni, A., & Venkataramanan, M. A. (2000). Enterprise resource planning survey of U.S. manufacturing firms. *Production & Inventory Management Journal, 41*(2), 52-58.

Manetti, J. (2001). How technology is transforming manufacturing. *Production & Inventory Management Journal, 42*(1), 54-64.

Rondeau, P. J., & Litteral, L. A. (2001). Evolution of manufacturing planning and control systems: from reorder point to enterprise resources planning. *Production & Inventory Management Journal, 42*(2), 1-7.

Chapter X

Using SAP for SCM Applications and Design:
A Study of the Supply Chain Management Process

Mahesh Sarma, Miami University, USA

David C. Yen, Miami University, USA

ABSTRACT

In order to maintain a competitive position in today's marketplace, companies must demand a greater level of enterprise efficiency. In today's rapidly changing market, experts argue that it is no longer about becoming a powerhouse but simply about remaining competitive. That is why automating and linking the supply chain has become so imperative. Supply chain management systems link all of the company's customers, suppliers, factories, warehouses, distributors, carriers, and trading partners. These systems integrate all the key business processes across the supply chain of a company. This chapter explains the objectives of supply chain management and how SAP's supply chain management system helps companies fulfill these objectives.

INTRODUCTION

Supply chain management is the delivery of customer and economic value through integrated management of the flow of physical goods and associated information, from raw materials sourcing to delivery of finished products to consumers (Viradix, 2005). There are many enterprise resource planning (ERP) and supply chain management (SCM) vendors in the market. Some of these vendors design ERP packages while some design SCM packages.

However, looking at the definition of supply chain management previously given, it sounds a lot like what an ERP system does. However, the difference between ERP and SCM systems is in the detail. Usually, SCM systems provide companies with planning capabilities for their supply chain. SCM systems can not only plan the supply chain but it can optimize the whole supply chain so that all the business processes are linked together to form part of one single activity. It does so because it can look at the demand, supply and the constraints simultaneously and then find an optimal solution. Traditional ERP vendors have started developing and supplying SCM solutions in order to gain a foothold in the SCM market. This chapter will look at the details of a SCM system more specifically SAP's SCM system.

The purpose of this chapter is to study the different features and functionalities in an SCM system. Users of this chapter will be able to understand the various modules in a SCM system and how these modules are used across the supply chain by different departments. Users will also be able to understand the flow of data, the underlying business processes, how the data is stored and retrieved and how the same data can be used by both an ERP and an SCM system. The objective of this chapter is to focus on the business processes in the SCM system. People reading this chapter will be able to understand how the SCM process actually works. Integrated systems usually have centralized databases and this allows for the free flow of information. Any activity that takes place somewhere in the supply chain affects the other activities someplace else in the supply chain. This chapter will look at how these activities are linked together to form part of one big picture.

This chapter can be used by the users to start understanding the different parts of a supply chain management system and how this system can be used in different business activities. Usually, SCM implementations are very complicated because it involves integrating the business processes of more than one company. By understanding the business processes in one company, users will be able to better understand how the business processes work in other companies and how these processes can be integrated. They will also know the different data that is used in an SCM system. The best way to use this chapter is to understand the business process explained in this chapter and then try to implement it on an actual system. By doing this, users will be able to understand the important details of a SCM system. The intended audiences for this chapter are the faculty and students in schools interested in learning about a SCM system. People involved in implementing a supply chain management system can use this chapter as a starting point for understanding the business processes that take place in a supply chain. Most importantly, this chapter can be used by beginners just starting to work on the system as a reference in understanding the different departments involved in a supply chain. This chapter can be used in any course teaching the concepts of ERP and SCM systems. The SCM process is important for any company and users have to know what happens in an SCM process. Learning about an SCM system will give the users an idea of how business transactions occur within a company and how the data from these transactions is sent upstream and downstream to the company's suppliers and customers respectively.

Since there are many vendors who provide supply chain management systems, it is difficult to explain all the supply chain management systems in detail. So, this chapter will focus on SAP's supply chain management system. This chapter starts off with an introduction to supply chain management and SAP's SCM system. It explains the different modules in SAP's SCM system and then takes a look at the different business processes in an SCM system. It looks at the different departments involved in a supply chain and tries to explain how these departments can use SAP's SCM system to add value to the organization. In conclusion, it looks at the future trends in the industry and how these trends are helping companies change the way they do business.

From an academic point of view, this chapter can also be used as a case study for instructional purposes. Instructors can use this chapter to explain the concepts of supply chain management and to explain how the different operations in a supply chain come together so that companies can deliver the right products to the right customers at the right time. The supply chain management course can be conducted over the period of a semester with a class size of typically 35 students. These students should have a basic understanding of the different departments in a company and should have an idea of the business processes within a company. However, this knowledge is not essential as students should be able to pick up any details that they do not understand just by reading this chapter. A very important point to be noted is that this course covers the different parts of the supply chain and how all these parts are used together by companies to tighten their supply chains. This course does not go into the practical aspects of the supply chain (i.e., it does not explain how to actually use a supply chain management software). It is up to the discretion of the instructor to incorporate practical exercises using supply chain management software. Please note that the chapter explains the topics that are covered in the course but instructors may have to use additional readings or exercises to explain each module of the course in more detail. Another point to be noted is that there are many SCM softwares available in the market and this course primary uses SAP's supply chain management system to explain the concepts associated with a supply chain. Again, it is up to the discretion of the instructors to use any software that they think will explain the supply chain management concepts. Though it is possible to explain the concepts in supply chain management without the use of any softwares, SAP's SCM system is used here so that students have a better understanding of how exactly an information system is used to handle the supply chain of any organization. In most modules of the course, the course theory and the module itself are linked together, that is, the theoretical aspects of the course are linked and explained together with some of the systems used in SCM systems so that students have a better understanding of how supply chain management systems (information systems) are used in order to improve an organization's supply chain. Much of the concepts are explained using modules of an actual SCM system. However, students will be able to understand the theoretical aspects of a supply chain. They will learn about the different departments in a company involved in the supply chain and how these departments work together to create more efficiency. They will also be able to understand what the different tools are offered by software vendors to manage a company's supply chain. The different modules that are covered in the course are as listed below. Each module is explained in detail in the topics that follow. Each module explains in detail the theoretical aspects associated with the particular part of the supply chain and then tries to explain how students are able to benefit from this information.

1.   Background Information
2.   Concepts in Supply Chain Management
    a.   Supply Chain Planning
       (i)   Demand Planning
       (ii)   Advanced Planning and Scheduling
       (iii) Transportation Planning and Vehicle Scheduling
    b.   Business Procurement
    c.   Warehousing and Distribution

BACKGROUND INFORMATION

Supply chain management involves coordinating and integrating the business flows both within and among companies. Thus, supply chain management can be viewed as a pipeline for the efficient and effective flow of products/materials, services, information, and financials from the suppliers' suppliers through the various intermediate organizations/ companies out to the customers' customers. The inbound and outbound logistics are very important components of the supply chain and this helps in making any company financially viable. Supply chain management (SCM) integrates marketing, sales, and manufacturing with logistics. The integration of each business function helps to reduce lead times, making companies with supply chain management systems more competitive in the marketplace. However, implementing supply chain management systems involves spending a lot of time and money. Companies have the option of creating their own SCM system, but it makes more sense for companies to buy an SCM system from a vendor and then get it customized according to their needs. Many companies offer complete supply chain management systems, which can be used by companies without too much customization.

Though all these companies offer supply chain software, this chapter focuses on the supply chain management system offered by systems, applications, and products (SAP) in order to explain the different concepts associated with the supply chain. The advantage of SAP's SCM system is that it uses an adaptive supply chain network. What this means is that this network consists of many customer-focused companies that share resources and knowledge so they can better adapt to changing market conditions (SAP). These supply chain networks connect all the operations within a company like planning, manufacturing, distribution, etc and the data within these departments is visible immediately so decisions can be made and carried out immediately. The results are cost reduction, productivity gains, and higher profit margins. This chapter will focus on how a supply chain management (SCM) system helps companies fulfill its objectives. We will also look at some SCM components, look at the various business processes that can take place in a supply chain and see how these components fulfill those business processes. The main objective of SCM is to get the right product to the right place at the right time and at the right price. Some of the other broad objectives of SCM are to:

- Reduce lead times
- Increase customer satisfaction by providing products and services at the lowest possible cost

- Reduce operating expenses
- Understand the value chain and understand and eliminate those activities, which do not add value to the company's business processes
- Share information both up and down the supply chain in real-time
- Have accurate and flexible operations, which can be totally integrated with the suppliers' value chain

All these objectives can be achieved in a supply chain if information about product demand and service requirements is shared within the shortest possible time. These objectives arise out of the need to eliminate the "bullwhip effect." In the bullwhip effect, relatively small fluctuations in the actual demand among consumers is magnified through the supply chain which in turn has negative effects on the planning of transportation of the products and services and also on the production of the company's products.

Figure 1 explains how there is a distortion of demand information as this information passes up the supply chain and this is the bullwhip effect. The supply chain in the figure consists of customer, retailer, wholesaler, and supplier. The curve in the figure is the demand information that is received by each component of the supply chain.

Figure 1. The bullwhip effect — a distortion in demand

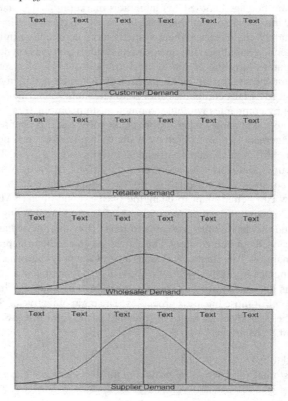

One of the main causes of the bullwhip effect is the break in the sharing of information between the different partners in the supply chain. Some of the solutions for reducing the bullwhip effect are to have real-time data up and down the supply chain, have just-in-time supply, reduce lead times, and so forth. Companies have come up with many solutions to reduce the bullwhip effect and to share information between the different partners of their supply chain. One of the solutions is to have an efficient and responsive supply chain system, which will integrate the different parts of the company's supply chain. However, just knowing that there is a bullwhip effect taking place is not the most important thing. Companies have to understand and change their business processes in order to reduce or eliminate this effect. Though it is important to understand the ramifications of the bullwhip effect and its possible solutions, it is more important to understand how supply chain management works within a company. There are many business processes, which take place when a company receives an order or wants to purchase an item from a supplier. In order to understand how supply chain management works, it is necessary to look at the various business processes within a company because it helps users understand how the flow of information takes place up and down the supply chain.

This is the background information that is explained to the students over the first week of the course. This helps the students understand the objectives of the course, that is, understanding how a company manages its supply chain. This background information helps the students to understand what the objectives of a supply chain management are and why companies decide to implement supply chain management systems. Please note that the topics in the rest of the chapter covers the theoretical aspects of the course (i.e., the topics that are taught to students).

CONCEPTS IN SUPPLY CHAIN MANAGEMENT

As previously explained, the main use of a supply chain management system is to link all of the company's customers, suppliers, factories, warehouses, distributors, carriers, and trading partners in one virtual enterprise. By doing this, a company can use an SCM solution to achieve a competitive advantage and broaden its profit margin. By providing greater visibility throughout the supply chain — from planning and procurement to point-of-purchase — businesses can reduce expenditures, improve operational efficiency, and respond more quickly to customer demands (Borck, 2001). A supply chain management system should have the capability to plan, implement and control any strategy that is necessary to advance the company's objectives. What this means is that the system should be able to respond to the corporate strategy (i.e., the SCM plan should be in sync with the plans of all the other departments in the company). The system should be good enough to put the plan into action (i.e., implementation should not be too much of an effort). The system should also be able to carry out checks of the processes and inform the personnel whether the plan was good or not and whether it was properly implemented.

Supply Chain Planning

The first thing to be done in any supply chain system is to have the capability to plan the supply chain functions. A supply chain planning system should house the functionalities to schedule and monitor all the processes that are necessary in the planning phase. It should also have a single common database and several modules that share this common database.

It should also provide the visualization capabilities for planning the inter- and intra-company logistical networks. All this is explained to the students using SAP's advanced planning and optimizer (APO). The different modules used in supply chain planning softwares are explained using SAP's software. The graphical user interface for SCM planning softwares in the SAP environment is explained to the students as given next:

- **Supply chain cockpit (SCC):** The SCC module is like the graphical user interface of SAP's SCM initiative. It consists of built in algorithms that can be used to optimize company networks. With the help of these algorithms, modeling of any logistics network [based on nodes (locations) and arcs (transportation lanes)] can be carried out and different business scenarios can be evaluated. It also has pre-defined exception conditions. When these conditions occur, the SCC sends a message to the workers or managers informing them of the problem in the business scenario. Since the SCC can be used to model a logistics network using advanced algorithms, managers can use these algorithms to access demand forecasts and to create business plans based on the supply and demand in each individual business unit (node). The detailed version of the SCC can be used for scheduling and control of products, which can then be assigned to specific locations.

Figure 2 explains a supply chain cockpit with locations and transportation lanes. It shows how the different parts of a supply chain are linked together. It also shows that information and materials can be passed through any part of the supply chain.

Figure 2. A supply chain cockpit with locations and transportation lanes (Knolmayer & Zeier, 2002)

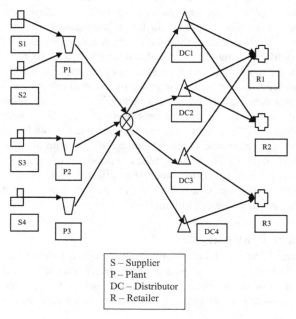

S – Supplier
P – Plant
DC – Distributor
R – Retailer

Supply chain planning consists of demand planning, advanced planning and scheduling and transportation planning and vehicle scheduling.

- **Demand planning:** Given the constraints within each company, the ability to forecast demand is one of the key functions in any SCM system. The demand planning sub-module in a supply chain is used to forecast the products that will be sold in the market. Then a sales plan is generated for any particular market. This forecasting and sales plan creation may be based on historical data collected over the years. This data can be taken from a business warehouse, point-of-sale systems, or online analytical processing servers providing the users with functionalities of data analysis. The demand planning is done based on the collaborative planning, forecasting and replenishment (CPFR) model. This model and in turn the demand planning sub-module is based on the idea of reducing the bullwhip effect (i.e., the effect of any problem at one end of the supply chain felt at some other end of the supply chain). If companies in the supply chain improve coordination and avoid multiple administration and repeated use of planning methods and databases, they can reduce the bullwhip effect. This increases the coordination between the different partners of the supply chain and helps them to make decisions which can benefit the whole chain. With demand planning systems in place, the supply chain partners are able to develop an outline plan in which core process activities can be assigned to the participating companies. These companies then jointly prepare a forecast of the consumers' demands. This forecast serves as a basis for the schedules to be agreed on. Finally, the partners try to avoid inappropriate schedules in the material flow.
- **Advanced planning and scheduling (APS):** This sub-module contains functions by which different planning methods for different time zones can be examined and appropriate steps taken. It consists of supply network planning which determines the procurement, production and distribution schedules. It also determines the optimal quantities that can be shipped and the advantages of using external suppliers. The APS also consists of deployment functionalities which can be used to determine the optimal usage of existing distribution and transport resources taking into account all the constraints. Finally, it contains the production planning and detailed scheduling system which is used to plan the sequence of the production and the scheduling of orders. This can be done with a very high amount of accuracy usually with accuracies as high as 99% (Morris, 2000).

Figure 3 explains the different parts of the advanced planning and scheduling cycle. It starts off with a company planning their supply chain model and setting the limitations and constraints. The company then defines its different locations for supplying products. It then prepares a sales forecast, that is, deciding the amount it plans to sell. It then determines the parameters for its sales plan, that is, the limitations for sales and distribution, then it looks at the orders that it gets and then compares the actual orders to its sales forecast. It then executes its orders. By comparing its actual and forecasted orders, it is then able to fine-tune its supply chain so that the next time around, it is able to try and equate demand and supply for its goods and services.

- **Transportation planning and vehicle scheduling (TP/VS):** The TP/VS sub-module helps in the simultaneous consideration of transportation constraints using the company's

Figure 3. APS cycle (Knolmayer & Zeier, 2002)

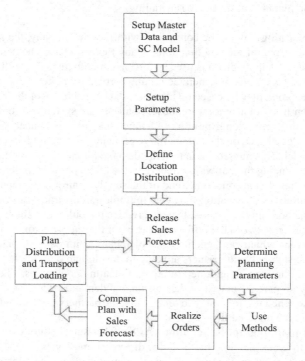

transport fleet or using external carriers. This module allows different members of the supply chain to design their transportation activities in such a way that everybody benefits because of the optimal use of transport loads, routes and carriers.

- **Available-to-promise (ATP):** The ATP sub-module can be used to investigate whether a promised delivery can be made. It can be used to determine whether an existing order can be fulfilled accurately. It takes into account all the market forces and determines the most favorable result for both the company and the customer. It works on the principle that the customer is always right and that the customer has to be satisfied under any circumstances.

By learning about the different aspects of supply chain planning, students are able to get an idea of the different terms factors involved in supply chain planning. They are able to grasp the fact that just to plan a supply chain; a company has to plan many different factors like demand and transportation. They are also able to understand the fact that implementation of a supply chain management system involves understanding the factors involved in the demand of a product. They understand that in order for a product to reach the customer the company has to start the supply chain in the planning stage and then move over to the execution stage.

Business Procurement

In today's business world, companies need to get raw materials at the right time so that they do now have to maintain excess inventory. Companies are realizing the importance of linking their processes to those of their suppliers so that there is free flow of information. By doing this, suppliers will be able to supply materials needed by the company at exactly the time that the company needs those materials. This concept is explained using SAP's business-to-business procurement module. The business-to-business module takes care of the electronic support for the procurement of goods and services and helps in integrating the purchasing process into the overall flow of goods and information. The advantage of this module is that purchases can be made by individual members of the company using the Internet from their own workplace. Since these tasks can be carried out by individual members of the company, the actual purchasing department can use their time on making strategic decisions beneficial to the company. This module can be used to control and monitor the purchasing process. Since the purchase orders are made by individual members without involving the purchasing department, the receipt of goods is streamlined. This also helps in making the invoicing and payment tasks simpler. It can also be used to connect various product catalogs so that there is a direct interaction between a purchasers and suppliers. This is based on the principle of free market economy where the order is one by the company, which offers the lowest price and the best quality product.

Figure 4 depicts a sales order process from demand of the product to the invoice. This sales order is fulfilled by the company by ordering products from its suppliers using and online catalog on the Internet. This is again linked to an internal ERP system within the company so that there is free flow of information between the different departments of the company.

Warehousing and Distribution

Once the company receives the raw materials and produces finished goods, it has to supply those goods to the customers where and when they need it. The company needs to have a good inventory management system in its warehouses and logistics system so that

Figure 4. Procurement of parts using the Internet (Knolmayer & Zeier, 2002)

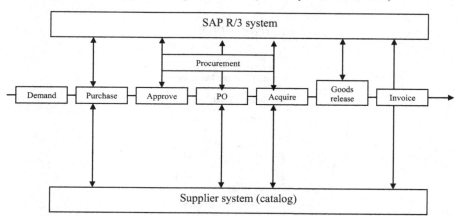

it does not have to maintain excess inventory while at the same time is able to supply its products to customers at the right time. This is the concept that is explained using SAP's logistics execution system (LES). The logistics execution system helps in efficient ware-housing and distribution using the warehouse management system (WMS) and the transport management system (TMS). The warehouse management system supports the use of various warehouse equipment like rack storage areas. This system is used to monitor the movements in the warehouse and for the management of warehousing activities like unloading, packing, dispatching loading vehicles to the appropriate ramps and the printing of necessary docu-ments. It is also used to maintain the inventory in the warehouse. When dangerous materials have to be handled, this system can be used for creating the regulations and circumstances for the handling of these materials. Warehousing technologies include the use of wireless terminals and mobile barcode scanners. SAP R/3 provides a tool called the radio frequency component which uses radio frequency terminals with scanning devices attached so that the data can be accurately and immediately transferred. These radio frequency terminals have the advantage that they can be mounted almost anywhere and that they receive the data directly from the SAP R/3 system.

The transport management system uses the plans and ideas developed in the transport planning and vehicle scheduling (TP/VS) system and using these ideas helps in providing the functionalities for scheduling, shipping, route planning, calculating freight charges and handling of the products. The transport management system also helps in selecting the best transport companies, determines the best possible routes for transporting materials and helps in scheduling the shipping of the materials. This system takes into account the various constraints imposed on the transportation process because of the nature of the goods being transported and gives the user the best possible solution. It takes into consideration the fact that transportation costs signify the largest portion of costs in any logistical system and so calculates the transportation costs in such a way that these costs are always minimized. It relies on the Internet to communicate with the suppliers and the customers and so can be used to transfer appropriate data in the minimal time possible.

Though the section above gives the user an idea of the different components that can be utilized to effectively fulfill some supply chain objectives, it is still not sufficient. It is more important to understand the flow of business processes within a company. The flow of business processes within a company can be integrated with the help of an enterprise resource

Figure 5. Porter's generic value chain (Porter, 1985)

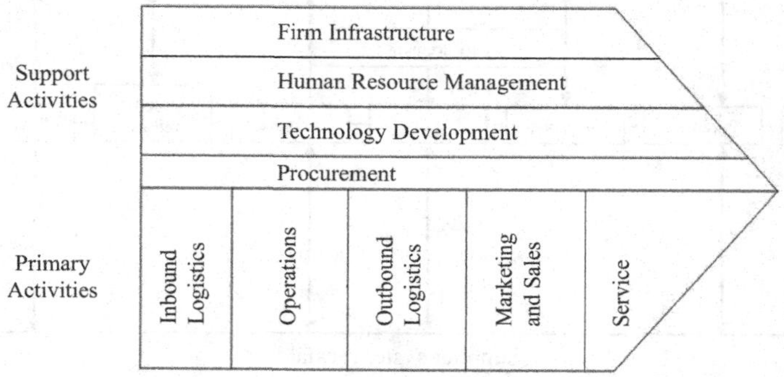

planning (ERP) system. Though the ERP system will help to link the different departments within a company, the necessary information has to be transmitted to the company's supply chain partners so that there is a smooth flow of information to suppliers and customers. A company can have all the resources and systems but a system that is implemented on top of a flawed business process is bound to fail and in the long run, create even more problems for the company. In order to implement a good supply chain system, a company has to know which business processes can be improved and then think about how to go about it.

THE BUSINESS PROCESSES
IN A SUPPLY CHAIN

The first step to study the company's business process is to understand the company's value chain. The value chain can be seen as a necessary tool for identifying the areas where a company can gain a competitive advantage over its rivals (Porter, 1985). Every firm can be broken down into a series of activities or categories that start at the design of the product and ends with customer support. By looking at each and every detail in terms of the value chain, a company will be able to understand its business process and identify potential sources where it can gain an advantage over its competitors.

Figure 5 depicts the value chain for a company with primary activities that process inputs and produce outputs and the support activities which support the primary activities.

A company's value chain can be divided into primary and support activities. The primary activities are concerned with manufacturing, sale and distribution of the product and can be divided into five categories viz. inbound logistics concerned with inventory, transportation, product returns etc, operations concerned with manufacturing etc, outbound logistics concerned with orders, deliveries etc, marketing and sales concerned with marketing the product or service and service concerned with customer service activities. The support activities support the primary activities and consist of procurement, human resources, technology, and procurement. These activities are again broken down further into different business processes and by understanding these business processes, a company can focus on the area it wants to improve.

Figure 6 illustrates the different departments within a company and the various activities that take place in each department. It depicts how information flows from one department to the other in order to fulfill the sales order. This shows the value chain thinking in action.

Using all the components of a supply chain management given above, a company will be able to design its network and supply chain effectively. However, the design part has to be followed by proper execution of the design. In order to maintain a competitive advantage, a company has to be able to improvise depending on the fluctuations in demand for its products and services. In order to understand how the supply chain works, let us look at the different departments that process the sales order and which ends with the delivery of the products to the customer. By looking at this process, students are able to understand the different processes within a supply chain and also have a general overview of different departments and its functions within a company and how the different SCM and ERP modules help these departments do their job more effectively and efficiently. Logistics, scheduling transportation and materials, procurement from external suppliers, warehousing, inventory management, production, and so forth are some of the areas in a supply chain. But the supply chain also includes areas like product design, sales, procurement, production and distribution.

Figure 6. Value chain thinking (Curran, 2000)

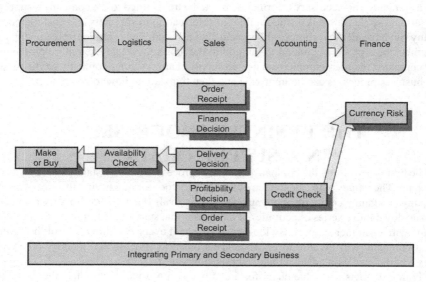

Product Design and Development

Product design and development is one of the most important activities carried out within a company. This includes research and development (R&D), design of the product and so forth. The reason why this part is so important because the data developed initially is sent to different systems to be used. For example: the bill of material (BOM) is sent to the materials resource planning (MRP) module, design data is sent to the computer aided design (CAD) systems and so forth. It is always better to have people from different companies and if possible employees from supplier and customer firms to work together in the design and development of a product. Having different people from different companies and departments in the development stage is beneficial because it will save the company time and money on the modifications of the products, if and when it comes up. Customers have their own preferences for products and this is always the main concern for the sales and marketing teams. Therefore, it is necessary to introduce a few variations in the products so that the customer is fully satisfied. However, by introducing variations in the product, the cost for the companies increases. This happens because it is difficult to forecast the demand for the products with variations, there may be differentiations in the logistics part and so forth. So it is always better to introduce these variations as late in the production process as possible. This concept is explained using SAP's product variant structure (PVS). Students are able to understand the importance of having standardized products as far as possible so that companies are able to cut down on their expenses and as a result, increase their profits. "In SAP, the Product Variant Structure (PVS) can be used to describe the different types of variants. PVS provides filter mechanisms to define function specific variants of products and structures" (Knolmayer & Zeier, 2002).

In Figure 7, each triangle is a part produced by the company and the circles next to the triangles represent the variations in the product. It shows how even though different products can be linked together during design and manufacturing, the variations are separate and may require a separate assemble line which in turn costs the company additional time and resources.

"Every triangle represents a part and points placed next to triangles indicates an alternative" (Knolmayer & Zeier, 2002). In addition to product variations, computer aided design (CAD) systems are used to develop the product. For product design, students are introduced to the CAD interface so that they understand that an SCM system contains not only the planning and execution components of the supply chain but also the design components of the supply chain. The SAP system includes an open CAD interface. It can be used to link different CAD systems so that the data needed to design the product and materials can be taken directly from the SAP system. After the design part of the system, students are explained that an SCM system also has components for documentation and project management. This is explained using SAP's product data management (PDM) sub-module. This sub-module helps in administering the documentation, master data for product classifications and project management.

Sales

Sales is another area which is very important to optimizing the supply chain. Among other things, sales include the pre-sale activities, the actual sales order, delivery, and customer relationship management.

The aim of marketing is to increase the customer base and at the same time reduce the costs of marketing the products to customers. This can be done by targeting specific customers, which reduces the costs of customer visits. The best way to do this is to tap into a large database and select customers to be targeted. Data mining can be used to create customer groups and identify patterns of customers within existing groups. It can also be used

Figure 7. Visualization of the product variant structure (Knolmayer & Zeier, 2002); triangle — part, point — alternative

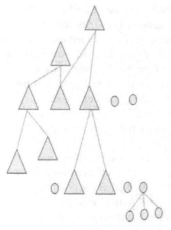

to forecast marketing strategies by looking at patterns between complimentary products. For example: companies selling furniture will be able to forecast future sales by looking at customers who purchase a house based on the fact that people who buy a house may at some time in the future decide to purchase furniture. Companies can target these customers for specific marketing strategies. SAP has included many marketing strategies like one-to-one marketing, data mining etc in its mySAP customer relationship management (CRM) module. Data mining can be run on a data warehouse for better results.

Depending on the number of customers in a company, recording a customer enquiry and processing customer quotations may be very important from the company's point of view. This is so because there are many quotations that may have to be processed every day and if the company can use standard quotation elements for processing quotations, it will be able to save a lot of money. Since the quotations involves taking data from materials management, customer master data and inventory management, it is important for the company to have a good system in place for developing quotations. This forms an important part of knowledge management. A data warehouse can contain data from many different sources and this data can be drawn upon to create new quotations.

In Figure 8, each box represents a factor to be considered for a sales quotation while the boxes above the original boxes represent the data within the different factors. This figure explains how data is drawn from different sources within the company to create new quotations.

Large, multinational corporations have a range of products and some of these products are designed even if there is no customer demand for these products or if the customer is not willing to pay enough for these products. In such cases, companies use something called product costing which depends on the maximum price a customer is willing to pay for a product rather than the costs of manufacturing the product. Depending on the market requirements, the products are designed and the maximum price that the customer is willing to pay is taken into account. Since the customer is not willing to go beyond a specific price, the company and its suppliers have to come up with ways to reduce the costs of developing and transporting the product. This involves a high degree of coordination between the different parts of the supply chain. Product costing can be carried out with the help of SAP's project system (PS) (Knolmayer & Zeier, 2002). Depending on the maximum allowable limits for the costs in the different business processes, the system generates messages when these limits are exceeded. This system is customized according to the customer requirements which help in building the customer base. Another way of providing total customer satisfaction is to introduce the concept of mass customization. Mass customization can take place successfully only when there is a free flow of information between the suppliers, the company, and the customers. If this happens, as soon as the customer places the order, it triggers an assemble-to-order process and by doing this, companies will be able to satisfy even the smallest customer demand thereby increasing its customer base. SAP provides the "Order Entry with configuration" system in which data is directly entered into the SAP system using the Internet and which triggers the production process immediately (Knolmayer & Zeier, 2002).

When an order is received from a customer, there are many checks that have to be performed before the order can be processed. If the customer requires a customized product, then checks have to be performed to see whether the company can manufacture the product on time and deliver it to the customer. Credit checks have to be performed in order to see whether the customer has a good credit standing with the company. SAP has credit man-

Figure 8. Checklist for quotation selection (Knolmayer & Zeier, 2002)

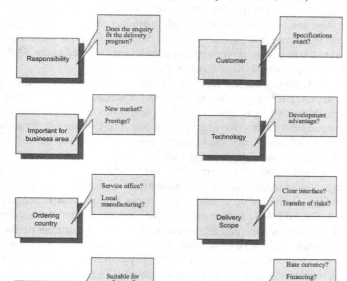

agement functionalities in the sales and distribution (SD) and the financial accounting (FI) modules. Also, these modules contain functionalities by which the customer can pay for the order using different kinds of payments. The important part here is that these systems are integrated with many different kinds of customer-centric systems and all the data is stored in a central database. Another check that has to be performed is whether the company will be able to meet the customers' required delivery date. If it does not, then the company has to schedule the production process and inform the customer accordingly of the new delivery date. In order to do this, it has to coordinate fully up and down the supply chains so that the production process and the logistics process can work simultaneously in tandem with each other. SAP permits the planned delivery time to be calculated depending on the availability of a product by calculating the inventory, production capabilities, resources, and so forth. It does this using the available-to-promise (ATP) module of the advanced planning and optimizer (APO) system. With the advent of the Internet, communication between different companies has become a lot easier and if a company has business customers (B2B e-commerce), then it can use the Internet to communicate with its business partners. Electronic trading exchanges and portals are one of the best ways to interact with business partners. SAP has developed the business-to-business procurement solution which uses the Internet for communication (Knolmayer & Zeier, 2002). "The Internet helps companies in the obtaining the raw materials, processing sales orders, the billing process, and so forth. In addition to this, e-commerce has grown on a large scale and has become a widely used form of selling products and services. Online stores are a predominant way of getting in touch with the customers and making a sale. This involves credit card transactions online and security measures like secure socket layer (SSL) and digital signatures are of paramount importance" (Knolmayer & Zeier, 2002). The SAP online store can be used to create an online product catalog on a company's Web site on the Internet (Knolmayer & Zeier, 2002). The data entered by customers on the Web site is transferred to a transaction server and this in turn is transferred to the SAP database where these orders are processed (Knolmayer & Zeier, 2002).

After the order is processed, it is necessary to have a good customer service system which involves the products to be stocked in stores and how much space to allocate to each item, good replenishment systems, good marketing and promotion systems and efficient new product introduction systems (Knolmayer & Zeier, 2002). Value can be added to the value chain only when all these things can be implemented correctly and this can occur only when there is total trust between the suppliers, the company, and the customers and when there is free flow of information in all parts of the supply chain. This can take place when the vendor manages the inventory so that any fluctuations in customer demand are directly visible in the vendor systems and by which the vendor can take immediate action to satisfy customer demand. The SAP APO system provides the tools for vendor managed inventory (VMI) and which is a very popular and efficient way of satisfying customer needs. In order to take care of customer needs, SAP offers tools to the sales people in a company as part of its mySAP customer relationship management (CRM) system. The sales people are able to retrieve to customer data anywhere from the data warehouse. They are also able to configure products based on a customer's needs and run queries and reports on the data warehouse in order to extract the exact data that they want.

Procurement

Procurement is an important part of the supply chain because only when the raw materials arrive on time is the company able to start producing the products. In procurement, it is very important to have a close relationship between the sales departments and the purchasing department. By sharing information, the demand can be anticipated by the sales department and this can be transmitted to purchasing which can take the necessary steps to procure the materials needed to complete an order. Just-in-time procurement and vendor managed inventory (VMI) are two methods by which companies can cut down on procurement lead times and fulfill customer orders. The advent of the Internet has greatly enhanced the way companies procure raw materials from its suppliers. By having a direct line of communication with its suppliers, a company is able to share demand information with these suppliers. By using procurement portals over the Internet, a company is able to provide a single point of access for its suppliers and at the same time share information cheaply using the Internet. The SAP business-to-business (B2B) component allows all the procurement tasks and activities to be conducted over the Internet. It also allows product catalogs to be offered over the Internet.

Figure 9 explains how users use Web browsers to access and search a company's online store. This search is done using a search engine on the company's online store and this search engine is linked to the company's product catalog and the company's online database in order to retrieve customer queries in the shortest possible time.

Good procurement techniques come into effect when all the parts of the supply chain including all the systems are linked together to form part of a big, cohesive system. This will allow the free flow of information between all parts of the supply chain and will go a long way in adding value to the value chain of a company.

Figure 10 shows how the different components of an information system are linked together right from an online store to the company (its value chain) and the different components of its SCM system. This results in a free flow of information up and down the supply chain.

Production

Once all the materials are available, the production process has to be started. The main goals of production are to reduce the lead times, to manage inventory in the production process and utilize all the resources efficiently (Knolmayer & Zeier, 2002). This can be achieved using the materials requirements planning (MRP) functionality in the production planning (PP) module. Projects can be managed using the project management (PS) system. It may so happen that a company may have different manufacturing facilities in different parts of the country or the world and it is necessary for the distribution of production to be partially or fully centralized. This will allow the company to get all the data required for production without the need to worry about where the data and materials are stored. However, MRP within standard ERP systems is used to plan the production within a company while SAP's advanced planning and optimizer (APO) provides algorithms that can be used to support the entire supply chain (Knolmayer & Zeier, 2002). The advanced planning and scheduling (APS) module provides much different functionality that can overcome the shortcomings of standard MRP systems. Production can also be improved using the Kanban and just-in-time systems. The production planning (PP) module in the SAP system supports the Kanban principle and this allows the external and internal procurement, production and supply from a warehouse (Knolmayer & Zeier, 2002). The SAP APO uses mathematical models which takes into account the problems in capacity planning, constraints in production, material stock-outs, inventory levels etc and tries to come up with an optimal solution that will allow the company to streamline its production process.

Figure 9. Use of the Alta Vista search engine in the SAP online store (Knolmayer & Zeier, 2002)

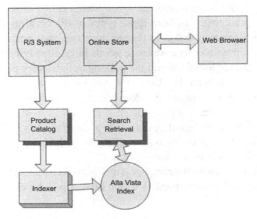

Figure 10. Cooperation of SAP components (Knolmayer & Zeier, 2002)

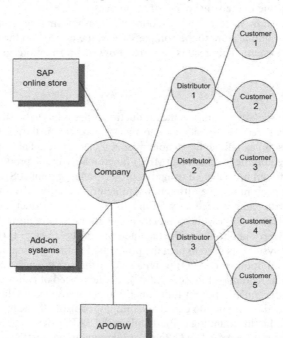

Distribution and Logistics

Once all the products, materials, and services are ready, it is necessary to package and distribute them to the company's warehouses and outlets and from there transport these products to the customers. Usually, products are supplied to the customers either from a central warehouse or from local warehouses. A systems called cross-docking distribution tries to combine the advantages of both these types of distribution (Knolmayer & Zeier, 2002). This works in such a way that even though goods are transported to warehouses, they pass through as fast as possible because these goods have already been assigned spaces in the warehouses and storage locations and the picking and delivery parts have already been decided. "This concept has been developed by Wal-Mart. The warehouses use laser-controlled transportation systems where barcodes indicate to which trucks the incoming goods have to be routed" (Knolmayer & Zeier, 2002).

Figure 11 explains the different options that a company has in order to distribute its products from its production facilities to its markets using different components like wholesalers and retailers who make up the supply chain.

The distribution systems include transport models which look at the optimal transportation techniques and route planning models which look at which vehicles should be used to satisfy demand. The SAP logistics execution system (LES) is an important component of the SCM system. Route planning is the trigger point in LES and by selecting the mode of transport; the resulting routes are calculated by the system. It also provides a graphical display of the planned routes on the screen for better visualization. It also includes distribution requirements planning systems, fleet management systems and shipment tracking systems. To determine where a company's vehicle is on the road at a given time, the fleet management systems are linked to global positioning systems (GPS). Using satellite technology, the exact location of a vehicle can be determined and this information is passed on to the customer using shipment tracking systems so that the customers know exactly where their ordered products are and the expected time of arrival of the products. For customer service, SAP also has a SAPPhone interface to provide data to call center personnel (Knolmayer & Zeier, 2002). "In addition, a help desk can be organized using SAP Call Center Components" (Knolmayer & Zeier, 2002). Logistics and distribution also involves reverse logistics by which goods that are damaged or not required by the customers can be returned back to the company. These goods travel up the supply chain and the system makes sure that this is done in the least possible time and at the minimum possible cost. The system automatically updates the data in all the modules of the ERP and SCM systems.

FUTURE TRENDS

The Internet is changing the way companies do business by providing a cheap and efficient form of communication. One of the most important trends to be noted is the convergence of ERP, SCM and CRM systems. Customers always like to have systems that compliment their existing systems for example; customers with SAP's ERP system prefer to have a supply chain management system developed by SAP so that they can be sure that both their systems will be compatible. So, ERP vendors are providing SCM and CRM solutions while SCM and CRM vendors are developing ERP solutions. In order to contain supply chain costs, it is necessary for companies to look beyond their existing borders and try and collaborate with different supply chain partners (Srikanth RP, 2003). Outsourcing has become very common in today's business world and companies look at ways to cut labor costs with outsourcing. Since companies outsource their business processes to different countries throughout the world, it has become all the more important to have an efficient and responsive supply chain to satisfy customer demand. Most companies have stand-alone business solutions for certain departments. However, companies are now realizing the benefits of having an integrated approach in which all the different software solutions are part of the same package. The Internet has made sure that geographical boundaries do not exist anymore and companies are able to track the cheapest suppliers anywhere in the world and also reach a customer anywhere in the world. This has led to a significant increase in the number of suppliers and also the number of customers. An increase in the number of suppliers and customers has led to an increase in the number of transactions carried out everyday. In order to maintain these transactions and gain a competitive advantage over their rivals, companies are investing in supply chain planning and supply chain execution systems. These systems not only help a company develop its customer base but also help in maintaining it over an extended period of time.

Figure 11. Options in planning of distribution systems (Knolmayer & Zeier, 2002)

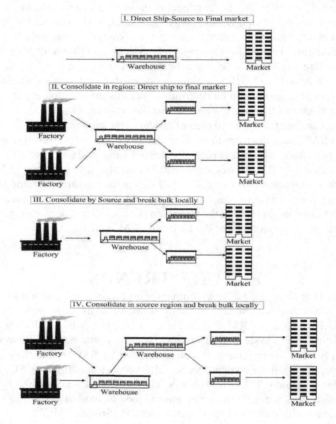

SUGGESTIONS TO LEARN THE
SUPPLY CHAIN MANAGEMENT PROCESS

There are many details, which the user can use in order to successfully learn the business processes involved in a supply chain. Some of these suggestions are:

1.   In order to understand how a supply chain works, users should try and understand the business processes in a supply chain.
2.   To understand the business processes in a supply chain, users can look at the business processes that take place within a company and try and understand those business processes. After understanding the business processes within a company, it will be easier to understand the processes that take place between two or more companies.
3.   There are many similarities in the transactions in an ERP system and an SCM system. If users are able to understand the transactions in an ERP system, they will also be able to understand the processes in an SCM system.

4.   A good way to learn how the system works is to actually work on the system. Users should try to implement what they learn in this chapter on an actual system.
5.   Another good way to learn about the SCM process is to create many companies within the system and carry out transactions between those companies.
6.   Before carrying out the transactions, users should try to use the design part of an SCM system. By using the different modules of a supply chain management system, users will be able to design their own supply chain between suppliers and customers.
7.   Once the supply chain is designed, users will be able to visualize how an actual supply chain looks like and how a change in one part of the supply chain affects all the different parts of the supply chain.

LESSONS LEARNED

There are many things that a user should be able to follow after going through this chapter. Users should:

1.   Understand the different modules in a SCM system and know how each module helps create an efficient supply chain
2.   Have an understanding of the business processes in a supply chain
3.   Understand how the SCM process and the processes within an ERP system are linked together
4.   Know how to fix the errors that may come up. By fixing these errors, users will be able to better understand the flow of data within the system
5.   Know the different departments that can be involved in a company's supply chain and how these departments can use the modules of an SCM system

STRENGTHS AND WEAKNESSES OF THE SYSTEM

Each system has its own strengths and weaknesses. Some of the strengths and weaknesses for a SCM system are listed next:

Strengths

1.   The main purpose of a training SCM system is that users can make mistakes and learn from the system rather than making a mistake during an actual implementation which can prove to be very expensive for the company.
2.   By understanding the different departments that can be involved in a supply chain, users will be able to grasp the significance of each department and focus on the business processes that interest them the most.
3.   By understanding the business processes, users can create their own companies and carry out transactions between those companies. Users will be able to learn the importance of having an efficient supply chain and know how a small change at one end of the supply chain is reflected at the other end.

Weaknesses

1.   The main problem with an SCM system is that users should have access to such a system. The design modules form an important part of the SCM system and users should be able to access those modules to learn how a supply chain can be designed from scratch.
2.   Another problem that the users can face is the lack of technical support or technical documentation. But by going through this chapter, users will have a basic understanding of how a supply chain works and this may help them in overcoming technical difficulties.
3.   Some users may encounter errors while going through the SCM process in the system. This happens because in a supply chain management process there are many different companies involved and users have to learn to coordinate between different departments.
4.   For users who are new to the system, getting familiar with the system may be time consuming. However, by going through this chapter, users should be able to understand the system better.

CONCLUSION

Companies are changing the way they do business by moving from vertically integrated enterprises to horizontally integrated enterprises. They do so by increasing the number of suppliers and procuring products and services from may different suppliers rather than produce everything in-house. This is achieved by having good supply chain management systems, which help in reducing waste between the company and its suppliers and the company and its customers. By having good supply chain management systems, companies can focus on their core competencies and improvise on it. This chapter looked at some SCM initiatives and how it can be used by companies to satisfy customer demand. However, though all these things are important from a broad perspective and though we have looked at the different components in a SCM system and studied their importance, it is always better to work on an actual implementation to gain a thorough understanding of how an SCM system operates. This will help the user to implement the theoretical knowledge and will go a long way in making certain that the user has totally understood the different internal and external business processes that take place in a company.

REFERENCES

Ayers, J. B. (2001). *Handbook of supply chain management*. Boca Raton, FL; Alexandria, VA: St. Lucie Press; APICS.

Bloomberg, D. J., LeMay, S. A., & Hanna, J. B. (2002). *Logistics*. Upper Saddle River, NJ: Prentice Hall.

Bolstorff, P., & Rosenbaum, R. (2003). *Supply chain excellence: A handbook for dramatic improvement using the scor model*. New York: AMACOM.

Boone, T., & Ganeshan, R. (2002). *New directions in supply-chain management: Technology, strategy, and implementation*. New York: AMACOM.

Borck, J. (2001). Supply chain success. *InfoWorld, 23*(17), 52.

Brewer, A., Button, K. J., & Hensher, D. A. (2001). *Handbook of logistics and supply-chain management* (1st ed.). Amsterdam; New York: Pergamon.

Chopra, S., & Meindl, P. (2001). *Supply chain management: Strategy, planning, and operation.* Upper Saddle River, NJ: Prentice Hall.

Chorafas, D. N. (2001). *Integrating ERP, CRM, supply chain management, and smart materials.* Boca Raton, FL: Auerbach.

Copacino, W. C. (1997). *Supply chain management: The basics and beyond.* Boca Raton, FL: St. Lucie Press.

Curran, T. A. A. L. (2000). Sap R/3 business blueprint: Understanding enterprise supply chain management (2nd ed.). New Jersey: Prentice-Hall.

Ellram, L. M. (1990). *Supply chain management, partnerships, and the shipper-third party relationship.* Columbus, OH: College of Business, The Ohio State University.

Frazelle, E. (2002). *Supply chain strategy: The logistics of supply chain management.* New York: McGraw-Hill.

Fredendall, L. D., & Hill, E. (2001). *Basics of supply chain management.* Boca Raton, FL; Alexandria, VA: St. Lucie Press; APICS.

Handfield, R. B., & Nichols, E. L. (1999). *Introduction to supply chain management.* Upper Saddle River, NJ: Prentice Hall.

Hugos, M. H. (2003). *Essentials of supply chain management.* Hoboken, NJ: John Wiley & Sons.

Knolmayer, G. P. M., Zeier, A. (2002). *Supply chain management based on sap systems* (1st ed.). Heidelberg, Germany: Springer-Verlag.

Lambert, D. M., Stock, J. R., & Ellram, L. M. (1998). *Fundamentals of logistics management.* Boston: Irwin/McGraw-Hill.

Mentzer, J. T. (2001). *Supply chain management.* Thousand Oaks, CA: Sage Publications.

Porter, M. E. (1985). *Competitive advantage.* New York: The Free Press.

Morris, C. E. (2000, November 1). *Scheduling software: A key b2b link.* Retrieved March 22, 2005, from http://www.foodengineeringmag.com/CDA/AriticleInformation/features/BNP_Features_Item/0,3330,95684,00.html

SAP. (n.d.). *Distell uses mysap scm to improve delivery performance.* Retrieved March 3, 2005, from http://www.sap.com/solutions/business-suite/scm/index.epx

Schary, P. B., & Skjott-Larsen, T. (2001). *Managing the global supply chain* (2nd ed.). Copenhagen, Denmark: Copenhagen Business School Press.

Shapiro, J. F. (2001). *Modeling the supply chain.* Pacific Grove, CA: Brooks/Cole-Thomson Learning.

Srikanth RP. (2003, November 24). *Enterprise APP vendors ride the economic boom wave.* Retrieved April 7, 2005, from http://www.sap.com/solutions/business-suite/scm/index.exp

Stadtler, H., & Kilger, C. (2000). *Supply chain management and advanced planning: Concepts, models, software, and case studies.* Berlin; New York: Springer.

Viradix. (2005). *Terminology.* Retrieved March 2, 2005, from http://www.viradix.com/terminology.html#s

Walker, W. T. (2005). *Supply chain architecture: A blueprint for networking the flow of material, information, and cash.* Boca Raton, FL: CRC Press.

Chapter XI

Using SAP for ERP Applications and Design:
A Case Study of the Sales and Distribution Process

Mahesh Sarma, Miami University, USA

David C. Yen, Miami University, USA

ABSTRACT

In order to become globally competitive in today's dynamic business environment, organizations have to come closer to customers and deliver value added services and products in the shortest possible time. The primary business process through which this is achieved is the sales and distribution process. However, the sales and distribution process is just one part of an enterprise resource planning (ERP) system. This chapter will focus on the sales and distribution (SD) process of SAP's ERP system. This chapter will assist in learning about the basic functions that make up this process and how it affects the other modules in the ERP system. This chapter will also look at the Purchasing process and the materials requirements planning (MRP) process and how all the three processes are linked together to form one complete business process.

INTRODUCTION

The aim of an enterprise resource planning system is to integrate different business applications from various business processes. Though there are many different ERP softwares available in the market, SAP is the market leader in ERP systems, especially in Europe, where it's 39% market share compares very favorably with the 11% held by the merged Oracle/ Peoplesoft (Lynch, 2005, February 21) . SAP is an acronym for "Systeme, Anwendungen, Produkte in der Datenverarbeitung" ("Acronym finder") which in English means systems, applications & products in data processing. The SAP R/3 system is divided into many modules with each module consisting of many business processes. In this chapter, we will look at the sales and distribution (SD) module in SAP's R/3 system. The main purpose of this chapter is to understand the sales and distribution process in an ERP system. It is important for the users of this chapter to understand the underlying business processes that take place when a company gets a sales order. Though it is easy to grasp what actually happens when a sales order is executed, it is more difficult to understand how the system gets the data, how the data is stored, how the flow of the order occurs and how the data in a simple sales and distribution process is used by the other modules in an ERP system and these are the things that this chapter tries to focus on. The objective of this chapter is to focus on the business processes in the sales and distribution module in the SAP system. People reading this chapter will be able to understand how the sales and distribution module works. Any activity that takes place in one module is reflected in the other modules in some way. Similarly, some of the activities that take place in the SD module are reflected in some other way in other modules. This chapter will also focus on how the sales and distribution module affects the production planning module and the financial accounting module.

This chapter can be used by the users as a starting point to understand the sales and distribution process. Usually, ERP implementations are so vast and complicated that it is very difficult to focus on one particular module. By understanding the business processes in one module, users will be able to better understand how the actual implementation occurs. They will know the different data that has to be implemented in the SD module. The intended audiences for this chapter are the faculty and students in schools interested in learning about the sales and distribution process of an ERP system. People involved in the implementation process of this module in a company can use this chapter as a starting point for understanding the business process in the sales and distribution process before actually proceeding with the implementation. Most importantly, this chapter can be used by beginners just starting to work on the system as a reference in understanding the business flow of the sales process. By learning about the SD module, users will also know the basics of how this module affects the other modules like the financial accounting module and the production planning module.

From an academic point of view, a long standing practice of universities has been to offer discipline specific courses. However, in order to survive in today's business world, students have to take a multi-disciplinary approach to study their courses. What that means is that even though a student may major in finance, they need to know how information systems affect the different financial areas of a business or if a student is marketing major, he or she still needs to know how marketing is affected by the production or operational areas of a business. It has become imperative for a student to understand the relationships between the different functional areas of a business and to have a working knowledge of how a business works. To try and achieve this, universities have started offering courses which integrate the functional areas of a business. One of the ways universities attempt to do this is to have enterprise resource planning (ERP) systems related courses in their curriculum. Universities do this because ERP systems are designed to bind the functional areas of a business together. Typically, students learn about their disciplines in a variety of courses and then take an integrative (ERP) course that emphasizes on the integration of different functional areas of a business. ERP related courses in universities incorporate a broad of functionalities and theories which aims at making the students proficient in the different areas of a company. However, ERP systems in general are highly complex systems composed of different modules. The actual implementation of an ERP system may take years and a large portion of the company's resources. From a career point of view in the business world, professionals who are highly proficient in any one or more modules are in high demand. As mentioned earlier, an ERP system is composed of different modules interlinked together. This chapter focuses on the sales and distribution (SD) module of an ERP system. The sales and distribution module described in this chapter is from SAP's ERP system in Miami University, Ohio. One of the primary aims of this chapter is to describe the different business processes used in the Sales and Distribution module in an ERP system more specifically SAP's ERP system. This chapter tries to explain the importance of the Sales and Distribution module to illustrate the functionalities of an ERP system, that is, how learning about the sales and distribution module will help in understanding the various business processes that take place in other functional areas of a business. An important point to be noted is that most of the exercises described in this chapter are taken from an SAP training session on Business Process Integration I attended by one of the authors at Louisiana State University, Baton Rouge. This training session was conducted by Stephen Tracy and many of the snapshots depicted in this chapter are from that training session. Typically, students who take an ERP related course do not have any significant experience in using an ERP system. This chapter has been designed by considering this limitation. A class size of around 25 students is ideal for this course. This helps the instructor to focus on each individual student. Students face many problems while using ERP software and a class size larger than this may make it difficult for the instructor to solve the problems faced by students. The different topics that are covered in the course are as listed as follows:

1. Background Information
2. Concepts in the Sales and Distribution (SD) Module
   a. Organizational Data
   b. Customer and Material Master Data
   c. Document Master Data
3. The Business Process
   a. Sales Order Process
   b. Materials Requirements Planning (MRP) and Transportation Scheduling
   c. Purchase Order Process
4. Future Trends
   a. Suggestions to Learn the Sales and Distribution Process
   b. Lessons Learned
   c. Strengths and Weaknesses of the System and the Processes
5. Conclusion

A very important point to be noted is that this chapter focuses mainly on the theoretical topics that are covered in a course teaching the Sales and Distribution process using an ERP system (i.e., this course tries to explain what happens in a Sales and Distribution process). Also, many snapshots of an actual SAP's ERP system are presented so that students have a basic idea of how the different screens look like in an actual ERP system. They also have an idea of what to look for while going through the different exercises and processes described in the chapter. However, these screens are taken from Miami University's SAP system and it is up to the discretion of the instructor to use any ERP system that they feel will best fit the business processes in sales and distribution. Please note that the chapter explains the topics that are covered in the course but instructors may have to use additional readings or exercises to explain each topic of the course in more detail. Also note that the terms sales and distribution and the sales and distribution (SD) module are used interchangeably.

BACKGROUND INFORMATION

In an ERP system, the different applications or modules of a business are integrated together. It is also a homogenous product with the same user interface irrespective of the module being used. Due to the tight integration of the different modules, users have the capability to go into depth into one of the modules while at the same time understanding the overall business process. One of the other advantages of using an ERP system is that information is transmitted and updated in real time allowing effortless communication between different areas of a business. Thus, for an example as soon as a company receives goods from its suppliers, not only is the inventory in the company updated but the accounting entries for that particular transaction are also updated immediately. This chapter uses SAP's ERP system at Miami University to explain the Sales and Distribution process and so, this chapter focuses on the business processes in SAP's system.

SAP's R/3 system is divided into three core functional areas viz. human resources, financial and logistics (Williams, 2000). The modules in the ERP system are part of these functional areas. The sales and distribution (SD) module is part of the logistics functional area. Other modules included in logistics are product data management (PDM), production planning and control (PP), project system (PS), materials management (MM), quality management (QM), plant maintenance (PM), and service management (SM) (commerce). Sales and distribution enables a company to have real-time information about the inventory of raw materials, the orders-in-process, the finished goods and so forth. The sales and distribution module is integrated with the other modules in the different functional areas including production planning and control (PP), materials management (MM) financial accounting (FI) and so forth (SAP). A basic diagram of the R/3 application structure is given in Figure 1.

Figure 1 shows the different modules that are integrated together in SAP's ERP system.

It is also important to understand the underlying business processes associated with the SD module in order to understand how the SD module works. The main objectives of this chapter are to focus on understanding the sales and distribution module and the underlying business processes that are associated with this module. Since the sales and distribution process touches the customer directly, this module is one of the core modules in the R/3 system. ERP systems consist of many different modules with each module having a multitude

Figure 1. R/3 Client-server integrated solution (Source: Tracy, 2005)

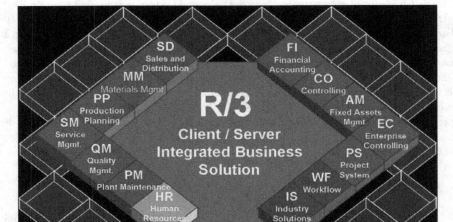

of business processes and functionalities. Also, since ERP systems encompass almost all the functionalities present in a company, it makes these systems very complicated and difficult to understand. The functional area that we are concerned with, that is, logistics is the largest functional area in the R/3 system. Within this functional area, the module we want to study is the sales and distribution (SD) module. It is very important to understand the business processes that occur during the sales and distribution process. Though this forms just a small portion of the whole system, understanding this process gives the user a better idea of how business transactions are carried out in a company. Understanding a part of this module will also aid the user in working with the other modules in an ERP system.

Logistics is that part of the supply chain process that plans, implements and controls the efficient, effective flow and storage of goods, services and related information from the point-of-origin to the point-of-consumption in order to meet customers' requirements (Knolmayer & Zeier, 2002). Within the logistics functional area, the sales and distribution (SD) module helps to optimize and automate the business processes associated with the sales and delivery of products and services. Some of the processes within this module include getting a sales quotation, processing the sales order, delivering the sales order and billing the customer for the order. In order to understand the business processes involved in the sales and distribution (SD) module, it is important to start at the beginning and understand the architecture and structure of the SD module.

This is the background information that is explained to the students at the beginning of the course. This helps the students understand what the course covers, what the different modules are in an ERP system and what is going to be covered in the course.

CONCEPTS

The basic element in SD processing is the SD master data. It is the highest element of data and so has the largest effect on the standard business process (Williams, 2000). The organization of this master data determines how the module and the system work. It is important to note that the SD master data can be accessed from many other modules like PP, FI, and so forth, master data forms the basis of the sales and distribution processing. Each module in SAP has some element of master data in it. Since this is the highest level of data, it has a significant effect on the business processes and it determines how the business processes will take place. The master data is further divided into three main types of data:

Organizational Data

The structure of the company is represented in the organizational data. A hierarchical format is used to depict the different areas within the company. For example: In a company, one part of the business is a sales area which handles all the sales transactions. This sales area can be composed of a sales organization, a distribution channel and a division.

Figure 2 shows a sample company structure with sales organizations, distribution channels and divisions.

SAP links the data between different modules using the master data. The company code is the highest level of data in the financial accounting module.

Figure 3 shows a company code structure in a particular SAP ERP client. This figure is depicted here just to show the organization of the company code within an ERP client.

The SD module is linked to this module using the sales organization (i.e., the sales organization is linked to the company code). The SD organizational data is very important because without this the transactions cannot proceed. This is so because in order to get a sales order from a customer, there has to be some department like the sales organization within the company which actually processes that sales order. This department forms part of the organizational data. Every transaction occurs within this structure and is stored in the database. A sales organization is that part of the company which processes the customer orders and deals directly with the customer. A distribution channel is a pathway by which the company's products actually reach the customers. Some of the examples of distribution

Figure 2. Sample organizational structure (Williams, 2000)

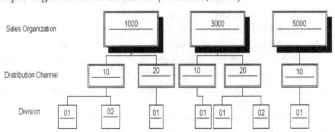

A Sample organizational structure with
sales organizations, distribution channels and divisons

Figure 3. Company code data structure (Williams, 2000) © SAP AG

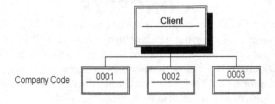

Figure 4. Plant and storage location structure (Williams, 2000) © SAP AG

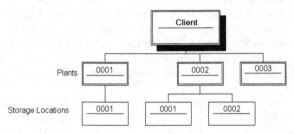

channels can be wholesale or retail. In wholesale, products are sold in bulk and which are utilized for resale purposes. In retail, the products are sold directly to customers. A division is just a group that can be defined for a group of products. This can include specific customer rebates or agreements, pricing terms specific to products or customers and so forth. Please note that a distribution channel can belong to more than one sales organization (i.e., each sales organization can sell the products either in wholesale or in retail). Similarly, since each sales organization can sell the same products, the material master records can be maintained in different sales organizations and distribution channels. A sales organization, a distribution channel and a division make up a sales area. All the data that is important for making a sale is defined in a sales area. From the context of an ERP system, since the company code in the FI module and sales organization in the *SD* module are linked together, the system is able to post a particular sales transaction in the correct sales organization.

A company has an organizational structure for different modules. In the organizational structure for Accounting, the company code is the highest level of data. The SD module is linked to this module because each sales organization is assigned to a company code.

Similar to the organizational structure in sales and distribution, there is an organizational structure in materials management.

In Figure 4, the plant is the place where the materials are kept. The storage location is the area to store the inventory. Each plant can have more than one storage location and each company code can have more than one plant. In order to deliver the products to the customers, the products have to be shipped to the customers. These are carried out from shipping

Figure 5. Assignment of sales organizations and plants (Williams, 2000) © SAP AG

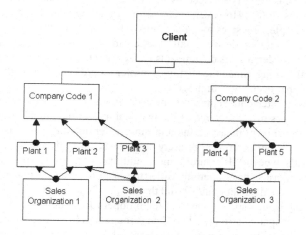

points. So each shipping point can be assigned to one or more plants. Similarly, the loading and unloading of materials takes place at loading points. A loading point is a sub-section of a shipping point. Since the shipping and loading points are part of the transportation process, it is enough to just understand what they are and what they represent.

The organizational structures of the SD module and the materials management module are discussed above. The figure below explains how these different modules are linked together.

In Figure 5, the client is the highest level of data. The company code belongs to the financial accounting module, the plants belong to the materials management module and the sales organizations belong to the sales and distribution module. All these modules are linked together to form part of the bigger picture. In the figure "Plants 1, 2, and 3 belong to company code 1. Sales organization 1 uses plants 1 and 2. Sales organization 2 uses plants 2 and 3. Sales organizations 1 and 2 can make cross company sales for goods from plants 4 or 5 because according to the design and structure of SAP's ERP system, a sales organization can sell from a plant belonging to a different company code. According to the structure of the SAP system, there is a one-to-one relationship between sales organization and company code and a many-to-many relationship between sales organizations and plants" (Williams, 2000).

Customer and Material Master Data

The customer is the most important part of any company. The customer master data creates the base for creating sales orders and carrying out sales transactions. The customer master data includes the general customer data like the customer number, name, address and phone numbers. It also includes data like the sold-to-party, ship-to-party and the payer records, payment transactions records, the contact person in the company and loading and unloading points. It includes the company code data (for the accounting department) and the sales and distribution data (for the sales department). Each customer will have a customer number even if the customer is serviced by one more than one company code or sales organization (Williams, 2000). However, each customer may have different data in different sales area. For example, one sales area may deliver the products wholesale to a customer while another sales area may deliver retail products to the same customer. As soon as the customer places and order, a sales document is created and the customer master records are copied into the sales order. Since the customer master records are used in the sales orders, it makes these records even more important.

The material master data represents the data about the product or service that the company manufactures or sells. Some of the material master data includes data about the type of material, the units of measure, the minimum order quantity, the minimum delivery quantity, the price of the material, the safety stock level (used in materials requirements planning [MRP]), the type of MRP, purchasing conditions, storage conditions and delivering conditions. The system also has something called the customer material information records. These records represent data about a material that is specific to a particular customer. It can be anything ranging from a specific price of the product for the customer to the customers description of the company's product. This data is the first to be copied in the system when creating the sales order. To sum up, the customer and material master data represents the data relating to the goods and services sold by the company. This helps the company keep a track of the products or services being sold and also helps to track the trading partners of the company.

Document Master Data

There are many transactions that occur in a company and all these transactions are stored in the form of documents. The document master data makes sure that all the documents are stored in a systematic manner. In the SD module, it is very important to understand where

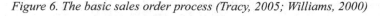

Figure 6. The basic sales order process (Tracy, 2005; Williams, 2000)

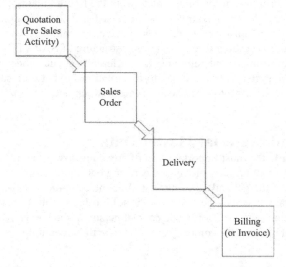

the data is coming from in these transactions and from where the data is being accessed. Generally, the data flow follows the normal principle, that is, data flows from the top level to the bottom level. So for example, if an employee of the company is creating a sales order and enters the material to be sold, the ERP system will check the organizational data first, then the customer data , then the material data and then the document data (Williams, 2000).

It is important to note that working in an actual ERP implementation is one of the best methods to learn the business process in a company. However, gaining a basic understanding of the SD business process and then working on an actual system greatly reduces the time needed to understand the business process. In order to fully understand the flow of information and the organizational structure, it is important to look at the sales order process. We will look at the sales order process, understand how information flows through different parts of the company and how the company is able to update its records in real-time.

This is the theory that is covered in this topic of the chapter. By understanding this topic of the chapter, students gain an understanding of the structure of an organization from an ERP system's point of view. Even though students have an idea of the different departments in a company, this topic helps the students to understand how the different functional areas within a company are organized within an ERP system. They gain a thorough understanding of some of the areas within a company and how these areas are linked together using an ERP system. They come to know the different types of data used in an ERP system and how all the data are linked together. Most importantly, they gain an understanding of the data flows within the company and how one functional area within the company is able to access data from some other functional area. By understanding this topic thoroughly, students are able to understand the inter-linkages between the different departments of a company.

THE BUSINESS PROCESS

In order to understand what happens in the sales and distribution process of a company, students go through various exercises that help them understand what happens during the sales and distribution process in a company. More importantly, students understand how a company fulfills an order using an ERP system.

"A sales order is a contractual agreement between a sales organization and a customer for the supply of services or products over a specific period of time and in certain quantities" (Williams, 2000). A sales quotation is a pre-sales activity in which the customer requests information from the company about the products the customer is interested in. A sales quotation can be defined as "A legally binding agreement to deliver specific products or a selection of a certain amount of products in a specified time-frame at a pre-defined price" (SAP). Every quotation has a validity period within which the customer can either place the order according to the conditions specified in the contract or can cancel the contract. If the customer decides to purchase a product, a sales order is created. The sales order is created with reference to a sales quotation. It can also be created without any reference to another document. When the sales order is created, the system automatically copies all the data from the specific customer and material master records for the particular sales area. Data is also copied from the customer material data records. Once the products are ready to be shipped to the customer, the data from the sales document is copied to the delivery note which includes the delivery information. Once the products are delivered, a billing document

Figure 7. Create material screenshot in Miami University's SAP system (University, 2005)

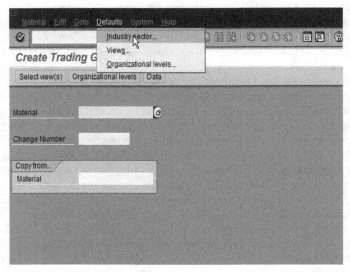

is created and the customer is billed for the sales order. In the following topics, all of these documents are looked into in detail from a business process point-of-view.

Sales Order Process

Step 1: Creating the Material Master Records

The first step is to create the material master records. Usually, this is a set of records of the products and services sold by the company. An authorized employee of the company creates the material master records.

Figure 7 shows a snapshot of the create material screen in an ERP system.

This contains the data about the industry sectors, the company code, the plant, sales organization and the distribution channel. There are many views created in the material master records. Each view contains some data necessary for some module. Among other things, the basic views contain the information about the name of the material, the units of measure and the dimensions of the material. The sales view include such information as the delivering plant, the tax data, the minimum order and delivery quantities, the selling price of the product, the sales organization, plant and distribution channel. The MRP and plant views include data like the MRP type and the inventory on hand. It is important to be noted that these are just some of the data that is included in the material master records. These records contain a lot more data than is listed above. Similarly, in all the master records the system actually contains a lot of data. We just look at the data that is most relevant to understand the basic sales and distribution process.

Figure 8. A pricing condition screenshot in the material master screen (University, 2005)

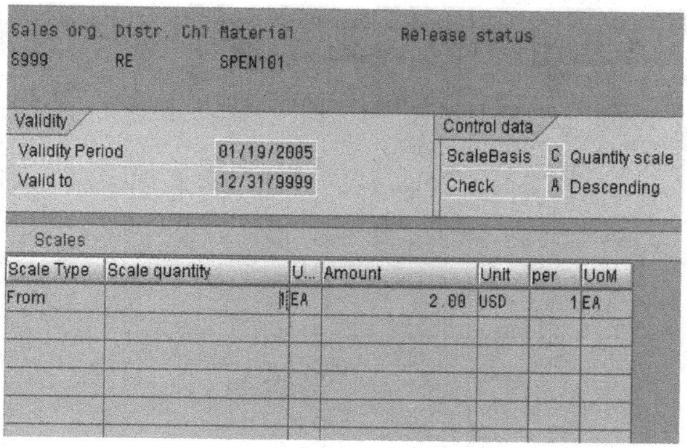

Sales org.	Distr.	Chl	Material	Release status		
S999	RE		SPEN101			

Validity			Control data		
Validity Period	01/19/2005		ScaleBasis	C	Quantity scale
Valid to	12/31/9999		Check	A	Descending

Scales

Scale Type	Scale quantity	U...	Amount	Unit	per	UoM
From		1 EA	2.00	USD	1	EA

Figure 8 shows a snapshot of the pricing condition screen in an ERP system. This is the screen where the price of the material is set and entered into the system by the company.

Step 2: Creating the Customer Master Records

The customer master records include all the data about the customer. This includes data about the company code, the sales organizations, the distribution channel and the division. It includes general data about the customer like the customer name, the address, the language of communication and so forth. The company code data used in financial accounting contains data about accounting and payment information. The sales area data contains information about the sales order like the order currency and pricing data. It also contains the shipping information like the shipping conditions, the delivering plant, maximum deliveries and so forth. In addition to shipping, it will contain the billing data like the terms of payment, the tax classifications and so forth.

Figure 9 is a snapshot of the create customer screen. In this screen, the company enters all the data about the customer.

It is important to remember that a company has many employees serving in different locations. The material master and customer master records will be created by different people in different locations. However, as soon as someone updates the master records the database is automatically updated as a result of which people in different locations are able to see the same, updated real-time data.

Step 3: Creating the Quotation

When customers are interested in the company's products, they request information about those products from the company. This leads to the generation of a customer quotation. "The quotation is a sales document that comes before the sales order and after the sales enquiry and most quotations have a validity date" (Williams, 2000). Since the quotation is a contract that can be activated by the customer, it contains all the data relevant for the sales order to be created. Some of the data included in the quotation include the details about the

Figure 9. A customer master data screenshot (University, 2005)

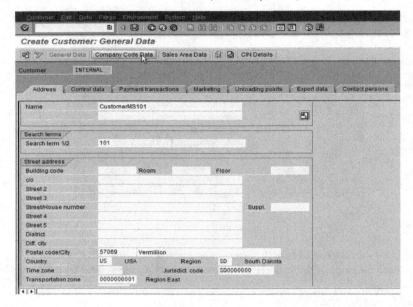

product like the quantity and the price of the product. It includes the requested delivery dates, plant, the shipping and unloading points, and so forth. It also includes the billing conditions and the details of the amount charged to the customer.

Figure 10 shows a snapshot of the customer quotation screen. This is the screen that is used by company employees to enter data about information requested by customers about the company's products or services.

It is also important for the company to know the probability whether the customer is going to place an order or not based on the sales quotation. The system already has an order probability for all the different types of sales documents and the system then combines this probability with the probability from the customer's previous records to create an order probability.

Figure 13 shows how the information in the system about the customers and quotations is combined together to calculate the probability of the quotation being converted into the sales order.

So, the system actually creates a sales quotation which has the highest probability of turning into actual sales orders.

Step 4: Creating a Sales Order

If the customer is satisfied with the quotation, the customer orders the product. If not, the customer can cancel the quotation. If the customer places the order, a sales order is created. Since the company already has a sales quotation available, it creates the sales order with reference to the quotation. When it does that, the system copies all the material from the sales quotation into the sales order. If the company does not have a sales quotation, it

Figure 10. A customer quotation screenshot (University, 2005)

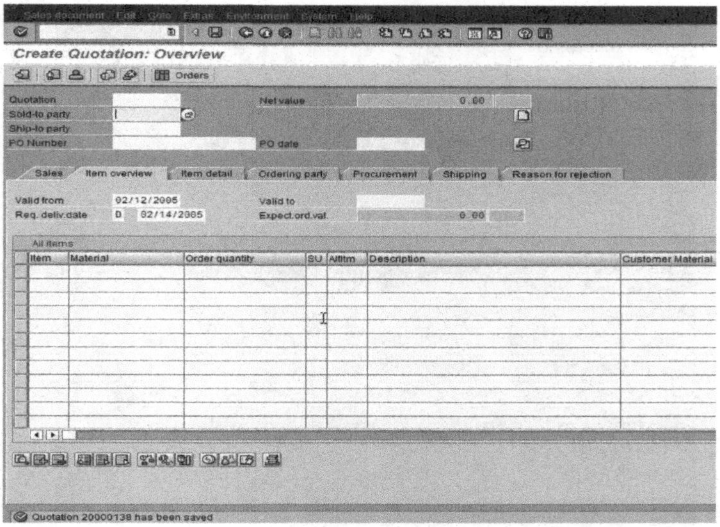

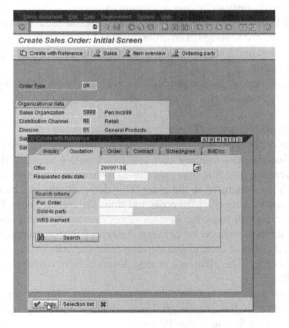

Figure 11. A sales order created with reference to a quotation screenshot (Tracy, 2005; University, 2005)

Figure 12. Creating a delivery note screenshot (University, 2005)

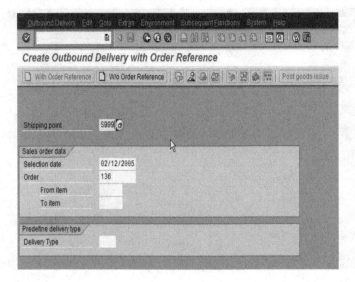

always has the option of creating a standard sales order without the quotation, the only difference being someone has to enter all the relevant information into the sales order. The sales people now have the option of either delivering the entire product on the proposed date or staggering the delivery over a period of time depending on the customer requirements. Once the order is created, it is assigned an order number. Note that the order contains all the data present in the quotation like the customer number, the order quantity, delivery dates, product price, ad so forth.

Figure 11 is a snapshot of the sales order screen. This sales order has been created with reference to a customer quotation.

Step 5: Creating a Delivery Note

Once the sales order is created, the inventory for that particular material is checked. If the material is available in inventory, then a delivery note is created. If the material is not available in inventory, then it is either purchased from a vendor (initiating the purchase transactions) or it is manufactured in the plant. This delivery note can be used a proof of delivery when the customer receives the order and signs the delivery note. If the material is available in inventory, it will show the number of items available for unrestricted use, the sales order and the items scheduled for delivery. Assuming that the material is available in inventory, the delivery note is created and the data from the sales order is taken automatically from the sales order. The plant and storage location from where the products are to be supplied are selected.

Figure 12 shows a snapshot of the delivery note screen. This delivery note is created by the company to indicate that the material is available in the company's inventory and that it can be delivered on time to the customer.

Figure 13. Determination of an order probability (Williams, 2000)

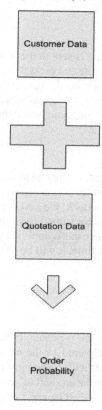

Once the delivery note is created, the inventory level is checked once again. What happens now is that the amount in the unrestricted use column goes down while that in the scheduled for delivery goes up. For example, assume that the company has a stock of 1000 items and it has an order for 200 items. Before the creation of the delivery note, the inventory data will be:

Unrestricted use: 1000
Sales order: 200
Scheduled for delivery: 0
After the creation of the sales order, the inventory data will change to:
Unrestricted use: 1000
Sales order: 0
Scheduled for delivery: 200

Note that as soon as the delivery note is created the system automatically updates the inventory data.

Step 6: Picking the Materials

Once the delivery note is created, it is sent to the plant or the warehouse. Someone in the plant or the warehouse receives the note and picks the amount of material to be delivered. Picking involves actual picking and selecting the materials to be delivered. This material is then packed in the form needed by the customer and scheduled for dispatch. The items can be picked in batches or at one time. Picking usually interfaces with the warehouse management (WM) module.

Step 7: Posting the Goods Issue

Goods issue is an event that indicates a change in the ownership of the product (Tracy, 2005). This ends the shipping process and prevents changes to the shipping document (Tracy, 2005) . Once the items are picked from stock, the goods are issued. This is done by posting a goods issue. In this step, the order is consumed from the warehouse and it results in the reduction from the warehouse stock. Once this is done, the goods are shipped to the customer. If the inventory data is checked at this time, it will be something like this:

Unrestricted use: 800
Sales order: 0
Scheduled for delivery: 0

Note that as soon as the goods issue is posted, it means that the material has left the company warehouse and is being delivered to the customer. The system automatically updates the inventory level for that particular stock in the company (i.e., the stock of that material in the company goes down by the amount of goods that have left the warehouse or storage area). On the accounting side, in the General Ledger accounts, the system decreases the value of the stock on hand and increases the cost of goods sold.

Step 8: Billing the Customer

Once the goods issue has been posted, a billing document (invoice) is created listing the details of the order and the amount to be billed to the customer. As soon as it is confirmed that the customer has received the order, the customer is billed by sending the billing document to the customer. Again, the general ledger accounts are updated by updating the revenue accounts and the amount to be received from the customer. The system also updates the stock requirements.

Step 9: Receiving Customer Payment

Once the customer receives the invoice, the customer may choose to pay the total amount in the invoice or stagger payments over a period of time. In either case, once the customer makes the payment, the accounting and financial entries are automatically updated (i.e., on the accounting side) the balance in the customers account goes down while the revenue entry for the company goes up.

The topic covered previously is a hands-on part of the course and which are performed by students individually. The previous topics explain what happens in each step of the sales process within a company. Students gain an understanding of what are the different business processes that take place right from the time a customer wants to buy a product or service from a company right to the time the payment is received from the customer after the order is delivered. An important point to be noted here is that the steps above explain in brief what happens in each step of the process. However, students are provided with step-by-step instructions of carrying out each business process so that they gain an understanding of the business process and also gain experience in using an ERP system. By carrying out these exercises, students are able to implement the theoretical aspects that they studied in the previous topic using and actual ERP system. Even though the initial topics are theoretical, with the help of this hands-on approach, students understand how things work within a company and how the different areas within a company are linked together. Though they work only on a basic sales order process, they understand how even a simple sales order process uses data from different areas within the company and how this data is used to link the different departments in a company. Another point to be noted is that students start off with creating materials and customers which help them understand the business processes from the very bottom. They understand the importance of entering the data in the system so that any functional area can access this data provided they have the necessary rights to do that within the system.

Materials Requirement Planning (MRP) and Transportation Scheduling

In *step 5* of the sales order process, after creating the sales order and before creating the delivery note, the inventory level for the particular material is checked and the delivery note is created when the material is available in inventory. However, it may so happen that the required material may not be available in inventory. At this time, the company may either manufacture the item or purchase it from a vendor (or supplier) in order to increase its stock. When the sales order is created, a schedule line is created. The schedule line gives the details about the customers order like the amount to be delivered and the delivery date. This information is sent to materials requirements planning (MRP). MRP then determines whether there is enough material in inventory to fulfill the sales order. In order to do this, there are many business processes that have to be scheduled properly like purchasing the materials, transportation planning, packing and loading the materials and so forth. There are two types of scheduling that can be carried by the system:

- **Backward scheduling:** This happens when the system schedules all the business processes backwards from the requested delivery date to meet a specific delivery date. For example, if the customer places an order on April 1 and wants the item on April 7, the system will carry out backward scheduling from April 7. If the transportation time is 4 days, packing time is 1 day and the loading time is 1 day, and then with a delivery date of April 7 less 6 days gives April 1. So the system estimates that if the materials are available on April 1, then the materials can be delivered to the customer on April 7.
- **Forward scheduling:** However, if the materials are not available on April 1, then the system will carry out forward scheduling, in which it will calculate the time the goods can be delivered depending on the time needed to complete all the business processes and depending on the availability of the materials. So, if the materials will

be available only on April 4 then the delivery date will be April 4 plus 6 days (i.e., April 10).

A case where the material is purchased from a vendor initiating the procure-to-pay process is looked into.

In this step, students perform the MRP exercise. Again, please note that the details of the exercise are provided to the students so that they can perform this hands-on activity. By doing this, students are able to understand what happens in the production department of the company. They realize that though the process starts off with a sales order to be delivered to the customer, it has moved to the production department if the material is not available in inventory. Again, they understand how the different departments in a company are linked together and how these departments work together to fulfill a customer's requirements.

Purchase Order Process

Step 1: Creating a Vendor

The first step in creating the purchase order process is creating a vendor. This works the same way as creating a material or customer master data. Some of the data that is entered in the vendor master data include the general data like the name, address, and so forth, the tax information, accounting information data, the payment terms and methods and any other extra conditions.

Step 2: Creating a Purchase Order

When the MRP is carried out, the system checks for the inventory level of that particular material. If the material is not in inventory, then the system creates a purchase requisition that can be converted to a purchase order. A purchase order can also be created without the purchase requisition. In either case, the company code, the purchasing organization, the vendor number, the quantity to be purchased, the price, and so forth, are all entered and the purchase order is created. A purchase order is nothing but a document which specifies the supplier to deliver a certain number of products by a certain date at a specified price and which becomes a legally binding document once the supplier accepts it. Since the purchase order contains the details of the materials to be supplied, the supplier delivers the material according to the terms of the contract.

Step 3: Creating the Goods Receipt

When the goods supplied by the supplier are received at the company's warehouse or storage location, somebody acknowledges the physical receipt of all the goods according to the conditions specified. The storage location is specified so that the material can be stored at the correct location. This step involves interfacing with warehouse management and is an important part of materials management. Now, once the goods are received by the company, the inventory level in the company for that particular material goes up, the sales order can be completed and the materials can be supplied to the customer.

Step 4: Invoice Receipt

Once the goods have been received by the company, the supplier creates an invoice and sends it to the company where it is received. This works the same way as the sales order. The only difference being, in the sales order the company creates an invoice and sends it to the customer while in the purchase order process the invoice is created by the supplier and sent to the company. So, the accounts payable for the company goes up.

Step 5: Paying the Vendor

Once the invoice is received by the company, the company pays the vendor by entering the amount to be paid, the vendor number, the account number, and so forth. The payment can be made automatically by electronic funds transfer (EFT) when the goods receipt and invoice receipt match the invoice. In the accounting module, the matching of the purchase order, the goods receipt and the invoice receipt is known as the "three-way match" and once these match; the payment transactions with the vendor are completed. By interacting with the accounting module, the accounting transactions are automatically updated.

Students perform the purchase order process using the ERP system. They understand that to fulfill the sales order, some other department has to purchase the required materials so that production can be started or the finished goods can be delivered to customers. They understand the link between the purchasing department and the sales department. Again, note that the steps to be used in this process are provided to the students so that they are able to carry out these exercises. The snapshots for the purchase order process and the MRP process are not provided because this chapter focuses mainly on the sales order process. However, the snapshots and all the exercises used by students are available with the instructors and which can be provided to the students anytime during the hands-on activities. With all these above steps, students realize that the process starts off with the customer enquiry and sometimes ends with purchasing. In between, the company may have to manufacture products too to fulfill the sales order. Students gain a thorough understanding of the different business processes that take place within the sales order, the purchase order and MRP. They understand how the company utilizes an ERP system to fulfill customer requirements and how there is always a free flow of information within a company by using an ERP system. By performing these exercises over the course of a semester, students gain an understanding of not only how a company and its data are organized but also understand the different business process that take place within the sales and distribution module of the company. They understand the different functionalities of an ERP system by looking at the sales and distribution process. They understand this process thoroughly, that is, right from getting a request from a customer to delivering the product to the customer. They also look at how a company manages its inventory with MRP and also look at the purchase order process. Though, all these exercises are carried out by each student, it is possible to divide the students into teams representing different functional areas of a company and carry out these exercises. By doing this, students are able to simulate real-world conditions where different data is entered into the system by different people and which is linked together within the system to take care of the company's customers.

FUTURE TRENDS

Since this chapter focuses on the sales process using SAP's ERP system, the future trends of this particular system are discussed. Again, instructors are free to use any ERP system that they see fit to explain the sales process. The SAP system is based on a three tiered client/server system with the data being stored on a separate database, the application code written in ABAP/4 and running on application servers and the presentation server. However, now SAP has come up with the web-based mySAP which is powered by the SAP NetWeaver platform. "mySAP ERP takes the R/3 Enterprise stable application core, augments it with additional functionality and supports it with the full SAP NetWeaver software stack, which includes Web Application Server 6.20, SAP enterprise portal, SAP exchange infrastructure (XI), SAP business information warehouse (BW) and SAP collaborative master data management. Powered by SAP NetWeaver, mySAP ERP is fully interoperable with Microsoft .NET and IBM WebSphere, and supports portal and mobile technology, business intelligence and knowledge management technology" (Unisys). Every enterprise system contains many modules and sales and distribution is just one module in the SAP R/3 system. Though the SD module is an important module in the R/3 system, it is more important to understand how this module integrates with the other modules of the system and how the flow of business processes take place. In order to really understand the importance and the business processes involved in the SD module, it is necessary to have a basic understanding of the other modules and business processes in an ERP system. A good way to learn about the business processes is to work on an actual implementation of an ERP system. However, in the absence of access to an actual implementation project, SAP has a system designed for educational purposes. The screen shots used here are taken from Miami University's SAP system used for learning the processes used in an ERP system. Though this chapter tries to explain the overall sales and distribution process, there are many variables which are used in the module which are not covered here. However, by gaining an overall understanding of how the sales and distribution process works, it becomes a lot easier to understand the rest of the business processes and the other variables in the R/3 system. Those interested can use this data to understand more about how the mySAP system works and how the internet can be used in the sales and distribution process.

SUGGESTIONS TO LEARN THE SALES AND DISTRIBUTION PROCESS

There are many little details and suggestions that will help the user understand the sales and distribution process and allow the users to successfully complete this process on an actual system. These suggestions are just some tips to help the students proceed through the exercises faster. It is always better to pause after each step and try to understand the processes in each step, look at how the data flows and know how that step is related to the overall business process. Some of these suggestions are listed below:

1.   After each step of the sales and distribution process is carried out, users should look at the different variables involved in each step and try to understand the significance of each piece of data.
2.   SAP provides an online help system for users. It is always good to use this help system to understand the variables involved in each step.
3.   In order to go back to the SAP easy access (main) screen directly from any of the exercises, the "UP" key has to be pressed:

4.   Since the inventory level has to be checked after each step of the process, it is better to create a new session. This new session can be used exclusively to check the inventory level while the rest of the exercises can be carried out in the original session. The new session can be started by going to Session -> Create Session on the Main toolbar. A new session is just a new screen that opens up in the system.

5.   If the users have two or more sessions running simultaneously, logging off from one session will close all the sessions or windows. In order to close one session, System -> End session has to be accessed to close just that one session.

6.   Since the SAP system consists of many different users using the same processes, it is always useful to use the user's user number in the search criteria. The search criteria is included in most of the master data, so using the user number in the search criteria will allow the user to look up their own data immediately.

7.   In order to save time while going through the business process, it is always good to note all the document numbers which are created. It is also good to note the system messages for future use.

8.   If an error comes up, it is good practice to capture the error screen and forward it to the instructor or administrator so that they can solve the problem and fix the error.

9.   The sales process and the purchasing process are sometimes linked when there is no inventory on hand. In order to understand these processes, they have to be completed separately. Once that is done, these processes should be linked together and the exercises should be completed.

10.   In the Goods Receipt section, the storage location has to be entered. The place to enter the storage location can be found in the "Where" tab of the Goods Receipt screen.

LESSONS LEARNED

There are many things that the students should be able to follow after going through this chapter. Students should:

1.   Have a thorough understanding of the business process of the SD module

2.   Understand the architecture of the SD module and know where the system picks up each part of the data from

3.   Understand what happens if one of the steps is not completed and know whether the business flow can proceed if this happens

4.   Know how to fix the errors that may come up; by fixing these errors students will be able to better understand the flow of data within the system

5.   Understand how the sales and distribution process and the purchasing process are linked together

6.   Understand the significance of the sales process, the purchasing process and the MRP process

7.   Create their own materials, customers and vendors and be able to buy goods from the vendors and sell it to the customers using an ERP system

STRENGTHS AND WEAKNESSES
OF THE SYSTEM AND THE PROCESSES

Each system has its own strengths and weaknesses. Some of these for this particular SAP system are listed below:

Strengths

1.   The exercises are carried out in the IDES R/3 system which has been created by SAP for training purposes. So, the main strength of this system is that users can make mistakes and learn from the system rather than making a mistake during an actual implementation which can be very expensive to the company.
2.   By going through the same set of exercises, students are able to understand the business process thoroughly.
3.   By understanding the business process, students create their own materials, vendors and customers and buy and sell goods. By doing so, students learn the significance of having multiple vendors and customers and how a company manages these business relationships.
4.   By understanding how the sales and distribution process is linked to other modules, students are able to understand the business processes in other modules.
5.   As the students' gain an understanding of the different modules, architecture of those modules and the different business processes, after a period of time, they are able to set up their own company using the SAP system. This helps them not only to develop their technical expertise but also helps them gain a business perspective of looking at things.

Weaknesses

1.   One of the main problems is lack of documentation to understand the business process. Hopefully, by going through this chapter, students are able to understand the business processes that take place in the SD module.
2.   Some students may encounter errors while going through the SD process in the system. Some of these errors will help them know more about the system while other errors have to be fixed by the administrator or instructor.
3.   Understanding the business process is a time consuming but interesting process. Students should be able to devote a certain amount of time in order to understand the flow of business documents.

CONCLUSION

The main use of an ERP system is to allow a company to use a single integrated system for all the different business processes. By using an ERP system, users will realize the importance of such a system while at the same time understanding the difficulties in using and implementing such a system. This chapter focuses on explaining the business processes involved in sales and distribution. Overall, this chapter will bring the users a little closer to the SD module with a focus on sales orders, distribution, MRP, purchasing and accounting. By understanding this system, users will realize the time a company saves by using this system.

A suggestion for the user would be to access the SAP ERP system and try and work through some of the processes explained in this book. This will not only help the users to understand the business process but will also help in familiarizing the user with an Enterprise system.

A better project for any user would be to get more involved in the system than just the sales or distribution process. Users should delve deeper into different areas of businesses that would allow them to achieve a bigger overall experience with the SAP R/3 system.

REFERENCES

Acronym finder. (2005). Retrieved March 1, 2005, from http://www.acronymfinder.com/af-query.asp?p=dict&String=exact&Acronym=SAP

Bargas, J. (1998). *Commerce, C. F. V. O. a. Sap history. Best Practices*. Retrieved February 26, 2005, from http://isds.bus.lsu.edu/cvoc/learn/bpr/mprojects/bp/bpsap.html

Knolmayer, G. P. M., & Zeier, A. (2002). *Supply chain management based on SAP systems* (1st ed.). Berlin: Springer-Verlag.

Lynch, M. (2005, February 21). *In enemy territory*. Retrieved March 1, 2005, from http://www.computeractive.co.uk/features/1161388

SAP. (2004). *Quotation and inquiry*. Retrieved February 26, 2005, from http://help.sap.com/saphelp_crm30/helpdata/en/29/c1f339c67ff216e10000000a114084/content.html

Tracy, S. (2005, January 4). *R/3 client-server integrated solution*. Paper presented at the Business Process Integration - 1, Baton Rouge, LA.

Unisys. (2005). SAP services. Retrieved April 1, 2005, from http://www.optimum.unisys.be/solutions/Upgrades_and_Consolidations-03.asp

University, M. (2005). *SAP system*. Oxford, OH: Miami University.

Williams, G. C. (2000). *Implementing SAP R/3 sales & distribution* (1st ed.). New York: McGraw-Hill.

FURTHER READING

Barrett, L., & Guengerich, G. (1991). *Sales and distribution*. New York: F. Watts.

Dunn, C. L., Cherrington, J. O., & Hollander, A. S. (2005). *Enterprise information systems: A pattern-based approach* (3rd ed.). Boston: McGraw-Hill/Irwin.

Grambo. (2005). *SD and financial accounting integration*. Retrieved February 26, 2005, from http://academic.uofs.edu/faculty/gramborw/sap/sdandacc.htm

Greenberg, P. (2002). *CRM at the speed of light: Capturing and keeping customers in Web real time* (2nd ed.). New York: McGraw-Hill/Osborne.

Hamilton, S. (2003). *Maximizing your ERP system: A practical guide for managers*. New York: McGraw-Hill.

Ptak, C. A., & Schragenheim, E. (2004). *ERP: Tools, techniques, and applications for integrating the supply chain* (2nd ed.). Boca Raton, FL: St. Lucie Press.

Sagner, J. S., & NetLibrary Inc. (2001). *Financial and process metrics for the new economy.* Retrieved from http://www.netLibrary.com/urlapi.asp?action=summary&v=1&book id=57013

SAP. (n.d.). *Sap quotation and order analysis.* Retrieved February 26, 2005, from http://help. sap.com/saphelp_crm40/helpdata/en/87/0ebc0297cale43aebd8a419215881a/content. htm

Sharpe, S. (1997). *10 minute guide to SAP R/3.* Indianapolis, IN: Que.

Wallace, T. F., & Kremzar, M. H. (2001). *ERP: Making it happen: The implementers'guide to success with enterprise resource planning.* New York: Wiley.

Section III

Examples —
How to Teach Specific
IT Topics in ES

Chapter XII

Putting Enterprise Systems in a Larger ICT Context:
A Pedagogical Framework

Thomas Rienzo, Western Michigan University, USA

J. Michael Tarn, Western Michigan University, USA

James Danenburg, Western Michigan University, USA

ABSTRACT

Many business schools are attempting to integrate their curricula with enterprise software, particularly enterprise resource planning (ERP) software. Although the introduction of ERP into the undergraduate academic curriculum offers students a potentially deeper under-standing of business processes, it cannot by itself provide for students a connection between the adoption of robust information systems and a paradigm shift in the way that business organizations operate in a global, information-centric environment. Connecting a new global economy with enterprise systems requires a course much broader than ERP that places enterprise systems in a much larger information-communication technology (ICT) context. This chapter presents a teaching model that provides that context, emphasizing the critical role of systems components and relationships, the central function of information in problem solving, and business perspectives of information from infrastructure to applications.

INTRODUCTION

Technology has consistently been applied to the education process, with differing levels of success. In many areas, real-world technology applications are being used in teaching, including applications like CAD/CAM software, simulation languages, and enterprise resource planning (ERP) software packages. Industrial trends in IT have been moving from traditional models with disconnected applications to complex integrated models involving enterprise systems (ES). Changes in industrial practice have prompted changes in business information technology education resulting in a potpourri of teaching and learning methods, but academic institutions are increasingly focusing on enterprise software as a means of integrating curricula (Hejazi, Halpin, & Biggs, 2003; Johnson, Lorents, Morgan, & Ozmun, 2004; Markulis, Howe, & Strang, 2005; Michaelsen, Hobbs, & Stead, 2000). Joseph and George (2002, p. 51) suggest that ERP software can bring about more effective pedagogy in higher education enabling deeper understanding of course materials and a clearer vision of interlinked aspects of business activity. Practical experience with ERP software may help students appreciate related business processes, but the effects of the global information infrastructure extends far beyond integrated business software. Training with ERP and customer relationship management (CRM) systems do not communicate the economic, political, and social revolutions spawned by world-wide telecommunications, robust wide area networks, prolific and effectual hardware and software, and the incredible power of the Internet to connect everything to everything. Students should appreciate the paradigm shifts occurring in the way people live and work, which are every bit as liberating and tumultuous as the shifts that were initiated by the invention of printing in the 15th century and the industrial revolution in the 18th century. In this chapter, a high-level framework is presented to incorporate enterprise systems in a larger picture of evolving and adaptive organizational structures, and the business processes that enable them. The authors present a pedagogical model that links enterprise systems to information and communication tools, an understanding of systems, and the role of information in problem solving.

CONNECTING BUSINESS PROCESSES

Businesses judge their performance by outcomes produced by entire business systems, not individual components. While control and optimization of integrated business processes have been goals of business managers since the Industrial Revolution, tools *capable* of complex control and optimization of diverse business functions developed only recently. Prior to about 1990, little attempt was made to integrate large scope business activities because:

- Computer processing capabilities were limited.
- Computer hardware and software were costly.
- Specialized business activities needed customized software code created from scratch.
- Robust computer networks did not exist.

The 1990s was a watershed decade. It produced:

- Robust computer networks
- Greatly enhanced computing power

- The World Wide Web
- Expanded multi-nationalism and globalization

Businesses first encountered software capable of connecting the enterprise during the 1990s, and many were compelled to move forward with enterprise computer systems because they did not trust the ability of the information islands created by their computer legacy systems to be able to cope with the year 2000. There is no doubt that enterprise software is changing the face of business. Manufacturing companies who have been under siege from "the China Price" are using enterprise software to improve productivity an astounding 4% *per year* since 1994 (Frichol, 2004). The top 100 SCM vendors generated about $4 billion in supply chain application revenue in 2002. The Yankee Group estimates that supply-chain integration reduced total cost of ownership of value-added networks by about 15%. Forrester Research expects U.S. firms will spend an average of $4.8 billion a year through 2008 to tune their entire supply network processes. International Data Corp estimates that the U.S. market size for CRM applications was about $5.6 billion in 2002 with projections of $10 billion by 2006. Giga Information Group approximates sales of core ERP software at $13 billion, and it predicts growth of 4.8% annually through 2006 (Targowski & Rienzo, 2004). American business schools must address enterprise software to stay relevant to current business practice.

Enterprise systems should be taught as a discipline because corporate emphasis is currently focused on the enterprise. This emphasis will remain because there is great potential for wealth creation. Enterprise focus is a formidable undertaking, and tools and techniques required to truly integrate the enterprise are still developing. When learning about enterprise systems, students should develop an appreciation of the way businesses create and employ information, regardless of its source. And they should also develop an appreciation of the relationships that system components have to the larger whole.

Systems are infinite in their expansion and regression, and business managers responsible for systems must draw system boundaries in an appropriate scale and scope that affords them prediction, control, and performance needed to achieve their objectives. Business systems are engineered to accomplish a goal, and significant resources are employed to get them to work together smoothly. Business corporations have evolved into economic dominance through coordination of nearly-decomposable hierarchical divisions and organizational identification (Simon, 2001). Nearly-decomposable systems maximize component independence and minimize the cost and effort of coordination and communication. Companies have separate, and nearly independent, departments optimizing sales, production, and logistics. Near-decomposability allows a corporate department to independently change many of its processes and procedures without concern for effects on other departments. As systems become more complex, nearly-decomposable architecture with its hierarchical subdivisions has been shown to be much more effective than architecture with less departmentalized interconnections. Simulations with genetic algorithms, have confirmed the dominance of near-decomposability in complex biological ecosystems (Simon, 2001). Near-decomposability can apply to any business system of activities. Once coordination and communication demands are minimized, the responsibility for the system can be assigned to any group that can accomplish the activities effectively. The phenomena of outsourcing and offshoring are direct consequences of near-decomposability.

As effective as nearly-decomposable systems are in business, they minimize rather than eliminate the need for coordination, communication, and control of different departments, divisions, or activities in a business. As the quality focus of the 1970s and 1980s demonstrated, there is wealth to be created, and competitive advantage to be gained, from coordination and communication of business component systems. Successful businesses ensure that the products obtained by the purchasing department perform well in production, and that accounting and sales personnel know when raw materials are in transit, production is scheduled, shipments are made, deliveries can be expected, and invoices issued. As business systems expand from individual to multiple companies, the demands of coordination, communication, and control intensify. If sufficiently robust methods of coordination, communication, and control exist, then nearly-decomposable activities can occur wherever they can be carried out most efficiently. Enterprise systems provide those robust methods.

CURRENT STATE OF ENTERPRISE INFORMATION INSTRUCTION

Implementing a curriculum focused on the connections of enterprise systems as opposed to the more traditional management information systems approach can be very challenging and expensive. Many universities have undertaken the process by introducing enterprise or ERP business software packages into the classroom, focusing on hands-on exercises with gradually escalating requirements for student understanding of process activities and implications. Many universities recognize that direct enterprise software experience can be helpful to students, but utilizing software to provide students with an opportunity to learn business processes experientially is a challenging effort. Antonucci, Corbitt, Stewart, and Harris (2004) observed that some universities flourish in their implementation of enterprise or ERP business software packages and others flounder. Academic champions of enterprise software must struggle through the same exasperating climb up the ERP tower as their industrial counterparts. Holland and Light describe an industrial ERP maturity model (as cited in Antonucci et al., 2004) with three stages:

- **Stage 1:** Planning and implementation.
  - o   Stage 1 has an operational focus, concentrating on tasks and tracking. Planning should include a long-term strategic vision, but the vast majority of time and energy in phase 1 involves operational tasks.
- **Stage 2:** Adoption and utilization.
  - o   Stage 2 expands operational thinking to tactical use of real-time data spread throughout the enterprise to improve quality and efficiency.
- **Stage 3:** Strategic use of ERP.
  - o   Stage 3 takes a broad strategic focus involving all elements of the business supply chain. The ERP system is used to coordinate the business value chain and is often linked to other enterprise systems including Supply Chain Management and Customer Relationship Management software packages.

Academic institutions can expect to experience a similar journey of maturity with ERP implementations, progressing from operational tasks to strategic thinking and learning. Most are still at stage 1. Some universities have made significant progress in integrating enterprise or ERP business software packages courses in their curricula. Fedorowicz, Gelinas, Usoff, and Hachey (2004) provide a dozen tips to guide institutions of higher learning to integrate enterprise systems in their curricula in order to illustrate current best practices of business processes and expose students to technology they can expect to use in their business careers. They can be summarized as follows:

- Develop infrastructure.
- Train the converted.
  - o Spend training money on those who will incorporate material and share information with other faculty.
- Start with concrete and develop more sophisticated learning.
- Build networks.
  - o Within faculty, industry practitioners, ERP trainers and support people.
- Share information through academic alliances.
- Give students support.

Even though universities implementing ERP systems in their coursework can expect to move from less sophisticated to more sophisticated uses of the software, core coursework must provide a larger framework under which the connections of enterprise software can be appreciated, and the capabilities of these systems can be seen as drivers for organizational transformation. Enterprise systems are not just making traditional business processes more efficient. They are contributing to the design and engineering of new processes. The impact of enterprise systems cannot be appreciated without recognizing organizational changes underway in the corporate world.

ENTERPRISE SYSTEM TEACHING MODEL

A model for enterprise teaching is shown in Figure 1. Infrastructure lays the foundation for enterprise system instruction. Students should receive a general overview of the components and tools of networks and the Internet, but a broad array of subjects can satisfy this requirement. Students cannot understand the connections of enterprise systems unless they recognize the technology systems that enable them. The unifying theme is *infrastructure*, lower level systems that allow higher level ones to operate. Relating the familiar transportation infrastructure to components and relationships that form our modern information/communication infrastructure can be a useful analogy. Topics like telecommunications, LAN topology, network technologies, client-server systems, operating systems, programming languages, e-mail, electronic data interchange, and groupware prepare students to think about the roles of communication and information in modern businesses.

Following infrastructure, students should be introduced to generic business systems emphasizing the role components play in the larger business. General systems theory can be introduced to the students by explaining the characteristics of historic Cold War development of systems design and engineering. General systems understanding precedes the introduction of the systems life cycle and system development life cycle. Systems instruction is also an appropriate place to introduce organizational complexity and the increasing demands placed upon managers to balance the interests of shareholders and stakeholders in modern business. Information systems make it possible to cope with unprecedented demands to control and monitor many diverse aspects of business. An understanding of the role information plays in

Figure 1. Enterprise systems teaching model

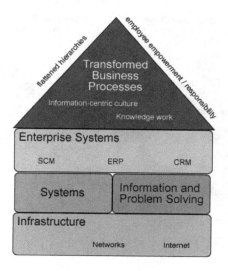

problem solving complements students' awareness of system components and relationships. Many business activities are problem solving activities. Students must understand that data can't solve problems but data is a critical starting point. Data must be analyzed, processed, and transformed into information, concepts, and knowledge in order to make prudent business decisions. Information systems play a critical role in process and analysis.

Infrastructure, systems, and problem solving prepare students for a discussion of enterprise systems that coordinate and integrate outputs from the many nearly-decomposable systems operating in business. By preceding the introduction of enterprise systems with the role of information and communication technology (ICT) in systems and problem solving, students can see enterprise software as part of business evolution. Enterprise systems can be seen as links in the business value chain. Supply chain management (SCM) links inbound logistics, operations, and outbound logistics. Customer relationship management (CRM) links outbound logistics, sales/marketing, and service. Enterprise resource planning (ERP) links outputs of theses systems as well as human resources, financial, and infrastructure support. Enterprise portals and electronic enterprises are included in enterprise systems discussions. The teaching focus involves moving from traditional business school discipline silos to integrated business processes as shown in Figure 2. Students should have an opportunity to work with enterprise software in class projects. Transformed business processes are the end result of enterprise systems. Paradigm shifts are occurring in business strategy, outsourcing, and substitution of technology for labor. Organization structures are experiencing flattened hierarchies, disintermediation, and networked alliances. Management is moving from task control to culture control with a pursuit of paradoxical goals. Knowledge is increasingly a source of wealth and knowledge workers are increasingly valued in the workplace. Information systems affect both our professional and personal lives with

Figure 2. Moving from academic silos to integrated business process

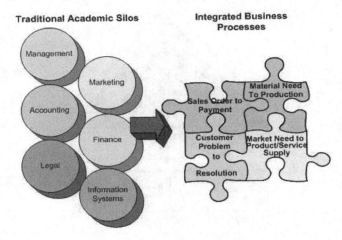

or without our knowledge or cooperation. The effects of the Information Age touch us all, and some of the changes in skill requirements, training, and attitudes occurring in modern workplaces are not comfortable.

TEN LEARNING MODULES

Following the enterprise systems teaching model of Figure 1, a modern undergraduate business program can support the fundamental characteristics of presenting enterprise systems in a larger ICT context through the use of the following 10 learning modules:

Infrastructure

Network Infrastructure and Business Processes

An information infrastructure model is introduced with layers involving telecommunications, computer networks, the Internet, computer hardware/software, communication programs, and business application programs. Investments in telecommunications are described and different types of networks are discussed along with the role of servers and clients in those networks. Communication systems like e-mail, groupware, teleconferences, and electronic data interchange (EDI) are covered.

The Internet and its Business Applications

Internet technologies are introduced along with their history, governance, and protocols. Top-level domains of the World Wide Web are described. Languages of the Internet including HTTP, FTP, HTML, and XML are covered as are services like Internet search. Intranets and Extranets are introduced along with security concerns and network protection. Typical uses for each are presented. E-commerce and business models associated with e-commerce are described. Web services are described as heirs to e-commerce technologies pioneered by EDI. Architecture is modeled for e-commerce from a B2C and B2B perspective, and revenue associated with each is discussed. Online payment systems are covered, as is public key infrastructure for secure on-line transactions. A short history of dot com companies is also provided. Students complete an Internet Services/E-Commerce project in which they compare service and commerce Web sites by specific criteria including ease of use, content/scope, privacy policies, customer service, and marketing techniques.

Systems
From Components to Business Process Integration

The systems perspective is introduced with general systems theory and a focus on components, relationships, and the role of components in a larger whole. A system definition is provided, expanded to information systems, and complexity of modern business systems is addressed. Information systems are presented as a means of coping with complexity. The system life cycle and system development life cycle are introduced with a brief history of system analysis and engineering. Quality management and project management are presented from a systems perspective. Students complete a systems project focusing on components and relationships of views relating to their majors. They create an input-process-output model of a company and examine critical perspectives for that particular business. Students calculate system complexity by calculating the number of pair-wise comparisons resulting from components they place in the views they believe are critical to their businesses.

Information and Problem Solving
From Data to Business Intelligence

The role of information in decision making is presented, exploring the way we move from data to choices. Information richness and methods of problem solving are introduced. This module has a cognitive science focus and history. It looks at ways in which problem solving methods utilize traditional outputs of computer information systems, and more recent incorporation of artificial intelligence.

Transformed Business Processes
From Enterprise to Extended Corporation

Enterprise systems are introduced and connected to the business value chain introduced by Michael Porter (1985). Enterprise systems are presented as the glue of business activities from inbound logistics to customer service. They also impact Porter's support activities of procurement, technology, human resources, and infrastructure. Management information systems are introduced as well as their gradual evolution to knowledge management systems. Enterprise portals are presented as a gateway to the electronic enterprise controlled and optimized by supply chain management (SCM), customer relationship management (CRM), and enterprise resource planning (ERP) software systems. Enterprise software is also aligned with the Porter value chain.

Enterprise Systems Classification and Project

Characteristics of enterprise information systems are presented for accounting, human resources, marketing, legal, and operations. ERP components are categorized as business, operations, or management information systems and related to the Porter value chain. Students complete an exercise with ERP software working through an entire business process like purchase to payment or sales order to payment.

IT/Communication and Evolving Business Organizations

Shifts in business structure resulting from the control and optimization capabilities of integrated information systems are presented. Trends involving shifts in strategic resources, flattening hierarchies, network-centric work relationships, and virtual enterprises are addressed. Attendant changes in management responsibilities are described. The role of information in outsourcing and off-shoring is discussed, and knowledge workers are presented as a source of creating wealth.

IT for Business Transformation

The transformation of business from an industrial to an information mindset is explored. An industrial enterprise model is compared with an information enterprise model. The work system of the industrial model is focused on in-house standardization, hierarchical and task management, a disposable labor force, and separation of thinking and doing. The business organization is concerned with economies of scale and mass production. In contrast, the work system of the information model is focused on flexibility, immediacy, outsourcing, network and culture management, high trust relations, and the integration of thinking and doing. Its business organization involves economy of scope and mass customization.

Information — Past and Future

A historic look at information in society beginning with the invention of printing with movable type to the electronic global village of the 21st century is presented. This section deals with the movement from goods to services, increasing reliance on theoretical knowledge and creation of new "intellectual technology" based on computers and other smart machines. The "digital divide" which separates information "haves" from information "have nots" is discussed.

Social/Ethical Information Issues

The role of information in our culture is presented: values, life styles, security, privacy, cyber crime, and ethics. Global communication networks are both bringing the world together and driving it apart at the same time. Broadband and convergence are changing the way we work, shop, and entertain ourselves. Privacy and security are important issues in cyberspace with wide-spread information dissemination, protection of intellectual property rights, and identity theft. Ethics have new dimensions in the age of blogs and billions of pages on the World Wide Web. Information systems bring new problems from the standpoint of bioethics.

CONCLUSION

Enterprise systems provide an opportunity for students to experience the complexity of integrated business processes, but the complexity of business extends beyond the connections of enterprise systems. Technology provides new tools that permit businesses to re-engineer systems and relationships that offer new and exciting means of building wealth. Students must prepare to work in a global business environment that is continuously evolving, and they need a context to frame enterprise systems in new economic paradigms. As business students prepare to enter a connected world, they should do more than experience the technology that enables it. They should consider what technology means to their professional and personal lives. This chapter describes a course that is designed to position enterprise systems within the trends and challenges that are shaping the post-industrial age.

REFERENCES

Antonucci, Y. L., Corbitt, G., Stewart, G., & Harris, A. L. (2004). Enterprise systems education: Where are we? Where are we going? *Journal of Information Systems Education, 15*(3), 227.

Bransford, J. D., Brown, A. L., & Cocking, R. R. (2000). *How people learn brain, mind, experience, and school*. Washington, DC: National Academy Press.

Bosco, J. (2004). *Is it possible to reform schools*? Paper presented at the New Futures for Learning in the Digital Age, Dublin, Ireland.

Fedorowicz, J., Gelinas, U. J., Usoff, C., & Hachey, G. (2004). Twelve tips for successfully integrating enterprise systems across the curriculum. *Journal of Information Systems Education, 15*(3), 235.

Frichol, M. (2004, November 17). *Microsoft business solutions manufacturing update*. Paper presented at the 2004 Microsoft Manufacturing Summit, Orlando, FL.

Gackowski, Z. J. (2003, June). *Case/real-life problem-based experiential learning with information system projects*. Paper presented at the Information Science and Information Technology Education Joint Conference, Pori, Finland.

Hejazi, S. S., Halpin, A. L., & Biggs, W. D. (2003). Using SAP ERP technology to integrate the undergraduate business curriculum. *Developments in Business Simulation and Experiential Learning, 30*, 122-125.

Johnson, T., Lorents, A. C., Morgan, J., & Ozmun, J. (2004). A customized ERP/SAP model for business curriculum integration. *Journal of Information Systems Education, 15*(3), 245.

Joseph, G., & George, A. (2002). ERP, learning communities, and curriculum integration. *Journal of Information Systems Education, 13*(1), 51-58.

Markulis, P. M., Howe, H., & Strang, D. R. (2005). Integrating the business curriculum with a comprehensive case study: A prototype. *Simulation & Gaming, 36*(2), 250

Michaelsen, L. K., Hobbs, J., & Stead, R. (2000). *Experientially integrating the undergraduate curriculum*. Paper presented at the Academy of Business Education, Villanova, PA.

Porter, M. (1985) *Competitive advantage creating and sustaining superior performance*. New York: The Free Press.

Roschelle, J. M., Pea, R. D., Hoadley, C. M., Gordin, D. N., & Means, B. M. (2000). Changing how and what children learn in school with computer-based technologies. *Children and Computer Technology, 10*(2), 76-101.

Schacter, J. (1999). *The impact of education technology on student achievement.* Retrieved October 10, 2004, 2004, from http://www.milkenexchange.org

Simon, H. A. (2001). Complex systems: The interplay of organizations and markets in contemporary society. *Computational & Mathematical Organization Theory, 7,* 79-85.

Targowski, A., & Rienzo, T. (2004). *Enterprise information infrastructure* (4th ed.). Kalamazoo, MI: Paradox Associates.

Chapter XIII

Enterprise Architecture and Information Architecture:
What is It and How to Teach It

Frank Lin, California State University of San Bernardino, USA

Leo Liu, Oracle Corporation, China

ABSTRACT

Companies around the world are using enterprise systems. Universities are following the trend by integrating enterprise systems into their curricula. The main role of enterprise systems is to support business operations efficiently and effectively and to create competitive advantage. Nevertheless, to reap the benefits of using enterprise systems, it is essential to align the information technology goals with business goals and to establish appropriate enterprise architecture (EA) and enterprise information architecture (EIA) support. For students to understand the linkage between the EA and EIA and to learn the subject, a hybrid academic and industrial approach to teach EA and EIA is proposed. This proposed hybrid approach covers theory, framework, principles, and best practices of the EA and EIA in the beginning, evolving to a practical and comprehensive approach in delivering the subject matter — EA and EIA. A real world EA and EIA project is used to illustrate the efficacy of these architectures.

INTRODUCTION

The initial publication of the Zachman framework in 1987 has generated great interest for educators, researchers, and practitioners in the subject of enterprise architecture, enterprise information architecture, and enterprise systems (ES) (Brancheau, Janz, & Wetherbe, 1996; Zachman, 1987). Companies around the world have implemented and/or are continuously implementing enterprise systems. Universities are following the trend by integrating enterprise systems into their curricula. Among various topics related to enterprise architecture, enterprise information architecture and enterprise systems, the need to align information systems (IS) and information technology (IT) with business goals is among the top key issues in organizations as ranked by information systems executives over the last decade (Luftman, 2005). The challenge sounds simple yet it is seemingly difficult to achieve given the dynamic nature of the competitive environment. This also has been evidenced by the much debated productivity paradox, resulting from inconclusive findings in research on information technology investment and organizational productivity (Broadbent & Weill, 1997; Ross & Beath, 2002).

Enterprise information architecture is built with the intention of supporting business goals and objectives. Alignment of information technology and business strategy requires sound enterprise architecture (Buchanan & Soley, 2002; Crossan, 2000; Laartz, Monnoyer, & Scherdin, 2003; Nolan, 2002). In the commercial world, many large corporations around the world such as Intel, Texaco, Best Buy, Delta, Hewlett-Packard, General Motors, DHL, Land O' Lakes, CAN Insurance, Vertex, and so forth, have developed and implemented their enterprise architectures and enterprise information architectures to support their operations in this world of "extreme competition." Even non-profit organizations such as the U.S. Internal Revenue Service, the U.S. Department of Veterans Affairs, the Coast Guard, the U.S. Department of Agriculture, the U.S. Forest Service, the Kansas Department of Transportation, the U.S. Air Force, and the U.S. Federal Aviation Administration are involved in enterprise architecture. Accordingly, it is apparent that enterprise architecture is a pertinent linking component of enterprise systems education in the 21st century.

Research has shown that strategic alignment theory and practice are in synchronization and there is little conventional academic wisdom to challenge, except for the need to document IS strategy and plans (Chan, 2002). Such a need calls for an adoption of an enterprise architecture software tool to document the IS strategy and plans. Popular frameworks such as the Zachman framework, DoDAF (C4ISR framework), and TOGAF (The Open Group Architecture framework) already have software tools available to promote their application. This chapter focuses on laying the foundation of why we cover enterprise architecture and enterprise information architecture in teaching enterprise systems and the importance of deriving an enterprise architecture and enterprise information architecture in achieving alignment between IT and business.

Any student who wants to understand and grasp the concepts, knowledge, integration, and application of enterprise systems has to understand the EA and EIA well.

Most approaches to EA and EIA have been far too complex and theoretical. The fundamental assumption in teaching this subject is: (1) a need for a simpler approach in teaching enterprise systems, and (2) the subject can best be learned through learning by doing. We recommend a hybrid academic and industrial approach that combines EA and EIA to teaching enterprise systems. We propose covering theory, framework, principle, and best practice of the EA and EIA in the beginning, and then moving to a practical and comprehensive approach to delivering the subject matter — EA and EIA combined with a case study to illustrate the efficacy of the architecture. Throughout the term, students should also carry out a comprehensive real world project involving building an EA and EIA for a real business. This can be best achieved through partnering with industries, professional organizations, and businesses.

The next section presents background information for this chapter. After that, we define enterprise architecture, enterprise information architecture, enterprise systems, and ultimately how they are all related. Next we discusses the issues, controversies, and problems regarding enterprise systems education, as it is today. Then a suggested alternative approach of teaching enterprise systems is presented, in which we also outlines the topic into 10 modules. Finally, we conclude the chapter by summarizing the efficacy of the proposed approach of teaching enterprise systems; a sample syllabus is presented in the Appendix.

BACKGROUND

The 1980s and 1990s were notorious for intensifying business competition. With the emergence of globalization and technology, coupled with the networking and communication infrastructure created in the 1990s, and economic liberalization and digitalization, we became a world of "extreme competition" as we proceeded into the 21st century (Fingar, 2005; Huyett & Viguerie, 2005). In order to compete or even just to survive, businesses have responded with new business models, new strategies, flatter organizational structures, more efficient and integrated processes and functions, new performance management systems, and six-sigma quality management programs among others. All of the aforementioned initiatives require proper infrastructure support, particularly the EA and EIA.

Businesses have also been quickly implementing ES to track the business, understand the business, improve the business, and predict the business. These ES implementations often included enterprise resource planning (ERP) with integrated business processes across functions in the 1990s; in the 2000s, it was customer relationship management (CRM), supply chain management (SCM), business intelligence (BI), e-business, e-commerce, and enterprise application integration (EAI). All these initiatives require proper infrastructure support, particularly enterprise architecture and the information systems and technologies-enterprise information architecture.

In this new economy, the skills, knowledge, and tools required for an employee to function efficiently and effectively are very different from those in the traditional economy. There have been some joint efforts by enterprise systems vendors and academic institutions in integrating enterprise systems into curricula in business, engineering, and information technology schools (Rosemann, 2004). Nevertheless most academic institutions that are still using a curriculum based on functional departmental operations seem to be slow in responding to these new requirements compared to the business world (Bennis & O'Toole, 2005; Bliss & Potter, 2000; Bradford, Vijayaraman, & Chandra, 2003; Dudley, Dudley, Clark, & Payne, 1995; Elliott, Goodwin, & Goodwin, 1994; Gosling & Mintzberg, 2004; Hamilton, McFarland, & Mirchandani, 2000; Michaelsen, 1999; Stover, Morris, Pharr, Reyes, & Byers, 1997; Wheeler, 1998).

According to the Clinger-Cohen Act of 1996 (Clinger-Cohen Act of 1996, 1996), the chief information officer (CIO) of federal agencies in the U.S. are required to develop and maintain an EA and use it to make investment decisions when acquiring a large automation system. Furthermore, the Clinger-Cohen Act mandates that all federal agencies' information systems align with the organization's strategic goals and objectives. Ensuring such an alignment requires sound enterprise architecture. In the commercial world, many large corporations around the world have also developed their EA to support their operations in this world of "extreme competition." Accordingly, the EA is a pertinent linking component of the enterprise systems education in the 21st century.

Globally, numerous universities have implemented some kind of enterprise systems education in the last 10 years or so (Antonucci, Corbitt, Stewart, & Harris, 2004). Yet, the integration of enterprise systems into the curriculum of business, engineering, and information technology schools is a major challenge for many universities (Rosemann, 2004). One of the biggest problems encountered by most universities in addition to the issues related to curriculum, training and outside support is the availability of a comprehensive case to be used in the classroom setting (Fedorowicz, Gelinas, Usoff, & Hachey, 2004; Johnson, Lorents, Morgan, & Ozmun, 2004).

However, little attention has been paid in the college curriculum to the architecture of an enterprise — either from the business perspective or the IT perspective. With traditional emphasis more about the functions of business than the practice of managing, students tend to lack of an overall understanding from an integrated perspective (Gosling & Mintzberg, 2004). It seems that students just understand certain business functions or certain IT products designed for a particular business process such as marketing, accounting, human resource, and so forth. Many information systems and/or information technology curricular in colleges and universities are set up according to the development path of the ES: MRPII-ERP-ERPII-CRM/SCM/BI. As a result, after completing the program, students are programmed into the module mind-set rather than a process-integrated and solution-oriented perspective that is required by organizations in this extreme competitive environment. Consequently, students often cannot meet the actual requirements of business after they complete their study of enterprise systems.

The importance of students having a comprehensive and strategic view of an enterprise when providing enterprise systems solutions can not be undermined. It is believed that an understanding of EA and EIA is a necessity in guiding students to not only appreciate the benefits of enterprise systems but also to evaluate and design an enterprise solution for a business. EA, EIA and their relationship is discussed in the next section.

ENTERPRISE ARCHITECTURE

Zachman brought the importance of EA to the attention of academia and practitioners when he published his article, "A Framework for Information Systems Architecture," in 1987 (Zachman, 1987). What is enterprise architecture? In general terms, an enterprise is a business or organization formed to produce product(s) or provide service(s). Architecture is the design of any type of structure.

Bernard (2004) defines an EA as "… (it) is both a management program and a documentation methodology that together provides an actionable, coordinated view of an enterprise's strategic direction, business processes, information flows, and resource utilization." Dennis A. Stevenson (n.d.), section editor for IS World Research, defines an EA as "a complete model of the enterprise; a master plan which acts as an integrating force between aspects of business planning such as goals, visions, strategies and governance principles; aspects of business operations such as business terms, organization structures, processes and data; aspects of automation such as application systems and databases; and the enabling technological infrastructure of the business such as computers, operating systems and networks."

Although the literature provides us with numerous definitions of what EA is, they are more or less similar. EA is the explicit description and documentation of the current and desired relationships among business and management processes, information systems, and information technology. It describes the "current architecture" and "target architecture" to include the rules and standards and systems life cycle information to optimize and maintain the environment which an organization wishes to create and maintain by managing its information technology portfolio. The EA must also provide a strategy that will enable an organization to support its current state and also act as the roadmap for transition to its target environment (VA Enterprise Architecture Innovation Team, 2001). Thus EA is a comprehensive blueprint of an organization by which we analyze and plan changes and make additions with respect to the business and information technology.

Enterprise Architecture and Enterprise Information Architecture

EA creates the ability to understand and determine the continual needs of integration, alignment, change, and responsiveness of the business to technology and to the marketplace through the development of models. "The essence of EA is much more than a series of models. Behind each model lie the policies, processes, and procedures through which each area or organization of the enterprise can articulate interests, exercise rights, meet obligations, and mediate differences for the collect whole" (O'Rourke, Fishman, & Selkow, 2003). Thus, EA serves as an input to the development of EIA.

EIA, with the focus of data, application, and technology requirements, is the foundation to support the design, development, and implementation of business strategies through an integrated enterprise system. EA is the linking pin to ensure an alignment of enterprise systems objectives and business objectives as illustrated in Figure 1. A well-designed EA and

Figure 1. Enterprise architecture (Lin, 2004)

Business and IT Are Related Through Enterprise Architecture

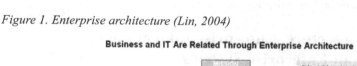

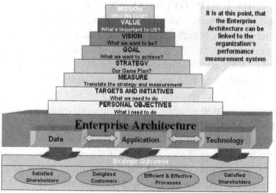

EIA ensures the alignment of enterprise system objectives and business strategic goals and objectives through the integration of mission, vision, goal, strategy, structure, and process in an organization. Clive Finkelstein (1997), chief scientist of Visible Systems Corporation states, "The only way an organization can manage strategic information, implement interoperable systems, and establish true data sharing is by using an EIA."

Data architecture, application architecture and technological architecture comprises the EIA. EIA also establishes guidelines, standards, and operational services that define the enterprise's systems development environment. Thus, a well-documented EA and EIA is a logical organization of information pertaining to the following corporate-level, enterprise-wide elements (Finkelstein, 1997):

- Strategic goals, objectives, and strategies
- Business rules and measures
- Business processes and workflows
- Information requirements
- Application systems
- Relationships between applications and data elements
- Technology infrastructure

When EA is so documented, it can be used to accomplish the following:

- Evaluate information systems and information technology investment
- Develop enterprise systems based on the requirements stipulated
- Facilitate change management by linking strategic requirements to systems that support them and by linking the business model to application designs
- Enable strategic information to be consistently and accurately derived from operational data
- Promote data sharing, thus, reducing data redundancy, and reducing maintenance costs
- Improve productivity through component development, management, and reuse
- Reduce software development cycle time

Enterprise Architecture, Enterprise Information Architecture, and Enterprise Systems

Researchers and practitioners have approached architecture from two different perspectives: business perspective, which often is labeled as enterprise architecture, and information technology perspective, which is described as enterprise information architecture. Nevertheless, EA and EIA are complementary to each other, like two sides of a coin. The EA serves as the basis for developing EIA and the EIA can be used to stimulate the innovative ways of achieving business objectives as stipulated in EA. Combined together, they serve as the basis for an organization in guiding its information system investment, development of enterprise systems and deployment of information technology.

Enterprise systems can be defined as customizable integrated application software that supports the core business processes and the main administrative areas of enterprises in different industries (Rosemann, 2004). Klaus, Rosemann, and Gable (2000) state that these systems have been viewed from a variety of perspectives:

- First, and most obviously, an enterprise system is a commodity, a product in the form of computer software.
- Second, and fundamentally, an enterprise system is seen as a development of mapping all processes and data of an enterprise into a comprehensive integrative structure.
- Third, an enterprise system is seen as the key element of an infrastructure that delivers a solution to business. This is the perspective embraced by information systems professionals, and the perspective we endorse in the context of this chapter.

As a commercial product, enterprise systems are offered by a range of vendors that specialize in this segment of the software market. The main enterprise systems vendors are SAP and Oracle which has acquired J. D. Edwards and PeopleSoft as of the writing of this manuscript. Gartner Group, prior to the recession in 2000, forecasted that this market would grow to more than $20 billion by 2002 — approximately half service revenue and half license revenue (Eschinger, 2004). They further estimated that more than 90% of Fortune 500 enterprises had purchased a module or a set of modules from an enterprise systems vendor. Gartner Group also forecast that the small and medium-sized enterprises (SME) market is the main customer group, as more than 50% of these enterprises have yet to select a next-generation enterprise system. A recent survey by AMR Research and Gartner Group (AMR Research, 2003; Eschinger & Pang, 2004; Soejarto & Eschinger, 2004), which tracks the enterprise software market indicates that the number of companies that intend to buy a new ERP suite or upgrade their current one is on the rise. According to AMR Research, such rebound of ERP spending partly is triggered by the availability of new modules, such as portals, SCM, and CRM, being incorporated into the ERP system by vendors and partly by the government regulation requirements such as HIPPA and Sarbanes-Oxley (Morgan, 2003). A 2004 survey published by Input Inc. of Reston, VA., finds that the federal market for ERP solutions will grow to $7.7 billion in fiscal 2009. This figure marks a 37% increase over fiscal 2004 spending of $5.6 billion (Grimes, 2004).

The Linkage of Enterprise Architecture and Enterprise Information Architecture

First and foremost, an enterprise system has to support an organization's strategy in achieving its goals and objectives. Developing business strategy involves the assessment of current state of the business, designing the target state of the business and developing strategies accordingly; all to achieve goals and objectives within the context of the organization's mission, value, and vision. The business strategy then serves as the input in building EA where metrics are constructed, targets and initiatives of achieving strategic goals and objectives are prioritized and ultimately designed. Furthermore, essential rules, policies, standards, and procedures are specified to ensure individuals in an organization work towards the company's goals and objectives. Necessary information, processes, and technologies requirements to support the business operation and achieve its goals and objectives are modeled into the EIA that is comprised of data architecture, application architecture, and technological infrastructure. The EA and EIA then serve not only as the basis for evaluating the information systems and technology investment but also as the guideline for developing and deploying enterprise systems in organizations. Figure 2 provides the detailed steps involved in building enterprise systems. Figure 3 further illustrates the component interactions within, and between, EA and EIA .

Business is typically organized into a number of functions including finance, accounting, sales, marketing, human resource, purchasing, receiving, inventory, research and development, manufacturing, planning, and so forth. Business processes are procedures, activities, and workflows that are organized to manage the business and to deliver products/services to customers. The business processes blueprint is the model of the organization's business processes, workflows, and all relevant policies, standards, procedures and guidelines that are used to ensure efficient and effective operation of the business. Business functions/processes blueprint, as one of the key components of EA, provides standards for building data and application access interface. Through data and application access interfaces, EA interact

Figure 2. Architecture development process

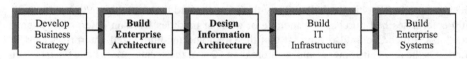

Figure 3. Strategy, architecture, and infrastructure

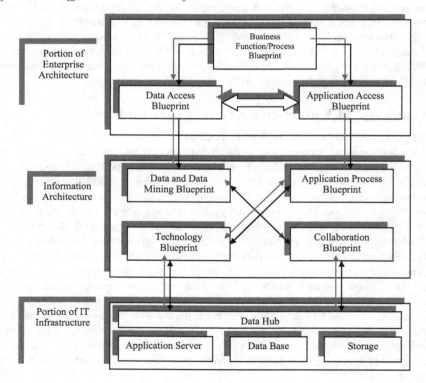

with the EIA, which encompasses the application architecture represented by the application process blueprint, data architecture represented by data and data mining blueprint, and technological architecture represented by technology blueprint. The interaction between various architectures is accomplished by collaboration blueprint. The Data Hub encompasses application server, data base, and storage illustrates one of the most component of the technology used by enterprise in accomplishing its goals and objectives.

ISSUES, CONTROVERSIES, PROBLEMS

The world is changing to become both global and process oriented. The competition and cross-functional integration in organizations has led businesses to look for individuals who have broad knowledge, problem solving skills and integrative view of a business rather than those who specialize in a functional area only. Enterprise system education as it is today has its limitations. The following discuss these limitations.

The New Enterprise: Moving From Pieces to Process

Achieving any overall business objective, such as retaining customers or increasing supply chain visibility, requires information to flow back and forth constantly among many organizations. For example, discovering customer requirements for a product, designing the product, managing the production process, shipping the finished goods, and collecting payment from the customer crosses multiple organizations within a business and requires a seamless flow of information.

To execute such a complex process efficiently requires that many organizations be able to exchange data quickly and easily. Achieving that ease and speed requires one of two actions: companies must either go to the expensive, time-consuming trouble of integrating and customizing applications, or they must adopt flexible applications that are designed, developed, and supported as a system that works together.

Usually, the establishment of enterprise systems is carried out in a proper sequence. To achieve the goal of an integrated system consists of flexible and scalable applications; one has to start the first step with a picture of total architecture in mind. Therefore, the design of the enterprise architecture is critical for the ultimate success of the enterprise.

Business Function Based, Not Business Process Based

Most of the college curricula are based on the business functions not on process (Bennis & O'Toole, 2005; Elliot et al., 1994). Students usually fail to have a sound and comprehensive understanding of business process. In most cases, the development of a certain enterprise system is to meet the requirement of a certain process not just a business function such as accounting or order entry. Many students who have taken study courses in information management still cannot analyze and examine the enterprise systems with a view of "business process." Although there have been some efforts in offering an integrated view of business in classes, particularly in teaching ERP (Hajnal & Riodan, 2004; Johnson et al., 2004) it is suggested that the foundation of such integration (i.e., EA and EIA) needs to be incorporated into teaching enterprise systems. There has been little coverage of EA and EIA in university curricula. For those do cover the topics, most approaches to delivering EA and EIA have been far too complex and theoretical. A suggested alternative approach is discussed in the next section.

SOLUTIONS AND RECOMMENDATIONS: AN ALTERNATIVE APPROACH TO TEACH ENTERPRISE SYSTEM

Based on the aforementioned discussion and the experiences of the authors with respect to integrating enterprise systems into university's curriculum, the following fundamental assumptions in teaching this subject are prescribed: (1) need for a simpler approach in teaching enterprise systems, and (2) the subject can be best learned through learning by doing. We recommend use a hybrid academic and industrial approach to teach enterprise systems in general and EA and EIA in particular. This hybrid covers theory, framework, principle, and best practice of the EA and EIA in the beginning, and then moves to a practical and comprehensive approach in delivering the subject matter — EA and EIA. A real world enterprise architecture and information architecture project is used to illustrate the efficacy of these architectures.

Topics to be covered include:

- The EA and its linkage to EIA
- EA and EIA toolkit
  1. Business framework
  2. Architecture framework
  3. Implementation framework
  4. Approach: each module contains major theme and includes exercises

As an illustration, recommended modules for teaching EA and EIA are listed below (please also see the Appendix for a sample syllabus, adopted from Carbone, 2004).

- **Module 1:** Introduction — best practices
  Objective — Understanding which strategies for enterprise architecture and enterprise information architecture work and why.
- **Module 2:** Linkage between enterprise architecture and information architecture.
  Objective — Understand the linkage between enterprise architecture and information architecture and the toolkit.
- **Module 3:** Using the business framework
  Objectives — Understanding what business information to collect and how to collect and analyze it
- **Module 4:** Using the architecture framework
  Objectives — Understanding how to translate business drivers to architecture outputs, understanding how to develop architecture outputs, and architecture modeling
- **Module 5:** Translate architecture to projects
  Objectives — Identifying and selecting viable architecture projects
- **Module 6:** Project implementation strategies
  Objectives — Understanding how to intentionally minimize architecture scope
- **Module 7:** Key implementation activities defining metrics, gaining concurrence and governing compliance.
  Objectives — Understanding what to measure and how to create metrics, how to gain concurrence for the target architecture and defining architecture governance

- **Module 8:** Key architecture processes, roles and human resource policies
  Objective — Assessing and defining key processes, policies and roles that enable architecture
- **Module 9:** Case study
  Objective — Understanding the process of building Enterprise Architecture and its benefits
- **Module 10:** A comprehensive enterprise architecture and enterprise information architecture project.
  Objective — Developing the knowledge of analyzing, creating, designing and developing an enterprise architecture and enterprise information architecture

CONCLUSION

Companies around the world have implemented or are implementing enterprise systems. Universities around the world are following this trend by integrating enterprise systems into their curriculum. The limitations of current curricular of enterprise system education are discussed. The main role of enterprise systems is to support business operation efficiently and effectively and to create competitive advantage. The requirements of alignment of information systems and information technology goals and business goals and an appropriate EA and EIA support are stressed and a hybrid academic and industrial approach to teach EA and EIA is proposed. This hybrid approach covers theory, framework, principles, and best practices of the EA and EIA in the beginning, and then move to a practical, simple, and comprehensive approach to delivering the subject matter — EA and EIA. When teaching EA and EIA, it is suggested to combine with a case and a real world project to illustrate the efficacy of the architecture and to facilitate students' learning of the subject.

REFERENCES

AMR Research. (2003). *Enterprise application outlook for 2003: The performance-driven enterprise*. Boston: AMR Research.

Antonucci, Y. L., Corbitt, G., Stewart, G., & Harris, A. L. (2004). Enterprise systems education: Where are we? Where are we going? *Journal of Information Systems Education, 15*(3), 277-234.

Bennis, W. G., & O'Toole, J. (2005). How business schools lost their way. *Harvard Business Review, 83*(5), 96-104.

Bernard, S. A. (2004). *An introduction to enterprise architecture*. Bloomington, IN: Authorhouse.

Bliss, R., & Potter, M. (2000). Integrating the undergraduate business curriculum: The case of Babson College. *Journal of Business Education, 1*(1), 1-13.

Bradford, M., Vijayaraman, B. S., & Chandra, A. (2003). The status of ERP implementation in business school curricula. *Communications of the Association of Information Systems, 12*(26), 437-456.

Brancheau, J. C., Janz, B. D., & Wetherbe, J. C. (1996). Key issues in information systems management — 1994-1995 SIM Delphi results. *MIS Quarterly, 20*(2), 225-242.

Broadbent, M., & Weill, P. (1997). Management by maxim: How business & IT managers can create IT infrastructure. *MIT Sloan Management Review, 38*(3), 77-92.

Buchanan, R. D., & Soley, R. M. (2002). *Aligning enterprise architecture and IT investments with corporate goals*. Stamford, CT: Meta Group, Inc. and the Object Management Group.

Chan, Y. E. (2002). Why haven't we mastered alignment? The importance of the informal organization structure. *MIS Quarterly Executive, 1*(2), 97-112.

Clinger-Cohen Act of 1996. (1996). (formerly, Information Technology Management Reform Act [ITMRA]). *Public Law*, 104-106. Division E, The Information Technology Management Reform Act (Clinger-Cohen Act) of 1996.

Crossan, Jr. R. M. (2000). Enterprise architecture: A must on the road to enterprise value. *Instrumentation & Control Systems, 73*(4), 35-39.

Dudley, S., Dudley, L., Clark, F., & Payne, S. (1995). New directions for the business curriculum. *Journal of Education for Business, 70*(5), 395.

Elliott, W. J., Goodwin, J. S., & Goodwin, J. C. (1994). MBA programs and business needs: Is there a mismatch? *Business Horizon, 37*(4), 56-60.

Eschinger, C. (2004). ERP license revenue and forecast: Worldwide, 1998-2008 (Executive Summary). Third party report, Gartner Group.

Eschinger, C., & Pang, C. (2004). Market trend: Enterprise Resource Planning, worldwide, 2003-2004. Third party report, Gartner Group.

Fedorowicz, J., Gelinas, Jr., U. J., Usoff, C., & Hachey, G. (2004). Twelve tips for successfully integrating enterprise systems across the curriculum. *Journal of Information Systems Education, 15*(3), 235-244.

Fingar, P. (2005). *Extreme competition: Innovation and the great 21ˢᵗ century business reformation*. Tampa, FL: Meghan-Kiffer Press.

Finkelstein, C. (1997). *Enterprise information architecture*. Retrieved March 22, 2005, from http://members.ozemail.com.au/~visible/papers/Architecture.html

Gosling, J., & Mintzberg, H. (2004). The education of practicing managers. *MIT Sloan Management Review, 45*(4), 19-22.

Grimes, B. (2004). *Report: Government spending on ERP will rise*. Washington Technology, November, 15, 2005. Retrieved November 22, 2005, from http://www.washington-technology.com/news/1_1/daily_news/24297-1.html

Hajnal, C. A., & Riordan, R. (2004). Exploring process, enterprise integration, and E-business concepts in the classroom: The case of petPRO. *Journal of Information Systems Education, 15*(3), 267-275.

Hamilton, D., McFarland, D., & Mirchandani, D. (2000). A decision model for integration across the business curriculum in the 21ˢᵗ century, *Journal of Management Education, 24*(1), 102-126.

Huyett, W. I., & Viguerie, S. P. (2005). Extreme competition. *The McKinsey Quarterly*, (1), 47-57.

Johnson, T., Lorents, A. C., Morgan, J., & Ozmun, J. (2004). A customized ERP/SAP model for business curriculum integration. *Journal of Information Systems Education, 15*(3), 245-253.

Klaus, H., Rosemann, M., & Gable, G. G. (2000). What is ERP? *Information Systems Frontiers, 2*(2), 141-162.

Laartz, J., Monnoyer, E., & Scherdin, A. (2003). Designing IT for business. *The McKinsey Quarterly*, (3), 77-84.

Lin, F. (2004). A comprehensive approach of enterprise architecture planning: Leveraging lessons from the industry, government, and research. In *Proceedings of International Conference on Pacific Rim Management* (pp. 321-325).

Luftman, J. (2005). Key issues for IT executives 2004. *MIS Quarterly Executive, 4*(2), 269-285.

Michaelsen, L. K. (1999). Integrating the core business curriculum: An experience-based solution. *Selections, 15*(2), 9-10.

Morgan, T. P. (2003). *ERP software spending seems to be picking up.* IT Jungle. Retrieved November, 22, 2005, from http://www.itjungle.com/tfh/tfh111703-story03.html

Nolan, D. P. (2002, September-October). Creating strategic alignment and readiness for IT. *Balanced Scorecard Report*, Harvard Business School Publishing.

O'Rourke, C., Fishman, N., & Selkow, W. (2003). *Enterprise architecture using the Zachman framework.* Boston: Course Technology.

Rosemann, M. (2001). Industry-oriented design of ERP-related curriculum — an Australian initiative. *Business Process Management Journal, 7*(3), 234-242.

Rosemann, M. (2004). The integration of SAP solutions in the curricula — outcomes of a global survey. *Queensland University of Technology,* 1-36.

Ross, J. W., & Beath, C. M. (2002). Beyond the business case: New approaches to IT investment. *MIT Sloan Management Review, 43*(2), 51-59.

Soejarto A., & Eschinger, C. (2004). *User survey: New initiatives show promise.* North America. Third party report, Gartner Group.

Stevenson, D. A. (n.d.). Enterprise architecture: Business theme and enterprise architecture. Retrieved March 6, 2005, from http://users.iafrica.com/o/om/omisditd/denniss/text/busthem0.html

Stover, D., Morris, J., Pharr, S., Reyes, M., & Byers, C. (1997). Breaking down the silos: Attaining an integrated business common core. *American Business Review, XV*(2), 1-11.

VA Enterprise Architecture Innovation Team. (2001). *Enterprise architecture: strategy, governance, & implementation.* Department of Veteran Affairs. Retrieved from http://www.va.gov/oirm/architecture/EA/strategy/VAEAVersion-10-01.PDF

Wheeler, B. (1998). The state of business education: Preparation for the past. *Selections, 14*(2), 19-21.

Zachman, J. A. (1987). A framework for information systems architecture. *IBM Systems Journal, 26*(3), 276-292.

APPENDIX

Syllabus (A Sampler)

Readings

1. Carbone, J. A. (2004). *IT architecture toolkit.* Upper Saddle River, NJ: Prentice Hall.
2. Spewak, S. H. (1992). *Enterprise architecture planning: Developing a blueprint for data, applications, and technology.* New York: John Wiley & Sons.
3. Other relevant materials:
   - Bernard, S. A. (2004) *An introduction to enterprise architecture.* Bloomington, IN: Authorhouse.

- Buchanan, R. D., & Soley, R.M. (2002). Aligning enterprise architecture and IT investments with corporate goals, Meta Group, Inc. and the Object Management Group.
- Cook, M. (1996). *Building enterprise information architecture: Reengineering information systems.* Upper Saddle River, NJ: Prentice-Hall.
- Earl, M J. (1988). IT and strategic advantage: A framework of frameworks. In M. J. Earl (Ed.), *Information management: The strategic dimension.* Oxford, UK: Oxford University Press.
- IBM. (1984). Business systems planning: Information systems planning guide (4th ed.).
- Laartz, J., Sonderegger, E., & Vincker, J. (2000). The Paris guide to IT architecture, *The McKinsey Quarterly*, (3), 118-127.
- Labovitz, G., & Rosansky, V. (1997). *The power of alignment.* New York: John Wiley & Sons.
- McFarlan, F. W. (1984). Information technology changes the way you compete. *Harvard Business Review, 62*(3), 98-103.
- McGrath, R. G., & MacMillan, I. C. (2005). Market busting: Strategies for exceptional business growth. *Harvard Business Review, 83*(3), 80-89.
- Nolan, D. P. (2002, September-October). Creating strategic alignment and readiness for IT, *Balanced Scorecard Report.* MA: Harvard Business School Publishing.
- O'Rourke, C., Fishman, N., & Selkow, W. (2003). *Enterprise architecture using the Zachman framework.* Boston: Course Technology.
- Porter, M. E., & Millar, V. E. (1985). How information gives you competitive advantage. *Harvard Business Review, 63*(4), 149-160.
- Porter, M. E. (1985). *Competitive advantage: Creating and sustaining superior performance.* New York: The Free Press.
- Rackoff, N., Wiseman, C, & Ullrich, W. A. (1985). Information systems for competitive advantage: Implementation of a planning process. *MIS Quarterly, 9*(4), 285-294.
- VA Enterprise Architecture Innovation Team. (2001). *Enterprise architecture: strategy, governance, & implementation.* Department of Veteran Affairs.
- Zachman, J. A. (1987). A framework for information systems architecture. *IBM Systems Journal, 26*(3), 276–292.

Goals and Objectives

Goals

The goal of enterprise architecture is to help organizations do the right things better and to win competition. The course focuses on the aspects and issues of building of enterprise architecture and enterprise information architecture.

Objectives

Information systems and information technologies play a critical role in the products' creation, operations, decision-making, and learning of modern organizations. In the service industry, for example, almost half of all new capital investment involves information systems and information technologies. The topic is therefore of considerable interest to senior

IS executives, managers in all functional areas of business, and students. Understanding the strategic potential of information systems and information technologies is arguably the key to obtaining significant value from information system and information technologies expenditures. This has been, and will continue to be, one of the most significant challenges facing IS professional.

The specific learning objectives a student will obtain from this course are:

1.   Understanding of business success factors and the role information systems and information technologies can play in shaping and/or supporting business strategies
2.   An appreciation of the fact that the benefits of information systems can only be unleashed when one understands a company's internal strengths/weaknesses, the external environmental challenges (threats/opportunities), its vision, mission, strategies, tactics, and management style; this includes an understanding of the competitive environment and the competitive forces within an industry
3.   Understanding of the relationships between a company's vision, mission, strategy, tactics, business plan, and how the information systems plan, including enterprise architecture and enterprise information architecture, fits in
4.   Ability to analyze where strategic use of information systems in a company can bring competitive advantage
5.   Ability to apply the strategic business planning process, the enterprise architecture planning (EAP) framework to develop an information system plan and build an enterprise architecture and enterprise information architecture

Class Sessions

The learning methodology used in this course consists of lecture, class discussion, article review and report, presentation, group project report & presentation, and exams.

Course Outline

The course outline provides an overview of the topics to be covered.

*   **Module 1:** Introduction — course overview and best practices
    Objective — Understanding which strategies for enterprise architecture and enterprise information architecture work and why
*   **Module 2:** Linkage between enterprise architecture and information architecture
    Objective — Understand the linkage between enterprise architecture and information architecture and the toolkit
*   **Module 3:** Using the business framework
    Objectives — Understanding what business information to collect and how to collect and analyze it
*   **Module 4:** Using the architecture framework
    Objectives — Understanding how to translate business drivers to architecture outputs, understanding how to develop architecture outputs, and architecture modeling
*   **Module 5:** Translate architecture to projects
    Objectives — Identifying and selecting viable architecture projects
*   **Module 6:** Project implementation strategies
    Objectives — Understanding how to intentionally minimize architecture scope

- **Module 7:** Key implementation activities defining metrics, gaining concurrence and governing compliance
  Objectives — Understanding what to measure and how to create metrics, how to gain concurrence for the target architecture and defining architecture governance
- **Module 8:** Key architecture processes, roles and human resource policies
  Objective — Assessing and defining key processes, policies and roles that enable architecture
- **Module 9:** Case study
  Objective — Understanding the process of building enterprise architecture and its benefits.
- **Module 10:** A comprehensive enterprise architecture and enterprise information architecture project
  Objective — Developing the knowledge of analyzing, creating, designing and developing an enterprise architecture and enterprise information architecture.

Requirements

1. *General Class Participation*
    The class participation grade will reflect an evaluation of the quality and quantity of students' contributions during class sessions over the course of the term. Students are expected to have thoughtfully read and studied all assigned readings prior to class. Some class sessions will begin with instructor or student led presentation, questions, and answers. Therefore, students should be prepared to discuss the assigned readings, answer questions, and contribute to group discussions at every class. It is unlikely that a simple read of the chapters and assigned materials will sufficiently equip students for class. Look for opportunities to apply the chapter's concepts to situations in class discussions and take time to write down any unanswered questions.

    The following are some general guidelines that I use to grade class participation: If you almost never speak out in class or miss several classes, you will receive a participation grade of C. If you speak occasionally but rarely say anything inspired, your participation grade will be some sort of B (depending on how "occasionally" and how well prepared you are). "Inspiration" — the path to an "A" participation grade — involves things like, (1) applying conceptual material from the readings or the presentation/lecture, (2) doing a bit of outside reading and applying it in the discussion, (3) integrating comments from previous students, (4) reaching back to something said previously in the discussion that is pertinent to the discussion at the moment, (5) taking substantive issue with a classmate's analysis, (6) pulling together material from several places in the readings and assigned materials, (7) drawing parallels from previous discussions and readings and experiences from the on-going projects, (8) tying in briefly an experience you have had that is relevant to the discussion, (9) generally demonstrating that you have carefully read the assigned readings and given them careful thought, or (10) not dominating class discussions. I will cold-call — particularly on students from whom the class has not heard in a while.

2. ***Strategic Information Systems Planning (ISP) — Enterprise Architecture Project Report and Presentation***

This is a group project. Students will form groups of 5 or 6 members during the first day of the class. Students may form their own groups. The instructor will assign any student needing a group to a group. Each group will be responsible for a Strategic Information Systems Planning study for a real organization. The instructor will assign organizations to student groups. Students will use the Strategic Business Planning process for building enterprise architecture by Jane A. Carbone (2004) and complement it with the EAP methodology discussed by Spewak (1992) as well as materials discussed in class. Students are expected to use enterprise architecture modeling tool such as ProVision by Proforma Corporation or System Architect by Telelogic & Popkin. Students are expected to make an oral presentation and submit a written report on this project. Each group has to select a group leader and prepare a Gantt chart for the project schedule by the third week of class.

3. ***Industry Analysis***

Each student group will conduct an industry analysis. Students may use Porter's 5 forces model, Porter and Miller's Information Intensity Matrix, the Strategic Grid and SWOT analysis for industry analysis.

4. ***Article Reports***

You will be expected to prepare a total of three article reports based on outside readings and related to topics covered in class. The articles you research should come from journals (i.e. *Sloan Management Review*, *Harvard Business Review*, *Information Systems Research*, *MIS Quarterly*, *Journal of Management Information Systems*, etc.) rather than the 'popular press' (i.e., *PC Magazine*, *LA Times*). The top of the report should note the citation, followed by a half page summary of the article. The rest of the report should cover your analysis of the topic including any issues you believe are relevant to the topics discussed in class. A copy of the article should be attached to your report.

5. ***Examination***

Each student will participate in a comprehensive final examination. The examination will evaluate the student's comprehension and retention of the topic areas and subject matter in the field being studied.

Chapter XIV

Teaching ERP
with Microsoft Business
Solutions — Great Plains™

Muhammad A. Razi, Western Michigan University, USA

ABSTRACT

Enterprise resource planning (ERP) systems have become indispensable software systems for many corporations worldwide. As more and more companies implement ERP to support daily business transactions, the need for ERP trained employees are increasing as well. Industry demand has prompted many universities to consider incorporating ERP into their curricula. Information systems curriculum in many universities have started offering courses that include ERP education; however, most universities have faced multi-faceted challenges related to lab setup, training, software support, and curriculum design. In this chapter, a guideline for development and teaching an ERP based course with MS Great Plains™ is provided. Teaching approach is discussed and an ERP based business curriculum is proposed. Effectiveness of the curriculum design in the classroom is analyzed based on a single semester trial of the course in two classrooms.

INTRODUCTION

In today's highly competitive business environment, employers expect business graduates to understand business processes and underlying technologies that support them. As businesses are going global, the complexity of business processes and the interdependent relationships that are needed to support globalization are also going beyond traditional boundaries. Understanding of business processes is not complete without the proper knowledge of data flow associated with each business process. As Antonucci, Corbitt, Stewart, and Harris (2004) put it "As educators, we must bring the issues and practices of industry to the classroom" (p. 227). Traditional education methods are often task-oriented rather than process oriented (Boykin & Martz Jr., 2004). This creates a paradoxical situation where businesses demand new hires have knowledge and understanding of process so that they can take part in projects with minimal training and within the shortest possible time. Enterprise resource planning (ERP) systems software is used by most manufacturing and service organizations and is able to provide a comprehensive business process experience to students. ERP systems seamlessly integrate information generated and used by various functional departments within an organization, such as manufacturing, inventory control, accounting, purchasing, sales and marketing, finance and human resources. ERP systems provide accurate and real-time data, which is vital for a company's day-to-day business operations, decision making and ultimately, its success. Desire for data sharing among manufacturers, sellers, vendors, and customers is pushing manufacturers and vendors alike toward installing compatible systems such as ERP, supply-chain management (SCM) and customer-relationship management (CRM). Yet, according to Watson and Schneider (1999) "Most IS curricula do not provide significant coverage of ERP concepts, nor do they graduate students who are knowledgeable about these systems and the impact that these systems have on industry" (pp. 1-48).

Typically, an ERP system is supported by a single or multiple relational databases. Inclusion of ERP systems in the business curricula could essentially provide:

- Students with knowledge in management information systems that integrate and automate many of the business practices associated with the manufacturing, buying and selling operations of a company.
- Students with better understanding of how a business works within and across functional areas.
- Student opportunity to learn skills with high demand in the job market.
- Increased visibility of the academic program and thereby, increased visibility of students among business and industry leaders.

Corbitt & Mensching (2000) also mentioned several of the reasons above as objectives of an ERP implementation course. A conceptual diagram of ERP curriculum that shows integration of the Business Core is shown in Figure 1.

Large ERP software systems such as, SAP are being used by many universities into their curriculum (Antonucci, Corbitt, Stewart, & Harris, 2004; Boykin & Martz, 2004; Fedorowitz, Gelinas, Usoff, & Hachey, 2004; Hawking, McCarthy, & Stein, 2004; Johnson, Lorents, Morgan, & Ozmun, 2004). Instead of using a large and complex ERP software, we use a smaller business solution named Great Plains™. Great Plains is a Microsoft product that mainly targets small-to-medium size companies (SMEs). In this chapter, a guideline

Figure 1. ERP curriculum (Adapted from Boykin et al., 2004)

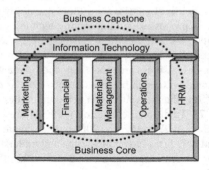

for teaching ERP systems with MS Great Plains™ is provided. The rest of the chapter is organized as follows.

The next section provides a literature review followed by a brief introduction of MS Great Plains™. Section four discusses pedagogy and suggests an ERP based business curriculum. Section five provides a reflection of the effectiveness of the curriculum design in the classroom. The chapter ends with concluding remarks.

LITERATURE REVIEW: ERP IN EDUCATION

ERP systems evolved from material requirement planning (MRP) systems over the past 3 decades. The American Production and Inventory Control Society (APICS) has been a strong advocate for ERP systems (Watson et al., 1999). APICS (1998) defines ERP as "an accounting-oriented information system for identifying and planning the enterprise-wide resources needed to take, make, ship, and account for customer orders. An ERP system differs from the MRPII system in technical requirements such as graphical user interface, relational database, use of fourth generation language, and computer-aided software engineering tools in development, client/server architecture, and open-systems portability."

Inclusion of ERP in business curriculum is a relatively new phenomenon. In addition to the information systems (IS) programs, accounting, supply-chain management and human resources management programs are showing interest in the inclusion of ERP in their curriculum. Watson et al. (1999) discuss opportunities for incorporating ERP knowledge into an IS program. The authors proposed a curriculum that focuses on providing ERP knowledge through hands-on experience by students on a real ERP system. The curriculum development approach discussed by authors is referred to as the "KnowDule" (know-jewel) approach. "A KnowDule is short for a 'knowledge module' and is, ideally, designed to be an on-line learning module." The KnowDule approach exposes students to key elements of the ERP system (e.g., functionality, business process, integrated system concept, common development environment, and ERP technical architecture [client/server architecture]). The authors also discussed costs and critical success factors.

Hawking, Ramp, and Shackleton (2001) examined the potential use of an ERP system within the context of a broad IS curriculum model referred to as the IS'97. Authors provided brief outlines of possible courses where ERP can be used. They also provided discussions on physical design and implementation issues. In their approach, the authors claim to have refined the KnowDule concept of Watson et al. (1999). Universities that decided to introduce ERP curriculum were helped by ERP vendors (notably SAP and Microsoft). SAP established the largest alliance with more than 400 universities worldwide (Hawking et al., 2004). Microsoft is also getting into the ERP academic alliance with its mid-to-low end ERP product named Great Plains™. Hawking et al. (2004) mentioned five different curriculum approaches that are developed by universities:

1. ERP training
2. ERP via business processes
3. Information systems approach
4. ERP concepts
5. The hybrid (hybrid of the four)

The authors think that irrespective of the approach adopted by universities, the curriculum is often dependent on just a few faculty. While understanding ERP system is crucial, the focus is shifting from the system to the business processes (Antonucci, Corbitt, Stewart, & Harris, 2004). Even though many universities in the world have implemented ERP education in their curriculum, the depth of system, technology, business process, and web integration into the curriculum varies. Stages of ERP education deployment are discussed by Antonucci et al (2004). Fedorowitz, Gelinas, Usoff, & Hachey (2004) provide twelve tips for ERP integration into curriculum. Tips are grouped into three categories: (1) curriculum, (2) training and outside support, and (3) faculty and student. They conclude that, "effective planning and efficient use of time and resources in these areas will help reduce start-up time and bolster success."

MS GREAT PLAINS™

More and more organizations see strategic advantage in functional integration and therefore, seeking to move away from the traditional silo (functional independence) mentality. In order to align students' academic preparation with the demand of business, educators see ERP as a vehicle that will enable the change in educational delivery from functional orientation to business process orientation (Becerra-Fernandez, Murphy, & Simon, 2000).

Microsoft business solutions (MBS) — Great Plains™ operates as both a Windows software application and as a Web Portal. Users may operate the system from either a Windows PC or launch it using an Internet browser. The number of users may range from a single user to several hundred users. Great Plains™ offers powerful features, compatibility and reliability. In addition to providing a multi-user environment, Great Plains™ supports multi-language, multi-currency, multi-tax, multi-server, as well as multi-processor. Great Plains™ imposes an integrated system by establishing a set of applications supporting business operations. Microsoft Great Plains™ modules and functions are shown in Table 1.

One of the advantages of using Great Plains™ as a teaching tool for ERP is that it has familiar Microsoft Office™ (MS Office) look. The system also comes with a wide range of user configurable features, object oriented design, flexible menu structure, configurable security, and a wide set of integration tools including tools for integration with MS Office.

Table 1. Great Plains modules and functions within each module (Source: http://www.mi-crosoft.com/BusinessSolutions/GreatPlains/factsheets.mspx [Click on the Microsoft Great Plains Overview link])

FINANCIAL MANAGEMENT	MANUFACTURING
General Ledger	Sales Forecasting
Account Level Security	Master Production Scheduling
Analytical Accounting	Capacity Requirements Planning
Multidimensional Analysis	Materials Requirement Planning
Fixed Asset Management	Sales Configurator
Intercompany with Interfund	Manufacturing Bill of Materials
Accounting	Manufacturing Order Processing
Payables Management	Engineering Change Management
Receivables Management	Quality Assurance
Bank Reconciliation	Job Costing
Cash Flow Management	
Collections Management	
Customer/Vendor Consolidations	
eBanking	
eExpense Management	
Revenue/Expense Deferrals	
Refund Checks	
Multicurrency Management	
DISTRIBUTION	**FIELD SERVICE MANAGEMENT**
Sales Order Processing w/Advanced	Service Call Management
Invoicing	Contract Administration
Invoicing	Returns Management
Advanced Distribution	Preventive Maintenance
Advanced Picking	Depot Management
Available to Promise	ManagerAssist
Landed Cost	eTech
Inventory Control	TechAssist
Bill of Materials	eService Calls
Extended Pricing	eReturns
Purchase Order Processing/Receiving	
PO Generator	
Demand Planner	
MICROSOFT BUSINESS SOLUTIONS BUSINESS PORTAL	**CUSTOMIZATION AND INTEGRATION TOOLS**
Microsoft Business Portal	eConnect
HRM Self-Service Suite	Integration Manager
Key Performance Indicators	Modifier with Visual Basic® for
Project Time and Expense	Applications
Requisition Management	Dexterity
Electronic Document Delivery	Software Development Kit (SDK)

Table 1. continued

ANALYTICS	HR MANAGEMENT
Microsoft Business Solutions for Analytics–FRx® Professional Microsoft Business Solutions for Analytics–Forecaster Microsoft Business Solutions for Analytics–Enterprise Reporting Crystal Reports 10 Professional	Human Resources (US & Canada) Payroll (US & Canada) Direct Deposit (US & Canada) Payroll Connect (US) Federal Magnetic Media (US)
FOUNDATION	E-COMMERCE
System Manager Report Writer Advanced Security Field Level Security Process Server	eConnect eOrder
PROJECT ACCOUNTING	
Project Accounting	

Figure 2. Great Plains™ architecture (Source: http://msdn.microsoft.com/library/)

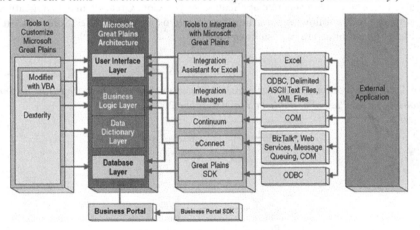

Familiar, easy-to-use environments help improve productivity and minimize training costs. Great Plains™ architecture that shows available integration methods is shown in Figure 2.

TEACHING ERP WITH MS GREAT PLAINS™

This chapter proposes a curriculum that adopts an information systems approach with business processes in the background. The approach basically works in four steps:

1.   Students are introduced to the ERP software, different modules and functions within each module.
2.   Lectures are given on specific business processes.
3.   Students work on business processes in class using MS Great Plains™ functions.
4.   They work on challenging assignments outside the class that involves understanding business processes and use of ERP software. Emphasis is given to the strategic use of ERP to:
     a.   Support integrated, cross-functional business activities
     b.   Optimize ERP benefits
     c.   Support decision making

Projects and assignments also involve teamwork. Some setup issues and a detailed teaching strategy follow.

Setting Up the Lab

The structure of the core Great Plains™ application is shown in Figure 3.

•   **Single-user installation:** All components are installed on a single workstation.
•   **Multi-user installations:** The runtime engine and Great Plains™ application diction-ary are installed on individual workstations while data for the system is managed by a separate server that hosts SQL server database. However, application dictionary may also be installed on a separate application server. Core Great Plains™ application is composed of the following parts (http://www.microsoft.com/BusinessSolutions/Great-Plains/gp_architecture_wp_summary.mspx).

Figure 3. GP application structure (Source: Architecture White Paper, Microsoft Business Solutions — Great Plains™, published in November 2004)

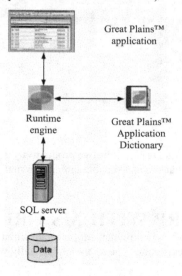

Great Plains™ application

Runtime engine

Great Plains™ Application Dictionary

SQL server

Data

- **Dexterity runtime engine:** Normally a client side software component that displays the functioning application to the end user and works as the subsystems that access the SQL database. The runtime engine also provides the modifier, report writer, VBA environment, and COM interface. It relies heavily on Microsoft's Visual C++ but also includes graphical tools for tasks such as user interface design and report creation. The runtime engine is also integrated with Microsoft Office, allowing data transfer from Great Plains™ software to Excel, Outlook or other Office applications.
- **Great Plains™ Application Dictionary:** The Application Dictionary, considered as the middle tier, contains the business logic for the core application. This tier separates the business logic from the application presentation, thereby, insulating the application from technology changes.
- **Microsoft SQL server database:** Microsoft Great Plains™ uses Microsoft SQL server database to store and manage data for the application. Great Plains™ installation allows sample data (Fabrikam, Inc.) to load on the SQL server database.

Account format setup in financial accounting for Fabrikam data requires account length to be at least nine characters with a minimum of three segments per account. Once installation is complete, user accounts must be created through Great Plains™ administrative functions (shown in Figure 4).

User accounts are stored in SQL server database. Lab setup should be tested by logging in as an end-user and executing transactions that are to be presented in class. The GP users will note that the activation date for items in the test company Fabrikam, Inc. is set to a future date (for GP version 8.00g7, the date is set to April 12, 2007). Therefore, if the transaction date is before the activation date, a user may encounter warnings and may not be able to complete certain transactions. However, the activation date for individual items may be set to an earlier date from the main menu as follows:

Cards → Manufacturing → Inventory → Engineering Data

Fiscal periods for years 2000 through 2008 exists, however, none of the periods are closed.

Teaching Strategy

Teaching strategy is based on maximization of critical pedagogical issues such as, learning objectives, student participation, teamwork, and effective communication. This course is designed to underscore applied concepts such as, business activities, economic events, and information processing requirements with software that supports integration

Figure 4. User account creation

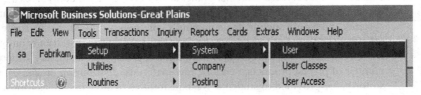

and real time information processing. Depending on the technical skill of target students, ERP curriculum may include application development/modification through GP modifier (Tools → Customize → Modifier) and Visual Basic Editor (Tools → Customize → Visual Basic Editor). Students are required to have prior programming and database exposure for them to be able to add modification to Great Plains™ functions. At the end of the course, students are expected to have some understanding of the architecture, modules, implementation, setup, and management of enterprise resource planning systems. Recommended course components follow:

1. **Discussion:** Fundamentals of business processes, company structure, system integration and ERP architecture.
2. **In-class practice assignments:** With in-class assignments, students gain first hand knowledge of ERP systems. Assignments may cover transaction processing in the areas of purchase order (PO), sales order (SO), inventory management and others. Students may also work on report writer, modifier and administrative functions. In-class practice assignments need to be relatively short, easy to follow ("click-by-click" instructions) and well understood by students. On one hand, this approach may expose students to different parts of the system with minimum support from the faculty, on the other hand, the risk is that many students may resort to blindly following the instructions without understanding the material. As suggested by Stacy E. Kovar (http://info.cba. ksu.edu/skovar/greatplains/), negative effects of "click-by-click" instruction may be reduced if students are required to answer frequent questions throughout the assignment.
3. **Homework assignments:** In-class assignments may be followed by more in-depth and challenging homework assignments. Depending on the depth and complexity, assignments may be designated for individuals or team.
4. **Team projects:**
    a. The first approach is more suitable for technically sound computer science (CS) and computer information systems (CIS) students. In this approach, a class project is divided among several teams. Each team is responsible for developing end-user applications using any programming language for various business processes within a department, for example, accounting, purchasing, sales, inventory, and so forth. Students also develop a back-end database using Oracle™ or SQL server or any other database engine that supports front-end applications. Data modeling techniques are used in the development of the database. End-user applications are then put together into an integrated software system, just like a real world ERP system. This approach gives students a unique project development experience that emphasizes team dynamics, IT and business knowledge, knowledge in system integration and management skills.
    b. The second approach is also a class project divided among several teams and is suitable for all business students. Students are given a case that involves a company in need of a software that would be able to replace the existing information systems and would support the company's continuous growth and its stride for efficiency and competitive advantage. Students are asked to install and configure MS Great Plains™. All relevant information regarding the company structure, number of plants, products, vendors, raw materials, distribution processes, and so forth, are provided to students. Responsibilities of students are as follows:

- Install MS Great Plains™
- Create a new company within MS Great Plains™
- Setup all accounting, financial and other parameters
- Create employee, vendor, warehouse, raw material, product and other required data following the guideline in the case
- Setup work centers and create routing and bill-of-materials (BOM) for manufacturing
- Create transactions, for example, purchasing, production (manufacturing order entry), sales, warehouse transfer
- Check to see if journal entries are correct
- Perform period-end/year-end closing

For this project to be successful, students should be able to map actual flow of business processes with functional steps of ERP.

Suggested Course Components

Component		Percentage
1.	In-class practice assignment	25
2.	Take-home assignments	25
3.	Term project	25
4.	Exams	25

Suggested Discussion Topics and Assignments

Discussion Topics
- Introduction to enterprise resource planning (ERP) systems
- Great Plains™ architecture
- Business process re-engineering
- ERP system planning design and implementation–critical issues
- Great Plains™ installation (single-user/multi-user) and related issues
- Great Plains™ navigation (class demonstration suggested)
- Material management (MM)
- Purchase order
- Billing/accounts receivable/cash receipts process
- Sales and marketing
- Accounts payable/cash disbursements process
- Manufacturing

Assignments
- Case-business process re-engineering
- Great Plains™ system admin/security management
- MM (vendor, item, site [warehouse] maintenance)
- Purchase order
- Billing/accounts receivable/cash receipts process
- Sales order process
- Accounts payable/cash disbursements process

- Great Plains™ System modification-customize Great Plains™ Windows
- Great Plains™ System modification-report generation and modification
- Great Plains™ System modification-advanced report generation and modification

Term Project
- Project case presented to the class
- Project leader and assistants to project leader identified
- Teams are formed and responsibilities of each team member, project leader, and assistant to project leader identified

Instructors may include functions such as human resources management (HRM) and payroll processing (PP). A sample homework assignment and a project case is provided in Appendices A and B.

Effectiveness of the Curriculum Design in the Classroom

This approach has been used in two sections of a capstone course at an undergraduate business program with CIS majors during Spring 2005. No formal survey was conducted to evaluate the effectiveness of this approach; however, informal student interviews and results of teaching evaluations indicate that most students liked this approach and they thought the assignments were useful. The project was seen as too complex to be coordinated, completed and executed within a semester with the participation of whole class. Students also felt that it was difficult to maintain fair participation from all students at all levels of the team project. By and large, students accepted the curriculum as a capstone course for undergraduate business students with CIS majors.

CONCLUSION

MS Great Plains™ has advanced, but still very easy to use modules and features. Installation and maintenance of Great Plains™ is relatively easy compared to other ERP products. MS SQL server does an excellent job as back-end database. Easy navigation and windows-like familiar menu layout is an added advantage. In this chapter, a guideline for an ERP based curriculum for business students is presented. Informal response from students was positive. MS Great Plains™ was well accepted by students; however, care must be taken during installation and lab setup.

REFERENCES

Antonucci, Y. L., Corbitt, G., Stewart, G., & Harris, A. L. (2004). Enterprise systems education: Where are we? Where are we going? *Journal of Information Systems Education, 15*(3), 227-234.

APICS. (1998). Defining enterprise resource planning. Retrieved June 30, from http://www.apics.org/OtherServices/articles/defining.htm

Becerra-Fernandez, I., Murphy, K. E., & Simon, S. J. (2000). Integrating ERP in the business school curriculum. *Communications of the ACM, 43*(3), 39-41.

Boykin, R. F., & Martz Jr., W. M. (2004). The integration of ERP into a logistics curriculum: Applying a systems approach. *Journal of Enterprise Information Management, 17*(1), 45-55.

Corbitt, G., & Mensching, J. (2000). Integrating SAP R/3 into a college of business curriculum: Lessons learned. *Information Technology and Management, 1*(4), 247-258.

Fedorowitz, J., Gelinas, U. J., Usoff, C., & Hachey, G. (2004). Twelve tips for successful integrating enterprise systems across the curriculum. *Journal of Information Systems Education, 15*(3), 235-244.

Hawking, P., McCarthy, B., & Stein, A. (2004). Second wave ERP education. *Journal of Information Systems Education, 15*(3), 327-332.

Hawking, P., Ramp, A., & Shackleton, P. (2001). IS'97 model curriculum and enterprise resource planning systems. *Business Process Management Journal, 7*(3), 225-233.

Johnson, T., Lorents, A. C., Morgan, J., & Ozmun, J. (2004). *Journal of Information Systems Education, 15*(3), 245-253.

Watson, E. E., & Schneider, H. (1999). Using ERP systems in education. *Communications of the Association for Information Systems, 1*(9), 1-48.

APPENDIX A

Purchase Order

In this assignment, you will generate purchase order, receive materials from vendor, enter purchasing invoice, post purchasing invoice, pay vendor and post payment entry. During the process, you will check the inventory of purchased items to see when purchased quantity gets added to the inventory. You will also need to check status of documents. Following are some information that you will need for this assignment:

1. Items to purchase:
    a. ACCS-CRD-12WH
    b. ACCS-HDS-2EAR
2. Vendor to purchase from: AMERICAN0001
3. Site ID: WAREHOUSE (vendor will ship items to this site)
4. Purchase quantity = 100 units for each item
5. 6% tax must be added to obtain total purchase cost

For your convenience, some steps are provided as a guideline. You may need to do some research of your own to figure out solutions if you face transactions related problems. At each step, you need to cut-and-paste some screen shots on a word document (No need to cut-and-paste every screen shots, use your judgment). If the system requires you to generate outputs, direct outputs to the screen. Cut relevant information from the 1st output and paste it on the word document. Close other outputs (if there are more than one). Guideline is as follows:

1. Check inventory (quantity on hand) for items ACCS-CRD-12WH and ACCS-HDS-2EAR (provide documentation of the inventory).

2. Generate purchase order (PO) to purchase 100 units of each item. Add 6% tax to obtain total purchase cost. Save the purchase order. At this point, notice that the status of the PO is NEW. Document the PO and the status.

3. We need to release the purchase order so that we may receive items shipped by the vendor. Figure out how to release the PO so that the status is changed to "Released." Document the change.

4. Assume that the vendor has sent full quantity of both items. There are no returns. Receive 100 units/each for both items. You need to figure out what to do next so that inventory gets added in the WAREHOUSE for these items.

5. Check the quantity on hand for both items. Make sure that the inventory has increased by 100 units for each item. Document the increase.

6. Now, you need to create purchasing invoice. Receipt number for the invoice entry will be automatically generated. You need to enter vendor doc. number, batch ID, vendor ID, PO number, vendor item and tax. Other fields may be required as well. Look at the distributions (document it). Save the purchasing invoice entry (document the invoice).

7. We need to post purchasing Invoice so that we are able to pay the vendor. Figure out how to post purchasing invoice. During posting process, notice that the receipt no. related to the invoice has been posted (document may be obtained from the output generated by the posting procedure).

8. Generate payment entry. You may use payments of your choice for this purpose. Pay the entire amount that is on the invoice by applying the payment to the proper invoice. Provide documentation that shows the selection of appropriate invoice. Save the entry.

9. Check the status of the payable transaction. Note that the status is still OPEN.

10. Post the payment entry. Provide documentation that the payment of the appropriate document has been posted accurately (document may be obtained from the output generated by the posting procedure).

11. Check the status of the payable transaction. Note that the status is now HIST (history).

APPENDIX B
ERP Case Study: XYZ Corporation
Introduction

XYZ Corporation is a manufacturer of pumps such as, Air Lift pump, Bucket pump and Hand pump. The company has more than 70 finished products under the XYZ brand. The company has recently taken steps to expand distributorships in countries including USA, Canada, and the United Kingdom and to grow its presence in the Asian market, with plans to double its output over the next two years.

With distributorships in four countries and continued growth in global market, XYZ Products recognized that its disparate financial and manufacturing systems were not compatible to support today's global business processing needs, and therefore, hindering export growth. They needed a new ERP system.

The Business Case for an ERP

Currently, XYZ's information system is run by a bunch of legacy systems. To manage its production planning and scheduling, XYZ had been using multiple unrelated spreadsheets in conjunction with a financial accounting system called Solution-One. Solution-One, however, does not have manufacturing, purchasing, sales, and distribution modules. Payments to vendors, billing and invoicing of customers are handled through Solution-One. Lack of integration among functional departments caused the duplication of information–making accurate information sharing and decision making impossible. For example, inventories are maintained with spreadsheets while logistics are run by an outdated shipping system and, clip boards are used to track production data. In a word, the company is in need of an integrated Information Systems that is user friendly, can support business expansion, provide real-time information, and is able to replace all out dated systems currently in place. Having a purchasing operation that provides real-time purchasing information to manufacturing is vital for the efficient production planning and scheduling. Currently, payroll and related human resource (HR) functions are outsourced. The management, however, have decided to bring HR operations in-house once an ERP system is fully functional.

After a thorough evaluation of the current business processes and several ERP systems, the management decided to have a group of their developers, database administrators and system administrators design, develop and implement an ERP system with required modules along with a back-end relational database. The database is also to be designed, developed, and implemented by the same group. The whole ERP development project should be completed in two phases. Phase I of the project includes the following modules:

1. Accounting and financial processes
2. Purchase order processing
3. Inventory control (material management)
4. Sales order processing
5. Human resources

This phase has been approved by the top management. Don Miller, the chief information officer (CIO), authorizes, and allocates financial and human resources. It has been agreed on principle that five functional teams will be formed and each team will have the responsibility of developing a module. In order to preserve the integrated nature of an ERP system by providing functional dependence among modules, a team of coordinators will supervise the work and coordination among functional teams. A team of project leaders will have the overall responsibility of managing the project.

Phase II will include manufacturing and advanced production planning. However, management has not made any firm commitment about Phase II of the project. The decision to develop Phase II will depend upon the successful development and implementation of Phase I. Don says the company has some unique processing needs that are unavailable in existing ERP software. "We also like to use our own resources to develop the product so that we are in control of the product and the company doesn't have to pay recurring licensing fee to a software vendor" says Don.

Potential Benefits:

After development and implementation of the proposed ERP systems, XYZ expects to gain following benefits:

1. Reduced data entry
2. Enabling staff to focus their time on completing non-administrative tasks
3. Efficiencies within product scheduling and planning, resulting in more informed business decisions
4. Improved inventory and purchasing control, leading to a reduction in inventory overheads and thereby, more inventory turnover
5. More flexibility in invoicing and acknowledgment of sales orders, allowing the company to deliver better service to their customers
6. The new software will position XYZ to successfully compete with local competitors as well as expand into international markets.

Some Relevant Information

1. **Company Profile:** XYZ Corporation is a manufacturer of pumps such as, Air Lift pump, Bucket pump and Hand pump. The company has more than 70 finished products under the XYZ brand. The company has recently taken steps to expand distributorships in countries including USA, Canada, and the United Kingdom and grow its presence in the Asian market.
2. **Challenges:** XYZ Inc. recognized the right technology was necessary in helping it expand into international markets, and the company sought a new integrated solution to supersede the limitations of its previous financial and manufacturing systems.
3. **Challenges:** Home grown ERP solution named ERPXYZ.
4. **Functional Areas:**
   a. Accounting and financial processes
   b. Inventory management
   c. Sales order processing
   d. Purchase order processing
   e. Human resources
5. **Hardware and software platform, workstations, and consultants:** n/a.

APPENDIX C

Explanations of Acronyms

- **SDK:** Software Development Kit.
- **BizTalk™:** A Windows server system product that helps customers integrate systems, employees, and trading partners.
- **Component object model (COM):** A software architecture that allows the software components developed by different software vendors to be combined and used into a variety of applications. COM provides a standard for component interoperability.
- **Visual Basic for Applications (VBA):** A development software.
  Open database connectivity (ODBC) = A software component that makes data access possible from any application.
- **American Standard Code for Information Interchange (ASCII):** ASCII is a character encoding based on the English alphabet. ASCII codes represent text in computers, communications equipment, and other devices that work with text. Source: http://en.wikipedia.org/wiki/ASCII
- **Extensible markup language (XML):** XML is a simple, very flexible text format. Originally designed to meet the challenges of large-scale electronic publishing, XML is also playing an increasingly important role in the exchange of a wide variety of data on the Web and elsewhere. Source: http://www.w3.org/XML/One integration method used to integrate the enterprise to the Internet in Great Plains™ is Microsoft BizTalk Server. It unites enterprise application integration (EAI) and business-to-business (B2B) integration. In the next section, the teaching approach and course outline are briefly discussed, followed by assignments and projects. The teaching approach is a combination of understanding business processes and hands-on learning.

Chapter XV

Teaching Integrated Business Processes via ERP Configuration

Bret Wagner, Western Michigan University, USA

Thomas Rienzo, Western Michigan University, USA

ABSTRACT

The business world has recognized the importance of managing business processes rather than functions. Business education has begun to embrace this transformation, although the organizational barriers between departments in most business schools have limited the success of teaching business from a process-oriented perspective. ERP technology provides an opportunity to illustrate the management of integrated business processes. One approach to using ERP software to teach business processes is through a dedicated configuration class. In this class structure, students configure an ERP system to manage the basic business processes of a small company. Because of the integrated nature of ERP systems, students must configure the system in a number of functional areas — accounting, operations, sales, and so forth — many of which are not in a student's major. The necessity of configuring an ERP system in a number of functional areas illustrates the importance of having a background in all basic business functions to successfully manage a business enterprise. This chapter will provide a review of an ERP configuration course that is currently being taught at Western Michigan University using SAP R/3 business software. The context of the course, its mechanics, key learning points, and areas for future development will be presented.

INTRODUCTION

Enterprise resource planning software is gaining momentum in business school curricula as a means of integrating business processes and traditional functional disciplines (Antonucci, Corbitt, Stewart, & Harris, 2004; Hawking et al., 2002; Hejazi, Halpin, & Biggs, 2003; Johnson, Lorents, Morgan, & Ozmun, 2004; Nelson & Millet, 2001). While numerous business process exercises have been designed for student use, literature involving ERP configuration is scarce. Davis and Comeau (2004) describe configuration exercises as part of an enterprise integration course. They use configuration to provide students with a high-level appreciation of the functional connections provided by ERP software. The Western Michigan University SAP R/3 configuration course follows a similar philosophy. Working with material management, purchasing and sales organizations, plant parameters, financial accounting, and controlling areas helps students understand the relationships of interconnected business processes.

ERP CONFIGURATION — WHAT IS IT?

Enterprise resource planning (ERP) software is standard business software designed to manage a company's key business processes in an integrated fashion. Because all businesses are different, ERP software must be designed to manage a variety of business processes. When enterprise software is configured, data settings are selected so that business processes can be managed in ways suitable to the particular companies who utilize the enterprise software. ERP configuration at Western Michigan University is accomplished through the SAP R/3 system. Its structure is shown in Figure 1. The SAP software establishes relationships among enterprise organizational elements in a hierarchical structure. The client sits at the top of the SAP hierarchy. All business functions requiring integration should exist under one client. All components under the client share the same vendor, customer, and material designations. They also share databases, database tables, and a common general ledger number and description. The chart of accounts (list of accounts used for financial reporting) is assigned at the company level. Each company must be associated with one or more company codes. A company code is the level in which transactions are processed and accounts managed. Financial statements are created for company codes, but they can be consolidated at higher levels if needed. Master data of the company is stored at the company code level. Master data is relatively static (e.g., names and addresses of customers and suppliers) compared with dynamic transactional data (orders, shipments, inventory levels). All subordinate logistics and production elements are associated in some way with a company code.

Credit control areas manage customer credit. Multiple credit control areas can be associated with a company code. Controlling areas link the FI and CO modules. They are the highest reporting level under cost center accounting. Both company codes and controlling

Figure 1. Structure of SAP R/3 (Source: Targowski & Rienzo, 2004)

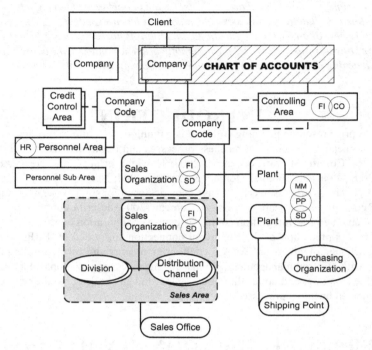

areas are assigned to a chart of accounts during configuration. Once they share a common chart of accounts, company codes can be assigned to controlling areas for managerial accounting purposes. Depending upon configuration, one controlling area can be associated with multiple company codes and deliver data across business entities represented by the company codes.

Organizational elements of human resources are represented in personnel areas and subareas. Pay scales and work schedules are controlled in personnel subareas. Organizational elements representing the logistics and operations of the business are subordinate to company codes. The plant is the heart of the production system. Materials are planned at the plant level and inventory is valued and tracked there as well. Although plants most commonly represent production facilities, distribution and storage facilities can also receive a "plant" designation in SAP. A plant can be assigned to one or more company codes. Shipping points are assigned to plants. A purchasing organization must also be assigned to one or more plants. They can be assigned to multiple company codes as well.

The plant and purchasing organization integrate the materials management (MM) production planning (PP) and sales & distribution (SD) modules of SAP R/3. The sales organization is the selling unit responsible for revenue and product liability. The sales organization links the financial (FI) and SD modules, holds master data for customers, and also controls pricing data. Sales organizations are assigned to only one company code, and plants are assigned to one or more sales organizations. Each sales organization must have at least one division, but divisions can be assigned to multiple sales organizations. Divisions are categorized by particular products or services. Distribution channels describe disbursement methods (e.g., wholesale or retail). One or more is assigned to a sales organization. An individual sales order belongs to one division and one distribution channel. A sales area consists of a sales organization, and its accompanying divisions and distribution channels. Sales offices are assigned to one or more sales areas. They can be assigned human resources elements. Configuration exercises can include any or all of the areas under company codes.

ERP software companies face a difficult challenge in deciding how to structure their software to handle business processes. An ERP company needs to determine what represents a "best practice" for each business process. Once an ERP company determines what "best practices" they will support, their customers are limited to choices within those best practices. For many industrial ERP software customers, adjusting their business processes to fit these best practices is a formidable task. They may face significant change management issues as they seek the benefits of employing integrated software.

Managing customer expectations of process management is one of the key challenges an ERP software company faces. On one hand, an ERP customer must be convinced that its software package will be able to deliver a return on investment by making business processes more efficient, yet on the other hand the company typically does not want to change the way it does business. This schizophrenic behavior is frequently related to objectives sought by different management levels. Senior management is looking at return on investment from a strategic perspective, while middle- and lower-level management is looking at the software from a tactical or operational perspective and may be resistant to the changes required to achieve the return on investment sought by senior management.

Implementing an ERP system is different from the typical business software project due to its broad scope and focus on business process improvement. Parr, Shanks, and Darke (1999) observed that ERP systems are more complex than other software packages, because users are involved in re-engineering processes to fit software best practices. Configuration of ERP software helps students develop models for business process best practices. Configuration can also provide insight into the connectivity of procurement, logistics, operations, sales, and finance.

CONFIGURATION TOOLS OF SAP

SAP has responded to the challenge of ERP implementation by providing a variety of tools to allow for configuration of its software product. The primary means of configuring the software is through the implementation guide (IMG). The IMG is a collection of software transactions that determine how the business software will function. Figure 2 shows the structure of SAP's IMG. Configuration activities in the IMG can be categorized into three general areas:

1. Defining and assigning organizational structures
2. Making business process settings
3. Entering master data

Figure 2. Implementation guide structure

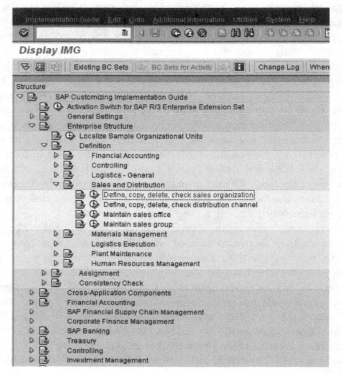

Defining and Assigning Organizational Structures

The first set of activities, defining and assigning organization structures, defines the hierarchical organization of a company. For example, in the sales area, organizational structures must be defined to determine the terms and conditions of sales to a customer. The organizational structure can determine pricing, delivery terms, minimum order quantities, and so forth. Figure 3 shows the transaction where a sales organization is defined and Figure 4 displays the transaction where distribution channels and divisions are assigned to a sales organization. Terms and conditions in sales processes can be defined uniquely for each combination of sales organization, distribution channel, and division. As a result, the definition and assignment of organizational structures provides a very flexible set of "building blocks" that a company can use to define its business processes.

Making Business Process Settings

The second type of configuration activities, making business process settings, defines how the ERP software will manage a business process. Figure 5 provides an example of this type of configuration activity in the area of customer credit management. This screen

Figure 3. Transaction to define a sales organization

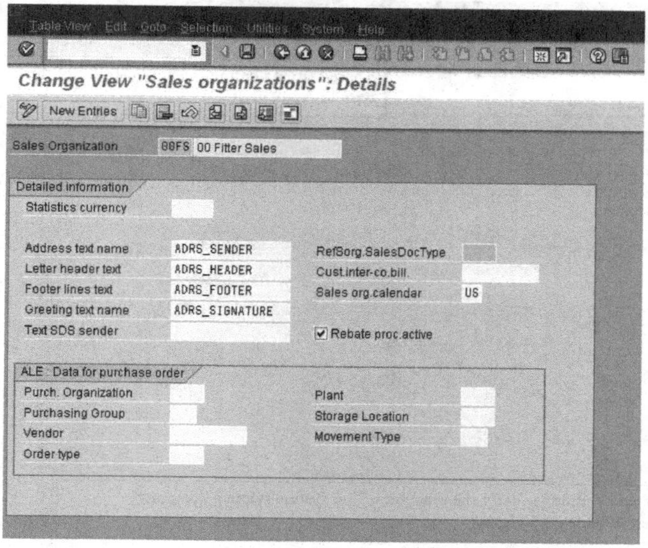

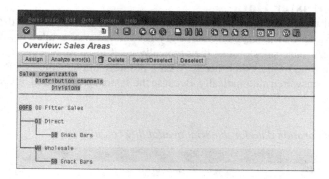

Figure 4. Assignment of distribution channel and division to sales organization

defines one type of credit checking response. In configuring credit checking, an unlimited number of credit checking responses can be defined for any type of customer. For example, the system may be configured to provide one type of response for a new customer, a different response for a high risk customer, and yet another response for a critically important customer. In the example in Figure 5, the settings determine that a customer sales order will be blocked if the credit limit is exceeded, and a warning will be issued to the employee that is saving the sales order indicating that the credit limit has been exceeded and specifying the amount by which the customer's credit limit has been exceeded.

Figure 5. Credit checking

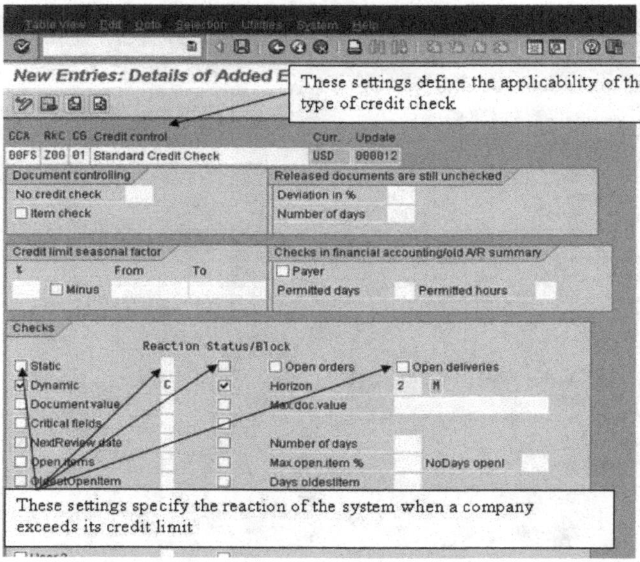

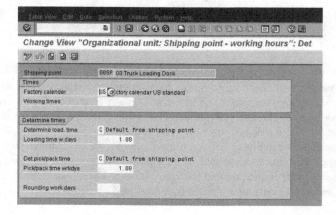

Entering Master Data

The third type of activity in configuration involves entering master data. Figure 6 provides an example of this type of data entry used in material availability calculations. When customers place sales orders, they typically want to know whether the orders can be delivered in time to meet their needs. With a properly implemented ERP system, this question can be answered automatically. Because the system is integrated, inventory and/or

Figure 6. Configuration data for material availability calculations

Figure 7. SAP easy access menu paths

production plans can be analyzed to determine when the customer's material will be available in the manufacturing facility. This information can be combined with the data shown in Figure 6, which indicates that one day should be allowed for picking and packing the order, plus another day for loading the order onto the delivery truck. Additional master data about shipping routes and calendar information (working days vs. holidays) can all be combined to determine when the order will reach the customer.

While a significant amount of master data for configuration is entered into the SAP R/3 system through the IMG, a significant amount of master data is entered through SAP's Easy Access menu paths. Figure 7 shows the SAP Easy Access menu path system.

In a production SAP system, users do not access any of the configuration settings in the IMG. Any IMG changes are imported into the system after testing in a separate quality assurance system. As a result, master data that is entered in the IMG is generally data that would not be modified regularly by the average company employee. Much master data, like customer information or information about the company's products, changes over time and might be modified by a number of the company's employees. This type of master data is accessible through the SAP Easy Access screen so that it can be changed directly in the production system.

ERP CONFIGURATION AT
WESTERN MICHIGAN UNIVERSITY

ERP Configuration has been taught at Western Michigan University since 2003. This configuration class consists of two parts. In the first part of the course, the students configure a company using a detailed set of instructions. In the second part of the course, the students configure a second, different company using the instructions from the first part of the class as a guide.

PART 1 — CONFIGURING THE
FITTER SNACKER COMPANY

Figure 8 gives an example of the level of detail in the instructions for the first part of the course, where students configure the SAP R/3 system to manage the key business processes for the fictitious Fitter Snacker Company. This fictitious company is used as an example throughout the text *Concepts in Enterprise Resource Planning.*[1] This textbook is used in the course to give students an overview of ERP systems, and having students configure the SAP system to manage the same company used in the textbook provides a common context.

The ERP configuration class is conducted in a computer lab classroom, and the detailed exercises simplify the configuration task for the students. Extensive use of screen shots of the SAP R/3 system provides the student with continuous feedback to show them that they have correctly followed the instructions. Callouts and arrows direct the student's attention to the appropriate part of the screen for data entry.

Each student must configure his/her own company within the SAP system. To allow for multiple companies in the same system, each student's company data is identified by a two-digit prefix. For example, when defining their company in the SAP system, the students use company codes are **00FS, 01FS, . . .** with description **00 Fitter Snacker, 01 Fitter Snacker, . . .** as shown in Figure 9. Using the two-digit code as a prefix facilitates the use of SAP's search tools in finding data. All configuration exercises are designed to use search tools to find their data (materials, customers, vendors, etc.). Students are discouraged from writing down document numbers as they complete an exercise. This approach has three benefits. First, it emphasizes the fact that the SAP system is a database application system

Figure 8. Example of detailed configuration instructions

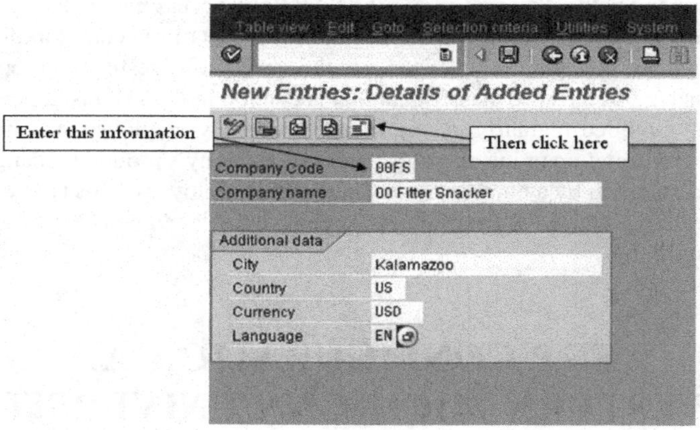

Then click on the address icon (🖃) to display additional data fields:

Figure 9. Company data numbering convention

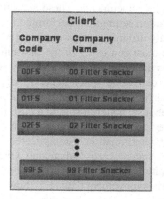

and not document processing software like Microsoft Word or Excel. Second, it teaches searching skills that are useful when working with an actual production system that might contain hundreds of thousands of data entries. Finally, it tends to keep students from seeing, and potentially misusing, other student's data. It is perhaps somewhat surprising that in teaching configuration for a number of years the author has never experienced malicious behavior from students. It may be that students are ill-equipped to behave maliciously in an unfamiliar software package, or it may be that they realize early that the SAP system thoroughly documents each user's activities and that there will be a record of their activities. In any event, once the students understand the data naming conventions, there are no problems with having multiple students working in the same system.

The configuration exercises are grouped into thirteen modules. The first nine modules configure basic company information, accounting data, materials and vendors:

Module	Activities
1	Define the company
2	Define the materials management organizational structure
3	Define the general ledger accounts
4	Define vendor master data
5	Define material master data
6	Configure document posting data
7	Configure materials management for goods receipts
8	Configure automatic general ledger account assignment for materials management transactions
9	Configure controlling (managerial/cost accounting)

While initially confusing for the student, the goals of the first five modules are generally straightforward. In Module 6, the students must be introduced to the documents concept. In the SAP system, every business transaction creates an electronic record, or document.

Each document is unique, and requires a unique document number. In addition, limits and controls must be set for recording documents. These activities are performed in Module 6. In Module 7, basic configuration settings are performed for managing material receipts, including tolerances for quantity differences between ordered and received quantities.

Module 8 is perhaps the most confusing of the first nine modules, but it is also the module that fully demonstrates the value of an integrated system. In Module 8, the system is configured to automatically determine which general ledger account(s) are affected by transactions involving materials (i.e., goods receipt from a supplier or vendor), goods receipt from production into the warehouse, material sold to a customer, material returned from a customer, and so forth. The key point that should be emphasized to students is that, while configuring automatic account determination is complicated (and confusing), it provides a company with a tremendous business process advantage. Once this module is configured, then accounting records are automatically updated whenever material is handled. Rather than having to maintain materials movement data (e.g., how many items do I now have in inventory) and accounting data (e.g., how much money do I have invested in raw materials) separately, each materials movement transaction will automatically create the appropriate accounting transaction. Combined with bar-code or RFID technology, automatic account determination can turn an onerous manual task into an easily automated activity. Automatic account determination provides a clear example of the cost-saving benefits of an integrated ERP system.

In Module 9, students configure the CO (controlling) module of the SAP system, which is the module that handles managerial accounting. In this module, students need to be reminded of the role of managerial accounting in business. For a business to understand whether it is profitable, it must be able to assign costs to activities. For every expense, a cost object (sales order, production order, project, cost center, etc.) must be defined to "absorb" the cost. Analysis of the costs "absorbed" by each cost object will allow a company to determine where it is spending its money. Combined with revenue data, this allows the company to determine which activities are, in fact, profitable.

After the first nine modules are completed, the students have configured enough of the fictitious Fitter Snacker Company to test the system by running business transactions. At this point, students are required to run two sets of transactions, which are referred to as Transaction Test 1 (TT1) and Transaction Test 2 (TT2). In TT1, students perform basic accounting transactions that test their configuration activities, including posting and paying invoices, posting and reposting invoices to costs centers, and allocating costs. In TT2, students further test their configuration by creating a purchase requisition for raw materials, converting the purchase requisition into a purchase order, recording the goods receipt, recording the invoice receipt, then posting the payment. In attempting TT1 and TT2, many students learn that their attention to detail is not sufficient for ERP system configuration. They frequently learn that something as simple as an asterisk missing from a field in a general ledger account is enough to block a goods receipt transaction. System errors resulting from configuration mistakes can be very frustrating for the student and the instructor. For the first time instructor, deciphering an SAP error message and determining where the student made a mistake in the hundreds of pages of exercise instructions is not an easy task. Yet debugging student problems is one of the best ways to learn the SAP system. As SAP Co-founder Klaus Tschira said about his experiences teaching COBOL to clients at IBM, "Never again did I learn so much in such a short time, because twenty participants made mistakes for me! You cannot make so many mistakes all alone."

For the student, it is critical to emphasize that SAP error messages, while annoying, are exactly what you want the system to do. An error message says that the system is being asked to do something it was not configured to do. If the system is properly configured, then the error message is preventing an employee from making an improper entry. If the system is not properly configured, then the error message is providing this information. Some error messages provided by the SAP system are quite detailed and may even provide a link to the portion of the IMG where the error is located. Unfortunately, some error messages are cryptic. It should be emphasized that the programmer that wrote the code was not a mind reader or futurist, and was not really in a position to understand what the user was intending to do when they made their mistake. The key to solving error message problems is to teach students to carefully read the error messages and look for clues on where (e.g., which module) the error is likely located. Students should also be advised to question all of their assumptions. An error message indicates that students did not perform every task in the exercises correctly, and they must methodically check each exercise to find their mistakes.

After completing TT2, students frequently have "learned their lesson" about attention to detail. At this point, many students have multiple copies of master data (materials, vendors, etc.) as they frequently think that, when confused, the best approach is to start over. When helping students, the instructor should consistently reinforce the idea that the student is working with a database system. If the student is unsure whether they have created the data for a vendor, they should be taught how to search for the vendor and correct any data problems rather than rushing in to enter the data again and ending up with two versions of the same vendor. To prevent fraud, the SAP system frequently does not allow data to be simply deleted. If that was the case, an employee could create a fictitious vendor, record a false invoice, issue payment to the employee's bank account, then delete all records of the transaction. In the SAP system, much of the data cannot be deleted directly, but must be flagged for deletion. Only after system administrators complete an archiving process can the data then be removed from the production system.

Because of these protections against fraud, students frequently may have working systems configured, but often there are significant amounts of extra copies of key master data. In addition, there may be configuration errors that won't be discovered until the production or sales modules are configured and tested. To give students a second chance, after TT2 their data is replaced with a clean copy of data that is properly configured through Module 9.

The configuration process continues with Modules 10 and 11, which have students configure the SAP system for production and enter all of the required master data (for workcenters, routings, etc.). After Module 11, the students test their configuration by running TT3, which tests the production planning settings by having them run the material requirements planning (MRP) process, and TT4, which has them process production orders. At the end of TT4, the students will have seven cases of finished snack bars in finished goods inventory. Students conclude the first portion of the class by configuring the sales and distribution using the instructions in Modules 12 and 13, which are tested by selling the finished snack bars using the instructions in TT5.

PART 2 — CONFIGURING THE MARSHALL MUFFLER COMPANY

One definition of a lecture is "information passed from the instructor's notes to the student's notes without being processed by either participant's brain." Similarly, a teacher can explain a topic but they can't understand it for the student. It is not uncommon for students to complete the configuration of the Fitter Snacker Company without having a very good grasp of what they have done. ERP configuration is a complex task. First, it involves all basic business functional areas, and business students, unfortunately, frequently view topics outside their major as unimportant. Second, students are configuring real software, which must be capable of dealing with all of the complexities of real world businesses. Configuring the Fitter Snacker Company is similar to taking a tour of Germany at 110 mph on the autobahn. The scenery rushes by without much time for appreciation. Finally, the detail in the instructions used in Western Michigan University's ERP configuration class can facilitate data entry without necessarily facilitating understanding. The instructions allow students to get through the assignments more easily and quickly, but they also allow them to get through without fully understanding what they have done.

Detailed instructions guide students to configure the Fitter Snacker Company within the first seven weeks of the course. This allows the last five weeks of the course to be devoted to a project, which is to configure the fictitious Marshall Muffler Manufacturing Company. The students are given a fourteen page project description, which provides the necessary data for configuring the Marshall Muffler Company. The data is purposely presented in tables and text that are not matched to the Fitter Snacker exercises. This mimics industrial reality, where finding the relevant data for a configuration project is a major part of the task. To successfully complete the project, students must configure the SAP system for the Marshall Muffler Company so that they can buy the required raw materials, manufacture mufflers, and sell them to the customer.

In addition to project instructions, the students are given a set of PowerPoint slides that review the instructions in each module and give key points on how the configuration task should differ for Marshall Muffler. As an example, automatic account determination in SAP

Figure 10. Valuation grouping codes and account assignment

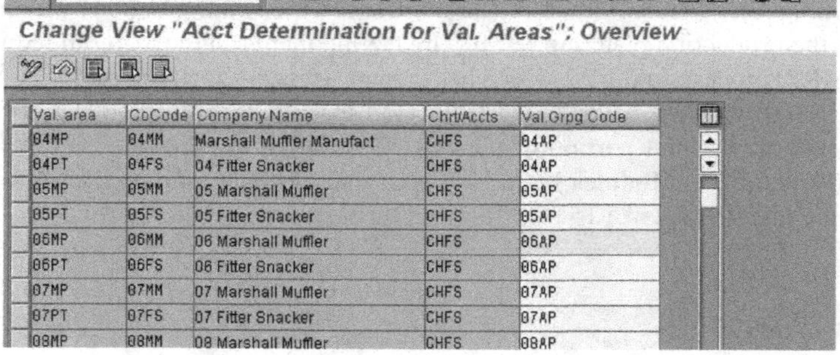

Val. area	CoCode	Company Name	Chrt/Accts	Val.Grpg Code
04MP	04MM	Marshall Muffler Manufact	CHFS	04AP
04PT	04FS	04 Fitter Snacker	CHFS	04AP
05MP	05MM	05 Marshall Muffler	CHFS	05AP
05PT	05FS	05 Fitter Snacker	CHFS	05AP
06MP	06MM	06 Marshall Muffler	CHFS	06AP
06PT	06FS	06 Fitter Snacker	CHFS	06AP
07MP	07MM	07 Marshall Muffler	CHFS	07AP
07PT	07FS	07 Fitter Snacker	CHFS	07AP
08MP	08MM	08 Marshall Muffler	CHFS	08AP

is not defined in terms of a company or a plant, but a valuation grouping code. Rather than going through all the detailed steps to configure automatic account assignment for Marshall Muffler, they can have the Marshall Muffler Company use the same account assignment logic they defined for the Fitter Snacker Company by simply assigning the Marshall Muffler plant to the Fitter Snacker valuation grouping code. While this saves student's time, it also provides an opportunity to discuss the practical advantages that were gained from having account assignment being defined for the valuation grouping code rather than a company code or plant. Valuation group codes are shown in Figure 10.

Similarly, the PowerPoint slides instruct students to create their general ledger accounts by copying the accounts defined for the Fitter Snacker Company. This means that they will avoid mistakes in creating Marshall Muffler's general ledger accounts. At this point, the author usually reminds students that almost all mistakes occur when humans enter data through a keyboard. Minimize keyboard data entry tends to minimize mistakes.

The Marshall Muffler configuration project forces the students to think about what configuration activities mean. While they have the detailed instructions from the Fitter Snacker exercise to follow, they have to think about how the Marshall Muffler Company is different, and what that means for each step in the instructions.

CONCLUSION

ERP configuration is a new pedagogical technique. There have been no research studies on its effectiveness, which would be extremely challenging as it is currently in a state of constant change. ERP configuration as a teaching tool is less than 5 years old, and the course taught at Western Michigan University has changed significantly in the two years that it has been taught. For a faculty member considering an ERP configuration task, the value of the effort must be based on judgment and faith rather than scientific evidence.

The task of teaching ERP configuration is challenging. Instructors have to be comfortable teaching about functional areas in which they are not experts, and configuration involves accounting, production, materials management, sales and marketing, and so forth. In addition, teaching ERP configuration, even after attending workshops, is still primarily an on-the-job training experience, usually without a trainer handy.

In spite of this, there are rewards. The challenges of learning and understanding an ERP system are intellectually stimulating. A faculty member can learn a lot by seeing how business concepts have been executed in state-of-the-art business software. In addition, the software confirms the relevance of the material being taught — to both the instructor and the student. Finally, the best rewards come when students take their experience in ERP configuration and use it in the business world.

REFERENCES

Antonucci, Y. L., Corbitt, G., Stewart, G., & Harris, A. L. (2004). Enterprise systems education: Where are we? Where are we going? *Journal of Information Systems Education,* *15*(3), 227-234.

Davis, C. H., & Comeau, J. (2004). Enterprise integration in business education: design and outcomes of a capstone ERP-based undergraduate e-business management course. *Journal of Information Systems Education, 15*(3), 287.

Hawking, P., Foster, S., & Basset, P. (2002). *An applied approach to teaching HR concepts using an ERP system*. Paper presented at the Informing Science & IT Education, Cork, Ireland.

Hejazi, S. S., Halpin, A. L., & Biggs, W. D. (2003). Using SAP ERP technology to integrate the undergraduate business curriculum. *Developments in Business Simulation and Experiential Learning, 30*, 122-125.

Johnson, T., Lorents, A. C., Morgan, J., & Ozmun, J. (2004). A customized ERP/SAP model for business curriculum integration. *Journal of Information Systems Education, 15*(3), 245.

Nelson, R. J., & Millet, I. (2001). *A foundation course in ERP and business processes: Rationale, design, and educational outcomes*. Paper presented at the 7th Americas Conference on Information Systems, Boston.

Parr, A. N., Shanks, G., Darke, P. (1999, August 21-22). Identification of necessary factors for successful implementation of ERP systems. In O. Ngwerryama, L. Introna, M. Myers, & J. DeGross (Eds.), *New information technologies in organizational processes: Field studies and theoretical reflections on the future of work*. IFIP TC8 WGB8.2 International Working Conference on New Information Technology in Organizational Processes: Field Studies and Theoretical Reflections on the Future of Work, St. Louis, MO.

Targowski, A., & Rienzo, T. (2004). *Enterprise information infrastructure* (4th ed.). Kalamazoo, MI: Paradox Associates.

ENDNOTE

[1]   Monk, E., & Wagner, B. (2005). *Concepts in enterprise resource planning* (2nd ed.). Course Technology.

Chapter XVI

Teaching ERP Programming Using SAP ABAP/4

Bernard Han, Western Michigan University, USA

ABSTRACT

In this chapter, a teaching pedagogy for ERP programming using SAP ABAP/4 is presented. While object-oriented (OO) programming techniques have received increasing attention in new ERP module development, learning and mastering of traditional ABAP/4 code will continue to play an important role especially in maintaining SAP R/3 systems for necessary extensions that are required to meet end-user needs of SAP adopters. The pedagogy presented is essentially a three-threaded teaching approach that involves a stepwise learning of ABAP/4, selective hands-on investigation of SAP R/3 modules, and an accumulative simulation of a simplified R/3 module. A simple ABAP/4 program is also presented to highlight how an online report could be easily generated through using both internal tables and the sample database (flight) available in SAP R/3. Limitations, suggestions, and future trend of ABAP/4 application development are also addressed with a concluding remark.

INTRODUCTION

SAP is the world's leading provider of ERP software solutions. Today, more than 18,000 companies in over 120 countries run more than 50,000 installations of SAP R/3 software (Hewlett-Packard, 2002). Noticeably, SAP is offering Business-One and mySAP All-in-One solutions to meet enterprise information needs from small to median to large corporations over the whole world (SAP, 2005). While SAP R/3 has the capacity in providing full information processing for companies of different sizes, it is of course not a *one-size-fits-all* solution package that can be put into use without necessary configuration and/or customizations, which often involve undesirable code modifications, addition of client-specific business functional extensions, and separate development of business modules. Hence, knowing the programming fundamentals of R/3 systems becomes important for prospective SAP adopters.

ABAP/4 is a fourth-generation application programming language and ABAP, an acronym of *advanced business application programming*. Though today more and more new R/3 modules are coded using ABAP Objects (Keller and Kruger, 2002), any customizations to existing modules cannot be conducted without a good knowledge in or even using ABAP/4. It is for this very reason this chapter is dedicated to teaching methodologies that are effective for CIS/MIS majors or IT professionals to develop ABAP/4 skills in managing or maintaining R/3 systems. As common to most programming languages, ABAP/4 evolved from a third-generation "procedural" language to a fourth-generation non-procedural one that embeds SQL statements to retrieve data from remote relational database servers. However, when compared to others, the uniqueness of ABAP/4 is its client-side programming capability along with team-shared features. That is, an ABAP/4 programmer only needs Internet access to a SAP developer server with a developer's privilege, then he/she can work from anywhere to conduct coding and share developed modules with other programmers on the same development environment. Furthermore, much of the programming knowledge (e.g., examples, syntaxes, etc.) can be acquired easily over the Internet by visiting free Web sites offered by many ABAP/4 consulting professionals or searching the help facility provided by SAP — http://help.sap.com. Therefore, ABAP/4 programming could be made possible by a simple setting — a client-side interface and a developer account that allows access to the ABAP workbench on a SAP server.

Since the set-up of ABAP/4 programming environment is relatively straightforward, this chapter is primarily focused on the teaching pedagogy for a one semester course designed for students with minimal programming knowledge in any third-generation languages (e.g., FORTRAN, COBOL, etc.). The goal of this course is to develop students' skills in ABAP/4 programming and knowledge in appropriate customizations for an existing R/3. The remaining of this chapter is organized as follows: First, a brief background is given to highlight the importance of learning ABAP/4. Second, three different levels of customizations for R/3 are addressed, followed by a teaching pedagogy fulfilled by a three-threaded teaching approach. Teaching subjects, take-home assignments, and a semester long-term project are proposed to simulate the development of a scale-down ERP module. Challenging issues and potential extensions are discussed. Finally, concluding remark is given in the end.

BACKGROUND

Business schools have long been criticized for not adequately preparing their students to satisfy the needs of their future employers. Business faculty members steadfastly cling to silo-based outdated methods, teaching functional know-how rather than integrated business knowledge (Bain, 1992; Lau, Rosacker, & Tracy, 2000; Stover, Morris, Pharr, Reyes, & Byers, 1997). Over the past few years, many integrative curricula have been proposed to fix the silo-based business education through proper use of some ERP solutions such as SAP R/3 and Microsoft Great Plains (Antonucci, Corbitt, Stewart, & Harris, 2004; Cannon, Klein, Koste, & Magal, 2004; Corbitt & Mensching, 2000; Fedorowicz, Gelinas, & Usoff, 2004; Hejazi, Halpin, & Biggs, 2003; Johnson, Lorents, Morgan, & Ozmun, 2004; Joseph & George, 2002;). As suggested by these integrative curricula, ERP software is considered an effective tool to teach business processes that involve multiple business functions. Through hands-on exposures to an ERP, learning business and its processes becomes a direct reflection of real world business operations. As a consequence, students will have an integrated understanding of business across multiple functions rather than a specialized training in some functional area. Therefore, understanding ERP becomes increasingly appealing in today's business education.

In addition to ERP's capacity of integrating business processes across various functions, the recent evolving global economy has significantly affected the U.S. 'domestic' corporate hiring that motivates IT education to focus more on business than technology itself. As more U.S. companies outsource basic IT tasks (e.g., coding, testing, etc.) overseas for possible cost reductions (Elmuti & Kathawala, 2000; Lee, Huynh, Kwok, Pi, 2003), CIS/MIS graduates with only IT skills but weak *business* knowledge become less employable (Parikka and Ojala, 2004). As suggested by IT executives, balanced CIS/MIS education in both "business" and IT is needed for the future job market (Head, 2004).

An ERP is essentially an enterprise-wide software that supports information processing for all business functions within a firm. Learning ABAP/4 will grant students programming skills that allow them to explore SAP R/3 and then have a solid grasp on how business processes can integrate business functions. With little doubt, learning ABAP/4 becomes one of effective ways for CIS/MIS students to acquire knowledge in both business and IT. Hence, more knowledge in ABAP/4 will improve CIS/MIS students' employability and in turn their expertise in ERP will assist the U.S. industries in becoming more efficient to cope with the challenges imposed by the global market.

Three Levels of Customizations for R/3

ABAP/4 can be used to develop I/O interfaces to support data entry, summary reports for middle management, dynamic programs (i.e., DynPro) to enhance existing R/3 applications, and separate modules with BADI (business add-in) and BAPI (business application interface) for further extension to the given functionality in R/3. By and large, ABAP/4 can be used at three different levels for R/3 modifications. They are:

- **Source code modification (Level 1):** For interface/display personalization and report generations that meet specific customer needs. It involves code changes in given original application program. Coding effort is relatively easy. However, modifications to be made at this level are often discouraged if system upgrades are expected since modified components may not work after the system upgrade.

- **Application enhancement (Level 2):** Rather than a direct source code modification, enhancements are done by integrating customer-defined data (tables) with application modules at customer-exits and screen-exits. While no guarantee, customized codes may still be useable when there are system upgrades. It is because of the coding independence between R/3 and customer add-ins.
- **Customer Development:** To further enhance the code reusability and the use of any available object-oriented modules, BADIs and BAPIs could be developed as integral parts in ABAP/4 program in support of R/3 customization. Code development done at this level has least concerns with SAP system upgrade, and hence "customer development" using BADIs and ABPIs and ABAP objects is considered the most attractive ways in support of R/3 customization.

Although there are three levels of customizations, the key decision is which level of modifications should be conducted for system tailoring. In practice, Levels 2 or 3 modifications are considered more appropriate than Level 1 since the latter will cause concerns in system upgrades.

As a one semester ABAP/4 programming course, it is unrealistic to cover all topics that are useful in support of all three levels modifications. A pedagogy is presented below that ensures students, once complete the course, will own the ability for level 1 and some level 2 customizations. Details follow.

Teaching Pedagogy for ABAP/4

The fundamentals of ABAP/4 are no different than any other traditional procedural programming languages. In fact, most of its syntaxes resemble COBOL in terms of data definitions, logic statements, and programming structures, though the language has been enhanced by database inquiring capability through embedded SQL and other remote function calls to some existing modules (e.g., BADIs, BAPIs, etc.). Nevertheless, ABAP/4 is the key language used in developing SAP R/3, which deals with 80,000 database tables and contains more than 100 million lines of code (Gilbert, 2002).

While SAP R/3 is very comprehensive, the primary purpose of teaching ABAP/4 is to give students knowledge and skills in understanding how ABAP/4 could be used to interface with an existing R/3 for functionality enhancements. However, without knowing the basics of ABAP/4, there is no way to conduct coding that is required for advanced application development. To ensure a doable pedagogy, the learning objectives and details of a three-threaded teaching approach are presented next.

Learning Objectives

The proposed ABAP/4 course is designed for seniors of CIS/MIS undergraduate or MBA students with an ERP systems concentration. The objectives for this introduction course are:

1. To introduce students with hands-on knowledge about the infrastructure of SAP R/3
2. To cover ABAP/4 programming skills that involves database access and processing with proper interface/report design using internal tables and online databases
3. To develop dialog programming (DynPro) application modules that access to both system and user-defined database to extend ERP functionalities

4.   To provide students with further experiences on how ABAP program could call BADI/BAPI modules to accomplish defined business needs

Given the previous objectives, students who complete this course will have solid knowledge and skills in ABAP/4 to conduct both Level 1 and/or some Level 2 system tailoring for a R/3 system. In fact, the fourth objective (i.e., hands-on with BADI/BAPI) is relatively aggressive and it could only be achieved for those fast learners. The above objectives can be achieved through a tested three-threaded teaching approach. Details follow.

A Three-Threaded Teaching Approach

It is critical for instructors to keep in mind that this course is not just focused on the programming skills. Rather, from the very beginning, students should be reminded that all subjects covered in the class will be reapplied in a term project to solidify their knowledge in ABAP and it could be used to support a SAP R/3 system. Therefore, an ideal teaching environment for this course requires two independent instances of R/3 — one, a pre-configured R/3 for students to navigate and conduct transaction postings, and the other, a developer client that supports a full-range of ABAP/4 application development. Throughout the semester students are expected to get familiarized with a pre-configured R/3 in order to understand the relationships among business processes and R/3 modules, and, in the mean time, students will learn ABAP/4 skills to develop I/O interfaces, reports, dialog modules, and programs with remote functional calls (e.g., BADI, BAPI, etc.). Moreover, a simulated scale-down ERP term project is progressively implemented in the second half of the semester to provide students opportunities in combining all skills learned to experience the development of a simplified ERP business process across two or more business functions.

To cultivate an effective learning and use of ABAP/4, a three-threaded learning approach has been used. A description on each thread of learning is given below:

*   **Thread one:** Learning by experiencing (15%). Knowledge in an existing SAP R/3 system is important. This component is focused on general knowledge about SAP R/3 interface and relationships among business modules and processes of a configured production system. With the time limit, students are not expected to learn the configuration of a R/3 system. Luckily, there are many ready-to-use production systems — one of them (Fitter-Snacker) could be found and provided by Monk and Wagner (2006). As known, there are more than 20 SAP application modules could be implemented in an R/3 system. Any of these modules could be used as teaching components for students to understand the basic construct of R/3.
*   **Thread two:** Learning by coding (60%). Coding is the most effective way to grasp a solid understanding about any language learning. Essentially, ABAP/4 is a pure client-side language that supports both remote database processing and object-oriented modeling. To ensure that students' learning of ABAP/4 is truly useful, subjects to be covered in this course should include from the basic coding such as simple interface or report programs to advanced ones that include ABAP dialog modules with a full range database processing and remote functional calls.
*   **Thread Three:** Learning by simulating (25%) — To avoid students' learning falls into the case of "seeing the trees but the forest,' it becomes necessary and challenging for students to combine all knowledge learned in Threads one and two by doing

a scale-down ERP project (i.e., a dialog application (DynPro) that mimics a real life business operations across multiple functions via multiple business processes).

Some specific teaching subjects and associated assignments are detailed in the next section to highlight how the above three-threaded teaching approach implemented at Western Michigan University.

Teaching Subjects and Assignments for ABAP/4

Effective teaching of ABAP/4 shall be based on a balanced coverage of subjects along with a set of take-home assignments for learning reinforcement. Key learning subjects, hands-on exercises, and assignments for each thread are detailed below.

Thread 1 (learning by experiencing). Understanding all SAP modules will be extremely difficult and is not the objective of this course. A pre-configured R/3 system — Fitter Snacker (Monk & Wagner, 2006) is used by students to experience the R/3 system. Specifically, three hands-on exercises are given throughout the semester:

- **#1 - SAP R/3 Navigation — (Due week 2):** An overview lecture of R/3 is given and a set of handout with necessary icons and navigation screens are given. This exercise require students to get acquainted a R/3. Defined search and output screens are to be delivered as an evidence of learning outcomes.
- **#2 Business processing cycle — (Due week 5):** While students are picking up coding basics towards interface and report development, a second R/3 hands-on focused on a "business process" is given. Students are required to follow a step-by-step procedure to enter data and post transactions. In specific, the "purchasing cycle" exercise is given for students to generate expected transaction results. This exercise is to highlight a process that involves the following five transactions:
  o   Create a purchase requisition.
  o   Create a purchase order.
  o   Create a goods receipt.
  o   Create an invoice receipt.
  o   Conduct an outgoing payment.

Through this exercise students shall have sufficient exposure to R/3 screens. More importantly, it provides students about the concept of a "business process" and its impacts on multiple business functions.

- **#3 R/3 Business module study — (Due week 8):** This exercise is to force students to have an in-depth look of a specific SAP R/3 business module. Detailed findings in terms of its subcomponents and interactions are required to be submitted for instructor's evaluation. The purpose of this hands-on is to get students have a clear view on the construct of a selected ERP module.

Thread 2 (learning by coding). Due to the frequent upgrade of SAP R/3, little update has been done by the publisher on the existing ABAP/4 textbook. One of the most easy-to-read textbooks written by de Bruyn and Lyfareff (1998) is highly recommended. However, this book has 21 chapters and it is not possible to cover the whole book without missing the learning components in threads one and three. Fortunately, many subjects can be easily

Table 1. Major teaching subjects for learning thread two

Week	Teaching Subjects	Assignments
1-3	**Basics:** Simple I/O, Data display, Output formatting/manipulation, and Decision logics (IF/ELSE and CASE)	#1 and #2
4-5	**Looping and Internal Table** (demo of sample database — **Flight**)	#3
6	**SAP SQL** and Processing of **Flight** database	#4
7	**Functions/Subroutines** and Logical Database	#5
8	Tread 1 (Exercise #3 – Intermission on ABAP)	
9	**User-defined database creation**	#6
10 - 11	**Dialog Programming** (Screen/Menu painters)	#7
12	Intro and demo on **BADI/BAPI**	Class Demo

picked up by the readers. Only selected subjects are instructed in detail. Table 1 summarizes the major subjects covered and the seven required assignments.

As seen on Table 1, the ABAP/4 language basics (i.e., Chapters 1-12 in de Bruyn & Lyfareff, 1998]) are covered in the first seven weeks. Since this course is designed for CIS/MIS undergraduate seniors and MBA students, most ABAP/4 basics, including data types, data structures, I/O formatting, decision logics, SAP SQL, and functions/subroutines, could be easily absorbed by students through in-class examples, hands-on exercises, and take-home assignments. An example of ABAP/4 program completed in week seven is given below to highlight students' learning.

An Example of ABAP/4 Application

In any SAP R/3 IDES environment, it is come with a sample airlines database–"Flight." A portion of the ER diagram associated with "Flight" database is displayed in Figure 1.

Figure 1. Some tables in the IDES Airline database — Flight

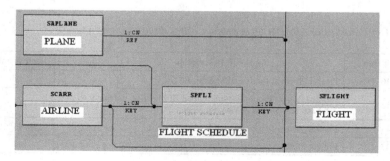

Figure 2. An ABAP/4 screen for interactive data entry

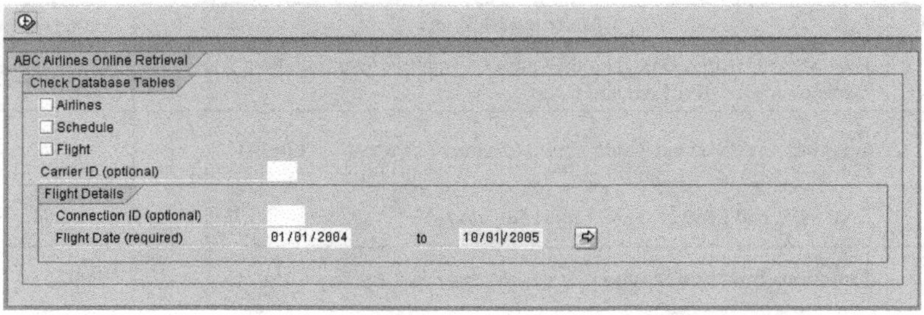

This sample database is very useful in teaching ABAP/4 programming. With a proper ABAP screen design and the use of internal tables and SAP SQL statements, an ABAP application can be easily developed with the following I/O interface (Figure 2):

Figure 2 contains three check-box parameters, two single-valued parameters, and one range parameter. Users are given many possible ways to enter the data to retrieve airlines information from the given "Flight" database. Some online reports produced by the ABAP/4 program are given in Appendix A for further reference.

In contrast to the first seven weeks, the second half of the semester is dedicated to the integration of knowledge and skills learned about SAP R/3 and ABAP/4 coding. Note that the learning activities with respect to *SAP hands-on*, *ABAP programming*, and *ERP term project* are intermingled throughout the semester. This "threaded" teaching pedagogy is very effective and quite appreciated by undergraduate seniors and MBA students.

By the end of week eight, students are expected to have a fundamental understanding of certain selected SAP R/3 module, from which a term project was derived for simulation. More details are given in the next section.

Thread 3 (Learning by Simulating). While R/3 hands-on and ABAP/4 coding give students a first-hand experience in using R/3 and the knowledge of programming, a term project that simulates the development of some SAP module will reinforce their true understanding on how business processes are could integrate multiple business functions. Table 2 summarizes the major deliverables required by a term project that aims at the implementation of a scale-down business process using ABAP/4.

Note that the term project proposal (deliverable #1) shall be initiated after students have sufficient knowledge about a selected R/3 module. The first deliverable — project

Table 2. Deliverables of ABAP/4 term project using dialog programming

Week Due	Description	Deliverable
10	Project Proposal (with a BPM & an ERD)	#1
12	Refined Project Proposal (with refined BPM, ERD, user-defined database, and proposed ABAP screens.)	#2
14	Final Report with a completed Dialog Program	#3
15	Project Presentation (with a demo of the developed dialog program)	#4

Figure 3. A business process map about service acquisition process

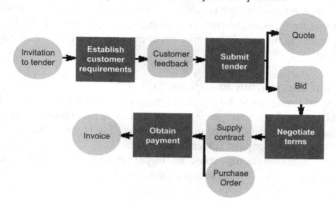

proposal should be tightly coupled with the first hands-on exercise required in Thread one. The scope of the term project shall be confined to a certain business process that supports transactions affect at least two business functions (e.g., accounting and marketing, etc.). The end-product of this term project is a dynamic program (DynPro) that deals with data processing from/to a 'user-defined' database hosted by a SAP server.

During the project design and analysis, a *business process map* (BPM) shall be derived based on the project proposal along with an ERD for a user-defined database. At present, no textbook is available for BPM modeling, though BPM has been extensively used by industries for ERP module development. For this course, a very practical example was found on the Web (Business Process Map, 2005). As shown in Figure 3, a service acquisition process is detailed by a diagram that is composed of a number of transactions (rounded rectangles), sub-processes (rectangles), and I/O documents (ovals). This BPM diagram was used as a reference example for students to develop their own BPM for the term project.

The details of all deliverables required by the term project are compiled into one document, which is given in Appendix B for further reference.

Covering the proposed teaching subjects with all required learning deliverables is no easy task. Nevertheless, the pedagogy presented in this chapter has been tested by the author over the past three years. For readers' easy reference, an integrated outline that lists all proposed teaching subjects, hands-on exercises, ABAP/4 assignments, and term project deliverables is given in Appendix C. This outline may serve as the sample syllabus for this course.

Learning Outcomes

The presented pedagogy shall provide students with a solid grounding in ABAP/4 and an in-depth understanding of how it could be used to support the modifications of an existing R/3 system. Once completing this course, students shall develop their ability in:

1.   Providing level-1 SAP R/3 customization, that is, knowing how to modify the source code to present input/output data in a user-preferred format, and generate reports for middle management.

2.   Applying the dialog programming for level-2 customizations, i.e., developing a DynPro that supports extension of functionalities to an existing R/3 system. Of course, there are always rooms for possible expansion of students' learning of ABAP/4. Limitations and suggestions to the current teaching environment of ABAP/4 are addressed in the next section.

Limitations and Suggestions to Expand Learning

A fundamental limitation to the effective teaching of ABAP/4 was caused by the fast upgrade of SAP R/3 and the emergence of new modeling/programming techniques for software development. A brief discussion on each limitation is given below, followed by some suggestions to further expand students' learning.

Limitations. Other than the time constraint on covering a rich set of topics as proposed, major limitations encountered by the author in teaching this course are:

- **Lack of updated ABAP/4 programming textbooks:** Due to fast changes in SAP R/3, very few authors and publishers are dedicated to the update of existing ABAP/4 textbooks. Most available ABAP/4 textbooks are outdated by at least three years. While recently a few ABAP books with a focus on ABAP Objects have been published, they are not easy for beginners to learn within one semester. Good textbooks are needed to speed up the knowledge acquisition of ABAP/4 — from traditional syntaxes to new object features.
- **Lack of SAP system documentation:** It is very important for ABAP/4 learners to have some easy-to-access secondary documentations to investigate the application modules in R/3 in regard to the coding structure of the underneath ABAP/4 programs and their programming features. Such support is often provided by the software vendor in various forms. Unfortunately, SAP AG has seldom made its application documentations to the public. This increases the difficulty for both instructors and students to learn ABAP/4.
- **Complexities and fast updates of SAP R/3:** Unlike most other monolithic applications, SAP R/3 is a very comprehensive ERP that cannot be understood without some in-depth instruction. Recent addition of many extended modules (e.g., business warehouse, etc.) makes R/3 even more complex and triggers a number of system upgrades. These frequent changes have significantly impacted the teaching and learning of ABAP/4. It becomes unrealistic for students to learn all subjects within one course.

Overall, the lacks of updated textbooks, SAP documentations, and increasing complexity of SAP R/3 make it extremely hard to teach ABAP/4 programming. Suggestions are given below to alleviate potential teaching and learning hindrances.

Suggestions. As agreed by most IT executives, with the current trend that more corporations outsourced routine IT jobs overseas, teaching only ABAP/4 coding skills will not make our future CIS/MIS graduates more employable. Therefore, ABAP/4 instructors shall focus more on students' general understanding of R/3 and their discerning ability in deciding which modules shall be kept in house for self modifications and which else to be spec-out to an outsourcer. To support this kind of training, a more flexible teaching setting should be provided. Ideally, each student should be granted a "Sand Box" that allows him/her to modify a pre-configured R/3. All knowledge and skills learned from a separate developer client could be used for *code modifications/extensions/module additions* onto the pre-configured R/3 for testing. Teaching of ABAP in this manner will truly train students to become more as a "business analyst" than as an "ABAP programmer." A richer teaching setting with the following provisions becomes desirable.

- Provide a developer's account for each student on both a client for ABAP development and a pre-configured R/3 system. Note that students are allowed to conduct coding or modifications on both clients. This setting is quite costly. However, without it there will be no way to expand students' learning.
- Extend ABAP coding using a SAP Web application server (i.e., students are given more trainings in building platform-independent business solutions). Leveraging J2EE is a reality and SAP Web application server is the underlying technology for all new R/3 enterprise components (e.g., customer relationship management, business intelligence, etc.). The trade-off between basic and advanced ABAP skills becomes a judgmental issue to be resolved by the instructor in the future course redesign.

FUTURE TRENDS

SAP R/3 has evolved from an enterprise-wide solution to a one that supports global e-business with B2B, B2C, and B2E operations. The most recent release of SAP *NetWeaver* has delivered SAP a unique integration and application platform that is designed to be fully functioning on the Web and interoperable with Microsoft .NET framework. This interoperability embraces all three integration layers — people, information, and business processes–using an extensible application platform that is based on open standards and advanced Web services. With the given connectivity methodologies between SAP and Microsoft, future SAP R/3 consultants shall know how to integrate solutions between these two platforms seamlessly. Hence, extending ABAP/4 coding into Web services become the immediate item to learn. With the current ABAP workbench, it is possible to add this facility in creating Web Service objects using ABAP code. Further exploration and teaching component in this regard shall be pursued to meet upcoming demands.

In the mean time, J2EE has been used as a common technology in building new business modules for better extension of module functionality and module maintenance for software both online or offline. This technology is also incorporated into the recently released SAP NetWeaver architecture. In fact, ABAP objects and J2EE are also employed for any newly added application modules in SAP. With little doubt, learning more about ABAP objects is the next step after students accomplish the course proposed herein. It will grant students ability and more flexibility in using ABAP to solve business challenges today and tomorrow.

CONCLUSION

ABAP/4 programming will continue to play a critical role for the coming decades since it is the primary language used in coding fundamental business modules of SAP R/3. Effective teaching and learning of ABAP/4 becomes increasingly important for CIS faculty and students, in particular, towards the delivery and acquisition of integrated business knowledge through the use of the world leading ERP software — SAP R/3. While SAP R/3 is a powerful ERP system for companies of different sizes, it is not a one-size-fits-all solution that can be put into services without modifications. Knowing ABAP/4 becomes a must for both corporate IT and business consultants to know how to configure and customize R/3 to meet corporate specific needs.

In this chapter, a teaching pedagogy with a three-threaded teaching approach is presented to show how ABAP/4 skills could be effectively acquired by students through sufficient exposures to a pre-configured R/3 and the accomplishment of a dialog program that simulates business processes across two or more business functions. Limitations and suggestions are also addressed for the proposed teaching pedagogy to expand the learning of ABAP/4, if a more flexible and richer setting is provided.

Many new features and business modules are undertaken by SAP to enhance the functionality of R/3. Recent release of SAP *Netweaver* architecture provides a great potential for R/3 Enterprise to integrate people, information, and business processes. To ensure that students' learning of ABAP/4 is for tomorrow's needs, future design of ABAP/4 course is advised to include subjects such as ABAP Web services and ABAP objects for new SAP module development–the most appropriate customization of R/3 that is on demand by today's SAP R/3 adopters.

REFERENCES

Antonucci, Y. L., Corbitt, G., Stewart, G., & Harris, A. L. (2004). Enterprise systems education: Where are we? Where are we going? *Journal of Information Systems Education, 15*(3), 227-234.

Bain, G. S. (1992). The future of management education. *Journal of the Operational Research Society, 43*(6), 557-561.

Business Process Map. (2005). http://www.iqa.org/publication/c4-1-80.shtml

Cannon, D. M., Klein, H. A., Koste, L. L., & Magal, S. R. (2004). Curriculum integration using enterprise resource planning: An integrative case approach. *Journal of Education for Business, 80*(2), 93.

Corbitt, G., & Mensching, J. (2000). Integrating SAP R/3 into a college of business curriculum: Lessons learned. *Information Technology and Management, 1*, 247-258.

de Bruyn & Lyfareff. (1998). *Introduction to ABAP/4 programming for SAP revised and expanded edition.* Prima Tech Publisher.

Elmuti, D., & Kathawala, Y. (2000). The effects of global outsourcing strategies on participants' attitudes and organizational effectiveness. *International Journal of Manpower, 21*(2), 112-128.

Fedorowicz, J., Gelinas, U. J., & Usoff, C. (2004). Twelve tips for successfully integrating enterprise systems across the curriculum. *Journal of Information Systems Education, 15*(3), 236-244.

Gilbert, A. (2002). *SAP calls for software that coexists.* News.Com. Retrieved from http://news.com.com/SAP+calls+for+software+that+coexists/2100-1001_3-869941.html

Head, B. (2004). *Holistic education essential — to a degree.* Information Age. Retrieved December 10, 2004, from http://www.infoage.idg.com.au/index.php/secid;404956636

Hejazi, S. S., Halpin, A. L., & Biggs, W. D. (2003). Using SAP ERP technology to integrate the undergraduate business curriculum. *Developments in Business Simulation and Experiential Learning, 30*, 122-125.

Hewlett-Packard News Release. (2002). SAP and HP announce alliance to deliver SAP® business one to small and midsize businesses. Retrieved September 4, 2002, from http://www.hp.com/ hpinfo/newsroom/press/2002/020904f.html

Johnson, T., Lorents, A. C., Morgan, J., & Ozmun, J. (2004). A customized ERP/SAP model for business curriculum integration. *Journal of Information Systems Education, 15*(3), 245.

Joseph, G., & George, A. (2002). ERP, learning communities, and curriculum integration. *Journal of Information Systems Education, 13*(1), 51-58.

Keller, H., & Kruger, S. (2002). *ABAP objects — an introduction to programming SAP applications.* Addison-Wesley.

Lau, S. M., Rosacker, R. E., & Tracy, S. L. (2000). Three undergraduate courses were developed to integrate undergraduate curriculum. *The Business, Education, and Technology Journal, 2*(1).

Lee, J., Huynh, M., Kwok, R., & Pi, S. (2003) IT outsourcing evolution — past, present, and future. *Communications of the ACM, 46*(5), 84

Matzke, B. (1999). ABAP/4 Programming the SAP R/3 system (2nd ed.). Addison-Wesley.

McCarthy, B., & Hawking, P. (2002, June). Teaching SAP's ABAP Programming to IS Students: Adopting and adapting Web-based technologies. *Informing Science,* 995-1000.

Monk, E., & Wagner, B. (2006). *Concepts in enterprise resource planning* (2nd ed.). Thomson Course Technology.

Ottewill, R., McKenzie, G., & Leah, J. (2005). Integration and the hidden curriculum in business education. *Education & Training, 47*(2/3), 89.

Parriak, M., & Ojala, A. (2004, October 29-November 1). Challenges of the information society to entrepreneurial and technology education in the Finnish Comprehensive School. *Conference of Finnish Association of Research in Information Technology.*

SAP NetWeaver and Microsoft .NET Interoperability. (2005) Published by SAP AG.

SAP News Release. (2005). *SAP solutions for small and midsize enterprises: Bringing powerful software to the Fortune 500,000.* Retrieved from http://www.sap.com/solutions/sme/ index.epx

Stover, D., Morris, J., Pharr, S., Reyes, M., & Byers, C. (1997, June). Breaking down the silos: Attaining an integrated business common core. *American Business Review, 15*(2), 1-11.

Appendix Figure 1. If only the "Airline" checkbox is checked, then you will have the following outpu (Note: a portion is displayed)

	Airlines Information		
CarrID	Carrier Name	Currency	Web Site
AA	American Airlines	USD	http://www.aa.com
AB	Air Berlin	EUR	http://www.airberlin.de
AC	Air Canada	CAD	http://www.aircanada.ca
AF	Air France	EUR	http://www.airfrance.fr
AZ	Alitalia	EUR	http://www.alitalia.it
BA	British Airways	GBP	http://www.british-airways.com

Appendix Figure 2. If only the "Schedule" checkbox is checked, then you will have the following output

	Flight Schedules for All Airlines			
CarrID	City From	Airport	City To	Airport
AA	NEW YORK	JFK	SAN FRANCISCO	SFO
AA	SAN FRANCISCO	SFO	NEW YORK	JFK
AZ	ROME	FCO	FRANKFURT	FRA
AZ	ROME	FCO	TOKYO	TYO
AZ	TOKYO	TYO	ROME	FCO
AZ	ROME	FCO	OSAKA	KIX
DL	NEW YORK	JFK	FRANKFURT	FRA
DL	NEW YORK	JFK	SAN FRANCISCO	SFO
DL	SAN FRANCISCO	SFO	NEW YORK	JFK

Appendix Figure 3. If only the "Flight" checkbox is checked, then you will have the following output

	Current Available Flights							
Airline	Conn ID	Flgt Date	Price	Currency	PlaneType	MaxSeats	OccSeats	TotPayment
AA	0017	05252005	422.94	USD	747-400	385	37	193,419.15
AA	0017	06222005	422.94	USD	747-400	385	37	192,721.22
AA	0017	07202005	422.94	USD	747-400	385	37	192,877.82
AA	0017	08172005	422.94	USD	747-400	385	37	192,353.34
AA	0017	09142005	422.94	USD	747-400	385	37	194,307.30
AA	0064	05272005	422.94	USD	A310-300	280	26	132,012.44

APPENDIX A
Partial ABAP Application Output and Relevant Code

In fact, the users may check any combination of checkboxes with any additional information to confine the search. All specifications are taken to form into SAP SQL to access to the sample database, then present onto the screen with a proper format. For easy testing, some partial code is given next.

```
Partial ABAP code for the output generated in the previous section.
*** three tables from the sample database FLIGHT are used
Tables: Sflight, spfli, SCARR.

Data: Begin of INT_AIRLINE occurs 0,
          carrid like scarr-carrid,
          carrname like scarr-carrname,
          currcode like scarr-currcode,
          url like scarr-url.
DATA: end of INT_Airline.

data: color_code type I.
data: rec_cnt type i.
data: switch type i.
data: flip type i.

**** Beginning of Block 1 ****    This section is to partition the I/O screen
SELECTION-SCREEN BEGIN OF BLOCK BLOCK1
     WITH FRAME TITLE text-001.

**** Beginning of Block 2 ****
  SELECTION-SCREEN BEGIN OF BLOCK BLOCK2
     WITH FRAME TITLE TEXT-002.
     PARAMETERS:
       Airlines AS CHECKBOX,
       Schedule AS CHECKBOX,
       Flight   AS CHECKBOX.
*    SELECTION-SCREEN SKIP 1.
       Parameters:    P_carrid like sflight-carrid.

**** Beginning of Block 3 ****
       SELECTION-SCREEN BEGIN OF BLOCK BLOCK3
            WITH FRAME TITLE TEXT-005.
            Parameters:   P_connid like sflight-connid.
            select-options: S_FLDATE for sflight-fldate.

     SELECTION-SCREEN END OF BLOCK BLOCK3.
   SELECTION-SCREEN END OF BLOCK BLOCK2.
 SELECTION-SCREEN END OF BLOCK BLOCK1.

Initialization.
color_code = 3.
S_FLDATE-low ='20040101'.
S_Fldate-high = sy-datum.
append s_FLDATE.

clear s_FLDATE.
```

Start-of-selection.
*case 1: if only Airlines box is checked
    If Airlines = 'X' and schedule <> 'X' and flight <> 'X'.
        perform display_airlines.
    endif.

*Case 2: If only Schedule box is checked
    if airlines <> 'X' and schedule = 'X' and flight <> 'X'.
        if p_carrid <> ''.
            perform display_one_schedule.   "for one carrier only
        else.
            perform display_All_schedules.   "for all carriers
        endif.
    endif.

*case 3. If only Flight box is checked.
*   code is omitted

    if airlines <> 'X' and schedule <> 'X' and flight <> 'X'.
        message i000.
    endif.
End-of-selection.

** Subroutines below are used to produce outputs for various cases

Form display_airlines.
    WRITE: /40 'Airlines Information' COLOR = 1. SKIP.
    ULINE 5(95).
    WRITE: /05 SY-VLINE,
        07 'CarrID',   15 SY-VLINE, 18 'Carrier Name', 45 SY-VLINE,
        47 'Currency',   55 SY-VLINE, 57 'Web Site',   99 SY-VLINE.
    ULINE /5(95).
    if p_carrid <> ''.
        select * from scarr where carrid = p_carrid.
            WRITE: /05 SY-VLINE,
                07 scarr-carrid, 15 SY-VLINE, 18 scarr-carrname, 45 SY-VLINE,
                47 scarr-currcode, 55 SY-VLINE, 57 scarr-url, 99 SY-VLINE.
            ULINE /5(95).
        endselect.
    else.
        select * from scarr.
            WRITE: /05 SY-VLINE,
                07 scarr-carrid, 15 SY-VLINE, 18 scarr-carrname,45 SY-VLINE,
                47 scarr-currcode, 55 SY-VLINE, 57 scarr-url, 99 SY-VLINE.
            ULINE /5(95).
        endselect.
    endif.
endform.
*
Form display_one_schedule.
write: /20 'Flight schedules for ', 42 'Airline ', 51 p_Carrid color 1.
skip.
uline 5(71).
WRITE: /07 'CarrID', 18 'City From',   40 'Airport', 50 'City to',
        67 'Airport'.
ULINE /5(71).

color_code = 3.

```
rec_cnt = 0.
if p_carrid <> '' and p_connID = ''.
  select * from spfli where carrid = P_carrid order by CityFrom.
    format color off.
    write: / '     '.
    format color = color_code.
    WRITE: 07 spfli-CarrID, 18 spfli-cityfrom, 40 spfli-airpfrom,
           50 spfli-cityto, 67(5) spfli-airpto.
    rec_cnt = rec_cnt + 1.
    if color_code = 3.
       color_code = 4.
    else.
       color_code = 3.
    endif.
  endselect.
else.
    if p_carrid <> '' and p_ConnID <> ''.
      select * from spfli where carrid = P_carrid and connid =
        p_connid order by CityFrom.
        format color off.
        write: / '     '.
        format color = color_code.
        WRITE:  07 spfli-CarrID,   18 spfli-cityfrom,
                40 spfli-airpfrom,  50 spfli-cityto,
                67(5) spfli-airpto.
        rec_cnt = rec_cnt + 1.
        if color_code = 3.
           color_code = 4.
        else.
           color_code = 3.
        endif.
      endselect.
    endif.
endif.
if P_carrid = '' and p_connid <> ''.
  message i001.
endif.
format color off.

if rec_cnt = 0.
  write:/15 '****** No available schedule at this moment ******'.
endif.

ULINE /5(71).
Endform.

Form display_All_schedules.
write: /20 'Flight schedules for All Airlines'.
skip.
uline 5(71).
WRITE: /07 'CarrID',  18 'City From', 40 'Airport',
        50 'City to',  67 'Airport'.
ULINE /5(71).

rec_cnt = 0.
switch = 0.
select * from spfli order by carrid.
```

```
format color off.
write: / '      '.
if rec_cnt <> 0.
    If spfli-carrid <> p_carrid.
        switch = switch + 1.
    endif.
endif.
flip = switch MOD 2.
if flip = 1.
    color_code = 4.
else.
    color_code = 3.
endif.
format color = color_code.
WRITE:   07 spfli-CarrID, 18 spfli-cityfrom,
        40 spfli-airpfrom, 50 spfli-cityto,
        67(5) spfli-airpto.
rec_cnt = rec_cnt + 1.
p_carrid = spfli-Carrid.
endselect.

format color off.
if rec_cnt = 0.
    write:/15 '****** No schedule at this moment ******'.
endif.
ULINE /5(71).
Endform.
```

APPENDIX B

ABAP/4 Programming Term Project — Simulating a R/3 Application Module

I. The Objective

This term project is to provide you an opportunity to combine all your ABAP skills and knowledge in SAP R/3 to develop a dialog application (using Screen painter and Menu Painter) that supports multiple business processes across at least two major business functions. This project, while not comprehensive as R/3, will get you familiarized with an information solution that could be extended to an enterprise-wide ERP, given time and resources are available.

II. Implementation Approach

This term project shall be accomplished by a team of three (no more than four) members. The common methodology of project management shall be applied to conduct the implementation of this term project. To ensure a success of this project, the following principles shall be followed:

1.   Understand what you have and what you want to accomplish. If you do not know exactly where you stand, it is impossible for you to gather information through all possible means (e.g., navigation of SAP R/3, search on the Internet).

2. Define a clear, complete, and discrete set of processing requirements for your targeted application.

3. Revisit the solution plan among the team. The solution plan shall map to a set of business processes. Subsequently, it will trigger data modeling and application consolidation.

4. Develop a feasible project implementation plan. The plan should receive full commitment from the team and implemented by each team member. All work shall associate necessary documentation for future references.

5. Implement the system modules and submit both coding and documentation to the team lead for system consolidation and final testing.

6. Perform a post-project analysis to reflect learning and generate possible suggestions for future improvements.

III. Term Project Deliverables

A number of deliverables (see description below) are to be submitted to the instructor to ensure the success of this project. In general, the final deliverable shall contain a working ABAP/4 application supports business operations involving two or more business modules (e.g., Accounting (FI in SAP) and. Marketing (SD in SAP), or Marketing (SD in SAP) and. Production Planning (PP in SAP). The finished ABAP application shall be compiled into one module that can be triggered by an ABAP transaction code. A in-class presentation with a hands-on demo of the final system shall be delivered in the final exam week. Specifics about each deliverable follow.

- **Deliverable 1:** Term Project Proposal (15%). This deliverable shall define an ABAP/4 dialog application that is to be implemented by your team. The body of the deliverable shall include: (1) Application problem statement — what to be by your ABAP/4 application. Note that it is narrative of a major business process that supports business operations involving multiple sub processes and business functions; (2) A business process map (BPM) using the technique proposed by Institute of Quality Assurance (see http://www.iqa.org/publication/c4-180.shtml. This map shall highlight major sub-processes involved in your module; give a brief description about each sub-process and I/O needs. (3) Data requirement analysis. Provide a primitive ER model that is sufficient to support your BPM. (4) Possible ABAP screens that are needed to support all sub-processes involved in your module.

- **Deliverable 2:** Refined project proposal (with a defined database) (15%). After you have learned skills of Screen/Menu painters, you shall revisit your term project proposal and prepare a deliverable with the following components: (1) Revised application statement; (2) Revised business process map; (3) Revised ER diagram with definition of entities, relationships, and data fields; (4) Refined interface structure of ABAP screens that supports your business module; (5) A snapshot of implemented user-defined database that is to be used by your term project.

- **Deliverable 3:** Final project report (with a working ABAP/4 dialog program) (60 %) This deliverable shall present the following: (1) Application problem statement; 2) Major processes supported by this application accompanied by a BPM; (3) Final ER diagram with necessary data dictionary for each table and field; (4) Screen snapshots for each major sub-process; (5) Discussion on limitations and possible expansion;

(6) Learning reflections (post-implementation analysis) and suggestions for future ABAPers. Note that the final deliverable should be professional prepared with a spiral binding.

- **Deliverable 4:** Term project presentation (10%). All teams should give a PowerPoint presentation in class to the classmates. Major components addressed in deliverable 4 should be highlighted in your PowerPoint slides. An online demo is required. Necessary hand-outs should be prepared if they can enhance audience understanding of details that cannot be easily presented in your PowerPoint slides. More details on the evaluation of in-class presentation will be announced.

IV. A Reminder for all Deliverables

All deliverables must be submitted with all components described above. Moreover, it shall be preceded with the following:

- A cover page
- A table of contents
- An executive summary

The cover page should include the deliverable title, all team members' names, and the submission date.

APPENDIX C
Integrated Outline on Teaching Subjects and Class Deliverables

Week	Subjects Covered/SAP R/3 Hands-on	ABAP/4 Assignment
1	• SAP R/3 Overview • Introduction toABAP/4 **Topics:** SAP R/3 IDES Environment; ABAP/4 general structure and functions (Team Project & SAP R/3 Exercise #1 are distributed)	Readings only
2	• ABAP Basics **Topics:** Data Types, I/O formatting, Data manipulation. **SAP R/3 Exercise #1 Due**	Assignment #1 — simple coding and execution (distributed)
3	• ABAP Basics Topics: conditional operations, looping concept	Assignment #2 — data processing using IF/ELSE and CASE (distributed) **Assignment #1 Due**
4	• ABAP Basics • SAP Business Modules–An in-depth look Topics: Looping using Internal Tables (R/3 Business Module Exercise #2 distributed)	Assignment #3 — App. using internal tables (distributed) **Assignment #2 Due**
5	• ABAP Basics Topics: data operations using Internal Tables **SAP R/3 Exercise #2 Due**	Assignment #4 — app. using sample database (distributed) **Assignment #3 Due**
6	• ABAP–SAP SQL Topics: data operations sing SAP SQL	Assignment #5 — App. Using subroutines (distributed) **Assignment #4 Due**
7	• Review and SAP R/3 Infrastructure (SAP R/3 Exercise #3 is distributed)	**Assignment #5 Due**
8	Midterm Exam **SAP R/3 Exercise #3 Due**	Assignment #6 — Develop user database (distributed)
9	• R/3 Data Table and data organization Topics: domain, element, field, and table.	**Assignment #6 Due** Term Project Deliverable #1
10	• SAP R/3 Modules vs. Dialog Programming Topics: Business Process Mapping	**Project Deliverable #1 Due**

11	• ABAP/4 Screen Painter vs. Dialog Program Topics: Screen Painter and hands-on	Assignment #7 — Dialog Programming (distributed)
12	• ABAP/4 Menu Painter vs. Dialog Program Topics: Menu Painter and Hands-on	Refined Project Proposal **Project Deliverable #2 Due**
13	• Business Process Modeling Topics: BPM and ERD hands-on	**Assignment #7 Due**
14	• Term Project Consultation	**Project Deliverable #3 Due**
15	Final Exam (optional) Term Project Presentation	**Project Deliverable #4 Due**

Chapter XVII

A Course on Enterprise Portal Development and Management:
Issues, Challenges, and Solutions

Kuanchin Chen, Western Michigan University, USA

ABSTRACT

Enterprise portals present a great opportunity to bridge online applications with the back-end business systems. Although enterprise portals are now widely adopted in the business environment, the literature has been scarce in studies on how an enterprise portal course is better delivered in an information systems curriculum. The goal of this article is to discuss the potential issues and challenges arising from the delivery of such a course, and to propose a comprehensive teaching framework. The framework consists of three teaching modules (i.e., portal basics, portal management, and portal development) to better cover enterprise portals with topics ranging from technical details to business decisions.

INTRODUCTION

Internet applications started to gain popularity in the early 1990s, but many of these were standalone online applications with little reliance on each other. Despite the great benefits realized for this type of applications in the early Internet era, it falls short in today's business where data are integrated from multiple data sources and applications. Sharing of data as well as software components have been the key for multiple applications to work together. This not only saves development efforts, but also allows individual applications to excel in their respective areas. The results of this integrated approach are software suites and online portals that offer services with support from multiple software applications. Portals have been a modern buzz word grown out of business needs, but the literature has been scarce in how to deliver a portal design and management course. This article focuses on the issues involved in teaching portals and therefore offers a framework to enhance the teaching pedagogy.

A recent InfoWorld/TechFlow Portal Pulse Survey (2005) uncovered the current role of portals in the business world. The survey involved 444 respondents from more than 22 industries, of which 62.5% were using portals. Results suggest that the respondents considered that user satisfaction (95%) and operational efficiency (95%) were the most important benefits of enterprise portals. They also wanted a portal project to be highly customizable (94%), in low cost (91%), and faster to implement (86%). In addition, the technology that a portal system supports was considered part of the base line decision (78%). Although the preferences on faster implementation speed of a portal system is noted in the Portal Pulse Survey, it had no significant impact on the real enterprise portal implementation and e-business performance (Yang, Yang, & Wu, 2005). Therefore, decisions to adopt an enterprise portal should not simply focus on the features or functionality of portal systems. Rather, they should incorporate a wide range of business as well as technical factors that are most applicable to the target environment.

Although portals have gained popularity in recent years, there have been issues ranging from the fundamental definition of the word "portal" to the pedagogical options available to implement or extend a portal system. The current issues and challenges to bring such a new subject to the information systems education should be assessed before a comprehensive solution can be provided. The following section outlines the current issues involved in the use and implementation of enterprise portal systems. A section then follows to examine constraints and recommendations in bringing portal education to the information systems curriculum. Future trends are also explored.

PORTALS —
CURRENT ISSUES AND CHALLENGES
Definition of Enterprise Portals

The term "Web portals" was originally coined to describe Web sites of large online application or information providers (often search engine sites) that offer organized access to their online offerings (Smith, 2004). Although this early conceptualization of the term offers some insights about enterprise portals in practice, the literature has not been consistent in its definition (Cloete & Snyman, 2003). "Corporate portal," "enterprise portal," and "business portal" have all been mentioned in the past studies to refer to the similar technology (Yang et al., 2005).

Smith (2004) defines a portal as "...an infrastructure providing secure, customizable, personalizable, and integrated access to dynamic content from a variety of sources, in a variety of source formats, wherever it is needed." (p. 94). An enterprise portal "... is an enterprise-wide integration of business applications to the Web, specifically devised to avail the benefits of the Internet." (Hazra, 2002, p. 623) and includes "[a]pplications that enable companies to unlock internally and externally stored information, and provide users a single gateway to personalized information needed to make informed business decisions." (Shilakes & Tylman, 1998, p. 1). Choo, Detlor and Turnbull (2000) also suggest that "Common elements contained within corporate portal designs include an enterprise taxonomy of classification of information categories that helps organize information for easy retrieval...and links to other internal and external Web sites and information sources" (p. 72). An enterprise portal "...provides access—a single point of personalized, online access — to business information and knowledge sources, and real time access to core application and processes." (Yang et al., 2005, p. 349). Based on the above definitions, an enterprise portal (a) is rich in features (e.g., security, customizability, and collaboration), (b) makes heterogeneous business data sources accessible to its users, (c) integrates business and online applications, and (d) offers a single entry point to access such applications.

Current Technology Outlook of Portals

A wide range of portal products have emerged over the years. More than a dozen major enterprise portal vendors have been identified in previous studies (Hazra, 2002; Kakumanu & Mezzacca, 2005). This number is still increasing with smaller software vendors and open source developers joining the portals bandwagon. However, all portal products are not created equal. Some are comprehensive suites of applications that are tightly integrated with other enterprise systems, while others have evolved from traditional application servers with added e-commerce capabilities. This proliferation of portal products also suggests that compatibility and standardization may very likely be an issue.

Technology Difference Among Portal Servers

A portal displays its content in the form of Web pages, but an individual page component may obtain its content from external sources, legacy systems, or modern enterprise systems (e.g., ERP). The underlying portal system primarily determines how a page component is displayed, who is permitted to access such a page component, and how software programs interface with the component. For example, the term portlet refers to "... a Java technology based Web component, managed by a portlet container, that processes requests and generates dynamic content." (Abdelnur & Hepper, 2003, p. 13), but the portlet technology is not uniformly supported in all portal systems. Table 1 shows major enterprise portals that offer some integration with other enterprise systems. This table is by no means a comprehensive list of portal systems that are currently available on the market. As discussed before, some portal systems are small in scale and offer only a limited set of features. Table 1 nonetheless highlights some insights about the major portal vendors, their supported portal technologies, and the backend enterprise systems.

Table 1. Major enterprise portal servers

---

1. Microsoft SharePoint Server
- Portal technology: Web parts
- Backend enterprise systems: GreatPlains
- Supported Language: .Net languages

2. IBM WebSphere
- Portal technology: Portlets
- Backend enterprise systems: WebSphere and J2EE
- Supported Language: Java

3. Sybase enterprise portal
- Portal technology: Portlets
- Backend enterprise systems: Runs with other application
  servers; J2EE, COM, PowerBuilder Component model
- Supported Language: Java and .Net languages

4. Oracle application server portal
- Portal technology: Portlets and items
- Backend enterprise systems: Oracle application server, J2EE
- Supported Language: Java

5. SAP (mySAP) enterprise portal
- Portal technology: iViews (Portlets)
- Backend enterprise systems: SAP ERP, J2EE
- Supported Language: ABAP, Java, and .Net

6. BEA WebLogic Portal
- Portal technology: Portlets
- Backend enterprise systems: BEA WebLogic App. Server
- Supported Language: Java

Portal Standardization

As Table 1 shows, several big-name portal vendors support Portlets. In fact, the Portlets technology has been accepted as a standard in "Web Services for Remote Portlets Specification" by the Organization for the Advancement of Structured Information Standards (OASIS). A portal system that supports Portlets also adopts the Java language and its associated Web technologies. Although Microsoft's Web Part technology is still currently proprietary, the large install base of Windows servers makes it one major contender in the portals market. SAP appears to target the widest audience with support to .Net, Java, and SAP's propriety ABAP languages. Although not listed in Table 1, several open source portal servers (e.g., Apache Pluto, uPortal, and JBoss's portal component) are available. These open source portal servers appear to unilaterally support portlets.

Criteria for Adopting Portal Systems

The decision to adopt a portal system is a challenging task. First, companies may be lured by the immediate benefits (such as strong sales and financial savings) of enterprise portals without carefully identifying applicable functions of the portal system or establishing a sound strategy for portal implementation (Rose, 2003). Second, a simple estimate of ROI can be heavily influenced by many external factors. Many times these factors may be difficult to quantify or may be of unknown relevance to the result the adoption decision. Therefore, this section aims at offering insights on common features of portals and factors that are identified in the literature.

Common Enterprise Portal Features

Although portal products vary in features, the literature seems to agree on a list of common features of what an enterprise portal should deliver. An enterprise portal offers a single access point to various Internet tools. In addition to this feature, Van Brakel (2003) and Wege (2002) suggest the following:

- **Channeled information:** User-defined channels are made available from various information sources. Subscription is needed to view the channel content.
- **Pushed information:** The user-selected content is delivered to a particular user when the user is properly authenticated.
- **Customization of the content and the display layout**
- **Personalization to adapt to individual characteristics**
- **Content aggregation and syndication**
- **Support for multiple viewing devices**
- **Single-sign on:** Users are not required to authenticate each time a new service is used or a new application is invoked.
- **Administration of the portal server**
- **User management and access control**

Two Factors Relevant for Adoption Decisions

Kotorov and Hsu (2001) offered a practitioner's perspective on how the constituents of a portal system are similar to what are involved in a newspaper production process. They recommended a star model; where the center of the star is the editorial board/top management, the concave corners of the star are journalists/regular employees, and the convex corners of the star represent photographers/IT employees. The star model offers the relational structure for collaborations to produce an effective portal system. Although not specifically aimed at addressing factors for portals selection and adoption, Kotorov and Hsu's article nonetheless offers insights on the intangible human factors that are many times overlooked.

Kakumanu and Mezzacca (2005) suggested that decisions on portal selection should be based on four evaluation factors: customizability, vendor stability and reliability, platform environment, and security. After implementation, five end-user adoption factors (ease of use, usefulness, clear objectives, adaptability, and marketability to end-users) will improve the success of the portal system. Similarly, Hazra (2002) suggested that ease of integration, scalability, availability/reliability, robust development environment setup, and flexibility in implementation technology, are the main factors relating to the establishment of a portal environment and integration of the portal elements to the e-business infrastructure.

As seen from the previous discussion, previous studies have listed common features and factors that must be evaluated when a portal system is to be selected. This offers only a starting point for the portal adoption decision. After all, features not listed in the common core may also prove to be important to the target operating environment. Portal products also vary in their support to the common features. Therefore, it is recommended that a portal adoption decision be based not only on the features and factors listed, but also on the individual target environment. Furthermore, some of the factors (such as adaptability and marketability) cannot be readily quantified and thus require some subjective assessments.

Quality of Portal Deliverables

From the technology standpoint, portals are Web sites with a collection of online services. As portals are built on Web site technologies, they inherit the fundamental design and quality characteristics reported in the Web site design literature. However, the literature on the quality of Web sites is fairly disparate with focuses on issues such as interactivity, ease of navigation, usability, efficiency, and reliability (Bauer & Scharl, 2000). Although treating these individual aspects of design quality may be of some value, a more comprehensive treatment of portal quality with a focus on portal development would generate much value to the topic. Gounaris and Dimitriadis (2003) used the highly regarded quality assessment — the WebQual model, to assess the quality of portals. The results show three distinct portal quality dimensions: (1) customer care and risk reduction (customer concerns, ease of communication, security, response speed), (2) information benefit (reliability of information, completeness, good coverage of personal interests, security, updatedness, and good mapping to personal style), and (3) interaction facilitation benefit (portal technology, design, speed and functionality).

TEACHING ENTERPRISE PORTALS

Originated from the business world, portals now receive much attention in the education environment. Educational use of portals falls in three main categories, (a) portals as a tool to facilitate teaching, (b) portals as the central location to facilitate various educational activities, and (c) portals as a target of learning in IS/IT related courses. For example, UC Berkeley's OWL Project offers features, such as bulletin board, instant messaging, and chat, to facilitate teaching and sharing of college writing activities (McGrath, 2002). Similarly, Western Michigan University deployed a portal in 2004 as a campus-wide initiative to facilitate information sharing and transactions for various educational activities. Although the first two educational activities involve some use of portal systems, they do not concern about how a portal is developed, extended and managed. Students are at best the "consumers" for the portal products, rather than the administrators, managers and developers. The focus of this article is the third category of portal use — portal as the target of learning in IS/IT related courses.

Pedagogical Challenges

Based on the previous discussion, introducing enterprise portals as the focus of study to an information systems or related curriculum is also a challenging task. The educational challenges come from the current status of the portal market as well as educational constraints as discussed next.

Multiple Vendors, Proprietary Technologies

The current portal market is full of vendors that offer solutions from a comprehensive suite to a tailored collection of applications. Due to the novelty of the portal technology, there has not yet a single dominant vendor that offers a widely accepted solution. Yahoo Inc., as an early pioneer of portal sites, has been providing only services (or portal applications), rather than tailored business or educational solutions. Different vendors support different portal technologies. They strive to differentiate themselves from other portal products by adding proprietary features. Compatibility across systems becomes an issue.

Inconsistent Support for Portal Features

Most portal systems boasted features such as single sign-on, customization, navigation, access control, and security, but the support for these features are not consistent across portal products. For example, some portal products implement only basic password protections, while others offer a full flagship of security components.

Standardization Favors One Technology Vendor

The only current standard of portal technologies has been the OASIS' Web Services for Remote Portlets Specification. As the name suggests, this is a standardization effort on Portlets, which is primarily a Java-based technology. However, a language independent (and vendor independent) standard has not yet been a reality.

Portal Selection and Quality Assessment is Difficult

The many competing portal products and feature discrepancies in these products have made selection of a portal system a daunting task. The literature currently lacks a consistent assessment instrument to measure portal quality. Although portals are Web systems where a considerable amount of studies has built upon, it is not clear whether these existing Web site guidelines apply to portal systems. Furthermore, existing studies on Web site quality focus much on the quality of Web sites and individual Web pages, rather than on the quality of the information presented to the users. It is crucial especially for business users that the information is presented in a consistent manner and its quality can be ensured. Due to the above reasons, ROI becomes difficult to measure as a portal selection decision very likely involve factors that are semi-tangible or intangible (e.g., information quality and quality of software).

Scarce Precedence in Formal Curriculum

Adoption of a portal product as the focus of study can easily lose value when students are tied to a specific vendor's product and the technology later becomes obsolete. Although e-commerce and Web site design course have been popular in many computer related programs, portal as the main study focus has not widely entered the formal college curriculum.

An Innovative Framework

A new framework for teaching portals is offered in this section to overcome the issues and challenges listed in the previous section. In this approach, three separate modules are proposed: portal basics, portal management, and portal development. These three modules are suggested to be covered in the same order listed. See Figure 1 for a graphical overview of the framework. Note that the teaching modules are developed to cover major enterprise portal topics. Although they can be applied to most enterprise portal products, the discussions below are maintained to be vendor neutral.

Portal Basics

The portal basics module is designed to familiarize students with the fundamental components of portal systems. This module begins with the first unit (PB #1) that takes a Birdseye view on the compositions of a portal system and how the components work together. Basic terms used in Web systems are also introduced in this unit. The second unit (PB #2) then proceeds to a survey of modern enterprise portal systems and the current standard. This unit also prepares students with basic knowledge in Web server technologies so that they will be ready for the portal development module introduced later.

Portal Management

The portal management module includes three units. The first unit (PM#1) begins with a discussion of portal design and implementation strategies. It is followed by a series of discussions on traditional theories about interactivity, usability, navigation, and Web site design. This unit is concluded with a study on the quality assessment of enterprise portal systems. To most audiences, portal sites are also Web sites offering many services. It is crucial that the developers understand the Web site design theories to deliver better navigation experience for the users.

Since portal selection decisions cannot be properly measured with a single factor and many selection criteria may be difficult to quantify, it is important to also teach students formal methods on business decision-making. In the business environment, decision-makers often face a need to make decisions when the input data is incomplete, imprecise and/or non-quantifiable. Many times the decisions are made based on both quantitative and qualitative data. The decision sciences and other related disciplines have developed multi-criteria decision-making (MCDM) models to fit just the need. For example, the analytic hierarchy process (AHP) employs the pair-comparison technique to aggregate assessments on multiple criteria (quantitative and/or qualitative). Fuzzy logic-based decision models also allow for decisions to be made under both quantitative and qualitative factors. The second unit (PM #2) of this module introduces students one or more MCDM models with hands-on sessions to perform calculations and selections. The third module (PM #3) aims at teaching students basic administration skills to manage portal servers and portal sites. A portal system should be in place before starting this unit, since most activities in this unit aim at training students the first-hand experience on how to manage a portal server. The unit begins by training students to create simple portal sites and then proceeds to the topics on site and portal server administration (such as user management, access control, system backup and system security).

Portal Development

The portal development module includes a series of three units. This module trains students two fundamental building blocks of portal systems: (a) using and customization, and (b) building of extensions. Technical details are introduced in this module and some experience in extensible hypertext markup language (XHTML), cascading style sheets (CSS), and programming languages are required.

Figure 1. Course modules — portal development

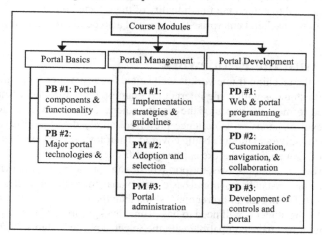

It is recommended that the instructor pick more than one portal product that supports different implementation technologies. For example, if the Oracle's enterprise portal server is the main product used in the course, the instructor might want to select Microsoft's Share-Point server to expose students to both Portlets and Web Parts. This module is designed to support teaching one or more portal products in the course.

The first unit (PD #1) familiarizes students with the basic Web technologies and programming techniques. This unit assumes some programming experience or coursework before taking the course, since the focus of the programming component here is on the ways to extend the selected portal system. If multiple portal products with different implementation technologies are to be introduced, this first unit will be a good place to survey Web server-side technologies and programming. The second unit (PD #2) focuses on common features that are seen in most portal products. Main topics include navigation, customization, collaboration, and membership management. The third unit (PD #3) studies portals

Table 2. Recommended proportion of time for each module

Type of Audience	Teaching Modules		
	PB	PM	PD
Business/Non-technical	40%*	50%	10%
Developers	10%	50%	40%
Mixed	20%	50%	30%

*Note: * 40% of time during a semester is to be used to cover the portal basics module*

implementation technologies and the programming API of the selected portal system(s). This unit is designed to extend the functionality of the selected portal product. In addition, integration with the backend enterprise systems will also be discussed in this unit.

Teaching with the Framework

Although the teaching framework is well suited for a semester-long three-credit hour course taught to students with some Internet programming background, some adjustments may be desired to meet the needs of the target audience. Student needs, the goals of the course, and level of hands-on experience preferred largely determine the class size and duration of each individual module being covered. Therefore, it is crucial that the instructor knows his/her target audience before applying the framework.

As the previous section shows, the portal basics and portal management modules focus on developing an understanding of portal basics, and management of portal sites/portal servers. They require a different type of prerequisite skills than the last module. To fully appreciate the last module, the students will need to have some background on Web development and a major computer language compatible with the selected portal systems. A one-size-fits-all approach to deliver the three modules is difficult and sometimes undesirable. Therefore, Table 2 shows the recommended proportions of time allotted for the three audience groups. The training focus for the business or non-technical students is on the knowledge of portal technologies and how to create and mange a portal system, whereas the training for developers would place more emphasis on the actual development of portal extensions and bridging of the portal systems with the backend enterprise systems.

Aside from administrative requirements and other external factors for class sizes, the portal technology itself may also be a constraint for class sizes. To be able to truly administer a portal server or to install portal extensions, a student needs some administrative rights to access the server systems. In addition, it may be highly desirable to have isolated portal servers for individual students so that they will not interfere with other's work. All these requirements could be costly to implement and could be a constraint on class sizes. The portal classes exclusively for general business or non-technical students may have 30 to 50 seats, but classes for portal developers may very likely be 20 or less to be efficient. Therefore, it is recommended that the instructors be aware of the technology constraints when planning for a portal course. A sample course syllabus is included in the appendix.

FUTURE TRENDS

The current state of the portals market is similar to the state of Web server side technologies in late 90s. Common gateway interface (CGI) was first popular. It was then replaced by in-process scripts such as active server pages (ASP) and java server pages (JSP) to improve efficiency. Eventually portal implementation technologies will converge to a handful of standardized technologies. Portal features will also move in the similar direction. The large number of portal selection criteria discussed in the portal management module will then include less of the technology components and perhaps more on business components, such as compatibility of the pre-packaged components with existing business logic. Off-the-shelf pre-bundled portal systems will start to emerge or even become popular. Although the composition of portal selection criteria may change over time to respond to business requirements, the need for a selection of portal products will still be required.

Another trend of the portal market may include vendors who specialize in niche sectors as suggested in Raol, Koong, Liu, and Yu (2003). As the standardization effort continues to strengthen, major portal servers will eventually support standardized technologies. This standardization movement also helps improve the compatibility of in-house portal applications that can make it easy to move from one vendor's portal product to another. Standardization also enhances the possibility of building portal applications that target special needs. Therefore, specialized portal systems and customized portal components may be popular.

CONCLUSION

Portal technologies are still evolving and the portal market currently consists of a large number of vendors offering products with competing but inconsistent features. It is too early to identify a dominant vendor and its products at this moment. Although standardization of portal technology has begun to emerge, the current effort favors a given technology vendor. With all these challenges, a well-designed enterprise portal course will not only reflect the major issues in the portal market, but also strive to be vendor neutral. Vendor neutrality is important in this early stage of portal technology until the technology converges.

Portals are gaining much attention in recent years. Due to the lack of efforts in the literature to report experience and guidelines in teaching enterprise portal, it is of much importance that this topic is given an appropriate attention. This article begins with a discussion of the issues and challenges involved in adopting a portal system. It then proceeds to the discussion of educational constraints to deliver an enterprise portal course. A teaching framework on essential portal topics is proposed. The three modules (portal basics, portal management, and portal development) listed in the framework are designed to familiarize students with various portal topics and portal related technologies. It is expected that this course be positioned at the junior or senior level in a college curriculum with prerequisites on basic programming and Web technologies. If the course targets the business or non-technical audience, the technical prerequisites may be dropped and the proportion of focus may be restructured.

REFERENCES

Abdelnur, A., & Hepper, S. (2003). *Java portlet specification* (Version 1.0). Retrieved December 20, 2005, from http://www.jcp.org/en/jsr/detail?id=168

Bauer, C., & Scharl, A. (2000). Quantitative evaluation of Web site content and structure. *Internet Research: Electronic Networking Applications and Policy, 10*(1), 31-43.

Choo, C. W., Detlor, B., & Turnbull, D. (2000). *Web work: Information seeking and knowledge work on the World Wide Web.* Dordrecht: Kluwer Academic Publishers.

Cloete, M., & Snyman, R. (2003). The enterprise portal — is it knowledge management? *Aslib Proceedings, 55*(4), 234-242.

Gounaris, S., & Dimitriadis, S. (2003). Assessing service quality on the Web: Evidence from business-to-consumer portal. *The Journal of Services Marketing, 17*(4/5), 529-546.

Hazra, T. K. (2002). Building enterprise portals: Principles to practice. In *Proceedings of the 24th International Conference on Software Engineering* (pp. 623-633).

Kakumanu, P., & Mezzacca, M. (2005). Importance of portal standardization and ensuring adoption in organizational environments. Cambridge. *Journal of American Academy of Business, 7*(2), 128-132.

Kotorov, R., & Hsu, E. (2001). A model for enterprise portal management. *Journal of Knowledge Management, 5*(1), 86-93.

McGrath, O. G. (2002). Building an instructional portal: Channeling the writing lab. In *Proceedings of the 30th Annual ACM SIGUCCS Conference on User Services* (pp. 199-203).

Raol, J. M., Koong, K. S., Liu, L. C., & Yu, C. S. (2003). An identification and classification of enterprise portal functions and features. *Industrial Management & Data Systems, 103*(8/9), 693-702.

Rose, J. G. (2003, September/October). The joys of enterprise portals. *Information Management Journal, 37*(5), 64-70.

Shilakes, C. C., & Tylman, J. (1998). *Enterprise information portals.* New York: Merill Lynch & Co.

Smith, M. A. (2004). Portals: Toward an application framework for interoperability. *Communications of the ACM, 47*(10), 93-97.

Van Brakel, P. (2003). Information portals: A strategy for importing external content. *The Electronic Library, 21*(6), 591-600.

Wege, C. (2002, May/June). Portal server technology. *IEEE Internet Computing, 6*(3), 73-77.

Yang, S. M., Yang, M. H., & Wu, J. T. B. (2005). The impacts of establishing enterprise information portals on e-business performance. *Industrial Management & Data Systems, 105*(3), 349-368.

APPENDIX: A SAMPLE MASTER SYLLABUS

Course number:

Course meeting information:

Professor contact information:

Course description:
This is an advanced course that focuses on the design issues and implementation details of Internet portals. Pertinent concepts of e-business, information retrieval & sharing, database integration and portal technologies will be discussed. Issues and strategies involved in developing successful portals are also discussed.

Course approach:
A portal system will be chosen as the core development platform. Students will learn the development stages of a portal using the selected portal system. Other portal environments will also be discussed to offer students a broader perspective of technical

varieties. About one-half of the class time will be spent in lecture and discussion. All remaining time will be spent in the Computer Classroom devoted to the "hands-on" application of current Internet programming labs and exercises.

Course objectives:
1. To provide the student with the knowledge and skills of a Web-based information sharing systems development.
2. To recognize the value of information sharing systems in today's competitive business environment and how to develop and manage them.

Required materials:
1. Sullivan, D. (2003). Proven portals: Best practices for planning, designing, and developing enterprise portals, Addison-Wesley, ISBN: 0321125207.
2. Buyens, J. (2005). Microsoft windows SharePoint services inside out, Microsoft Press, ISBN: 0735621713.
3. Reading materials and case studies.

Grading:
1. Labs (6 * 10%)
2. Project (10%)
3. Midterm (15%)
4. Final exam (15%)

A	92.00% or more
BA (A-)	87.00% – 89.99%
B	82.00% - 86.99%
CB (B-)	77.00% - 81.99%
C	72.00% - 76.99%
DC (C-)	67.00% - 71.99%
D	62.00% - 66.99%
E (F)	61.99% or below

Table 1. Class topics

Content module	Module number	Topic
Portal Basics (PB)	PB #1	1. Introduction 2. Portals, CRM, and home-grown online systems 3. Types of portals 4. Functionality of portals 5. Components of a portal system
	PB #2	1. Survey of major portal systems 2. Introduction to major portal technologies 3. Portal standards

Table 1. continued

Portal management (PM)	PM #1	1. Portal design and implementation issues. 2. Theories and guidelines 3. Quality assessment (interactivity, usability, reliability, navigation, scalability, etc.)

	PM #2	1. Criteria for portal adoption and selection.
		   a. Hierarchical breakdown of criteria
		   b. Assessment of tangible vs. intangible factors
		2. Theories on multi-criteria decision making and alternative prioritization

	PM #3	1. Creating of simple portal sites 2. Portal server administration 3. Custom administration tools 4. Backups, restoring, and migration 5. Security 6. Membership management 7. Access control
Portal development (PD)	PD #1	1. Introduction to Web architecture 2. Introduction to Web and portal programming
	PD #2	1. Navigation and customization 2. Collaboration and shared repositories 3. Single sign-on 4. Templates, controls, connections and deployment 5. Style sheets, lists and themes 6. Creating and managing libraries 7. Data sources and data views
	PD #3	1. Vendor specific technologies (Web part, Portlet, and Web channels) and programming API 2. Integration with backend enterprise systems

Section IV

Industrial Support
of ES Education

Chapter XVIII

The Status of SAP-Related Education:
Results of a Global Survey

Michael Rosemann, Queensland University of Technology, Australia

Amelia A. Maurizio, SAP America, Global Education Alliances, USA

ABSTRACT

This chapter focuses on the most popular enterprise system — SAP — and summarizes the outcomes of a global survey on the status quo of SAP-related education. Based on feedback of 305 lecturers and more than 700 students, it reports on the main factors of enterprise systems education including, critical success factors, alternative hosting models, and students' perceptions. The results show among others an overall increasing interest in advanced SAP solutions and international collaboration, and a high satisfaction with the concept of using application hosting centers. Integrating enterprise systems solutions in the curriculum of not only universities but all types of institutes of higher learning has been a major challenge for nearly ten years. Enterprise systems education is surprisingly well documented in a number of papers on information systems education. However, most publications in this area report on the individual experiences of an institution or an academic.

INTRODUCTION

Enterprise systems (ES) form the core of the application infrastructure of most large organizations. While the initial focus of these solutions was on the integrated support for all intra-organizational processes (logistics, accounting, human resource management), the scope has extended in three directions. First, complexity-reduced versions of those systems now target the market of small and medium-sized organizations. Second, ES now also cover advanced solutions for inter-organizational processes such as customer relationship management (CRM), supplier relationship management (SRM), and supplier chain management (SCM) (Klaus, Rosemann, & Gable, 2000). Third and most recently, the scope of ES extends to the technical integration platform that underlies the landscape of those applications as demonstrated in new ES platforms based on the idea of a service-oriented architecture.

ES education is an area demanding special attention for a number of reasons (Rosemann & Watson, 2002). Students have a strong interest in this subject hoping to gain market driven skills. While this often ensures high attendance, student perceptions and expectations must be managed carefully in that it is not the objective of such initiatives to enhance student skills via training activities. Managing ES is typically comprehensive and complex. The frequency of upgrades and innovations from one software release to the next characterizes the rapidly evolving nature of these IS solutions. Because of the frequency of changes in the functionality within the system, it is often difficult for the lecturer to stay abreast of these changes and to understand the implications of these changes to business practice, as well as research and education. By the time textbooks of satisfying quality are available, there are new system upgrades and innovation cycles to deal with almost making the text book obsolete. ES are used to support the learning of traditional business functions (e.g., accounting, cost management, operations management, human resource management), contemporary business process analysis (e.g., order-to-cash, plan-to-produce, procure-to-pay, hire-to-retire), and advanced technological solutions (e.g., data and knowledge management, systems administration, application development, Web services).

The increasing global implementation of ES since 1993 (Chung & Synder, 1999; Davenport, 1998; Davenport, 2000; Rosemann, 1999) did not initially correspond with a similar integration of ES into the curricula of universities and other institutes of higher learning (Gable, Scott, Erlank, & van Heer, 1997). The consequence was not only a shortage of graduates with a solid understanding of and appreciation for this kind of system, but also a lack of credible academic research on ES (Eder, Maiden, & Missikoff, 1999; Gable, 1998). A main reason for this development has been the tremendous complexity of ES that posed a significant challenge for many institutions. It wasn't until 1997 that ES found their way into the curricula of business, information technology/information systems and engineering schools (Gable & Rosemann, 1999).

This chapter provides a condensed overview about the status quo of ES education using SAP solutions as an example. The chapter is based on a global survey that was conducted between September 2003 and January 2004 involving responses from 305 lecturers and more than 700 students. It updates and extends a previous global survey on the integration of SAP solutions into the curricula from 1999 (Gable & Rosemann, 1999).

The chapter is structured as follows. Section 2 briefly summarizes previous related work on ES education. Section 3 provides background information in terms of the survey design and participants in this study. The discussion of current practices and experiences with SAP-related education in section 4 forms the core part of this paper. The perceived major issues and success factors are discussed in section 5. The final section summarizes the findings and provides a subjective outlook on future challenges in this area.

RELATED WORK

While ES were integrated quite late in the curricula in comparison with system implementations in practice, a high number of publications have been printed in this area. In fact, until four years ago, publications on ES education formed a large part of all ES-related academic publications (Esteves & Pastor, 2001). Comprehensive overview articles on ES education can be found in Watson and Schneider (1999) and Rosemann and Watson (2002). MacKinnon provides a brief overview about SAP-related offerings at 17 universities that are accredited by the Association to Advance Collegiate Schools of Business (MacKinnon, 2005).

However, the majority of papers reflect on individual experiences within a new program, such as a specific MBA program (Winter, 1999), or a certain discipline, such as Information Systems Master of Science programs (Holmes & Hayen 1999a, 1999b). The experiences of Louisiana State University in integrating SAP solutions into their IS curriculum have been documented by Watson and Noguera (1999). Becerra-Fernandez, Murphy, and Simon (2000), Elam, Becerra-Fernandez, Murphy, and Simon (1999), Lederer-Antonucci (1999), and Bradford, Chandra, and Vijayaraman (2003) report on experiences with the integration of ES into the curricula of Business Schools. Foote (1999) describes an SAP-accounting class and other SAP-related courses in the U.S. Shoemaker (1999) sketches a six-hour introduction to ES for sales and marketing professionals.

The practical nature of SAP solutions motivated many academics to create new educational models based on the notion of problem-based learning and involving current industry problems. Rosemann, Sedera, and Sedera (2000), Hawking and McCarthy (2000), Stewart and Rosemann (2000, 2001), and Rosemann, Gable, and Stewart (2001) discuss such ways of leveraging industrial work experiences and projects for ES courses. A number of academics contributed to the area of ES education with re-usable teaching cases (e.g., Brown & Vessey (2000). Initially, those case studies were often based on the easily accessible experiences of the ES implementation at the academic's university (Mahrer, 1999; Sieber, Siau, Nah, & Sieber, 1999).

An example of a syllabus for the remote delivery of an introductory subject via the Internet is given by Holmes and Hayen (1999a). Holmes and Hayen describe the design of a course consisting of 10 lessons that introduce the concepts, fundamentals and framework of ES (see also http://sap.mis.cmich.edu/sap-esoft00.htm). Rosemann (2001) compares effectiveness of the on-campus version of a post-graduate ES class with the corresponding off-campus version. McCarthy and Hawking (2004) discuss current technologies that facilitate e-learning experiences in the context of ES.

In some cases, the integration of ES into the curricula triggered innovative international collaborations. Stewart and Rosemann discuss an increased international collaboration at universities in order to deliver ES education more cost-effectively (Stewart & Rosemann, 2001). Klose et. al. (2004) report on a joint project between a German and an Australian university in the context of SAP-based supply chain management. Rosemann, Scott, and Watson (2000) summarize their experiences in a SAP-based collaboration between two American and one Australian university. Lederer-Antonucci and zur Mühlen (2001) outline the setup and experiences of an award-winning collaboration between an American and a German university. Tracy et al. (2001) report on a SAP-funded initiative related to the setup of a student marketplace.

The overall impact of reorganizing ES subject matter into existing curricula and the special challenges posed to faculty have been reported by Stewart, Gable, Andrews, Rosemann, and Chan (1999a) and Stewart, Rosemann, and Watson (1999b). The benefits and pitfalls of teaching conceptual knowledge with ES as a learning vehicle have been critically evaluated in terms of learning outcomes and effort by Watson and Noguera (1999) and Scott (1999).

As this brief overview indicates, most publications in this field reflect individual experiences. The core of all experiences is often similar and can be summarized as challenging for the involved academics and rewarding in terms of students demand. Papers that are actually based on more theoretical models of learning in the context of ES education have been the exception (e.g., Scott, 1999).

In summary, ES education is well discussed with a clear focus on papers reporting on individual experiences. However, the majority of these papers could be seen as case studies or action research.

BACKGROUND

This research project had the objective to identify the current and global status of the integration of SAP solutions into the curriculum of institutes of higher learning. SAP has been chosen as an example for an enterprise system due to its globally market leading status, the wide scope of its functionality, the mature SAP University Alliance Program, the comprehensiveness of the related research, and the support by SAP for this study. A survey was chosen as the research methodology as the focus was on collecting and analyzing a high number of responses in a well-understood domain (Gable, 1994).

Respondent Source and Controls

The SAP Global University Alliance Director developed questions and provided a comprehensive list of lecturers involved in the integration of SAP into the curriculum. SAP also provided funding for an Honor student for the development of an online survey, data collection and data analysis. With this online survey, it was possible to gather cost-effectively and quickly an international view on the current status of the integration of SAP solutions in the curricula. The survey was an extended update of a similar survey from 1999 (Gable and Rosemann, 1999).

The main difference between the study conducted in 1999 and the current study is that in addition to collecting information from faculty, information was also collected from students. The lecturers' contacts have been provided by SAP with the attributes name, university and e-mail address. Thus, there was no knowledge about the actual role of those individuals other than that they were members of the SAP University Alliance Program. We gained access to the student responses through these contacts. In the invitation to the lecturers, we included instructions to encourage the involvement of their students in answering the 5 minute survey as part of one of their SAP tutorials.

A total of 1,731 e-mail contacts have been provided by SAP through their SAP Global University Alliance Program. Table 1 shows the number of contacts per country reflecting the

Table 1. Invited lecturers per country

Country	Number of contacts
Australia	39
Brazil	20
Canada	226
China	9
Czech Republic	6
Finland	14
France	13
Germany	852
India	9
Japan	28
Malaysia	2
Mexico	9
The Netherlands	19
New Zealand	17
Philippines	2
Singapore	6
Slovenia	10
Spain	9
Switzerland	14
Thailand	2
UK	6
USA	416
Venezuela	3

true international character of this study. These are contacts of lecturers currently involved in teaching or administering SAP in their department and/or university. To ensure that the lecturers' survey was accurate and that complete control over the respondents existed, an authentication mechanism was put in place for the lecturers' online survey to identify and ensure that the lecturer only entered the response once and that only "invited" lecturers were able to complete the survey. Every respondent had to enter his/her e-mail address before he/she was able to complete the survey. The students' survey Web site, however, was only disclosed to the lecturers in their invitation e-mail. It did not include such a control mechanism.

Survey Design

The survey design was based on three sources. First, the core skeleton of the survey for the lecturers was based on the instrument previously developed and used by Gable and Rosemann in 1999. Second, a significant update of the survey took place based on new system developments (e.g., the development from SAP R/3 → mySAP Business Suite) as well as changes in the mode of system management (i.e., the increased popularity of mySAP Application Hosting Centers). Third, the survey for students was developed from scratch. A pilot test with six Australian lecturers involved in SAP-related education motivated only minor changes.

The Lecturer's Survey

The lecturer's survey was divided into these six sections:

(A)   Curriculum Implementation Issues
(B)   Learning SAP
(C)   Administering SAP
(D)   Cross-University Collaboration
(E)   Impact on Public Perception
(F)   SAP-Related Subjects

All the sections inquire about the respondent's overall experience and integration of SAP into the curriculum. In the following, each section is explained in more detail.

Curriculum Implementation Issues

This section consisted of two open-ended questions that were included in the original 1999 survey. The first question explored the major issues as perceived by the lecturers when introducing SAP into the curriculum. The second question captured the perceived success factors for SAP education. The respondent was required to fill in at least one answer for each question and had the opportunity to provide up to four answers for each of the two questions. This data provided qualitative information on the major challenges in establishing and delivering successful ES curricula. The purpose was to confirm issues and success factors as they have been reported in various papers.

Learning SAP

This section captured the lecturer's opinion regarding the best way to comprehend SAP solutions. The focus here was on the different learning instruments and methods for the lecturer and staff involved in SAP education. The data in this case was captured on a five point Likert scale ranging from "unimportant" (1) to "highly important" (5). The following alternatives represent a minor update of the alternatives as included in the 1999 survey:

- SAP training courses
- Workshops
- SAP Innovation Congress
- Third party training courses (classroom)
- CBT (computer based training)
- SAP Web pages (www.sap.com)
- SAP online help (help.sap.com)
- Hands-on (learning by doing)

A better understanding of the most effective training channels provides valuable guidance for new lecturers in the area of ES education, who regularly face the question of how to comprehend the SAP solutions in a restrictive timeframe. The feedback is also of significant importance for the SAP University Alliance Program.

Administering SAP: With the establishment of mySAP University Application Hosting Centers (a.k.a. University Competence Centers, UCC), it was important to include a new section that considered the alternative modes of system management. In September 2003, 13 SAP UCCs existed and it was of high interest to study the utilization of those centers as well as the perceived satisfaction. Four choices were set as options for the respondent:

Table 2. Questions on my SAP UCCs

No.	Option	Context-specific questions
1.	The university hosts own SAP application	• Do you plan to use a UCC in the next 12 months? • Number of staff and people involved in administering the SAP application.
2.	The university uses a UCC	• When did you become a member? • Degree of satisfaction with the UCC support in the following dimensions: - Response time - Quality of response - System performance - Value for money
3.	The university is a UCC	• Degree of satisfaction with the UCC in the following dimensions: - Response time - Quality of response - System performance - Value for money
4.	The university uses a third party ASP	• Degree of satisfaction with the ASP's support in the following dimensions: - Response time - Quality of response - System performance - Value for money

- The university hosts its own SAP application.
- The university uses a UCC (in which case a drop down list with the 13 UCCs was provided).
- The university is a UCC (in which case we asked which UCC they were).
- The university uses a third party application service provider (ASP) (in which case we asked which ASP and if any other parties are involved).

Depending on the selected choice, different sets of questions were presented to the respondent (see Table 2).

The section also included items related to the overall impression of SAP as a corporation.

Cross-university collaboration: The Global University Alliance Program helped to establish a close peer-to-peer network between the Alliance members. The intent of this section was to capture the actual status of collaborations between the members and the forms of such collaborations. This section is based on a very similar section in the 99 survey.

Impact on public perception: Also similar to the 99 survey, we included a section on the actual impact of the integration of SAP solutions in the curricula. This section used a

Table 3. Questions on the actual impact of the SAP integration

No.	Question	Scale
Q17	Increase in student demand	5: substantially 1: not at all
Q18	Increase in employer interest	5: substantially 1: not at all
Q19	Increase in employer demand for students with SAP knowledge	5: substantially 1: not at all
Q20	Reaction of students to SAP introduction	5: positive 1: negative
Q21	Reaction of industry to SAP introduction	5: positive 1: negative
Q22	Reaction of employers to SAP introduction	5: positive 1: negative

five point Likert scale in order to rate the impact on the public perception. The following table details different questions of this section.

The results of this section provide valuable indicators for the actual success of the SAP initiative. This is measured based on demand and employability of the students and also how receptive students are of the SAP education.

SAP-related subjects: This section forms the core of the entire survey as it collects detailed data on the individual units taught at the participating institutions. This section had to be substantially revised in comparison with the 99 survey as it investigates the integration of specific SAP solutions into the curricula. This section had to be completed for each unit in which the respondent is either currently referencing/using SAP or in which he or she plans to reference/use SAP in the future. For each unit, the respondent was required to provide details of the subject in terms of number of hours for lectures/tutorials and consultation. The respondent was also required to indicate the SAP modules the unit touched on and SAP support tools used in the course of this unit. Inputs were measured on a five point Likert scale from "casual" to "in-depth." The data collected in this section provided insights into the detailed design of the curricula and the most popular SAP solutions.

The Student Survey

A main motivation for the survey was the collection of feedback from the students. Exploring their feedback is similar to a customer satisfaction study. The student survey was a significantly reduced subset of the lecturer survey with some variations. Students were approached by the lecturers involved in this study within SAP-related tutorials. The Web-based design of the survey allowed an easy integration into hands-on sessions with the SAP system. The survey for the students has been very brief and on average it took five minutes to complete it. There were no incentives for the students to participate in this survey. In the end, students are the customers of the entire SAP education program. There were only two sections in the survey:

(A)   Major Issues and Success Factors
(B)   Learning SAP

Major Issues and Success Factors

Similar to the lecturer survey, this section included only two questions. The first was "Please list any major issues that you have experienced with learning SAP solutions as part of your courses." The student was required to provide up to five answers. This allowed us to compare the students' viewpoints with the lecturers' viewpoints. The second question was "Please list any key success factors you have identified for learning SAP solutions." Success is viewed very differently by individuals. With the data captured here, we could contrast the students' perspective with the lecturers' perspective.

Learning SAP

Successful ES education requires a deep understanding of the main challenges students face when they are exposed to SAP solutions. This section investigated a few of the main perceptions by students in this context.

DATA COLLECTION AND ANALYSIS
Issues Related to the International Nature of this Study

Data in this study had been gathered from lecturers from all over the world. This gave rise to many problems mainly in terms of language and the different semester structure in the different countries.

In order to increase the user acceptance and the understandability of the survey, it was decided that the two surveys also be translated by native speakers into Spanish and German. Once the data collection phase was completed, translators had to be engaged again to convert qualitative data back into English to maintain consistency for the entire data analysis.

The next problem was the different semester periods. As students were involved in the data collection, it was important to send out the survey at a time when the students could be approached (e.g. in a tutorial). Furthermore, students had to have a certain experience as consumers of ES education in order to develop an opinion. As German participants formed a significant percentage of the respondents and the German semester timeframe is quite different, we broke the invitation to complete the survey into different phases: global universities and German universities. The non-German participants received the first invitation on September 19, 2003. A reminder was sent out on 1 October 2003. The first invitation to the German participants was sent out on November 26, 2003 followed by a reminder on November 8, 2003.

Table 4. Questions on students' learning of SAP

Qn No.	Question	Scale
Q4	Please rate the ease of use of SAP software.	1: very difficult 5: very easy
Q5	Have you explored the SAP software beyond the classroom experience?	1: not at all 5: very much
Q6	Do you believe your SAP experience added value to your employability?	1: not at all 5: very much
Q7	Did the exposure to SAP software increase your interest in a SAP-related occupation?	1: not at all 5: very much
Q8	Overall, how would you rate your enjoyment of your experience with SAP software?	1: not at all 5: very much
Q9	What is your overall impression of SAP as a corporation?	1: positive 5: negative

Response Rate

Lecturer survey: 109 of the 1731 e-mails sent out did not reach their destination. Either the contact person was no longer with the institution or the e-mail bounced back because of an invalid address. A further 23 contacts replied stating that they do not have any SAP experience and asked to be excluded from the contact list. This leaves 1731-109-23 = 1599 valid contacts. During the course of the survey, 17 additional contacts were included due to recommendations from other contacts increasing the number to 1616. Of these 17 contacts 14 responded to the survey. At the end of the survey, 305 persons responded that leads to a response rate of 19%. Of these 305 responses, only 238 completed the entire survey (i.e., 15%. 20 participants indicated that they do not have any experiences in SAP education and 47 participants did not complete the entire survey). This could be because the person responding was heavily engaged with other tasks while completing the survey or the completion of the survey took longer that the participants expected and they were not able to finish the survey. Still, 15% is perceived as an overall satisfying response rate for the following reasons:

- We assume that a significant number of the 1616 contacts were not involved in SAP education, but did not bother replying to our two e-mails.
- In many cases we had a number of lecturers from the same institution. In some cases, this included more than 10 names. We are aware of a number of cases that those individuals pooled their answers.
- The collection of detailed data on the individual units can be quite time consuming that might have been an issue for some participants.
- Though we already offered the survey in three languages, barriers still may have existed for some regions, for example in Japan or France.

The 305 responses came from 205 different institutions and 19 different countries. 50.5% of the respondents came from Germany. Participants from Germany also represent

Figure 1. Respondents distribution

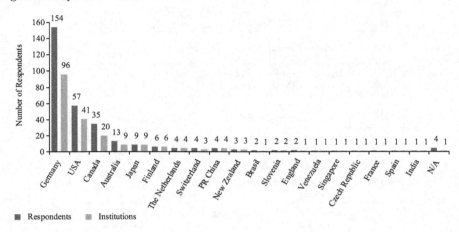

46.8% of the institutions responding though they only represented 35.3% of all institutions in the contacts provided by SAP. The absolute high number of responses from Germany can be explained by the long tradition of SAP education in Germany, which goes back to 1993, the mature German SAP University Alliance program with a full time University Alliance manager for more than 10 years, the high number of Fachhochschulen (universities of applied science) involved in SAP education and the overall German roots of SAP. USA comes in second with 18.7% of the respondents from 20% of the total institutions that responded. This is followed by Canada with 11.5% respondents and 9.8% institutions. Figure 1 provides a detailed view on the regional profile of the individual responses.

The Student Responses: 714 students from 8 different countries participated in the survey. 63% were German students, 18% American students, and 13% Australian students. Since the student's survey was conducted anonymously, many did not include the name of their institution. As we did not send the questionnaire directly to the students, we are not able to provide a response rate for the students' feedback. The ratio of lecturer to student is exactly 1:3. Students from 8 different countries responded to the survey and most came from Germany, USA and Australia. Since 50.5% of the lecturer respondents came from Germany, it is consistent to the result that the majority of students that completed the survey came from Germany as well. The second most responses came from USA also consistent to

Figure 2. Student's response distribution

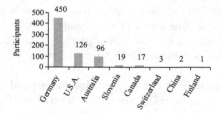

Figure 3. SAP teaching experience in years

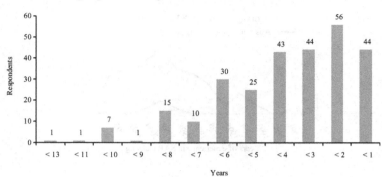

the lecturer's participation. Since this survey was initiated by an Australian university, we had direct access to lecturers and students in this region. This explains why Australia has 13.45% of the total student responses. Though we tried to time the survey according to the semester pattern, we had a number of responses from lecturers stating that their university's curriculum time does not coincide with the survey. This means that many of their students may not have sufficient experience in terms of exposure to SAP solutions. Therefore, they were unable to allow the students to respond to the survey.

Experiences

The average SAP teaching experience of the responding lecturers is 3.5 years with a 2.24 standard deviation. Fifty percent of all respondents have less than three years experience, 95% have less than eight years experience (see Figure 3).

Eighty-four percent of the respondents have at least one year of experience in teaching SAP. This shows that the results captured from the following sections seem to be sufficiently accurate.

We also investigated the status of the SAP version currently used. The results suggested that the applications being used were very current with 61% of the institutions using SAP 4.6 and 31% using SAP 4.7, the most current version at the time of this survey.

Taking an institutions' perspective on the experience with SAP solutions, we found an even higher maturity (Figure 4). The average teaching experience of the 206 responding institutions is 4.3 years with a standard deviation of 2.33. One of Canada's Universities has 13 years of SAP experience, while in Germany some institutions started teaching SAP as early as 1993. The first institutions in the USA followed in 1996. The following chart shows the distribution of the top five country's experience based on the year the country's institutions first implemented SAP solutions.

The pattern of distribution shows a general peak from 1998 to 2000. However, it also shows a general steady decline in implementation. This could be one of three reasons:

- Most institutions have already implemented SAP.
- There is a decrease in demand for implementing SAP solutions in the curriculum.
- Not all schools requesting membership in the University Alliance Program are accepted. Increasingly, SAP rejects applications for membership in the University Alliance Program for two reasons. First, an institution does not demonstrate the required

Figure 4. SAP experience by country's distribution

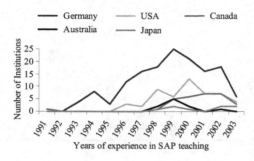

Figure 5. Learning SAP

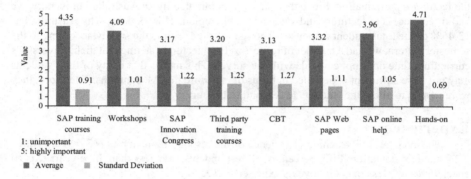

commitment (e.g., attending workshops). Second, the submitted curriculum plan for the integration of SAP into the curriculum lacks the required detail or is overall too weak.

Learning SAP

One of the key challenges in ES education is to develop the required knowledge of the selected ES solution. Thus, it was interesting to explore how the lecturers rate alternative ways of understanding SAP. It is obvious that hands-on experiences are the most important source of knowledge followed by SAP training courses. It is interesting to note that this is the same rating as in our 99 survey that clearly emphasizes the importance of hands-on experiences and training courses. At the same time, it characterizes the uniqueness of SAP as a curricula subject. Figure 5 shows the results based on a five-point Likert scale with five representing "highly important." The responses have been analyzed based on the simple arithmetic average knowing that this value has limitations in its validity when using ordinal scales.

In this section, there was an opportunity to provide other learning avenues. Thirty-three lecturers took this opportunity. Answers other than the given categories were grouped into the following answers:

1.   Exchange of experience with peers, trainers, mentors, specialists, consultants
2.   Literature, self-study
3.   Other material provided by the SAP University Alliance Program

A detailed breakdown of the answers categorized them into the following top six answers.

- Seven respondents state "training materials" including SAP training materials, books on SAP and other relevant literature.
- Six respondents state "exchange of experience."
- Four respondents state "consulting with specialists" such as professional SAP consultants.
- Three respondents state "practical experience" such as adopting industry processes and conducting case studies.
- Two respondents state "application help and support."
- Two respondents state attending "SAP events" such as SAPPHIRE and University Alliance workshops.
- There are respondents stating self-study, in-house training, virtual lessons as well as attending faculty workshops.

The results show that a number of respondents regard "training materials" and "exchange of experience" as highly important. This is followed by "consulting with specialists" and gaining "practical experience" as the primary training opportunities for learning SAP. All the additional suggestions repeatedly state the need for knowledge exchange through colleagues with common interests. This is seen in "exchange of experience," "consulting with specialists," "application help and support" and "SAP events." All these paradigms have some form of interaction and exchange involving parties of common interest. In this case it is teaching SAP. This is widely known as "communities of practice." These findings seem to support the need to form or join forums.

Administering SAP

Implementing and continuously maintaining and upgrading a SAP system is a challenging and time consuming activity that in many cases provided the single most significant hurdle on the way to successful ES education. Thus, it is not a surprise that hosting solutions are of increasing popularity in the context of ES education.

In this section we tried to find out the actual status of how SAP solutions are managed. An institution can either host its own SAP solution, use a SAP UCC, be a SAP UCC itself or use a third party to host SAP. The survey found that approximately 60% of all participating institutions are a customer of an SAP UCC. Around 30% of the institutions (still) host their own SAP solution. Twenty-two responses came from universities which are SAP UCC themselves. In total, 285 responses were received in response to this question. Figure 6 shows the detailed results.

The very high number of SAP UCC customers shows the successful roll-out of this concept. A few respondents stated alternative setups. This included also mixed solutions (e.g., hosting a part of the SAP landscape and accessing a hosted solution for other more specialized components) (e.g., CRM, data warehousing, and strategic enterprise management). In individual cases, solutions provided by an SAP lab or the official SAP training platform are used.

Figure 6. Distribution of SAP solution source

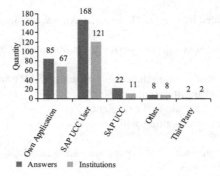

Figure 7. Will you consider being an SAP UCC costomer in the next 12 months?

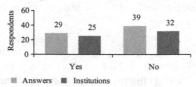

Hosting the Own SAP Solution

For the institutions that stated that they host their own SAP solution, we asked whether they would consider using a SAP UCC in the next 12 months. Only 68 of the initial 85 respondents answered this question (Figure 7).

A narrow majority of those who host their own SAP application stated that they do not plan to use a SAP UCC in the near future. However, 29 respondents from 25 different institutions answered "yes" to this question, stating that they may consider switching to a SAP UCC. A reason for not switching to a SAP UCC is often the significant investment made into the setup of the own solution.

In addition to the pure demographics, it was interesting to explore how satisfied the respondents were with their on-site SAP administration. Overall, the response indicated reasonable satisfaction in terms of response time, quality of response, and system performance as measured by a five point Likert scale with 1 being "very satisfied" (Figure 8).

SAP UCC Customers

For those respondents who were customers of an SAP UCC, we asked when they became a member. More than 90% became an SAP UCC customer in the last five years. The results show that there was a steady increase of members five years ago (Figure 9). The interest in a hosted solution is quite consistent over the last five years. The answers come from 115 participants in 91 institutions.

Again, we explored the satisfaction of users of an SAP UCC. The satisfaction was measured in terms of response time, quality of response, system performance and also value

Figure 8. Satisfaction of on-site SAP administration (hosting own application)

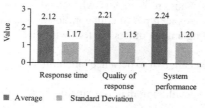

Figure 9. When institutions become an SAP UCC costomer

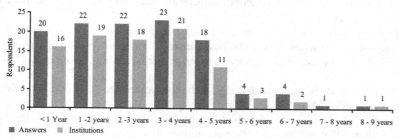

for money. The feedback came from 16 respondents who are an SAP UCC and 115 SAP UCC customers (Figure 10).

The general trend is that respondents who access SAP solutions through a SAP UCC that they host themselves, tend to be more satisfied with their own performance than their customers. However, it is important to note that in all of the three criteria — response time, quality of response, and system performance — customers of a UCC were more satisfied than those respondents who used their own system. The comparison of Figures 9 and 10 provides a convincing case for UCCs.

Cross-University Collaboration

The first question in this section was whether the respondents have entered into collaboration with any other institutions in their SAP-related teaching activities. Only 30%

Figure 10. General satisfaction with SAP UCCs

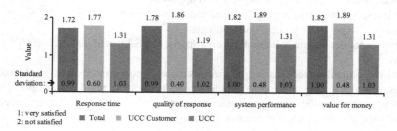

of the respondents answered "yes" for this question and 70% stated that they do not collaborate with other institutions. Those respondents, who stated that they do collaborate, had the chance to further specify the exact types of collaboration they experienced. Thirty-nine answers were received providing among others the following feedback:

- 15 respondents state "exchange of experience" including exchange of problems and ideas.
- Eight respondents state "developing material" including teaching and training material.
- Five respondents state "exchange of material" including teaching and training material.
- Four respondents state "collaborative lectures" such as having collaborative courses and joint lectures.
- Two respondents state "exchange of students and staff."
- One respondent states "create practical scenarios" such as depiction of a supply chain with different universities as players in the scenario (see e.g., Klose et al. 2004).

The top two items suggested were "exchange experience" (38%) and "developing teaching material" (21%).

The second question extended the first one. We asked the respondents if they would be interested in collaborating with other institutions in their SAP initiative. An impressive majority of 76% stated that they were interested in collaborating. Only 24% stated that they were not interested. The following answers are from those respondents who completed this part (140 answers were documented):

- 38 respondents state "exchange of experience" such as sharing teaching experiences and knowledge.
- 22 respondents state "exchange of material" including case studies, course material, exercises, and virtual learning material.
- 19 respondents state "exchange of courses" including exchanging and sharing curriculum.
- 18 respondents state "collaborative lectures" such as development of curriculum and conjoint courses.
- 18 respondents state "developing material" including teaching material, case studies and exercises.
- Eight respondents state "exchange of students and staff" including exchanging faculty members, lecturers and (research) students.
- Six respondents state "research" — some suggest research on ES adoption, institutionalization issues, and sharing research opportunities.
- Five respondents state having "regular meetings" such as attending workshops, discussion forums, user groups, and seminars.
- Four respondents state collaborating on a "particular SAP module" such as CRM, PS, PM.
- Two respondents state "creating practical scenarios" between schools to simulate actual business and setting up vendors and customers to simulate real-life examples.
- Others suggest collaborating on conferences and publications, teaching improvement and special skill set such as process modeling.

The results were placed into similar categories and irrelevant and erroneous answers were excluded in the analysis. The clustered results can be categorized into two broad dimensions. The first focuses on collaboration in teaching (54%). The second focuses on course material (29%), more specifically, the exchanging of it or its collaborative development. In the third and final question of this section, we asked if there was collaboration across faculties or colleges within their institution in their SAP-related teaching activities. 46% of the respondents answered "yes" to this question. The following is a list of answers (52 documented) from the respondents who provided further details:

- 14 respondents state "conjoint lectures" such as coordination of courses and development of case studies
- 13 respondents state "exchange of experience" such as having informal discussion, informal sharing of ideas and advice.
- 11 respondents state collaborating within "specific school or faculty" such as Accounting, Business, Engineering, IS, and Mechanical Engineering.
- Four respondents state "conjoint system" such as conjoint use of systems and conjoint administration.
- Four respondents state "developing materials" including coordination of course content, development of teaching materials, training materials, and exercises.
- Two respondents state "lecturer training" such as training and education for staff development.
- Two respondents state having "regular meetings" such as organizing interdisciplinary meetings.
- Two respondents state creating "special study program" like collaboration through student internships.
- There are a few responses about organizing workshops for students, creating a collaborative unit with faculty and exchange of lecturers.

Yet again the practice of exchanging experiences and conjoint lectures appears to be the most important (52%).

While some have collaborated across faculties internally, they still believe that collaborating with other institutions seems to be of great benefit to them. The results of this section on collaboration seem to indicate that although many institutions are not currently collaborating with other universities, they are interested in doing so. Many respondents acknowledge the need for such collaborative activities but have not sufficiently engaged in them.

Public Perception

This section explored the success of the SAP initiative as measured by public perception. Two hundred and eighty-five respondents answered this section. The following is a repeat of the questions posed and their respective scales (see also Table 3).

For question 17, there seems to be a slightly increasing student demand for SAP knowledge after it was introduced into the curriculum and the same is true regarding the increase in employer interest (Figure 11). Question 19 reports a higher rating. The lecturers found that there was an increase in employer demand for students with SAP knowledge; however, the highest ratings came regarding the student's reactions. The lecturers felt that there was a very positive reaction from the students after SAP was introduced into their

Table 5. Questions for impact on public perception of introducing SAP

Qn No.	Question	Scale
Q17	Increase in student demand?	5: substantially 1: not at all
Q18	Increase in employer interest?	5: substantially 1: not at all
Q19	Increase in employer demand for students with SAP knowledge	5: substantially 1: not at all
Q20	Reaction of students to SAP introduction	5: positive 1: negative
Q21	Reaction of industry to SAP introduction	5: positive 1: negative
Q22	Reaction of employers to SAP introduction	5: positive 1: negative

Figure 11. Section E ratings for impact on public perception

curriculum. Finally the reactions from the industry and the employers (questions 21 and 22) to the introduction of SAP were perceived as generally quite positive.

SAP-Related Subjects

In this last section of the survey, we captured details on the actual units. In total, 220 respondents answered this section. Overall, we collected details of 660 subjects which have references to SAP, of which 249 have been classified as undergraduate, 349 as post-graduate, and 62 as others including professional training, vocational school, and job training. This implies that the focus tends to be on graduate students instead of under-graduate students.

In order to evaluate the maturity of the offerings, we asked for each subject when it was first introduced into the curriculum (Figure 12).

The results show that approximately 80% of all classes were first offered between 1999 and 2003. There was a steady increase in the introduction of SAP-related subjects between the years 1997 and 2000. This result is consistent with the option of universities and schools utilizing the services of a university competency center.

Figure 12. Distribution of the subject's first introduction in years

Figure 13. Details of enrollment and curriculum hours

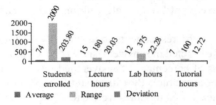

Details on Enrollment and Curriculum Hours

The respondents were required to enter the number of students enrolled for each subject, its lecture, lab and tutorial hours in total for each semester. Figure 13 shows the average, the range of values, and the standard deviation of all 660 subjects. The range indicates the highest value given. The lowest was 1 (students enrolled) or 0 (hours). The high deviation and range values seen here seem to indicate two possibilities:

- The questions we posed to capture this data was understood differently by individual respondents. This could cause inaccuracy in the data for these questions.
- Due to the diverse nature of this survey in terms of courses offered, the answers entered by individual lecturers may vary. For example, in specialized subjects, the enrollment and hours spent can be very different between undergraduate and graduate curriculum.

Considering possibility two, we classified each average to the different subject categories to compare the distribution. The trend here seems to be consistent with the majority number of subjects offered by graduate courses. However, the average number of hours cannot be analyzed accurately because of the diverse nature of the answers (Figure 14).

Figure 14. Details of enrollment and curriculum hours by course category

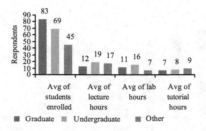

SAP Modules Used

In this part of the section we presented a list of SAP modules to the respondents and asked for a rating of their usage based on how detailed they would utilize a SAP module. The rating was done on a five point Likert scale with one being "casual review" and five being "in-depth review."

There was an option for the respondents to answer "N/A" for each module. In the analysis of the data, we also extracted the answers having "N/A" and calculated the number of "N/A" responses in terms of percentage. The averaged results indicate that MM (29% indicated this module is not available), PP (40%) and SD (36%) modules are the most popular solutions. The two least used modules were CRM (80%) and SRM (84%), bordering slightly below the two points margin. In general, it is clear that many lecturers have not yet ventured into an "in-depth" study of a SAP module. However, it could also be argued as how much "in-depth" really is in-depth? One lecturer's perceived depth of review of a module may mean a casual review to another lecturer.

The SAP Industry Solutions are practically non-existing in the landscape of SAP education. Only 1% of the respondents stated that they expose their students to industry solutions which would include banking, automobile, and retail.

SAP Support Tools

In addition to the implementation of specific functional modules, we explored the integration of additional SAP support tools in the curricula. We asked to respondents to rate the usage of these support tools and also to list any other additional support tools they may have reviewed/used for the purpose of teaching SAP (Figure 16).

Figure 15. Using ratings of SAP modules

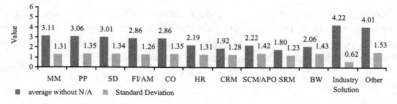

Figure 16. Using ratings of SAP support tools

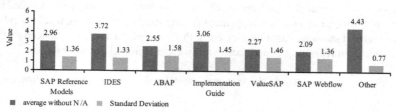

Again there was an option for the respondents to answer "not available (N/A)" for each tool listed. In the analysis of the data, we extracted the answers having "N/A" and calculated the number of "N/A" responses in terms of percentage. The averaged results indicate that the top three support tools are IDES (internet demonstration and education system) (24%), the implementation guide (IMG) (57%) and the SAP reference models (52%).

Respondents had the option to mention other tools. Only 3% of the respondents provided some feedback including ARIS, CBT Modules, Dolphin Group Integration and Configuration, Business Connector, and ALE.

MAJOR ISSUES AND SUCCESS FACTORS

In terms of qualitative feedback, we asked the lecturers "Please list any major issues that you have experienced with introducing SAP solutions into your curriculum" and "Please list any key success factors you have identified for teaching SAP solutions." The top four issues/obstacles introducing SAP solutions into the curriculum have been:

1. **Complexity of the subject:** 63 responses (12%) — The difficulty to comprehend the SAP solutions has clearly been the number one issue. This includes the initial knowledge acquisition as well as continuous knowledge management, that is, the need to keep up with system changes, upgrades and extensions. Typically, the lecturer has not attended ES classes himself/herself. In addition, this includes issues related to technical support (system administration as well as functional support), system issues (initial setup, system performance, maintenance), as well as training.
2. **Developing course material/curriculum:** 49 responses (9%) — Another main issue was the quality of material appropriate for tertiary education. Due to the release cycles, SAP-related material tends to be outdated quickly. Many publications are written for industry, simplified, and assume business knowledge. Available material for lecturers is often too much hands-on and lacks conceptual foundation. This item also included the requirement to customize the SAP solution beyond the IDES capabilities for specific needs and the corresponding efforts related to creating business scenarios.
3. **Student background/interests:** 25 responses (5%) — The student-related issues had two facets. First, the students' background has been perceived as critical when IT students did not have the required appreciation and understanding for the underlying business scenarios. Second, the overall interest of students in ES-related subjects matters.

4.   **Faculty support:** 21 responses (4%) — Finally, gaining the required support from the university or faculty has been perceived as a significant issue. This included interest, commitment and acknowledgement (recognition in promotion, teaching relief to comprehend software functionality, etc.). Furthermore, lack of experienced staff and difficulties in recruiting experienced staff were mentioned as major issues.

In terms of success factors, the lecturers mentioned among others the following factors:

- Employer feedback
- Experienced personnel
- Faculty support (administrative, management)
- Industry liaison
- Industry support
- Job market
- Learning approach
- Lecturer background (SAP experience/industry experience)
- Student enrolment
- Students interests
- Systems support (technical, administration)
- Teaching approach (real-world context, theory and practice)
- Training for lecturers (by SAP/faculty)

The results indicate that the following appear to be the top five key success factors identified for teaching SAP solutions (based on broad content analysis):

- Course materials — 23 responses (5%)
- Faculty support — 20 responses (4%)
- Systems support — 16 responses (3.5%)
- Students interests — 13 responses (3%)
- Training for lecturers — 12 responses (2.5%)

In a similar way, we have asked the students "Please list any major issues that you have experienced with learning SAP solutions as part of your courses."

Major issues stated in student responses included quality of course materials (manuals, books available, etc.), complexity of the system (hard to use/understand), system performance (too slow), accessibility of the system, user interface (hard to use/navigate), own motivation to learn (knowing the purpose of learning, etc.), differences in system versions, quality of lecturers and appropriateness of educational approaches (practical exercises, tutorials, etc.). It should be noted, however, that in the actual student responses, a significant number of them (close to 50%) quoted a specific SAP module as a major issue, for example, accounting, controlling, logistic, procurement, and so forth or a specific activity such as ABAP, customizing, and so forth. These responses are not taken into account as they do not correspond with the actual context of the question.

The consolidated results indicate that the following appear to be the top five issues students have experienced with learning SAP (based on a broad content analysis):

- Complexity of the system — (8%)
- System performance — (6%)
- User interface — (5%)
- Course materials — (4%)
- Learning approaches — (4%)

A list of key success factors stated in student responses:

- Job prospect.
- Good instructors.
- Class materials.
- Learning approaches (hands-on experience, teamwork, etc.).
- Practical application (applying the knowledge in practice).
- Foundation knowledge.
- Reduce and manage the complexity, extensive scope, or comprehensiveness of the SAP system for learning purposes.

Note: Again a good number of student responses (estimated to be more than 30%) do not correspond to the actual context of the question, or have no relevance to the key success factors. The results indicate that the following appear to be the top five success factors students have identified for learning SAP solutions (based on broad content analysis):

- Practical application — (8%)
- Learning approaches — (5%)
- Class materials — (4%)
- Job prospect — (4%)
- Good instructors — (3%)

CONCLUSION

This chapter reports on the outcomes of a global empirical analysis of the current status of ES education using the SAP solutions as a widely distributed example.

The results also show that students experienced major issues in (and are thus more concerned with) complexity of the system, system performance, system user interface, course materials, and approaches for learning SAP solutions as part of their courses. It also shows that students regard gaining practical experience, adequate educational approaches, helpful class materials, promising job prospect, and good instructors as key success factors for learning SAP solutions. The actual feedback shows that students are for most part satisfied with the outcomes of SAP education. They believe that having SAP as part of their curriculum makes them more recruitable. Overall, they also have a positive impression of SAP as a corporation.

The main outcome of this survey is a definitive sign for an increasing maturity in the field of SAP-related education. In comparison with five years ago, a much larger, more global and most of all more experienced group of lecturers is committed to engaging in such initiatives. Their challenges, however, remain in many areas the same. The willingness to get insights into the rich system functionality requires first of all hands-on experience and material appropriate for tertiary education is still an obstacle. However, the successful establishment of reliable application hosting solutions seems to relieve the burden related to financial and technical system support. Though ES might have been perceived as less popular during the dot.com era, they are now in high demand as indicated by strong students' demand and an overall very positive reaction. The participating lecturers also indicated that they perceived a positive reaction by industry to the introduction of SAP solutions into the curricula.

Comparing the results between lecturers and students, it seems that students experience more systems-related issues (such as complexity, performance, and user interface) than the course-related issues (such as different learning approaches) that have a total of 19% and 8% respectively. Lecturers, on the other hand, seem to experience more course-related issues (including faculty and student related) than the systems-related issues that account for 22% and 8% respectively.

With respect to success factors, students appear to be more concerned with "why and how to learn" rather than "what to learn" that account for 13% for the former and 4% for the latter. The former relates to knowing the purpose of learning, applying the knowledge in practice, acquiring hands-on experience while latter relates to better or improved class materials. A possible interpretation for the focus on the "why and how" instead of the "what" might be that students appreciate any form of SAP exposure. They understand the richness of the system and the demand to explore efficient ways to quickly comprehend this solution.

The outcome of this study also provides interesting insights into the future roadmap of education in the area of ES. From a number of possible predictions, we like to point out two: (1) The model of hosted solutions seems to be the core infrastructure for SAP-related activities. It can be expected that the use of hosting centers will be soon the only way to get hands-on access to SAP solutions. Future contracts between the involved parties will have to reflect the increasing complexity in the SAP landscape. UCC customers will also expect a fair and transparent price mechanism that takes student numbers, type of students, intensity of use, and so forth into account. Besides contractual issues, UCCs will also have to be selective as they continue to be exposed to an increasing number of SAP solutions. As a consequence, it can be expected, that UCCs will increasingly collaborate. This could mean that individual universities will use SAP-related services from a network of globally distributed UCCs. (2) The data indicated that collaboration and global knowledge exchange between universities will be the next wave that can be observed in this market. A marketplace could be established that facilitates the exchange of course material, case studies, assignment, exams, and overall experiences. However, competition between universities, intellectual property, reimbursement models, and so forth will be key challenges that have to be addressed in such a market for educational material related to SAP.

REFERENCES

Becerra-Fernandez, I., Murphy, K., & Simon, S. (2000). Integrating ERP in the business school curriculum. *Communications of the ACM, 43*(4), 39-41.

Bradford, M., Chandra, A., & Vijayaraman, B. (2003). The status of ERP integration in business school curricula: Results of a survey of business schools. *Communications of the AIS, 12*, 437-456.

Brown, C., & Vessey, I. (2000). NIBCO's big bang. *Proceedings of the International Conference on Information Systems (ICIS 2000)*, Brisbane, Australia.

Chung, S. H., & Synder, C. A. (1999). ERP initiation — a historical perspective. In *Proceedings of the Americas Conference on Information Systems*, Milwaukee.

Davenport, T. H. (1998, July-August). Putting the enterprise into the enterprise system. *Harvard Business Review,* 121-131.

Davenport, T. H. (2000). *Mission critical: Realizing the promise of ES.* Boston: Harvard Business School Press.

Eder, J., Maiden, N., & Missikoff, M. (1999, November 25-26). *Proceedings of the 1st International Workshop Enterprise Management and Resource Planning Systems: Methods, Tools and Architectures,* Venice, Italy.

Elam, J., Becerra-Fernandez, I., Murphy, K., & Simon, S. (1999, November 1-2). ERP as an enabler of curriculum integration. In T. Sinnott, G. G. Gable, & P. Hawking (Eds.), *Proceedings of the 3rd SAP Asia Pacific Institute of Higher Learning Forum — SAP-PHIRE 1999,* Singapore.

Esteves, J., & Pastor, J. (2001). Enterprise resource planning systems research: An annotated bibliography. *Communications of the Association for Information Systems, 3*(7).

Foote, P. S. (1999, August 3). *SAP R/3 curriculum development for undergraduate and graduate accounting information systems track.* Presented at the 1st Accounting Information Systems Educator Conference, Denver, CO.

Gable, G. (1994). Integrating case study and survey research methods: An example in information systems. *European Journal of Information Systems, 3*(2), 112-126.

Gable, G. G. (1998). Large Packaged software: A neglected technology? *Journal of Global Information Management, 6*(3), 3-4.

Gable, G., & Rosemann, M. (1999, November 1-2). ERP-software in teaching and research: An international survey. In G. G. Gable, P. Hawking, & T. Sinnott (Eds.), *Proceedings of the 3rd Institute of Higher Learning Forum "Maximizing the Synergy Between Teaching, Research & Business" SAPPHIRE 1999,* Singapore.

Gable, G. G., Scott, J., Erlank, S., & van Heer, R. (1997). Using large packaged software in teaching: The CASE of SAP. In *Proceedings of the Americas Conference on Information Systems,* Indianapolis, IN.

Hawking, P., & McCarthy, B. (2000, July 23-25). Transporting ERP education from the classroom to industry. In P. Hawking, M. Rosemann, G. Stewart, & T. Byrne (Eds.), *Proceedings of the 4th SAP Asia Pacific Institute of Higher Learning Forum — SAP-PHIRE 2000,* Brisbane, Australia.

Holmes, M. C., & Hayen, R. L. (1999a, August 13-15). An introduction to enterprise software using SAP R/3: A Web-based course. In W. D. Haseman & D. L. Nazarath (Eds.), *Proceedings of the 5th Americas Conference on Information Systems,* Milwaukee.

Holmes, M. C., & Hayen, R. L. (1999b, August 13-15). The master of science in information systems in a regional Midwestern University. In W. D. Haseman & D. L. Nazarath (Eds.), *Proceedings of the 5th Americas Conference on Information Systems,* Milwaukee.

Klaus, H., Rosemann, M., & Gable, G. G. (2000). What is ERP? *Information System Frontiers, 2*(2), 141-162.

Klose, K., Schallert, M., Holten, R., Becker, J., & Rosemann, M. (2004, June 14-16). Integrative teaching aspects for the IS profession: Development and application of a teaching framework. *Proceedings of the 12th European Conference on Information Systems,* Turku, Finnland.

Lederer-Antonucci, Y. (1999). Enabling the business school curriculum with ERP software: Experiences of the SAP university alliance. In *Proceedings of the IBSCA '99,* Atlanta, GA.

Lederer-Antonucci, Y., & zur Mühlen, M. (2001, August 3-5). Deployment of business to business scenarios in ERP education: Evaluation and experiences from an international collaboration. In *Proceedings of the 7th Americas Conference on Information Systems,* Boston.

MacKinnon, R. J. (2005, February 25-26). A comparison of the ERP offerings of AACSB accredited universities belonging to SAPUA. In *Proceedings of the 7th Conference of the Southern Association for Information Systems,* Savannah, GA.

Mahrer, H. (1999, August 13-15). SAP R/3 implementation at the ETH Zürich–A higher education management success story? In *Proceedings of the 5th Americas Conference on Information Systems,* Milwaukee.

McCarthy, B., & Hawking, P. (2004, December 1-3). ERP e-learning: If you can't take Mohammed to the classroom, take the classroom to Mohammed. In S. Elliot et al. (Eds.), *Proceedings of the 15th Australasian Conference on Information Systems,* Hobart.

Philippakis, A., & Hardaway, D. (1999, August 13-15). ERP in the MIS curriculum: A tri-perspective. *Proceedings of the 1999 Americas Conference on Information Systems,* Milwaukee.

Rosemann, M. (1999, June 23-25). ERP software — Characteristics and consequences. In J. Pries-Heje et al. (Eds.), *Proceedings of the 7th European Conference on Information Systems,* Copenhagen, Denmark (Vol. 3, pp. 1038-1043).

Rosemann, M. (2000b, August 10-13). Teaching ERP. Tutorial. In H. M. Chung (Ed.), *Proceedings of the 6th Americas Conference on Information Systems* (pp. 2159-2161). Long Beach.

Rosemann, M. (2001). Teaching enterprise resource planning in a distance education mode — experiences and recommendations. In R. Discenza, C. Howard, & K. D. Schenk (Eds.), *Distance education and telecommuting: Challenges and solutions.* Hershey, PA: Idea Group Publishing.

Rosemann, M., & Watson, E. (2002). Education in ES. *Communications of the AIS (CAIS),* April 2002.

Rosemann, M., Gable, G. G., & Stewart, G. (2001, June 27-29). Collaboration between industry and academe: The SAP-QUT example. In J. Becker (Ed.), *Proceedings of the University Alliance Executive Directors Workshop at the European Conference on Information Systems — ECIS 2001,* Bled, Slovenia.

Rosemann, M., Scott, J., & Watson, E. (2000, August 10-13). Collaborative ERP education: Experiences from a first pilot. In H. M. Chung (Ed.), *Proceedings of the 6th Americas Conference on Information Systems,* Long Beach.

Rosemann, M., Sedera, D., & Sedera, W. (2000, December 6-8). Industry-oriented education in ES. In G. G. Gable, & M. Vitale (Eds.), *Proceedings of the 11th Australasian Conference on Information Systems,* Brisbane, Australia.

Scott, J. (1999, August 13-15). ERP effectiveness in the classroom: Assessing congruence with theoretical learning models. In W. D. Haseman & D. L. Nazareth (Eds.), *Proceedings of the 5th Americas Conference on Information Systems,* Milwaukee.

Shoemaker, M. E. (1999). Introducing ERP systems to sales and marketing management graduate students: Discussion and exercises using SAP R/3. In *Proceedings of the 10th Annual International Information Management Association,* New Rochelle, NY.

Sieber, T., Siau, K., Nah, F., & Sieber, M. (1999, December 13-15). Implementing SAP R/3 at the University of Nebraska. In *Proceedings of the 20th International Conference on Information Systems ICIS.* Charlotte, NC.

Stewart, G., & Rosemann, M. (2000, August 10-13). Collaborative ERP curriculum developing using industry process models. In H. M. Chung (Ed.), *Proceedings of the 6th Americas Conference on Information Systems,* Long Beach (pp. 960-965).

Stewart, G., & Rosemann, M. (2001). Integrating industrial knowledge into IS curriculum. *Business Process Management Journal, 7*(3), 234-242.

Stewart, G., Gable, G. G., Andrews, R., Rosemann, M., & Chan, T. (1999a, August 13-15). Lessons from the field: A reflection on teaching SAP R/3 and ERP implementation issues. In W. D. Haseman & D. L. Nazareth (Eds.), *Proceedings of the 5th Americas Conference on Information Systems,* Milwaukee.

Stewart, G., Rosemann, M., & Watson, E. (1999b, August 13-15). An overview of teaching and research using SAP R/3. In W. D. Haseman & D. L. Nazareth (Eds.), *Proceedings of the 5th Americas Conference on Information Systems,* Milwaukee.

Tracy, S., Stewart, G., Boykin, R., Najm, M., Rosemann, M., & Carpinetti, L. (2001, August 3-5). SAP Student Marketplace for the Advancement of Research and Teaching (SAP SMART). In *Proceedings of the 7th Americas Conference on Information Systems,* Boston.

Watson, E., & Schneider, H. (1999). Using ERP systems in education. *Communications of the Association for Information Systems, 1*(1).

Watson, E. F., & Noguera, J. H. (1999, August 13-15). Effectiveness of using an enterprise system to teach process-centred concepts in business education. In W. D. Haseman & D. L. Nazarath (Eds.), *Proceedings of the 5th Americas Conference on Information Systems,* Milwaukee.

Winter, R. (1999, June 23-25). HSG master of business engineering program: Qualifying high potentials for IS-enabled change. In J. Pries-Heje, C. Ciborra, & K. Kautz (Eds.), *Proceedings of the 7th European Conference on Information Systems,* Copenhagen, Denmark (Vol. II, pp. 819-826).

ENDNOTE

[1]   A previous version of this chapter, "SAP-related Education — Status Quo and Experiences," by Michael Rosemann and Amelia Maurizio, appeared in the Journal of Information Systems Education, Vol. 16, No. 4, 2006.

APPENDIX

Abbreviations

AHC: Application hosting center
AM: Asset management
APO: Advanced planner & optimizer
CBT: Computer-based training
BW: Business warehouse
CO: Controlling
CRM: Customer relationship management
ERP: Enterprise resource planning
ES: Enterprise systems
FI: Financial accounting
HR: Human resource management
IDES: Internet demonstration & education system
IMG: Implementation guide
MM: Materials management
PM: Plant maintenance
PP: Production planning & control
PS: Project system
SCM: Supply chain management
SD: Sales & distribution
SRM: Supplier relationship management
UCC: University competence center

Chapter XIX

Supporting Enterprise Systems Across the Business Curriculum:
The Microsoft Dynamics™ Academic Alliance

Janelle Daugherty, Microsoft, USA

Sandra B. Richtermeyer, Xavier University, USA

ABSTRACT

This chapter discusses how enterprise systems supported by the Microsoft Dynamics™ Academic Alliance can be used by higher educational institutions in their business courses. The content is designed to be useful for both business educators and administrators as they plan and implement technology into their curricula. The chapter discusses the history and development of the Microsoft Dynamics Academic Alliance, a profile of its members, and key issues and challenges related to enterprise solutions use in the classroom.

INTRODUCTION AND BACKGROUND
OF THE MICROSOFT DYNAMICS
ACADEMIC ALLIANCE

A primary objective of any higher education business program is to prepare students for today's world and help them become lifelong learners who are able to implement best business practices and keep current on emerging trends. There are very few businesses that are able to achieve a competitive advantage through the use of best practices without a strong commitment to technology. A solid technological foundation is also a critical component of any business student's education. It can be challenging for many institutions to implement a curriculum that incorporates the use of technology in a manner similar to what is used by many leading edge organizations. The Microsoft Dynamics Academic Alliance helps address this challenge by donating business solution software to higher educational institutions for classroom use. This chapter discusses the background of the Microsoft Dynamics Academic Alliance and the types of systems available for its members. The chapter content is designed to be helpful for both business educators and administrators as they plan and implement technology into their curricula.

The Microsoft Dynamics Academic Alliance distributes leading edge business software and provides services to institutions of higher education that are interested in enhancing their academic curricula through the use of technology. This initiative is consistent with the Microsoft corporate mission "to enable people and businesses throughout the world to realize their full potential." The primary mission of the Microsoft Dynamics Academic Alliance is to help college and university students realize their full potential by enhancing and supplementing their theoretical knowledge through the use of real-world technology aimed at improving business activities related to financial, supply chain, and customer relationship management.

The Microsoft Dynamics Academic Alliance is championed by Microsoft Business Solutions (MBS), part of the Microsoft Business Division, a business group of Microsoft. The products offered by MBS help organizations with business activities related to financial, supply chain and customer relationship management, with a primary concentration on serving mid-sized organizations. The products are sold to end-users via a certified Microsoft partner channel.

This chapter is organized as follows: (1) the history of the Microsoft Dynamics Academic Alliance is explained; (2) a descriptive profile of Microsoft Dynamics Academic Alliance members is presented; (3) key issues related to enterprise solutions use in the classroom are discussed; (4) key challenges of the Microsoft Dynamics Academic Alliance are described; and (5) future challenges of the Microsoft Dynamics Academic Alliance are listed.

HISTORY OF THE MICROSOFT DYNAMICS
ACADEMIC ALLIANCE

The roots of the Microsoft Dynamics Academic Alliance began in 1996 with a broad initiative launched at Great Plains Software, located in Fargo, North Dakota, USA. The initiative was referred to as the Center for Organizational Excellence (CORE), and it was formed to help Great Plains partners build capacity in their organizations to sell and implement more software. CORE was comprised of three key impact areas: (1) Recruiting — which involved assisting Great Plains® partners in finding qualified candidates for opportunities working for their, or their customers', organizations; (2) Education Alliance Network (EAN) — which focused on the promotion of Great Plains solutions to local colleges and universities in an effort to increase product awareness and to help develop future employment candidates; (3) Business Consulting — which consisted of consulting services designed to help small businesses run more effective operations. The EAN laid much of the groundwork for the extensive college and university network that exists today. Prior to the EAN initiative in 1996, Great Plains Software donated its product for academic use on an ad hoc basis as requests were received from colleges and universities. There was no formal infrastructure within Great Plains to support these pioneering colleges and universities; thus in the early days, they were "on their own" in terms of software implementation and use.

After CORE was launched, a constituency of universities and professors were very eager to use the software in their curricula. The majority of the professors were teaching accounting or related subjects. Textbook publishers joined the initiative to create practice sets to enrich "hands-on" use in the classroom. As the software became easier to use in the classroom and as educational resources from textbook publishers and educators became available, the constituency grew rapidly. The EAN built the infrastructure that offered technical support, provided access to actual Great Plains training and materials, and assisted with educator attendance at Great Plains customer and partner conferences. The software and services were all extended to colleges and universities in the form of an in-kind donation from Great Plains through EAN.

In June 2000, Great Plains announced the completion of the acquisition of Solomon Software, located in Findlay, Ohio, USA. Prior to the acquisition, there were a limited number of colleges and universities that used Solomon Software products for academic purposes, and those institutions were added to the EAN membership. Solomon Software products also became part of the EAN product offering.

In April 2001, Microsoft announced the completion of the acquisition of Great Plains Software, and Microsoft Business Solutions (MBS) was formed. As mentioned earlier, MBS is now part of the Microsoft Business Division, one of seven business groups within Microsoft. Other groups include Windows Client, Server and Tools, MSN, Information Worker, Home & Entertainment, and Mobile & Embedded Devices. After the Microsoft acquisition in 2001, the EAN was renamed the Microsoft Business Solutions Academic Alliance (MBSAA).

In July 2002, Microsoft acquired Navision Software A/S, a company located in Vedbaek, Denmark. Navision Software A/S had previously merged with Damgaard Software and was a mid-market enterprise software leader in Europe with its Navision® and Axapta® products. With the Navision products added to the MBS range of product offerings, and the inclusion of other products over time such as Microsoft CRM, Microsoft FRx®, Microsoft Forecaster, Microsoft Retail Management System and Microsoft Point of Sale, MBS currently offers a complete spectrum of software and serves customers across an expanded geographic area.

In September 2005, Microsoft announced a new brand, Microsoft Dynamics, for its financial, supply chain, and customer relationship management solutions. The new brand replaced Microsoft Business Solutions. To align with the new brand, the Microsoft Business Solutions Academic Alliance was renamed the Microsoft Dynamics Academic Alliance. The Microsoft Dynamics Academic Alliance includes all MBS products.

Details on the program can be found online at http://www.microsoft.com/education/academic_alliance.mspx.

PROFILE OF MICROSOFT DYNAMICS ACADEMIC ALLIANCE MEMBERS

Members in the Microsoft Dynamics Academic Alliance are academic institutions, not individual academics; however, there is no limit to the number of individuals that can participate from each institution. Microsoft Dynamics Academic Alliance individual involvement is typically represented by both instructors and technology support personnel. The most extensive demographic information about institutions in the Microsoft Dynamics Academic Alliance profiles schools of higher education in North America, the core group that has evolved from the EAN to the Microsoft Dynamics Academic Alliance. This group consists of more than 250 higher education institutions, of which approximately 85% received donations of Microsoft Dynamics GP (formerly Microsoft Business Solutions — Great Plains®) software. Four-year universities make up approximately 75% of that sub-group, with 70% integrating the software into an accounting information systems or related course.

Obtaining demographics on the members of the academic programs that were previously sponsored by Navision, Damgaaard, and Solomon before they became part of the EAN or Microsoft Dynamics Academic Alliance is an ongoing and challenging endeavor. The licensing and tracking of software donated to educational institutions outside of North America (and prior to the acquisition by Microsoft) were handled very differently according to product line and geographic distribution. As the Microsoft Dynamics Academic Alliance grows in North America as well as globally, the demographic information is becoming more dependable.

USING ENTERPRISE SOLUTIONS IN THE CLASSROOM

Enterprise systems support an organization across many functional areas such as accounting, finance, marketing, human resource management, operations and logistics. Enterprise systems are frequently contrasted with functionally specific information systems of the past, such as accounting information systems, marketing information systems, or management information systems. Microsoft Dynamics products continue their evolution as components of an enterprise system. These systems have the capability to improve business processes and eliminate problems arising from non-integrated functional systems. Integrating Microsoft Dynamics products into the classroom offers students the opportunity to learn how technology supports an enterprise and also to learn how enterprise systems develop and improve. Business schools are typically organized in a functional manner, and the introduction of an enterprise system into the curriculum offers many unique opportunities to bring disparate areas of study together and allow for enhanced student learning regarding overall business operations. Figure 1 offers an illustration on how an enterprise system connects with four functional areas typically found in degree programs offered by business schools.

Figure 1. How an enterprise system connects with functional programs offered by business schools

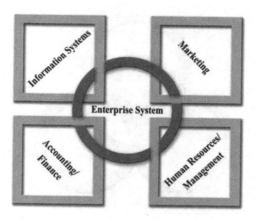

Information within an enterprise system flows across key business processes. Figure 2 illustrates how an enterprise system integrates with three primary business processes: (1) acquisition/expenditure, (2) conversion, and (3) sales/revenue. Acquisition and expenditure processes are used by an enterprise to acquire goods and services that are then converted into products and services sold in revenue generation processes. There are many types of processes supported by enterprise solutions; however, these three processes represent in aggregate the primary activities of virtually any organization.

Microsoft Dynamics products support primary business processes and are designed to improve and support three key business activities: (1) financial management; (2) customer relationship management and (3) supply chain management. Figure 3 illustrates how each of these activities offers solutions targeted at common business needs. Each of these three activities can be managed independently with software solutions; however, an organization has expanded opportunities when the technology supporting each activity is integrated. Figure 4 shows how integrating a solution targeted at the mid-market (such as the Microsoft Dynamics products) exposes the student to a system that is complex in functionality without being overwhelming to implement. A mid-market solution also offers the necessary components such as the ability to customize internal controls as well as many other features. The knowledge gained can be applied by the students if they work in a small business or a large enterprise. Following is a discussion of how financial, customer and supply chain management functions are supported by the Microsoft Dynamics products.

Financial Management Technology Solutions

Financial management is one of the original business activities supported by the Microsoft Dynamics product lines and consequently, the solutions are comprehensive and advanced in many ways. The financial management solutions support financial reporting,

Figure 2. How an enterprise system integrates with three primary business processes

Figure 3. Targeting business needs

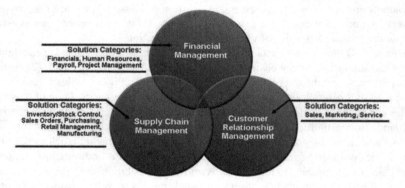

decision support, planning and control activities. Accounting and financial professionals use the solution to manage purchasing, budgeting, invoicing, forecasting, bank reporting, cash flow management, as well as traditional general ledger activities. The financial management products can provide a backbone for other business activities, and the potential business benefit from the products increases the more they are integrated with customer relationship or supply chain management solutions.

Figure 4. A mid-market solution

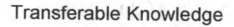

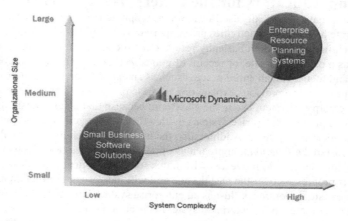

Customer Relationship Management Technology Solutions

Technology that supports customer relationship management (CRM) activities has emerged rapidly in the past several years. CRM solutions help businesses improve customer-centric activities by providing a technical backbone for functions such as sales support, customer service, customer valuation analysis, and marketing analysis. A CRM solution has the potential to help an organization communicate more effectively with customers and in turn accelerate sales, identify new sales opportunities and offer more consistent customer support. CRM solutions become even more powerful when integrated with financial management and supply chain management products.

Supply Chain Management Technology Solutions

Supply chain management (SCM) technology solutions empower organizations by allowing them to more effectively interact with customers, vendors and business partners. Many of the SCM products offer enhanced capabilities for organizations to improve management of distribution and directly affect inventory and order management. The benefits of an effectively implemented SCM solution are reduced cost, shorter fulfillment times, improved accuracy and stronger relationships with suppliers. More specific examples of SCM benefits are reduced inventory holding costs, improved purchasing, more flexibility in management reporting and increased ability to improve accuracy in forecasts. SCM products also increase the potential benefit to a business as they integrate with purchasing components in financial management as well as sales orders and inventory and stock control.

KEY CHALLENGES OF THE MICROSOFT DYNAMICS ACADEMIC ALLIANCE

Preparing Educators for the Enterprise Approach

Educators have historically used a *transaction* approach rather than a *process* approach to demonstrate how business activities are supported by an information system. A transaction approach in the classroom basically refers to instruction on one business activity at a time, such as a payment, a sale, or receipt of goods. A process approach groups activities into *events* and focuses on an entire process such as an expenditure/acquisition, conversion or revenue process (see previous explanation of these processes). The process approach is essential to enterprise system use in the classroom because that is how most organizations successfully implement enterprise systems, with a focus on overall business processes and not just individual transactions. Additionally, the traditional division of curriculum by discipline has fostered a *functional* approach as opposed to a process approach and it can be challenging for educators to move away from this style. Movement towards process-based curricula has progressed over the past decade and will increase as instruction and training on enterprise systems continues. Just as an enterprise system integrates across all business processes in an organization, enterprise system education needs to mirror that integration across the functional areas of a typical business school; such as, accounting, finance, information systems, marketing, operations management, and human resource management.

Providing Instructional Materials and Technical Support

Due to the varying methods of delivery, and the differences in desired outcome of each member, course material is not a component of the Microsoft Dynamics Academic Alliance program. The principal reason the Microsoft Dynamics Academic Alliance has not focused on developing and offering educational materials is that the software is suitable for use by all types of business or technology related disciplines and in varying degrees of complexity. For example, some members may use the software in entry level courses specific to a discipline such as introductory accounting geared for freshman or sophomores in a business school. Other members may use the software in more advanced courses designed for upper-level students who are near completion of their studies in degree programs in a specific functional area. ·

All faculty and technology personnel at member institutions have access to an extensive offering of Web-based courses and Microsoft training library resources for their own training and classroom preparation. Access to these Web-based resources, at no cost, is a benefit of Microsoft Dynamics Academic Alliance membership. The Web-based courses have time-limitations with respect to course access whereby faculty are typically given 30 days to complete each course. The Web-based courses are not available for student use.

Although educational materials are not a part of the Microsoft Dynamics Academic Alliance offering, members have the option of purchasing hard-copy training materials used by Microsoft solutions partners. The materials are designed for customer and partner training purposes and focus on specific functionality and nuances of the software and are not suited for supplementing a theoretical knowledge base linked to a curriculum.

Microsoft Dynamics Academic Alliance membership includes a service entitlement plan at no cost to the member institution. The plan includes product upgrades, access to customer support and an extensive set of resources available on the Microsoft customer portal.

The customer support feature can be essential to successful system use by both commercial customers and academic use customers because of the complexity and extensive options available within the products.

Finding textbooks that address the addition of technology to a course can be a challenge. Microsoft has developed relationships with leading publishers to develop instructional materials for use in many different instructional settings. Additionally, some of the instructional materials come pre-packaged with a version of the software that offers a less complicated installation and a way for students to maintain their own databases used to complete their coursework. Many instructors find using these pre-built instructional materials is a good way to introduce technology into their curriculum, without a major commitment from IT staff. The instructional materials that are provided with pre-packaged versions of the software are typically offered as a supplement to a more comprehensive textbook used in a course. There is ongoing demand and success using these supplements, and Microsoft continues to encourage and aid in their development. The use of publisher-supported instructional materials does not require involvement in the Microsoft Dynamics Academic Alliance. End-users of the pre-packaged software are not eligible for support by Microsoft; however, a publisher may offer some base of technical support that typically involves textbook specific issues. Many institutions that adopt textbooks with pre-packaged software still choose to join the Microsoft Dynamics Academic Alliance and install a complete version of the software in their instructional labs and actively collaborate with members of the Microsoft Dynamics Academic Alliance community.

Sharing course materials among Microsoft Dynamics Academic Alliance members is a common practice. A Web-based curriculum repository is readily available where educators from member schools post their materials for access by other members. The site is secured with password protection and accessible only to instructors at member schools.

Creating and Maintaining Data for Instructional Use

To simulate a real-world experience for students, it is important to provide sample databases of transactions and content similar to what is generated in an actual business setting. The appropriate instructional content can be difficult to create. Realistic transactions across all business processes (revenue, expenditure, conversion) that contain actual audit trail and transaction detail are an important feature requested by most instructors regardless of the course they are teaching. An ideal solution suggested by textbook authors and instructors is to modify data from actual organizations, but this can be impractical due to privacy concerns. Presently there are four options used for generating data for instructional purposes:

1. **Database provided with software:** Each Microsoft Dynamics software solution is packaged with a comprehensive sample database designed for both demonstration purposes and training of customers and partners. Many educators have found the sample databases to be adequate depending on their focus in the classroom; however, one of the drawbacks is that sample databases typically only contain a limited range of transactions which results in difficulty when students try to integrate and link information.

2. **Databases created with assistance from a Microsoft solutions partner:** The Microsoft Dynamics Academic Alliance contracted with a Microsoft solutions partner to create three databases representing three distinct industries: a distribution company,

a nonprofit organization, and a service-based enterprise. The partner modeled the databases after three of their actual clients. A primary benefit of this approach is a well balanced, historically complete set of data that allows for period analysis, comparison, and management reporting that is useful across various disciplines.

3.   **Creation of a database within a course:** One Microsoft Dynamics Academic Alliance member school's approach to developing data is through creation of a virtual enterprise that operates as a going concern and is an active component of instruction (see Chapter 9, Section II of this book, "Teaching Operations Management with Enterprise Software"). Transactions for the enterprise are created within courses in a continuous fashion, and the result is a company database that grows and develops each time the course is offered. It also has the potential to create a rich database for use in other courses.

4.   **Sharing of databases among educators from different institutions:** Some Microsoft Dynamics Academic Alliance members have created databases to support a specific discipline (e.g., a company that contains data for use in a managerial accounting course or a database suitable for use in an auditing course). Microsoft Dynamics Academic Alliance members are encouraged to share this information through the curriculum repository.

Nurturing a Community of Academic Users

Software and services are key components of an alliance between Microsoft and education, but beyond the donation, Microsoft Dynamics Academic Alliance believes in nurturing the development of a sense of community among the members. The curriculum repository provides a venue for sharing information. Sponsorship for educators to attend Microsoft Dynamics events, like Convergence, its annual customer conference, enables interaction among members, Microsoft team members, partners and customers. Convergence has emerged as the event most beneficial for the Microsoft Dynamics Academic Alliance members as they are considered a distinct customer group of Microsoft. The fee to attend is reduced for educators to encourage participation. A "Call for Presentations" is used to seek member presentations for delivery at Convergence. Along with these presentations, Microsoft team members and partners present topics of interest to the group. Microsoft Dynamics Academic Alliance members are encouraged to attend and participate in all aspects of the event.

A key component of this community is building a connection between educators and students with Microsoft solutions partners and customers. Examples of ways this could extend the opportunities for experiential learning include site visits, case studies, guest lectures, adjunct faculty work, co-ops and internships (both consulting and practical experiences). Since partner organizations are independently owned businesses, it can be challenging to garner involvement for a program that is non-revenue generating and can put a strain on channel capacity. However, the Microsoft Dynamics Academic Alliance recognizes the need and continues to find ways to promote involvement and growth in this area. By building awareness around the program, all parties can realize the benefits and find ways to work together.

Implementing the Technology for Educational Use

An ongoing challenge is the actual implementation of the software by the academic institutions. From the academic side, professors and IT personnel are implementing business solutions that, in a business setting, would be supported by a partner organization. If you consider the way a partner would install a business customer's product(s), academic users challenge the classic configuration. Many of these configurations would never be encountered in an actual business environment where users (students) are performing similar and/or simultaneous activities. For example, some installations are networked, some stand-alone, and some use a combination of both. The Microsoft Dynamics Academic Alliance has the backing of award-winning technical support teams to address these issues and work through various scenarios that are inherently different from a commercial user. Since many of these configurations have never been tested, technical support personnel frequently have to find a "work-around" to address academic issues.

From Microsoft's side, technology challenges include unique licensing issues, enabling academic users to perform non-standard installations, granting students the ability to access the software at home and in the classroom, the sheer size of the product which can impact processing speed and space limitations, the required technology stack, and accessing protected areas within a schools IT infrastructure. With the endorsement of Microsoft behind the program, there is ongoing work to improve these processes and extend the program in a more global reach.

Recognizing Excellence in the Classroom

Convergence, the Microsoft Dynamics aforementioned annual customer conference, is the venue for presenting the Pinnacle Awards, which recognize customers for excellence in a variety of areas. Customers are nominated by Microsoft partners or team members for their excellence in a number of categories, including Excellence in Education. The Excellence in Education award was initiated in 2003 for members of the Microsoft Dynamics Academic Alliance. There has been considerable interest generated in the program from this recognition, including a case study that was developed about the 2005 Pinnacle Award winner. This case study addresses the innovative way one school has implemented the software across disciplines, with plans to expand their very successful program and truly use the system in an enterprise fashion.

FUTURE CHALLENGES

The Microsoft Dynamics Academic Alliance has grown dramatically over the past five years and will continue to expand its base of members as Microsoft's business solutions continue to evolve and address the needs of organizations and as new technological capabilities emerge. One of the key future challenges the Microsoft Dynamics Academic Alliance faces is to facilitate stronger connections among Microsoft solutions partners, customers, and member schools. This will further enhance the experience of students in the classroom with the ultimate goal to help them become as prepared as possible for their careers. By offering students exposure to emerging technology such as Microsoft Dynamics products, they are better equipped to help organizations determine how technology is an enabler and how it can increase performance and productivity in all types of organizations.

Another future challenge for the Microsoft Dynamics Academic Alliance is to continue to encourage and support the development of educational materials suitable for use across the entire business curriculum. A further challenge is to develop methods for licensing that more readily enable remote access by students and for distance learning situations.

The Microsoft Dynamics Academic Alliance will continue to grow and adapt to the needs of all types of business curricula and educators from a variety of disciplines, and the program will continue to offer a variety of ways students can learn how technology supports business operations in today's rapidly evolving business community.

ACKNOWLEDGMENTS

The authors would like to thank Sarah Longfors, online experience, Microsoft®, for providing graphics and Kate Mund, Microsoft Dynamics marketing, Microsoft for advice and assistance with chapter content (http://microsoft.com/dynamics/product/productoverviews.mspx).

Chapter XX

Enterprise Systems Education:
A Vendor's Approach —
Oracle University's Practice

Frank Lin, California State University of San Bernardino, USA

Tony Coulson, California State University of San Bernardino, USA

ABSTRACT

SAP and Oracle (including PeopleSoft and J.D. Edwards) are the major enterprise systems vendors in the marketplace. Yet most of the universities within the USA, Canada, and Germany that have an enterprise system curriculum integrate SAP's enterprise systems. As a result of the recent PeopleSoft merger, Oracle is becoming a major player in the education industry. Oracle enterprise systems are not only suitable for large and medium companies but also small companies. Oracle enterprise systems are appealing alternatives for institutions to consider in regard to integrating enterprise systems into their curricula. Thus, we are going to introduce this global application vendor's Oracle Academic Initiative, Enterprise System and its related education — Oracle University's practice. An alternative approach to delivering enterprise system education, developed through experience and literature, using Oracle E-business Suite in higher education is discussed.

INTRODUCTION

Although the global marketplace is dominated by a few enterprise systems (ES) vendors, including SAP, Oracle, PeopleSoft, and so forth, most of the universities that provide enterprise system education integrate SAP's ES into their curricula (Strong, Johnson, & Mistry, 2004). One reason for such a widespread incorporation of SAP into university curriculum is due to the early introduction of the SAP Academic Alliance program.

In this chapter, we will briefly review the experience of teaching ES using SAP in universities. Challenges of integrating ES into university curriculum are discussed and four major ES vendor's academic alliance programs are also compared. Then an alternative approach, the Oracle Academic Initiative (OAI) program, incorporating their ES — Oracle E-Business Suite, will be discussed. It follows with a detailed introduction of the Oracle Academic Initiative. A comprehensive case, Vision Enterprise that Oracle University uses to train its customers, is proposed as a viable alternative to be used in a variety of courses in a business school curriculum. Finally, one university's experience of using the Oracle E-Business Suite 11i will be discussed.

The following section briefly reviews the literature in the integration of ES into university curriculum.

REVIEW OF LITERATURE

Numerous universities around the world have implemented some kind of ES education in the last 10 years or so (Antonucci, Corbitt, Stewart, & Harris, 2004). Despite the growth in ES education, the integration of ES into the curriculum remains a major challenge for many universities (Rosemann, 2004; Rosemann & Stewart, 2001). Although some have shown success by bringing students to appreciate the integrated nature of business operation (Hajnal & Riordan, 2004), a problem encountered by most universities, beyond issues related to curriculum, training and outside support, is the availability of a comprehensive case to be used in the classroom setting (Fedorowicz, Gelinas, Jr., Usoff, & Hachey, 2004; Johnson, Lorents, Morgan, & Ozmun, 2004).

By their nature, business operations are integrated. To better serve customers, businesses are changing their operational approach to process-oriented management. To ensure an efficient and effective operation of a business, the alignment of information systems (IS) and information technology (IT) with business goals is a necessity. Nevertheless, businesses have been struggling with such integration. A recently survey of key issues in organizations (as ranked by information systems executives) shows that the alignment required for integration has appeared at the top of the list for the last decade (Luftman, 2005). In education, to illustrate the interrelationships between functions and to fully demonstrate the efficacy of the linkage between organizational goals, strategies, performance measurement and processes, a comprehensive case is needed. Thus, the education of ES should move to a cross-functional orientation, rather than a modular focus.

In integrating ES education into university curriculum, prior experience demonstrates that it is important to have a hands-on laboratory component in the course (Coulson, Shayo, Olfman, & Rohm, 2003). Yet, frequently the abundance of detailed operational requirements to operate the system in existing lab-based ES courses hinders the teaching effectiveness (Davis & Comeau, 2004). Such operational requirements — non-business (technical) oriented, are necessary for effectively using the ES for classes, thus it is necessary to be incorporated into the ES curriculum or at least make it available to the students (Davis & Comeau, 2004).

It has been noted that integration relates to two separate concepts in the context of a business curriculum (Cannon, Klein, Koste, & Magal, 2004). First, the term references a curriculum in which integrated business processes are the focus of students' learning. In the context of integrated business process, the curriculum is frequently implemented through an integration of ERP systems into a business capstone course or a low-level Management Information Systems (MIS) course (Davis & Comeau, 2004; Hajnal & Riordan, 2004). The second concept of integration references a complete redesign of core business curriculum using integrated business processes as the theme (Rivetti, Schneider, & Bruton, 1999; Walker & Black, 2000). In this latter perspective of integration, numerous process-focused courses are typically designed to replace traditional functional "silo" oriented courses. Advanced discipline courses can still be taught in traditional method or integrated with the redesigned core business curriculum. Although either approach incurs tremendous efforts in delivering the curriculum, the task of the latter approach (i.e., a complete redesign of core business curriculum based on integrated business processes) is often overwhelming and particularly challenging.

Challenges to integrating ES into university curriculum are discussed in the next section.

CHALLENGES TO INTEGRATING ES INTO CURRICULUM

Literature has documented numerous challenges to integrating ES software into a university business curriculum. These challenges include (Bradford, Vijayaraman, & Chandra, 2003; Cannon et al., 2004; Guthrie & Guthrie, 2000; Johnson et al., 2004; Michaelsen, 1999; Walker & Black, 2000):

- Insufficient funds for hardware, training, and IT staff
- Lack of IT department experience
- Insufficient IT support
- Lack of knowledge by faculty
- Lack of interest by administration
- Lack of interest or even resistance by faculty
- Extensive time commitment is required by faculty
- Lack of incentives to encourage faculty participation
- Autonomy of faculty/departments in creation of curriculum
- Policies relating to changing curriculum
- Lack of a comprehensive case that is suitable for academic courses
- Lack of academic recognition for effort

Although many of these challenges are equally applicable in the business world, some of them are unique to academic settings such as policies relating to changing curriculum, extensive time commitment required by faculty, lack of incentives — such as released time, to encourage faculty participate, lack of suitable comprehensive case for academic curriculum, and autonomy of faculty/departments in creating curriculum. These challenges that act as constraints towards the integration of ES in university curriculum can be classified into technical, budgetary, and operational issues. In spite of these challenges, numerous schools have attempted integration through a variety of "home-grown" methods (Bliss & Potter, 2000, Cannon et al., 2004; Hamilton, McFarland, & Mirchandani, 2000; McKinney & Yoos, 1998; Stover & Byers, 2002).

During the initial stage of incorporating ES into curriculum, one of the major concerns of faculty members is the training required to develop working knowledge of the ES. One of the most commonly used training methods is attending instructor-led training offered by ES vendors. Unfortunately, for faculty, vendors' training is more practitioner-oriented with emphasis on ES operations and frequently lack the theoretical background and depth needed for academic purposes (Cannon et al., 2004; Coulson et al., 2003). An integrated case has been claimed to be most popular and effective in delivering integrated business curriculum (Michaelsen, 1999). In fact, to address this shortcoming, some examples of using an integrated case have demonstrated successful implementation integrating ES into university business curriculum (Cannon, et al., 2004; Johnson, et al, 2004).

In the next section, Oracle University's training case, Vision Enterprise, a comprehensive multi-country and multi-location organization that can be tailored easily to various levels of breadth and depth coverage provides for a variety of courses in integrated business curriculum (Guthrie & Guthrie, 2000). The Oracle Academic Initiative provides Oracle's Information Architecture (OIA) that supports Oracle's ES — Oracle E-Business Suite 11i, and Oracle University's practice in delivering its ES education training. These will also be discussed in the following section.

A VENDOR'S PRACTICE: ORACLE'S APPROACH

In this section, OIA that supports Oracle's applications and ES are introduced. Oracle's E-Business Suite 11i that supports the management and integration of major business processes, with a particular focus on Oracle's education department — Oracle University, with its training format, is then discussed.

Introduction to Oracle

Oracle's business is information — how to manage it, use it, share it, and protect it. For nearly three decades, Oracle, the world's largest enterprise software company, has provided the software and services that let organizations get the most up-to-date and accurate information from their business systems.

The 2005 combination of Oracle and PeopleSoft marks a major turning point in the evolution of the software industry. The combined companies are now positioned to deliver a more competitive offering in the enterprise applications market and increase innovation with a larger applications R&D budget.

Today, Oracle is helping more governments and businesses around the world become information-driven than any other company, enabling companies to use high-quality information to collaborate, measure results for continuous improvement, and align their stakeholders.

Figure 1. Oracle Information Architecture (Source: derived from Oracle Information Architecture, n.d., http://www.oracle.com/broadband/showiseminar.html?3175411)

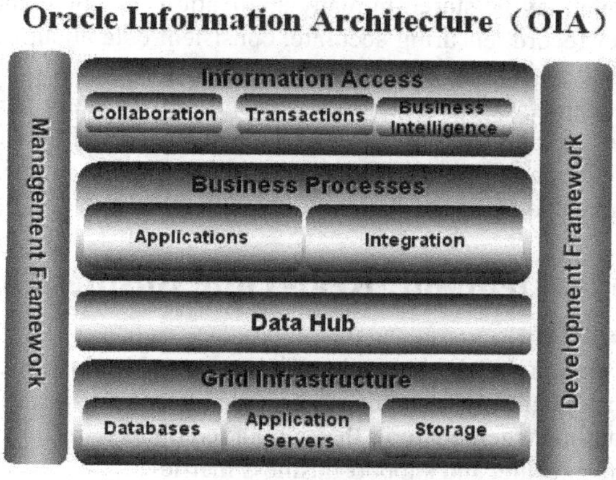

Oracle Information Architecture

OIA is the only enterprise data model available today with the capability of grid-ready database and application server. OIA supports information driven enterprises, provides a capability to store information in one place, and supports on demand information retrieval as illustrated in Figure 1. These are further discussed as follows.

Information Driven: Grid-Ready Database and Application Server

Grid computing is the foundation of the information-driven enterprise and the core of Oracle's Information Architecture. By pooling large numbers of inexpensive servers and storage, a grid-powered architecture continually analyzes computing demand and adjusts supply accordingly. Grid computing makes it possible to handle the exploding amount of information that businesses need to face every day. With OIA, IT department is equipped to respond rapidly to changes in business information needs.

Oracle Database 10g and Oracle Application Server 10g were the first database and application server platform built to support enterprise grid computing.

Oracle Database is the leading software for collecting, organizing, and protecting information. Oracle Application Server handles all application operations between users and back-end business operations or databases. Oracle Application Server Portal provides secure access to content across various functions in an organization.

Information in One Place: Data Hubs and System Management Tools

The success of all business processes depends on the availability of accurate master data to everyone who needs it and when they need it. However, information about a business often exists in several disconnected systems. Oracle's Enterprise Data Hub model helps to create a central repository that keeps key information about business continuously synchronized. Although data may be stored in many application-specific databases, the data hub provides the master record, ensuring accurate, consistent data about customers, products, and inventory among others.

Another component, Oracle Enterprise Manager, lets IT staff manage all Oracle software from a single console — from automated maintenance and the diagnosis and tuning of IT infrastructure to measuring quality of service. Information in one place for IT means fewer people can manage IT operations more cost effectively.

Information on Demand: Real-Time Business Intelligence and Collaboration

Quality information is of dubious value if it is not provided in a timely manner. Oracle's business intelligence platform is designed to provide information access, business-process-integration, and data-management tools that support complex reporting, query, and analysis capabilities to plan, execute, and support business metrics.

Oracle Collaboration Suite provides a set of integrated communication and reporting tools that aim to support communication regardless of time, place, or hardware. Oracle Collaboration Suite brings together components of collaborative productivity — Web conferencing, content management, e-mail, voice mail, and an integrated calendar.

Information Age Capabilities: Oracle Applications

An information-driven, integrated enterprise should be able to share information from all lines of business, from front to back office. Oracle E-Business Suite, an integrated family of business applications, collects, processes, and shares information from all lines of business; automates business processes so that information is shared across departments instantly; and provides a single source of truth about customers, partners, and employees and any other information in organization. Figure 2 depicts major functions supported by E-Business Suite.

Figure 2. Major functions supported by Oracle E-Business Suite (Source: based on Oracle E-Business Suite, n.d., Retrieved November 21, 2005, from http://www.oracle.com/webapps/ dialogue/dlpage.jsp?p_dlg_id=2903298&src=1252848&Act=51

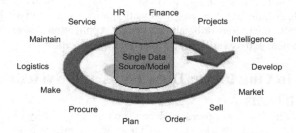

INTRODUCTION TO ORACLE'S
E-BUSINESS SUITE 11i

Oracle E-Business Suite is a fully integrated, comprehensive suite of business applications for enterprise. Oracle E-Business Suite is scalable where modules can be phase-implemented one a time, multiple modules at a time, or the complete suite at once ("Big Bang"). It also offers complete suite for large enterprises, specially packaged edition for mid market companies, and industry-specific functionality to meet specific industry requirements. The Oracle E-Business Suite provides integrated enterprise information that enables companies to manage their business cycles and to solve end-to-end business problems.

The Oracle E-Business Suite utilizes Oracle's full OIA technology stack, including database, application server, and open architecture development tools. The Oracle E-Business Suite also combines business functionality such as workflow and self-service applications.

Oracle E-Business Suite includes the following module families:

- Advanced procurement
- Contacts
- Corporate performance management
- Customer data management
- Customer relationship management
- Financials
- Human resource management
- Intelligence
- Interaction center
- Learning management
- Logistics
- Maintenance
- Manufacturing
- Marketing
- Order management
- Product lifecycle management
- Projects
- Sales
- Service
- Supply chain execution
- Supply chain management
- Supply chain planning

Each of the module families includes comprehensive sub-modules. For instance, the corporate performance management module family encompasses the following sub-modules:

- Activity-based management
- Balanced scorecard
- Business intelligence solution
- DBI (daily business intelligence)
- Demand planning

- Enterprise planning and budgeting
- Financial analyzer
- Financial consolidation hub
- Performance analyzer
- Profitability manager
- Sales analyzer

The financial module family includes the following:

- Activity-based management
- Advanced collection
- Assets
- Balanced scorecard
- Bill presentment architecture
- Cash management
- Daily business intelligence for financial
- Enterprise planning and budgeting
- Financial analyzer
- Financial consolidation hub
- General ledger
- iAssets
- Internal control manager
- Internet expenses
- iPayment
- iReceivables
- Lease management
- Loans
- Payables
- Property manager
- Receivables
- Sales analyzer
- Treasury

The human resources management module family includes:

- Advanced benefits
- Daily business intelligence for human resources
- Human resources
- iRecruitment
- Learning management
- Payroll
- Self service human resources
- Time and labor
- Tutor

When a module family is implemented one at a time, all necessary functions from other module families will also be included in the implementation. For instance, if a company implements only the financial module all necessary human resources management linked functions such as human resources and payroll will be included in the implementation. The Oracle E-Business Suite is an extremely complex system. To comprehend the whole Oracle E-Business Suite is mind boggling. The following section introduces the Oracle's education department and discusses Oracle's approach in teaching its E-Business Suite.

INTRODUCTION TO ORACLE'S EDUCATION DEPARTMENT — ORACLE UNIVERSITY

Oracle offers its education and training through Oracle University. Oracle University's curriculum is comprehensive, providing all lines of enterprise software products — from database to applications and business intelligence solutions. Oracle University's Curriculum is summarized in Table 1.

Table 1. Oracle university's curriculum

Database	Application Server	Development Tools
• Oracle Database 10g • Oracle9i Database • Oracle9i Real Application Clusters • Oracle8i Database • Oracle Enterprise Manager 10g • Oracle Enterprise Manager 9i • Linux	• Oracle Application Server 10g • OracleAS Discoverer 10g • OracleAS Portal 10g • OracleAS Web Cache 10g • Oracle Enterprise Manager 10g • Oracle9i Application Server Release 2 • Oracle9iAS Portal • Oracle9iAS Discoverer Web Development	• Oracle Developer Suite 10g • Oracle JDeveloper 10g • Oracle9i Developer Suite • Oracle9i JDeveloper • Oracle9i Forms Developer • Oracle9i Reports Developer • Oracle9i Warehouse Builder • Java • PL/SQL
Data Warehousing and Business Intelligence	**E-Business Suite**	**Collaboration Suite**
• Data Warehousing • OracleAS Discoverer 10g • Oracle9iAS Discoverer • Reports • Business Intelligence	• Technology • Financials • Procurement • Order Fulfillment • Projects • Advanced Planning • Manufacturing • Maintenance Management • Human Resources • Sales • Contracts • Service • E-Commerce • Business Intelligence • Interaction Center • Healthcare • Education	• Collaboration Suite

Table 1. continued

PeopleSoft Enterprise	JD Edwards EnterpriseOne	JD Edwards World
• Customer Relationship Management • Human Resources • Tools & Technology • Campus Solutions • Enterprise Performance Management • Financial Management • Supply Chain Management	• Asset Lifecycle Management • Customer Relationship Management • Human Resources • Supply Chain Management • Tools & Technology • Cross-Application • Financial Management • Project Management	• Financial Management

Oracle's training format includes instructor-led training, live WebClass, self-study CD-ROM, knowledge center, and private events. Instructor-led training, which is the most popular training format, provides students with hands-on experience to match job role requirements and to prepare students for Oracle certification exams. Topics covered in instructor-led training include concepts, in-class demonstrations, and hands-on-labs. Live WebClass training is delivered online. Students receive hands-on practice with an access to a live, hosted environment. Instructors also host live office hours to address students' questions. Many of the contents of instructor-led training courses are also available through self-study CD-ROMs which can be used to reinforce classroom learning. Self-study CD-ROMs also contain hands-on training. Oracle University also provides for private event training, designed to meet the specific needs of a team of employees who need the same training. The private event training is usually conducted at client's location. Finally, the knowledge center offers an on-demand access to self-paced Oracle E-Business Suite application courses and various advanced technology topics.

ORACLE ACADEMIC INITIATIVE

Oracle Corporation recognizes the needs of university students to be adequately prepared with information technology skills to meet the demands of the 21st century marketplace. Oracle Corporation through the Oracle Academic Initiative (OAI) partners with academic institutions worldwide to deliver Oracle Software — database, development tools, and application server, and curriculum resources to college and university classroom. OAI is a $1 billion commitment made by Oracle Corporation to provide Oracle software, curriculum and certification resources to the higher education community. Detail information of the OAI program can be found at http://oai.oracle.com. Oracle describes the mission of the OAI as:

> *Our mission is to enable every student of higher education across the globe to acquire industry-relevant skills and an introduction to Oracle certification pathway as part of a broader program of study.*

The OAI requires an annual membership fee of $500.00 or $3,000.00 to include E-Business Suite. The OAI membership is a department membership. A department equates to a single academic discipline within a school. The OAI membership allows faculty and students to access all software offered by OAI for instructional purposes on different platforms. The software is available to an unlimited amount of users. The usage of product, included in the membership fee, supports services (telephone, Web, and mail) and update. OAI faculty members are entitled for a 50% discount on instructor-led and technology-based training (self-study CD-ROM, Live WebClass). OAI curriculum resources include instructor and student materials, course and lab setup files. Each of the course materials costs $150.00. Copies of Oracle software under the OAI can be made for students use on their own machine. For students to participate in OAI Classes and use Oracle software, each is required to accept the terms and conditions of the OAI Student Software Agreement.

The software products offered by OAI include:

- Oracle 10g Enterprise Edition
- Oracle 10g Standard Edition
- Oracle 10g Personal Edition
- Oracle 10g Lite Edition
- Oracle JDeveloper
- Oracle Designer
- Oracle Forms Developer
- Oracle Software Configuration Manager
- Oracle Reports Developer
- Oracle Discoverer
- Oracle Warehouse Builder
- Oracle Business Intelligence Beans
- Oracle Application Server 10g Enterprise Edition
- Oracle Application Server 10g Standard Edition
- Oracle Application Server 10g Standard Edition One
- Oracle Application Server 10g Java Edition
- Oracle E-Business Suite 11i (only available for the $3,000.00 annual membership fee)

OAI resources are proving relevant across the academic spectrum. OAI faculty are using the resources in a variety of ways:

- Core component to an advanced database class
- Capstone course, in an MBA IT program
- Capstone course-enterprise systems, in an undergraduate information systems program
- Human resources management course in human resources program
- Project management tool in a project management course
- Inventory control course in an operation management program
- To build data warehouse application in an information systems course
- Introduce industry certification materials in an information systems course
- To track and aggregate results in chemistry experiments

- To store population data in urban planning courses
- Relational database illustration tool in introductory database courses
- Since the inception of the program in 1999 over 1500 institutions across more than 50 countries take part in the program.

Oracle University provides various means to facilitate the teaching and learning services to its customers and partners. Similar formats, for example revised Instructor-led instruction, Live WebClass and knowledge center offered by Oracle University, can also be applied in college and university education.

A comparison of OAI with other ES vendors' academic alliance programs is presented in the next section.

COMPARISON OF ORACLE ACADEMIC INITIATIVE WITH OTHER ES VENDOR'S PROGRAM

In 2003, the four top ES vendors, SAP, Oracle, PeopleSoft, and J.D. Edwards, offered academic alliance programs in which universities can become members for a nominal fee and receive the vendor software for academic use. Among the top four ES vendors, SAP was the first to introduce Academic Alliance Program in 1996. Since then PeopleSoft, Oracle and J.D. Edwards also joined the bandwagon in 1999, 1999, and 1998 respectively. The academic alliance programs were initiated by ES vendors in hope that their academic partners will:

Figure 3. SAP Academic Alliance Value Proposition (Bradford et al., 2003, Watson 2001)

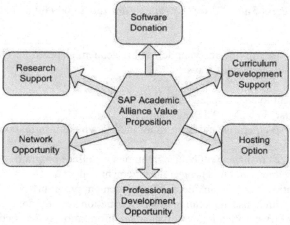

1. Expose future business leaders to the highly demanded skills and knowledge in the industry with their respective ES products, with the goal of selling more systems.
2. Alleviate the challenges faced by higher education to keep faculty and programs current with pace of the industry (Becerra-Fernandez, Murphy, & Simon, 2000; Cannon et al., 2004; Rivetti et al., 1999).

Thus, academic alliance programs are viewed as a critical business strategy of ES Vendors. By targeting potential users of the product, such programs can translate into a healthy investment in the future.

The value proposition of the academic alliance program presented by SAP is derived from six factors as shown in Figure 3 (Watson, 2001). In theory, these factors are equally applicable to other ES vendors' academic alliance programs. Software donation includes the licensing of software to member institutions. Hosting options is the availability of ES hosted by other institutions. Curriculum development and support includes faculty training. Research support includes user conferences, awards programs, and funding research projects. Professional development includes executive education. Networking possibilities enable the collaboration of multidisciplinary academics to leverage learning, research, and education. Overall, these six factors are not only pertinent in keeping faculty members aware of current and emerging developments but also critical in supporting curriculum development (Bradford et al., 2003; Watson, 2001).

Since the inception of academic alliance program by SAP in 1996, PeopleSoft acquired J.D. Edwards in 2003. Later, Oracle acquired PeopleSoft in 2005. Although Oracle is promising the industry users that PeopleSoft and J.D. Edwards's ES will continuously be supported until 2013, Oracle is no longer offering new PeopleSoft and J.D. Edwards academic alliance programs. For existing J.D. Edwards member institutions, Oracle offers an option to switch to PeopleSoft (for those institutions that are PeopleSoft customers) or Oracle. Thus, due to the acquisition of PeopleSoft by Oracle in 2005, there are only two major ES vendors, SAP and Oracle, which still offer academic alliance programs.

In comparing SAP and Oracle's academic alliance programs, it seems that the OAI offered by Oracle is relative inexpensive with respect to annual membership fee. OAI is also more flexible in terms of how the academic partners integrate OAI products. OAI partners can integrate Oracle database, Oracle E-Business Suite, or both into their curriculum. However, most of the OAI academic partners mainly implement database into their curriculum rather than E-Business Suite. This is evidenced by how OAI faculty is using the resources in their curricula as discussed in previous section. However, SAP has a much stronger curriculum support and larger industry and academic user base. SAP also offers hosting options for its ES software. This hosting service is an important consideration for many institutions that are short of funding and lack of experience and technical expertise in ES (Becerra-Fernandez et al., 2000; Bradford et al., 2003). Table 2 lists detailed information and brief evolution of the aforementioned top four ES vendors. PeopleSoft and J.D. Edwards are listed to provide readers with availability from a historical perspective.

A Case — Vision Enterprise Case

Apart from industrial training, university curriculum is educationally oriented which emphasizes both practical use and theoretical foundation. It's obvious that Oracle University,

Figure 4. Oracle application — Vision: General ledger

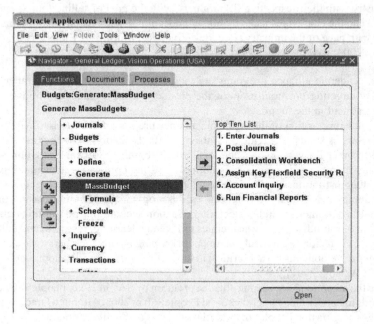

Figure 5. Oracle application — Vision: Generating budget journals

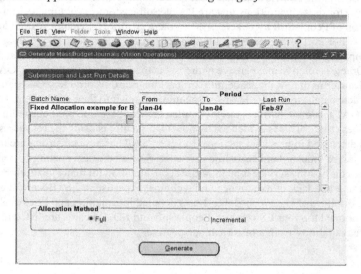

Figure 6. Oracle application — Vision: Workflows

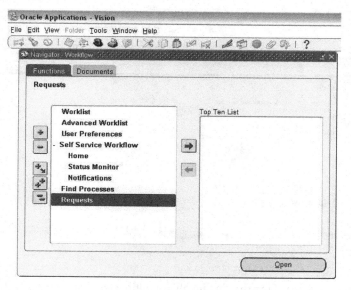

Figure 7. Oracle workflow — Status monitor (Search results)

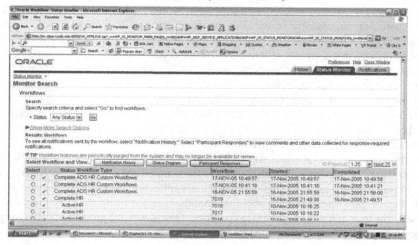

as the training and educational arm of Oracle Corporation, focuses on training its customers and practitioners how to use its products rather than supporting university curriculum. Nevertheless Vision Enterprise, developed by Oracle University to support training needs of Oracle customers, can be tailored for academic use easily.

Vision Enterprise is a preconfigured Oracle E-Business Suite application case populated with extensive data setup to cover a global enterprise. The Vision Enterprise case has training

Figure 8. Oracle workflow — Status monitor (Monitor diagram)

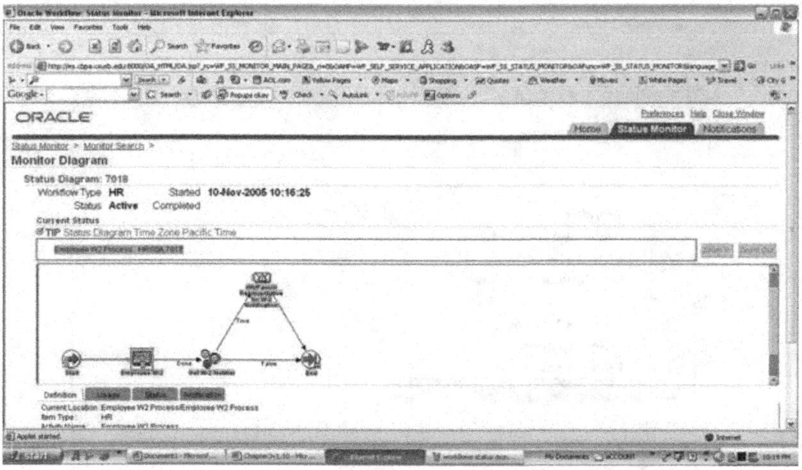

materials related to an enterprise that involves multiple currencies, global inter-company system, and specific integrated applications in a local location. Some example applications of Vision Enterprise case are: general ledger, account payables, accounts receivables, human resources, treasury, purchasing, order management, facility management, cash management, project management, customer relationship management, workflow, balance scorecard management, financial intelligence, and operation intelligence, and so forth. These applications can be integrated into a variety of university business courses.

Oracle's E-Business Suite supports two types of application. First, forms based operation which requires a helper, initiator, to be installed at the client machine to access Oracle applications. Figure 4 shows the forms based interfaces of general ledger functions and Figure 5 illustrates the access interface of budget generation report in general ledger.

The second type is the self-service application which uses a Web-based interface. Examples of self-service application include iAsset, iReceivables, iPayables, iProcurement, iRecruitment and iexpense, and so forth. Currently the interface of Oracle E-Business Suite operation is a hybrid operation which consists of forms based and self-service oriented operations. Figure 6 illustrates an example of workflow application using forms based interface. Figure 7 and Figure 8, representing workflows monitor search results and workflows monitor diagram, illustrate self-service interface operation. Oracle is in the process of converting all applications into self-service oriented interface.

At the authors' institution, business partners have indicated the need of business graduates with ES operation skills as well as the understanding of the concepts and theory of integrated business process. SAP and J.D. Edwards has been used in a variety of business classes in the College of Business and Public Administration. Recently due to the discontinued support of J.D. Edwards's University Relations Initiative, the Department committed to switch to Oracle E-Business suite as one of the tools besides SAP to integrate information management curriculum. Starting in Fall 2005, one of the authors of this chapter committed to use Oracle E-Business Suite for an undergraduate information management capstone course, in which

J.D. Edwards had been used for past three years. Two faculty members from the Department took Oracle E-Business Suite training for two weeks in E-Business Suite installation, administration and management, project management and workflow administration during summer 2005. Given the available time before school started (3 weeks or so) and resources related to hardware, software, and IT staff, it was decided to do a quick install of the Oracle E-Business Suite in a Windows 2003 server environment. During the installation, a number of difficulties, particularly with the needed utility for window to Linux command conversions, triggered the authors to change the platform to Linux environment. After receiving the Linux version of Oracle software, the installation went on smoothly and was finished about two weeks into the term. Despite these initial minor glitches encountered during the installation, there was no significant technical problem encountered during the term.

In this class, students were required to configure a company based on a scenario adopted from Vision Enterprise case. Then students used the company to setup up human resource and workflow operations. The purposes of these exercises were to explore students to an ES environment, setting up a company using ES software, learning the operation of an ES, and appreciate the integrated nature of a business operation. The outcome was rather satisfactory based on outcomes assessments and student feedback.

DISCUSSION

In summary, the comprehensive multi-country case, Vision Enterprise, can be used for developing class/laboratory hands-on projects. The operation of Oracle E-Business Suite is relative easy. Compared to the other ES products, Oracles E-Business Suite is extremely easy to install, configure and manage. The Oracle E-Business Suite could be very appealing to business departments who are interested in incorporating ES into their curriculum yet don't have either the department or college resources to commit to a large-scale project. Oracle could further assist by providing some of their instructor training tools for the faculty to develop further.

Nevertheless, literature has identified that when a software program, such as Oracle database or E-Business Suite, is used in a classroom or to be integrated into a curriculum, the technical support is crucial to ensure smooth and successful run of the program in class. Besides, limited available resources at colleges and universities have hindered the effectiveness of such integration. It is also important to differentiate the needs of practitioners and academic users. Faculty requires some other support that is unique to academic users. Some claim that most crucial is access to documentation (include tutorials and reference documentation) on the products being used (Flatto, 2000). These differences could be very significant, particularly the materials to be used in training versus education. Furthermore, Personnel training seem to be the biggest problem encountered by OAI partners due to limitation of fund available for such purpose.

CONCLUSION

In this chapter, we briefly review the current status of the integration of ES in university curriculum and the limitations as well as problems encountered in college/universities in the process of incorporating ES into their curricula. We propose an alternative — using Oracle E-Business Suite to integrate the business curriculum. An initial experience of using Vision

Enterprise case in integrating Oracle E-Business Suite into a capstone course of information management program at one university is discussed. It was found that the installation and operation was easy compared to ES from other vendors. The importance of developing a comprehensive case is also emphasized. Such a case should be able to be used in various courses, including production, marketing, sales, purchasing, accounting, finance, human resource management, decision making, and the capstone course. For complete curriculum integration from a process-centric perspective, Oracle E-Business Suite can also be used as a tool for such integration.

REFERENCES

Antonucci, Y. L., Corbitt, G., Stewart, G., & Harris, A. L. (2004). Enterprise systems education: Where are we? Where are we going? *Journal of Information Systems Education, 15*(3), 277-234.

Becerra-Fernandez, I., Murphy, E. E., & Simon, S. J. (2000). Integrating ERP in the business school curriculum. *Communications of the ACM, 43*(4), 39-41.

Bliss, R., & Potter, M. (2000). Integrating the undergraduate business curriculum: The case of Babson College. *Journal of Business Education, 1*(1), 1-13.

Bylinsky, G. (1999). The challengers move in on ERP. *Fortune, 140*(10), 306.

Bradford, M., Vijayaraman, B. S., & Chandra, A. (2003). The status of ERP implementation in business school curricula. *Communications of the Association of Information Systems, 12*(26), 437-456.

Cannon, D. M., Klein, H. A., Koste, L. L., & Magal, S. R. (2004). Curriculum integration using Enterprise Resource Planning: An integrative case approach. *Journal of Education for Business, 80*(2), 93-101.

Coulson, T., Shayo, C., Olfman, L., & Rohm, C. E. (2003, April 10-12). ERP training strategies: Conceptual training and the formation of accurate mental models. In *Proceedings of the 2003 SIGMIS Conference on Computer Personnel Research: Freedom in Philadelphia — Leveraging Differences and Diversity in the IT Workforce (SIGMIS CPR '03)*, Philadelphia (pp. 87-97). New York: ACM Press. Retrieved from http://doi.acm.org/10.1145/761849.761864

Davis, C. H., & Comeau, J. (2004). Enterprise integration in business education: Design and outcomes of a capstone ERP-based undergraduate e-Business management course. *Journal of Information Systems Education, 15*(3), 287-199.

Fedorowicz, J., Gelinas, Jr., U. J., Usoff, C., & Hachey, G. (2004). Twelve tips for successfully integrating enterprise systems across the curriculum. *Journal of Information Systems Education, 15*(3), 235-244.

Flatto, J. (2000). Implementing Oracle products in the curriculum: The good, the bad, and the ugly. In *Proceedings of the 2000 Annual Conference of the Association of Information Systems* (pp. 2153-2155).

Grygo, E. (2000, July 17). PeopleSoft seeks renewal. *INFOWORLD*, 18.

Guthrie, R. W., & Guthrie, R. A. (2000). Integration of enterprise system software in undergraduate curriculum. In *Proceedings of the ISECON 2000*, Philadelphia (pp. 301-307).

Hajnal, C. A., & Riordan, R. (2004). Exploring process, enterprise integration, and E-business concepts in the classroom: The case of PetPRO. *Journal of Information Systems Education, 15*(3), 267-275.

Hamilton, D., McFarland, D., & Mirchandani, D. (2000). A decision model for integration across the business curriculum in the 21st century. *Journal of Management Education, 24*(1), 102-126.

Johnson, T., Lorents, A. C., Morgan, J., & Ozmun, J. (2004). A customized ERP/SAP model for business curriculum integration. *Journal of Information Systems Education, 15*(3), 245-253.

McKinney, E. H., & Yoos, C. (1998). The one school rookhouse: An information and learning approach to curriculum integration. *Journal of Management Education, 22*(5), 618-636.

Luftman, J. (2005). Key issues for IT executives 2004. *MID Quarterly Executive, 4*(2), 269-285.

Michaelsen, L. K. (1999). Integrating the core business curriculum: An experience-based solution. *Selections, 15*(2), 9-10.

Oracle E-Business Suite. (n.d.). Retrieved November 21, 2005, from http://www.oracle.com/webapps/dialogue/dlgpage.jsp?p_dlg_id=2903290&src=195248&Act=51

Oracle Information Architecture. (n.d.). Retrieved November 21, 2005, from http://www.oracle.com/broadband/showiseminar.html?3175411

Rivetti, D. A., Schneider, G. P., & Bruton, C. M. (1999). Enterprise Resource Planning software as an organizing theme for MBA curriculum. *Academic of Information and Management Sciences Journal, 2*(1), 1-7.

Rosemann, M. (2004). The integration of SAP solutions in the curricula–outcomes of a global survey. *Queensland University of Technology*, 1-36.

Rosemann, M., & Stewart, G. (2001), Industry-oriented design of ERP-related curriculum — An Australian initiative. *Business Process Management Journal, 7*(3), 234-242.

Stover, D., & Byers, C. (2002, Spring). Integrated business curriculums do work: Assessing effectiveness five years later. *Journal of the Academy of Business Education, 3*, 26-37.

Strong, D. M., Johnson, S. A., & Mistry, J. J. (2004). Integrating enterprise decision-making modules into undergraduate management and industrial engineering curricula. *Journal of Information Systems Education, 15*(3), 301-313.

Walker, K., & Black, E. (2000). Reengineering the undergraduate business core curriculum: Aligning business schools with business for performance improvement. *Business Process Management Journal, 6*(3), 194-213.

Watson, E. F. (2001, November 17). *The SAP academic alliance: Preparing students for an E-Business world.* Panel presentation at the DSI Annual Meeting, San Francisco.

About the Authors

Andrew Targowski is a professor of business information systems at Western Michigan University, USA. He published 20 books on information technology, history, and political science in English and Polish. He is a pioneer of business computing and inventor of INFOSTRADA (Poland 1972), which triggered the Information Superhighway wave in the U.S. He published first books on enterprise information systems (1990) and electronic enterprise (2003). In his recent inter-disciplinary research and publications he investigates the role of info-communication in organizations and civilization. He is a member of the Executive Council of the International Society for the Comparative Study of Civilizations and former chairman of the Advisory Council of Information Resource Management Association (1995-2003).

J. Michael Tarn is an associate professor of business information systems at Western Michigan University, USA. He holds a PhD and an MS in Information Systems from Virginia Commonwealth University. Dr. Tarn specializes in multidisciplinary research, involving info-communication systems, e-commerce, strategic management, and modern organizational theory. He has published numerous research papers in academic refereed journals, book chapters, and refereed conference proceedings. His recent research has contributed to information security management and ERP/SCM integration. His areas of expertise are network security, data communication management, Internet research, integrative systems design, international MIS, business forecasting, and critical systems management. Dr. Tarn currently serves as managing editor of the *International Journal of Management Theory and Practices (IJMTP)* and was editor-in-chief of *Communications of the ICISA*. He is co-founder of the Telecommunications & Information Management (TIM) Program at Western Michigan University, the first interdisciplinary and inter-collegial TIM program in Michigan. Professor Tarn is former president of the International Chinese Information Systems Association.

***

Kuanchin Chen is an assistant professor of computer information systems at the Haworth College of Business, Western Michigan University, USA. He received his DBA in information systems from Cleveland State University and his MS in information systems from University of Colorado. His research interests include electronic commerce, applied artificial intelligence, data mining techniques, and WWW security. He has been promoting online interactivity, privacy, and security through research studies and grants. Dr. Chen's research appeared in such journals as *Information & Management, IEEE Transactions on Systems, Man, and Cybernetics, Communications of the AIS, Journal of Computer Information Systems*, and many others. He also serves on the editorial board of Journal of Website Promotion.

Tony Coulson has worked as an information system professional for the past 15 years as an executive, consultant, and academician. Most recently he was the director of information services for a major heavy equipment company with over $60 million in revenues. Dr. Coulson has led several major system implementations worked with large-scale business software systems and has a depth of experience with architecture planning and ERP training.

James Danenberg is an instructor of business information systems at Western Michigan University, USA. He is currently a doctoral candidate focusing on information and communications technology (ICT) in science education. In addition, James is a certified project management professional and has extensive experience at various companies as a mechanical and electrical product design engineer and project engineer.

Janelle Daugherty is the Microsoft Dynamics Academic Alliance (MDAA) program manager for North America. She has been involved with the MBSAA since its inception in 2002 and prior to that she was a program manager for the Great Plains Software Education Alliance Network (EAN). She has over 15 years of experience assisting higher education in the areas of professional development and the use of technology in various classroom settings. Her challenges as MBSAA program manager involve expansion of the program into the global market, maintaining and developing relationships with textbook publishers, assisting members of the MBSAA with integration of MBS products across business and technology-based curricula, determining processes for licensing and fulfilling MBSAA software and services, and promoting MBS products to all types of higher education institutions. She holds a bachelor's degree in university studies from North Dakota State University with an emphasis in communications and marketing.

Satish P. Deshpande is a professor of management at Western Michigan University, USA. His research includes applied psychology in human resource issues, unionization, and managerial decision-making. He has had over 50 refereed articles published in various journals including the *Academy of Management Journal, Compensation and Benefits Review, Human Relations, Journal of Small Business Management, Organizational Behavior and Human Decision Processes, Journal of Business Ethics, Journal of Labor Research,* and *Journal of Psychology.* He is also the faculty advisor of the Society for Excellence in Human Resources, a student chapter of SHRM.

Bernard Han is professor and chair of the Department of Business Information Systems. He earned his BS degree from National Chiao-Tung University, Taiwan, R.O.C. in 1977, his MBA degree from Arizona State University, Tempe, Arizona in 1981, and his PhD in Information Systems from University of Washington, Seattle, Washington in 1989. Dr. Han has served on the editorial board for the *Journal of Information Technology and Management.* His research has been published in journals such as *IEEE Transactions on Robotics and Automation, European Journal of Operational Research, Annals of Operations Research, Telecommunication Systems, Communication of the ACM,* and *European Journal of Information Systems.*

Paul Hawking is senior lecturer in information systems at Victoria University, Melbourne, Australia. He has contributed to the *Journal of ERP Implementation and Management, Management Research News* and contributed many conference papers on IS theory and practice. He is responsible for managing the university's strategic alliance with SAP and is coordinator of the university's ERP Research Group. In 2002, 2004, and 2005, Paul was a committee member of the SAP Australian User Group and in 2002 served as chairperson.

Stefan Koch is assistant professor of information business at the Vienna University of Economics and Business Administration, Austria. He received a MBA in Management Information Systems from Vienna University and Vienna Technical University, and a PhD from Vienna University of Economics and Business Administration. Currently he is involved in the undergraduate and graduate teaching programme, especially in ERP packages and software project management. His research interests include ERP systems, cost estimation for software projects, the open source development model and the evaluation of benefits from information systems.

R. Lawrence LaForge is alumni distinguished professor of management at Clemson University, USA. He received his BS degree in Industrial Management from Clemson, and his MBA and PhD degrees from the University of Georgia. Dr. LaForge has received numerous awards for innovative teaching of operations management with enterprise software, including recognition as South Carolina Professor of the Year. He is a certified fellow in production and inventory management by APICS — The Society for Operations Management, and he has been named a fellow of the Decision Sciences Institute for his teaching and research contributions to the field of operations management.

Frank Lin is a professor in the Department of Information and Decision Sciences at California State University, San Bernardino, USA. He received his PhD in Management Information Systems and MBA in Management Information Systems from SUNY-Buffalo. He has published articles and monographs in books and journals such as *MIS Quarterly* and *Journal of International Information Management* as well as international, national, and regional conferences. He has worked as an information systems professional for the last 20 years as an executive, consultant, and academician. He has received a number of grants and/or gifts from National Science Foundation, Department of Defense, Oracle Corp., GTE and Microsoft Corp., among others. His current research interests are in information systems and technology planning, organizational modeling, enterprise architecture, systems analysis and design, innovation and technological implementation, theory development, and research methodology in information systems.

Leo Liu graduated from the Graduate School of Business, University of International Business and Economics (UIBE), Beijing, China in 2004 with a master's degree in international business management. During 2001-2004, Leo participated in the research project of the Theory and Application of the Innovation in Chinese Enterprise, sponsored by the China National Natural Science Fund; Theoretical & Empirical Research of the Internationalization of Chinese Enterprise, sponsored by the National Social Science Fund and a Fulbright research project-The Capital Structure of Chinese Enterprises. Mr. Liu serves in Oracle China, and currently his work focuses on the e-business solution for the Chinese enterprises.

Amelia A. Maurizio joined SAP America as an associate manager of the University Alliance Program in 1998. In July 2001, she was given responsibility for the entire global SAP University Education Alliance program. Today, there are over 500 members of the University Alliance Program in over 39 countries. Prior to joining SAP, Dr. Maurizio spent several years in higher education where she held many positions including assistant vice president for Academic Administration and adjunct professor of Finance. Dr. Maurizio serves on the Board of Directors of AACSB and on other on numerous boards and advisory committees. In addition, Amelia is an adjunct professor at Stetson University in Florida where she teaches strategic management in the EMBA Program.

Brendan McCarthy is a lecturer in the School of Information Systems in the Faculty of Business and Law at Victoria University, Melbourne, Australia. He has contributed to the *Journal of Issues in Information Science and Information Technology*, Information Systems Education, Pan-Pacific Business Conference, PACIS Conference, and contributed many conference papers on IS theory and practice. His research interests include enterprise resource planning systems programming skills, development of E-learning technologies and end-user documentation. He is a member of the University's ERP Research Group and is co-ordinator of the Masters in ERP.

Kenneth E. Murphy holds a PhD in Operations Research from Carnegie Mellon University and is currently an associate professor of information systems at the Atkinson Graduate School of Management, Willamette University in Salem, Oregon. Recently, Dr.

Murphy has been investigating the implementation of integrated systems, specifically, ERP systems, in large enterprises. Dr. Murphy's work on integrated systems has followed several threads including the financial justification of large-scale systems using both tangible and intangible factors, and investigating the tools and methods for successful system implementation. He has published in *Operations Research*, *Communications of the ACM*, the *Information Systems Journal* and in other IS journals.

T. M. Rajkumar is an associate professor of MIS at Miami University, USA, where he teaches Enterprise Systems, Advanced Database Management Systems and other MIS courses. His teaching and research interests include offshore development of software, troubled projects, and enterprise systems.

Muhammad Razi teaches database, system analysis and design and programming courses at the Haworth College of Business at the Western Michigan University, USA. Dr. Razi received his BSc in Mechanical Engineering from the Bangladesh University of Engineering & Technology, MBA and PhD in Decision Sciences from Virginia Commonwealth University, Richmond, Virginia. He has worked as IT professional in manufacturing and service sectors in the U.S. His work has appeared in *Expert Systems with Applications*, *Logistics Information Management*, *Information Management & Computer Security*, *Journal of Small Business Strategy*, among other journals.

Sandra B. Richtermeyer, PhD, CPA, CMA is an associate professor of accountancy at Xavier University in Cincinnati, Ohio. She has over ten years of experience implementing technology into college courses. Her primary teaching experience is in accounting information systems, e-business, and systems analysis and design in addition to non-profit and managerial accounting. Her research focuses on enterprise systems, technology integration and professional issues for accountants. She holds a PhD, MBA, and MS from the University of Colorado and a BS from the University of Wyoming.

Thomas Rienzo is an instructor of computer information systems at Western Michigan University, USA, with more than 25 years of business experience in sales, technical service, and research. His research focuses on student learning through software and he has created several enterprise software exercises. He is currently pursuing a Doctor of Philosophy degree in Science Education.

Michael Rosemann is a professor at the School of Information Systems and the Co-Leader of the Business Process Management Research Group, Queensland University of Technology, Brisbane, Australia. His main areas of interest are enterprise systems, business process management, conceptual modeling and ontologies. He published more than 120 refereed papers in journals and conferences. Dr. Rosemann is teaching SAP solutions at universities since 1992 and published widely on his educational approaches. He is also the chief investigator of a number of SAP-funded research projects.

Mahesh Sarma is currently working as an instructor in the Department of Decision Sciences and Management Information Systems at Miami University, Ohio, USA, from 2004. He received his MBA in Management Information Systems from Miami University, Ohio. Prior to receiving his MBA, he worked as senior engineer designing real-time software simulation systems for the chemical industry. He is active in research, specifically the study of enterprise resource planning and supply chain management systems and the applications of these systems in academia and business.

Andrew Stein is a lecturer in the School of Information Systems in the Faculty of Business and Law at Victoria University, Melbourne, Australia. He has contributed to the *International Journal of Management, Journal of Information Management, ERP Implementation and Management, Management Research News, Virtual Education, ERP & Data Warehousing in Organisations* and contributed many conference papers on IS theory and practice. His research interests include enterprise systems, e-procurement and e-marketplace applications, reverse auction systems models and innovative use of emerging IS technologies like RFID. He is a member of the University's ERP Research Group, the Australian SAP user group and is co-ordinator of the undergraduate Information Systems degree.

Bret J. Wagner received a bachelor's degree in mechanical engineering from Michigan State University, USA, in 1983. While working for Newport News Shipbuilding on the Seawolf submarine design team, he earned a master's degree in engineering administration from George Washington University. He left Newport News Shipbuilding to return to Michigan State University, earning a doctorate in Operations Management. Dr. Wagner was assistant professor at the University of Delaware from 1994 to 2001, and is currently an associate professor at Western Michigan University, where he is director of the Integrated Supply Management program. Dr. Wagner's research is primarily in the area of production planning and scheduling, and his research has appeared in top academic journals, including *Decision Sciences* and the *European Journal of Operational Research*. Since 1998, he has been involved with SAP's University Alliance program, and has worked to integrate SAP's enterprise resource planning software into university curriculum. He has taught courses in production planning and scheduling, quality management, business process management and enterprise systems. He is the co-author of the textbook *Concepts in Enterprise Resource Planning* (with Ellen Monk) and is working on a textbook on integrated materials planning.

David C. Yen is a Raymond E. Glos professor in the Richard T. Farmer School of Business and a distinguished scholar of the Graduate Faculty at Miami University, USA. He was a professor of MIS and a chair of the Department of Decision Sciences and Management Information Systems at Miami University from 1995-2005. He received a PhD in MIS and Master of Sciences in Computer Science from the University of Nebraska. Professor Yen is active in research, he has published three books and many articles which have appeared in *Communications of the ACM, Decision Support Systems, Information & Management, International Journal of Information Management, Information Sciences, Expert Systems with Applications, Electronic Commerce Research and Applications, Journal of Computer Information Systems, Interfaces, Telematics and Informatics, Computer Standards and Interfaces, Information Society, Omega, International Journal of Organizational Computing and Electronic Commerce, Communications of AIS,* and *Internet Research* among others. He was also one of the co-recipients for a number of grants such as Cleveland Foundation (1987-1988), GE Foundation (1989), and Microsoft Foundation (1996-1997).

Index

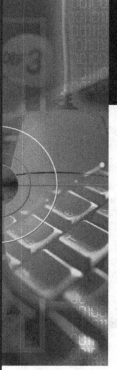